SAS® Companion for the Microsoft Windows NT Environment

Version 6
First Edition

SAS Institute Inc.
SAS Campus Drive
Cary, NC 27513

The correct bibliographic citation for this manual is as follows: SAS Institute Inc., *SAS® Companion for the Microsoft Windows NT Environment, Version 6, First Edition*, Cary, NC: SAS Institute Inc., 1993. 382 pp.

SAS® Companion for the Microsoft Windows NT Environment, Version 6, First Edition

ISBN 1-55544-562-4

1st printing, September 1993

Doc P19, 071393

Contents

Reference Aids

Figures

Output

Tables

Credits

Documentation

Composition	Candy R. Farrell, Nancy B. Mitchell, Blanche W. Phillips
Design	Design, Production, and Printing Services
Proofreading	Heather B. Dees, David Teal
Technical Review	Marilyn S. Adams, Dawn M. Amos, Stuart A. Austin, Brendan R. Bailey, Andy Barnhart, Patricia L. Berryman, Arthur P. Bostic, Douglas H. Brann, Ulrike Bumb, Mark Cates, Jennifer B. Clegg, Mark W. Craver, Katherine M. DeRusso, Rajen Doshi, Craig Drury, Ceci Edmiston, Brad Freeman, Cheryl Garner, Jodie Gilmore, Bonnie B. Horne, Sherri Humphreys, Lindi T. Ingold, David P. Jeans, Michael R. Jones, Kuo-Chung Andy Ju, Mike Kalt, Rich Lee, Julie Maddox, Jeffrey R. McDermott, Cynthia H. Morris, Patricia Mullins, Joy Polzin, Meg Pounds, Richard A. Ragland, Andy Ravenna, Kari Richardson, Carol Williams Rigsbee, Russ Robison, Jeff Schrilla, John Schroedl, Thomas E. Sherron, Lynne Overby Smith, Wes Smith, Linda J. Spanton, Tina Tart, Annette R. Tharpe, Wanda Verreault, Jim Watts, Holly Whittle, Dea Zullo
Writing and Editing	Brad Freeman, Jodie Gilmore, Hanna Hicks, Mike Kalt, Rich Lee

Software Development and Support

The system-dependent features and subsystems of Release 6.09 SAS software under Windows NT are designed, coded, built, tested, and supported by the PC Host Group within the Host Systems Research and Development Division. Implementation of the SAS System involves a variety of tasks and functions, including load, task, and memory management, I/O systems and engines, and user interface programming. A major effort has been made to research the advanced features of Windows NT, including Program Manager programming, Dynamic Load Libraries, Dynamic Data Exchange, and Object Linking and Embedding (OLE) to ensure that the SAS System fully exploits the powerful features of the Windows NT operating system.

An effort of this magnitude requires the cooperation of many individuals throughout the Institute. On these pages, the primary software developers and support personnel are identified. In addition, we extend our thanks to the many individuals, particularly in Technical Support and Quality Assurance, who participated in the testing and support of the product.

Development of the Host MVA Supervisor

Base Engine and V604 Engine	Steve Beatrous, Michael R. Jones, Lynne Overby Smith
BMDP Engine	Richard D. Langston
Code Generation	Michael R. Jones, David R. Stevenson
Communications	Steve Jenisch, David Kolb
Compiler Run-Time Support	Michael R. Jones
Control Break	Brian Corcoran, Russ Robison
Data Collection Features	David P. Jeans, Kuo-Chung Andy Ju, Julie A. Maddox
Debugging and Tuning	Michael R. Jones
Dynamic Data Exchange	David P. Jeans, Kuo-Chung Andy Ju
External I/O	David P. Jeans, Kuo-Chung Andy Ju, David Kolb
Floating Point Emulation	Michael R. Jones
Fonts and Icons	Jesse C. Chavis, David P. Jeans, Mike Pezzoni, Elly Sato, John Schroedl
Functions Specific to Windows NT	Arthur P. Bostic, Malinda McKee Adams, Michael R. Jones
Graphics Device Drivers	Malinda McKee Adams, Art Barnes, David P. Jeans, Russ Robison
Host Initialization	Arthur P. Bostic, Basil Qubain, Carol Williams Rigsbee, Russ Robison
Host Management	Mark W. Cates
Load Management	Arthur P. Bostic, Brian Corcoran
Memory Management	Brian Corcoran, David P. Jeans, Russ Robison
Numeric Formats and Informats	Michael R. Jones
Object Linking and Embedding	Jennifer B. Clegg, Ron Holanek
OSIRIS Engine	Richard D. Langston
Performance Tuning	Arthur P. Bostic, Tracy Carver, Michael R. Jones, Russ Robison
Printing	David P. Jeans, Kuo-Chung Andy Ju, Lynne Overby Smith
SPSS Engine	Richard D. Langston
SAS I/O	Michael R. Jones, Lynne Overby Smith
System Options	Brian Corcoran, Kuo-Chung Andy Ju
Task Management	Brian Corcoran, Russ Robison
Technical Management	Mark W. Cates, Carol Williams Rigsbee

Toolbox and Tool Bar	Kuo-Chung Andy Ju, Basil Qubain, John Schroedl
User Interface	Malinda McKee Adams, Andy Barnhart, Jennifer B. Clegg, David P. Jeans, Kuo-Chung Andy Ju, Carol Williams Rigsbee, Russ Robison, John Schroedl
Utility Application	Arthur P. Bostic, Brad Freeman, Julie A. Maddox, Randy Williams

Support of Development Process

Automation Tools	Tracy Carver, Brad L. Chisholm, Scott W. Ellis, Julie A. Maddox, Donald Major, Mark Schneider
System Support	Freda Cameron, Mitzi Krellwitz, Jeffrey R. McDermott, Leon Robbins
Help Windows	Brad Freeman
Installation Application	Arthur P. Bostic, Brad Freeman, Julie A. Maddox
Porting and Source Management	Robert Carpenter, Jere Judd, Wanda A. Lucas, Gary J. Mehler, John Asa Price
Quality Assurance	Marilyn S. Adams, Brendan R. Bailey, Douglas H. Brann, Jonathan Chapman, Katherine M. DeRusso, Meg Pounds, Linda J. Spanton
Technical Support	Dave Brumitt, Janice Kolb, Wes Smith
Testing Automation	Tracy Carver, Albert B. Cohen, Brad Freeman, David P. Jeans, Julie A. Maddox, Donald Major, Bob Overby
Documentation Development	Mark W. Cates, Anne Corrigan, Brad Freeman, Jodie Gilmore, Julie A. Maddox, Dea B. Zullo

Using This Book

Purpose

SAS Companion for the Microsoft Windows NT Environment, Version 6, First Edition provides information about how the SAS System is implemented under the Microsoft Windows NT operating system. This book includes both usage and reference material, and when used with other documentation provided by SAS Institute, it allows you to use the SAS System under Windows NT.

The usage and reference information are presented in separate parts of this book. The usage portion (Part 1) shows you how to perform common tasks and explains how these can be accomplished using the SAS System under Windows NT. The reference portion (Part 2) provides complete descriptions of all the features of the SAS System that have system-dependent behavior, but does not attempt to teach you how to use the software. Part 3 consists of several appendices.

This section describes the book's intended audience, the audience's prerequisite knowledge, the book's organization and its conventions, some general information about using the SAS System, and the additional SAS System and Windows NT documentation that is available to you.

Audience

This book is intended for users who have had some experience with the SAS System. System managers may also want to read this book to understand how the SAS System works under Windows NT and how they should administer the SAS System.

This manual is not intended to be a primer on the Windows NT operating system. Before you begin using the SAS System under Windows NT, you should have a basic knowledge of Windows NT concepts.

Prerequisites

The following table summarizes the concepts you need to understand in order to use the SAS System under Windows NT.

You need to know	Refer to
how to install the SAS System under Windows NT	*Installation Instructions for the SAS System, Release 6.08, under Windows NT*
how to reference SAS files	*SAS Language: Reference, Version 6, First Edition*
how to specify Windows NT filenames and pathnames	your Microsoft Windows NT documentation, including the online documentation
how to operate in the Microsoft Windows NT environment	*Microsoft Windows NT Graphical Environment User's Guide* or other Windows NT documentation.

Using the SAS System under Windows NT also involves these prerequisites:

- Microsoft Windows NT, Version 3.10 or later.
- the installation and CORE portions of the SAS System, Release 6.09 or later. (Under Windows NT, it is possible to selectively install portions of base SAS software.)

How to Use This Book

This section gives an overview of the book's organization and content. The book's parts and chapters are described, followed by a section on how to use each chapter.

Organization

SAS Companion for the Microsoft Windows NT Environment is divided into three parts. This section describes each of these parts and lists the chapters that appear in each part.

Part 1: Using the SAS System under Windows NT

Part 1 describes using the SAS System under Windows NT and gives examples of performing tasks commonly accomplished with the SAS System.

Chapter 1, "Introducing the SAS System under Windows NT"

Chapter 2, "Using Graphical Interface Features of the SAS System under Windows NT"

Chapter 3, "Using SAS Files"

Chapter 4, "Using External Files"

Chapter 5, "Accomplishing Common Tasks with the SAS System under Windows NT"

Chapter 6, "Using Advanced Features of the SAS System under Windows NT"

Part 2: System-Dependent Features of the SAS Language

Part 2 provides reference information on using the SAS System under Windows NT.

Chapter 7, "SAS System Options"

Chapter 8, "SAS Statements"

Chapter 9, "SAS Procedures"

Chapter 10, "Other System-Dependent Features of the SAS Language"

Chapter 11, "Performance Considerations"

Chapter 12, "Problem Determination and Resolution"

Part 3: Appendices

Six appendices follow Chapter 12.

Appendix 1, "Updating Your Licensing Information"

Appendix 2, "Graphics Considerations"

Appendix 3, "Network Considerations"

Appendix 4, "Moving Files Containing ANSI or OEM Characters between Windows NT, OS/2, and DOS"

Appendix 5, "Pop-Up Menu and Menu Bar Map"

Appendix 6, "Utility Application"

What You Should Read

This book is written for several types of users. The following table summarizes these users and their knowledge levels:

If you are	You should read
inexperienced with the SAS System or Windows NT	Chapters 1 through 6. Once you feel adept with Chapters 1 through 6, read Chapters 7 through 10.
experienced with either the SAS System or Windows NT, but not both	Chapters 1 through 12.
a system manager	the entire book, paying special attention to Chapters 11 and 12.

If you are unfamiliar with the SAS System or Windows NT, refer to "Additional Documentation" later in this section for more information.

Conventions

This section covers the conventions this book uses, including typographical conventions, icon conventions, syntax conventions, and conventions used in presenting output.

Typographical Conventions

In this book, several type styles are used. Style conventions are summarized here:

roman — is the basic type style used for most text in this book. It is also used for window names. Window names appear in mixed case.

UPPERCASE ROMAN	is used for references in the text to keywords of the SAS language, filenames, and variable names, and for operating system commands.
italic	is used for terms that are defined in text, for emphasis, for user-supplied values (in text or syntax), and for references to publications.
`code`	is used to show examples of programming code. In most cases, this book uses lowercase type for SAS code, with the exception of some title characters, and uppercase type for Windows NT commands. You can enter your own code in lowercase, uppercase, or a mixture of the two. The SAS System always changes your variable names to uppercase, but character variable values remain in lowercase if you have entered them that way. Enter any titles and footnotes exactly as you want them to appear on your output.
`monospace`	is used for items in windows and menus, such as field names and menu selections. Monospace is also used for character variable values that appear in text.

Icon Conventions

Three icons are used in the text to mark specific types of information:

indicates cautionary information.

indicates information that is especially important to SAS users in the Windows NT environment.

indicates that the information provided is supplemented by information in Appendix 4 about moving files between Windows NT, OS/2, and DOS and about files that contain national characters or graphics border characters.

Syntax Conventions

This book uses the following conventions for syntax, both for SAS statements and Windows NT commands:

UPPERCASE BOLD	indicates primary parts of the SAS language: statements, functions, and procedure names. For these terms, you must use the exact spelling and form shown. Note that you do not have to use uppercase when you type these elements.

UPPERCASE ROMAN	indicates arguments whose values have the exact spelling and form shown. The argument may or may not be optional, depending on whether it is enclosed in angle brackets (<>). Note that you do not have to use uppercase when you type these arguments.
italic	indicates arguments or items in statement syntax for which you supply a value.
<arguments in angle brackets>	are optional. Multiple arguments within one set of brackets means that if you use one argument, you must use all the arguments.
arguments not in angle brackets	are required.
. . . (ellipsis)	indicates that multiple sets of arguments can be specified. If the ellipsis and the final set of arguments are enclosed in angle brackets, they are optional.
| (vertical bar)	means to choose one item from the group of items separated by the bars.

The following example illustrates some of the syntax conventions described previously:

LIBNAME *libref <engine-name> 'SAS-data-library'*;

LIBNAME
is a primary part of the language, so it appears in uppercase boldface type.

libref
is required, so it is not enclosed in angle brackets; you must supply a value because it is in italics.

<engine-name>
is optional, so it is enclosed in angle brackets. If you use this argument you must supply a value because it is in italics.

'SAS-data-library'
is required and must be enclosed in quotes; you must supply a value because it is in italics.

Conventions for Examples and Output

Each page of output produced by a procedure is enclosed in a box. In each chapter, the procedure output is numbered consecutively starting with 1 and the output from each procedure is given a title. Dates in output are generic (for example, April 4, 19*xx*). Most of the programs in this book were run using the following SAS system options:

PAGESIZE=60	sets the length of the page to 60 lines.
LINESIZE=80	sets the length of the text line to 80 characters.
NONEWS	indicates you do not want installation-maintained news information to appear in your output.
NODATE	indicates you do not want the date and time to appear in your output.

Using the SAS System

This book describes how to use the SAS System in the Windows NT environment.

SAS Applications are Portable

This book helps you write SAS programs in the Windows NT environment. SAS software runs on many types of computers: personal computers, workstations, minicomputers, and mainframes. However, SAS applications and programs developed under one operating system are portable to other operating systems. In particular, you can easily move SAS programs between the SAS System for Windows NT and for Windows and OS/2.

Different Ways to Use the SAS System

There are two different ways to use the SAS System. One way is to use SAS/ASSIST software, an easy-to-use, menu-driven interface to SAS features; the other is to write your own SAS programs.

User Interfaces for the SAS System

The SAS System

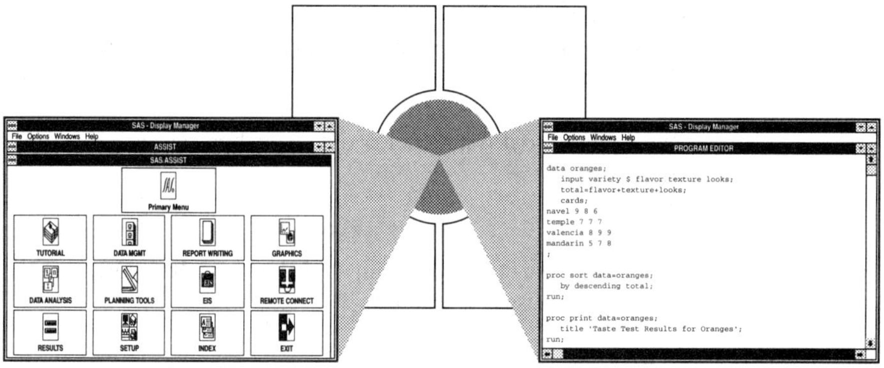

SAS/ASSIST Software　　　SAS Programming

SAS/ASSIST software is recommended for general users. General users and applications programmers may also want to use the SAS programming language to develop specialized programs and applications.

Methods of Running the SAS System

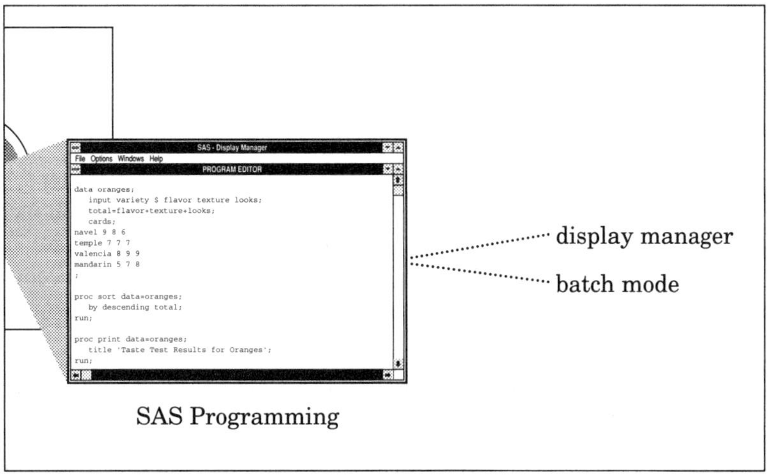

The SAS System also provides a fourth-generation applications development environment, which can be used to build customized information systems quickly and easily.

When you use SAS programs, you can choose between using the SAS Display Manager System or batch mode.

Additional Documentation

SAS Institute provides many publications about products of the SAS System and how to use them on specific hosts. For a complete list of SAS publications, you should refer to the current *Publications Catalog*. The catalog is produced twice a year. You can order a free copy of the catalog by writing to the address or calling the telephone number below:

SAS Institute Inc.
Book Sales Department
SAS Campus Drive
Cary, NC 27513
919-677-8000
Fax: 919-677-8166

SAS Software Documentation

The books listed here should help you find answers to questions you may have about general or specific aspects of the SAS System.

- *Getting Started with the SAS System Using SAS/ASSIST Software, Version 6, First Edition* (order #A56085) provides step-by-step instructions for using SAS/ASSIST software to access the power of the SAS System.
- *SAS/ASSIST Software: Your Interface to the SAS System, Version 6, First Edition* (order #A56086) provides a high-level overview of SAS/ASSIST software.
- *Doing More with SAS/ASSIST Software, Version 6, First Edition* (order #A56089) provides additional task-oriented instructions for using SAS/ASSIST software, building on the concepts presented in *Getting Started with the SAS System Using SAS/ASSIST*

Software.

- *Getting Started with SAS/EIS Software, Version 6, First Edition* (order #A56092) is a step-by-step, high-level overview to SAS/EIS software. This book introduces SAS/EIS software by showing how to complete the basic tasks necessary to build a simple EIS.
- *SAS/EIS Software: Reference, Version 6, First Edition* (order #A56090) provides reference information for Release 6.08 SAS/EIS software. It includes an introduction to SAS/EIS software, general features of the interface, information on the SAS/EIS metabase system, and a complete reference for all SAS/EIS objects, as well as other topics of interest.
- *SAS/CONNECT Software: Usage and Reference, Version 6, First Edition* (order #A56017) describes how to use SAS/CONNECT software under several operating systems.
- *SAS Guide to the SQL Procedure: Usage and Reference, Version 6, First Edition* (order #A56070) shows you how to use the SQL procedure, which implements Structured Query Language in Version 6 of the SAS System. You can use the SQL procedure to join and manipulate SAS/ACCESS views and other SAS data sets.
- *SAS Language and Procedures: Introduction, Version 6, First Edition* (order #A56074) gets you started if you are unfamiliar with the SAS System.
- *SAS Language and Procedures: Usage, Version 6, First Edition* (order #A56075) and *SAS Language and Procedures: Usage 2, Version 6, First Edition* (order #A56078) are users guides to the SAS System. They show you how to use base SAS software for data analysis, report writing, and data manipulation. They also include information on methods of processing and the LIBNAME statement.
- *SAS Language: Reference, Version 6, First Edition* (order #A56076) provides detailed information on base SAS software, the SAS programming language, and the types of applications the SAS System can perform.
- *SAS Procedures Guide, Version 6, Third Edition* (order #A56080) provides detailed information about the procedures available within base SAS software.
- SAS Technical Report P-195, *Transporting SAS Files between Host Systems* (order #A59112) describes how to move SAS files from operating system to operating system, in the context of both Version 5 and Version 6 SAS files.
- SAS Technical Report P-222, *Changes and Enhancements to Base SAS Software, Release 6.07* (order #A59139) describes Release 6.07 changes and enhancements to base SAS software.
- SAS Technical Report P-224, *SAS/CONNECT Software: Changes and Enhancements, Release 6.08* (order #A59141) describes Release 6.08 changes and enhancements to SAS/CONNECT software.
- SAS Technical Report P-242, *SAS Software: Changes and Enhancements, Release 6.08* (order #A59159) describes Release 6.08 changes and enhancements to SAS software.
- SAS Technical Report P-252, *SAS Software: Changes and Enhancements, Release 6.09* (order #A59169) describes Release 6.09 changes and enhancements to SAS software.
- SAS Technical Report P-255 *SAS/CONNECT Software: Changes and Enhancements, Release 6.09* (order #A59172, available first quarter, 1994) describes Release 6.09 changes and enhancements to SAS/CONNECT software.

Microsoft Windows NT Documentation

You may find the *Microsoft Windows NT Graphical Environment User's Guide* useful as you work with the SAS System under Windows NT. You can also find useful books on Microsoft Windows NT at your local bookstore.

Part 1

Using the SAS® System under Windows NT

Chapter 1 Introducing the SAS® System under Windows NT

Introduction

This chapter introduces you to the SAS System in the Windows NT environment. Some of the topics discussed in this chapter include a description of the relationship between the SAS System and Windows NT, details on how to communicate with your SAS session under Windows NT, a discussion of some files used by the SAS System under Windows NT, and an illustration of a sample SAS session under Windows NT.

Note: When you see the `App4` icon, be sure to read the appropriate section in Appendix 4 as well as the information provided in this chapter. You can ignore the icon if you do not need to move files between Windows NT, OS/2, and DOS, or if your files do not contain national characters or graphics border characters.

The SAS System and Microsoft Windows NT: Poised for Performance

Windows NT is an operating environment developed by Microsoft Corporation to allow more control over the capabilities of your personal computer. In the past, you have been limited by the capabilities of the PC DOS and MS-DOS operating systems. Windows NT provides a versatile environment with a friendly desktop interface.

Release 6.09 of the SAS System under Windows NT is a complete implementation of the SAS System. It adds many significant capabilities beyond what is available in Release 6.04 of the SAS System for the DOS operating system. Release 6.09 of the SAS System under Windows NT is similar to Release 6.08 under Microsoft Windows, except that it takes advantage of the improved performance of the operating system. For example, the following operating system improvements will positively affect your SAS programs:

- the 32-bit operating system enables your SAS programs to execute faster
- the improved fault isolation capabilities ensure that if another application fails, your SAS session is not affected
- the additional resources reduce resource contention, so your SAS programs execute more efficiently.

The SAS System is a comprehensive and flexible information delivery system that supports data access, data management, data analysis, and data presentation. The SAS System increases its power and flexibility by taking advantage of the features provided by Windows NT.

Windows NT enables you to communicate easily between applications. Enabling applications to share data concurrently is an important feature in Windows NT, and you can take full advantage of this feature. The SAS System supports this communication feature so that you can share information in other applications with the SAS System, share your SAS data with other applications, and share data between concurrent SAS sessions. The SAS System supports information sharing through the most powerful tools that Windows NT has to offer. These tools include the following:

- pipes
- named pipes
- Dynamic Data Exchange (DDE)
- Object Linking and Embedding (OLE)
- the Windows NT Clipboard.

A fundamental goal of Release 6.09 of the SAS System under Windows NT is to ensure that SAS data sets created by Releases 6.03, 6.04, 6.06, and 6.08 can be used by Release 6.09. Release 6.09 can read and write Release 6.03, 6.04, 6.06, 6.07, and 6.08 data sets. However, in order to bridge the upgrades in SAS catalog architecture and differences in operating system structure, catalogs must be converted from earlier formats (such as Release 6.04 under DOS or Release 6.08 under Windows) to Release 6.09 format using the transport procedures CPORT and CIMPORT. You do not have to convert SAS catalogs created by Release 6.08 under OS/2; these catalogs can be read directly by your Windows NT SAS session.

Compatibility with previous releases of the SAS System has been balanced against a desire to take advantage of Windows NT features. Specifically, the SAS System under Windows NT takes full advantage of the graphical interface. Most existing SAS Display Manager System commands are implemented, but where appropriate, interactive dialog boxes and various graphical user interface controls are used so the selection of operations is highly intuitive and interactive.

Communicating with Your SAS Session

The following sections briefly describe several important concepts involved in communicating with your SAS session. These include using the mouse to select items and determining if your SAS session is busy.

Selecting Items with a Mouse

Using a mouse with the SAS System under Windows NT greatly facilitates use of SAS System applications, especially if you are running the SAS System using display manager. Unless otherwise noted, it is assumed in discussions of SAS software in this book that you are using a mouse.

Within the SAS System under Windows NT, you make selections the same way you make selections in all other Windows NT applications. Therefore, if you are an experienced Windows NT user, you should find this mode of selection within the SAS System familiar and easy to use.

Use your mouse to make selections from menus and dialog boxes. To make a selection from these locations, single-click on your choice. Double-click on fields in windows such as fields in the LIBNAME and DIR windows. (*Single-click* refers to pressing the mouse button once; *double-click* refers to pressing the mouse button twice in quick succession. In future references, *click* is synonymous with single-click.) For example, to turn on an option in a dialog box, single-click on the option's button. If the SASUSER libref is listed in the LIBNAME window, double-click anywhere on the `SASUSER` line to display the contents of the SASUSER data library. See your Windows NT documentation for more information on selecting items.

★ ***When you bring up your SAS session, only the SAS AWS (Application Work Space) menu bar is present by default.***
If your preferences are set to pop-up menus, you can activate pop-up menus by clicking the right mouse button once. (The right mouse button is by default defined to bring up pop-up menus, but you can change this default using the KEYS window if you want.) For more information on pop-up menus and other methods of issuing display manager commands, see "Issuing Display Manager Commands" on page 55. ■

Wait Cursor

When the SAS System is performing a task, the arrow cursor changes to the wait cursor and your control of your SAS session is limited.* However, you can still move the pointer outside of the SAS AWS and execute other applications. If you move the pointer outside the SAS AWS (discussed in Chapter 2) or across a title bar, the wait cursor changes back to the arrow cursor.

Files Used by the SAS System

The SAS System uses many files while it is running; however, four of these files are especially important from a user's perspective. These files include the

- SAS configuration file
- SAS autoexec file
- user profile catalog
- WORK data library.

The system-dependent details of these files are discussed in the next four sections.

SAS Configuration File

The SAS *configuration file* enables you to specify SAS system options that are used to establish your SAS session. These options indicate, among other things, the location of your SAS System help and message files and the paths to SAS executable files. The SAS configuration file is particularly important because it specifies the directories that are searched for the various components of SAS products. See "Options for SAS Users under Windows NT" on page 177 for a list of system-dependent options you can use in your SAS configuration file. Also see Chapter 16, "SAS System Options," in *SAS Language: Reference, Version 6, First Edition* for more information on SAS system options.

A default SAS configuration file named CONFIG.SAS is created during the installation process and is stored in the !SASROOT directory. (The !SASROOT directory is the directory in which you install the SAS System. For more information on the !SASROOT directory, see "SAS Default Directory Structure" on page 11.) The SAS System requires a configuration file, so you must use a SAS configuration file regardless of whether you are using display manager or batch mode.

* By default, the wait cursor is an hourglass. The cursor can be changed via the Control Panel.

Specifying SAS System Options in the SAS Configuration File

You can specify any SAS system option in the SAS command when you start the SAS System. However, it is generally more convenient to place frequently used system options in your SAS configuration file rather than repeatedly specifying the same options at invocation. The syntax for specifying system options in the SAS configuration file is discussed in Chapter 7.

You can edit the default CONFIG.SAS file to add to or change the system option settings, or you can create your own SAS configuration file. The next section, "Naming Conventions for the SAS Configuration File" on page 7, discusses how to modify your SAS configuration file.

Your SAS configuration file is divided into two sections. The first section specifies system options that are not updated by the INSTALL application. The second section is used by the INSTALL application for updating information about where SAS software is installed. The sections are divided by the following text string:

```
/* DO NOT EDIT BELOW THIS LINE - INSTALL application */
/* edits below this line                             */
```

The INSTALL application deletes all data below this text string but does not affect the options specified above it. The INSTALL application appends the following system options below this text string: MAPS, PATH, PATHDLL, SASAUTOS, SASHELP, SASMSG, and SET. (The SET option defines the following SAS environment variables: SASROOT, INSTALL, LIBRARY, SAMPSIO, SAMPSRC, SASCBT, SASEXT01–SASEXT50, and USAGE).

Use the SAS Text Editor to edit your CONFIG.SAS file.
The text editor you choose to edit the SAS configuration file is important. The recommended method is to edit CONFIG.SAS using the SAS Text Editor and save it using the Save As dialog box. If you do not use the SAS Text Editor, be sure to use another ASCII text editor (such as Notepad). Do not use a specialized editor such as the WRITE application that comes with Windows NT. Using such an editor can insert carriage control characters into your CONFIG.SAS file or corrupt the characters that are there. ■

Naming Conventions for the SAS Configuration File

You can specify your own file to act as the SAS configuration file, overriding the default file, CONFIG.SAS. When you use a file named something other than CONFIG.SAS as your SAS configuration file, you must tell the SAS System where to find the configuration file. For example, the `Command Line` field in the Properties window for the SAS System may look like this:

```
C:\SAS\SAS.EXE -CONFIG C:\SAS\MYCONFIG.SAS
```

If the SAS System cannot find the SAS configuration file, an error message is displayed, and the SAS System does not initialize.

You must add several required system options if you create your SAS configuration file from scratch.
If you use your own configuration file instead of the default CONFIG.SAS file, you must add several required options. For example, you must either use the SET option to define the

environment variable, !SASROOT, or define SASROOT as a Windows NT environment variable. Therefore, if you do not want to use the CONFIG.SAS file, it is recommended that you copy the CONFIG.SAS file and modify the copy instead of creating your own file from scratch. ■

Search Rules for CONFIG.SAS

When you install the SAS System under Windows NT, a CONFIG.SAS file is created in the !SASROOT directory.

At invocation, the SAS System automatically searches for a file called CONFIG.SAS in the current directory (that is, the directory from which you invoked the SAS System). If a file by that name is not found, the SAS System searches for a CONFIG.SAS file among the paths specified in the Windows NT PATH environment variable and then in the root directory of the current drive. Finally, the directory that contains the SAS.EXE file is searched. For example, suppose your Windows NT PATH environment variable references the following directories:

```
PATH C:\MYSASDIR;F:\USERDIR
```

Now suppose you invoke the SAS System in the following manner:

```
C:\MYDIR>  D:\SASDIR\SAS
```

That is, you invoke the SAS System from the C:\MYDIR directory. In this example, the SAS System searches for a CONFIG.SAS file using the following rules:

1. Search the current directory (C:\MYDIR).
2. Search C:\MYSASDIR (from the Windows NT PATH environment variable).
3. Search F:\USERDIR (from the Windows NT PATH environment variable).
4. Search C:\(the root directory of the current drive).
5. Search D:\SASDIR (the location of SAS.EXE).

The SAS System uses the first CONFIG.SAS file it finds. If a CONFIG.SAS file is not found, an error message is displayed, and the SAS System does not initialize.

If you use the CONFIG system option, the SAS System uses the file you specify as the configuration file and does not use the previous rules to search for a file named CONFIG.SAS.

SAS Autoexec File

App4

The SAS *autoexec file* contains SAS statements that are executed immediately after the SAS System initializes and before any user input is accepted. Unlike the SAS configuration file, a SAS autoexec file is not required to run the SAS System, but if you do have a SAS autoexec file, the default name is AUTOEXEC.SAS. The SAS System uses the same search order rules for the AUTOEXEC.SAS file as it does for the CONFIG.SAS file:

1. Search the current directory.
2. Search the paths specified by the Windows NT PATH environment variable.

3. Search the root directory of the current drive.
4. Search the directory that contains the SAS.EXE file.

You do not have to name your SAS autoexec file AUTOEXEC.SAS, but if you name it something else, you must use the AUTOEXEC system option to tell the SAS System where to find the SAS autoexec file. For example, you can specify the following option after the path specification for the SAS.EXE file in the `Command Line` field of the Properties window:

```
-AUTOEXEC C:\SAS\INIT.SAS
```

If the specified SAS autoexec file is not found, an error message is displayed, and the SAS System terminates.

The SAS autoexec file is a convenient way to execute a standard set of SAS program statements each time you invoke the SAS System. You may want to include OPTIONS, LIBNAME or FILENAME statements, or any other SAS statements and options you want the system to execute each time you invoke a SAS session. For example, if you want to specify a script file for SAS/CONNECT software, you can place the following statement in the AUTOEXEC.SAS file:

```
filename rlink 'c:\sas\connect\saslink\vms.scr';
```

Or you can use the OPTIONS statement to set the page size and line size for your SAS System output and use several FILENAME statements to set up filerefs for commonly-accessed network drives, as in the following example:

```
options linesize=80 pagesize=60;
filename saledata 'f:\qtr1';
filename custdata 'l:\newcust';
filename invoice 'o:\billing';
```

Use the SAS Text Editor to create your SAS autoexec file.
The text editor you choose to create the SAS autoexec file is important. The recommended method is to create it using the SAS Text Editor and save it using the Save As dialog box. If you do not use the SAS Text Editor, be sure to use another ASCII text editor (such as Notepad). Do not use a specialized editor such as the WRITE application that comes with Windows NT. Using such an editor can insert special carriage control characters into your SAS autoexec file that the SAS System cannot interpret when it tries to execute the statements in the file. ■

Three other system options, in addition to the AUTOEXEC option, provide ways to send the SAS System information as it is starting up. These options are listed below in the order in which they are processed:

1. CONFIG
2. AUTOEXEC
3. INITSTMT
4. SYSIN.

See Chapter 7 for more information on the CONFIG, AUTOEXEC, and SYSIN options; see *SAS Language: Reference* for more information on the INITSTMT option.

Suppressing the SAS Autoexec File

If you have an AUTOEXEC.SAS file but do not want the SAS System to use it, specify the NOAUTOEXEC option in the SAS command, as in the following example:

```
C:\SAS\SAS.EXE -NOAUTOEXEC
```

Profile Catalog

Each time you invoke a SAS session, the SAS System checks the SASUSER data library for your user profile catalog (named SASUSER.PROFILE), which defines the start-up profile for your SAS session, including key definitions, display configurations, and so on. If you invoke the SAS System without accessing an existing profile catalog, one is created that contains the default key definitions and window configuration.

Use the SASUSER system option to specify a profile catalog other than the default. This option is useful if you want to customize your SAS sessions when sharing a machine with other users or if users are accessing the SAS System from a network.

The SASUSER option takes the following form:

-SASUSER *directory*

If *directory* does not exist, the SAS System attempts to create it. For example, if you specify the following option, a profile catalog is created in a directory named MYUSER that resides in the root directory of the C: drive:

```
-sasuser c:\myuser
```

(The profile catalog is not recreated if it already exists.) Any customizations (such as key definitions or color modifications) defined during subsequent sessions are stored in your profile catalog in the specified directory. Putting this same option in your SAS configuration file or specifying it in the SAS command yields the same results.

When you delete your profile catalog, you lose the key definitions, window configurations, and option settings you defined, as well as any other entries you saved to your profile catalog. In addition, any text you stored in NOTEPAD windows is erased.

For more information on the SASUSER option, see Chapter 7.

WORK Data Library

The SAS System requires some temporary disk space during a SAS session. This temporary disk space is called the *WORK data library.* By default, the SAS System stores SAS files with one-level names in the WORK data library, and these files are deleted when you end your SAS session. You can change the data library in which SAS files with one-level names are stored. See "Using the USER Libref" on page 84 for more information.

The WORK system option controls the location of the WORK data library. You can specify the WORK option in your SAS configuration file or when you invoke the SAS System. Usually, you use the WORK option specified in the default CONFIG.SAS file. The default specification for the WORK option is

```
-work saswork
```

This creates a directory called SASWORK beneath the current directory.

The SAS System creates temporary subdirectories under the directory you specify with the WORK option. These temporary subdirectories are created in the unique form #TD*nnnnn*, where TD means temporary directory and *nnnnn* is the process ID for each SAS session. These subdirectories enable multiple SAS sessions to be invoked using the same configuration file, and they prevent the WORK directory from being shared. The SAS System creates any temporary files required within each temporary directory. As with all temporary files that are created in the WORK data library during a SAS session, these temporary directories are deleted when you end the SAS session.

If you do not want the SAS System to create a temporary subdirectory under the specified WORK directory, but would rather use the actual directory specified in the WORK option, specify the USE suboption in the WORK option. For example, you can specify the following in the **Command Line** field of the Properties window:

```
-work saswork use
```

This creates a directory called SASWORK beneath the current directory and all temporary SAS files are stored in this directory, not in a subdirectory.

For more information on using the WORK data library and overriding the default location, see "Using the WORK Data Library" on page 83.

If the SAS System terminates abnormally, determine if the WORK library was deleted. If not, remove it by using the Windows NT File Manager. Do not attempt to delete the WORK directory while the SAS System is running.

If you want to verify the location of the current WORK directory, invoke the LIBNAME window to see the pathname for the WORK libref.

SAS Default Directory Structure

When the SAS System is installed, a number of subdirectories are created. Understanding the organization of the SAS directories helps you use the SAS System more efficiently. The SAS System can be installed on a single drive or across multiple drives. It is not recommended that a single product of the SAS System be split over multiple drives.

The root directory of the SAS System is the directory in which you install the SAS System. This directory has the logical name !SASROOT. Often this directory is called SAS, but this is not required. (The examples in this book assume the !SASROOT directory is called SAS.)

One important subdirectory of the !SASROOT directory is the CORE subdirectory. The CORE subdirectory in turn contains many subdirectories, two of which are described below:

!SASROOT\CORE\SASINST
: contains the installation process software.

!SASROOT\CORE\SASDLL
: contains the host executable SAS files as well as fonts and icons specific to the SAS System.

For each SAS product installed, the following subdirectories may be created:

!SASROOT*product*\SASEXE
: contains the SAS executable files.

!SASROOT*product*\SASHELP
: contains the SAS help files and many specialized catalogs and files.

!SASROOT*product*\\SASMACRO
contains SAS autocall macro files.

!SASROOT*product*\\SASMSG
contains the SAS message files.

!SASROOT*product*\\SAMPLE
contains the Sample Library programs.

!SASROOT*product*\\SASTEST
contains Test Stream programs.

!SASROOT*product*\\SASMISC
contains miscellaneous external files shipped with the product.

Some products, such as SAS/CONNECT software, also have other subdirectories associated with them. See the specific product documentation for details on each product's structure.

For more information about how the SAS directories are configured at your site, contact your SAS Software Representative.

Starting the SAS System

Under Windows NT, you can start the SAS System in the following ways:

- by selecting the SAS item in a program group in the Windows NT Program Manager
- by selecting the `Run` command from the `File` menu on the Program Manager or File Manager menu bar
- by issuing the SAS or START SAS command at the operating system command prompt

Starting the SAS System as a Program Item

To start the SAS System from a program group window, first create a SAS System item in the group of your choice. (At installation you are asked if you want to have the SAS System automatically added to a program group.) See your Windows NT documentation for information on creating groups and group items. Then, after setting the properties, double-click on the SAS item you have created. Figure 1.1 shows an example of a SAS item in a program group window.

You can create multiple SAS items within a group to represent several differently configured SAS sessions.

If you want the SAS System to start every time you log on to Windows NT, copy the SAS item to the Startup group.

Starting the SAS System from a Run Command

If you have not yet added the SAS System as a group item, or you want to start a SAS session with options other than those set up as a group item, you can start a session using the **Run** command.

To start a session using the **Run** command, select **Run** from the **File** menu on the Program Manager or File Manager menu bar. Type the path and the exact name of the program file, including the extension and options, in the Run dialog box. Select OK to submit the request.

Note: When starting the SAS System using the **Run** command, unless the directory that contains CONFIG.SAS is in your Windows NT path, you should specify the SAS configuration file location using the CONFIG system option, even if you use the default name of CONFIG.SAS.

Starting the SAS System from the DOS Prompt

You can start the SAS System from the DOS prompt by typing the SAS command. You can also use the START SAS command.

Unless you specify the WORK and SASUSER system options as part of your SAS or START SAS command, the WORK and SASUSER SAS data libraries are created in the directory specified for SAS.EXE, which is C:\SAS in the following examples.

Using the SAS Command

You can start either a display manager session or a batch SAS job by typing the SAS command at the command prompt. For example, the following command starts a display manager session, specifies the page size and line size, and indicates the location of the SAS configuration file:

```
C:\SAS\SAS.EXE -LS 80 -PS 60 -CONFIG C:\SAS\CONFIG.SAS
```

This next command starts a batch SAS job in a similar manner:

```
C:\SAS\SAS.EXE -SYSIN C:\SAS\PROGRAMS\PROG1.SAS -CONFIG C:\SAS\CONFIG.SAS
```

When you issue the SAS command from a DOS prompt, you cannot issue other commands at that DOS prompt until you close your SAS session. Of course, you can open another DOS prompt window and issue commands there.

Using the START SAS Command

If you want to be able to continue to issue commands at the DOS prompt after you begin your SAS session, use the START SAS command, as in the following example:

```
START C:\SAS\SAS.EXE -LINESIZE 80 -NODATE
```

When you issue this command, Windows NT opens a separate session to run the SAS System, and immediately returns to the DOS prompt, where you can issue further commands, such as starting other applications.

Options You Should Specify When Starting the SAS System

Table 1.1 provides examples of information you should enter when adding a SAS item to a Program Manager group, issuing a `Run` command, or otherwise invoking the SAS System.

Table 1.1
Options for Invoking the SAS System

Mode	Command	Parameter
display manager	<*path*> SAS.EXE	none required
batch	<*path*> SAS.EXE	-SYSIN *filename*

The *path* should be the drive, directory, and any subdirectory in which the SAS System is installed. If your SAS configuration file is not located in any of the search locations specified in "Search Rules for CONFIG.SAS" on page 8, or is named something other than CONFIG.SAS, you should also include the CONFIG option in your SAS command. Add other options to your SAS command as necessary, such as page size specification, location of SAS autocall macros, and so on.

When running the SAS System under Windows NT, you can use display manager or execute batch SAS jobs. You can use any of the previously discussed methods to start the SAS System in either mode. The default method of running the SAS System under Windows NT is display manager.

Submitting a Batch SAS Job

When you run a batch SAS job, a Status window is associated with the SAS job. This window tells you what SAS job is running and where your log and procedure output files are written. This window remains until the SAS job is complete.

You can run windowing procedures, such as those associated with SAS/FSP, SAS/GRAPH, SAS/INSIGHT, and SAS/ACCESS software, in a batch SAS job. When the SAS System reaches a point in your program where interaction is required, the SAS AWS is opened.

If you do not want to see the Status window while your batch SAS job is running, invoke the SAS System with the ICON system option so that the Status window becomes an icon when your job is running. You can also iconize the Status window by selecting [Icon] when the window appears. The icon is an hourglass while the SAS job is running and disappears when the job is complete. You can cancel a batch job by either pressing CTRL BREAK or choosing [Cancel] in the Status window.

There are several ways to submit a batch SAS job. One way is to specify the SYSIN system option in the SAS command to specify the SAS program to submit. You can issue the SAS command from the DOS prompt, or from the Run dialog box. Another method of submitting batch SAS jobs is to use the File Manager and drag your SAS program icon and drop it on the SAS.EXE file icon. Or, if the proper file associations have been set up, you can double-click on a file with a .SAS or .SS2 file extension.

Determining the Working Directory for the SAS System

Under Windows NT, the following rules are used for determining the working directory for the SAS System:

1. If a working directory is specified in the Windows NT Properties window, the SAS System uses that path as the working directory.
2. If Windows NT successfully loads the SAS.EXE file from the path specified in the SAS command, that path is the working directory.
3. If Windows NT cannot find the SAS.EXE file in the specified directory, the directory specified in the SAS command still becomes the working directory and Windows NT searches for the SAS.EXE file using the Windows NT PATH environment variable.

For example, if you specify the following in the **Command Line** field of the Properties window, C:\SAS is the working directory, whether or not the SAS.EXE file is actually in that directory:

```
C:\SAS\SAS.EXE -CONFIG C:\SAS\CONFIG.SAS
```

You can change the SAS working directory from within your SAS session by using the X statement or command with a CD or change drive command. See "Changing the SAS Working Directory" on page 21 for more information.

Note: Do not confuse the SAS working directory with the SASWORK data library. See "WORK Data Library" on page 10.

Sample SAS Session

This section illustrates invoking the SAS System from the **Applications** group, submitting a sample SAS program, looking at the program output, and ending the SAS session.

Figure 1.1 shows a possible configuration of the SAS item in the **Applications** group. Double-click on **SAS Session** to start the SAS System.

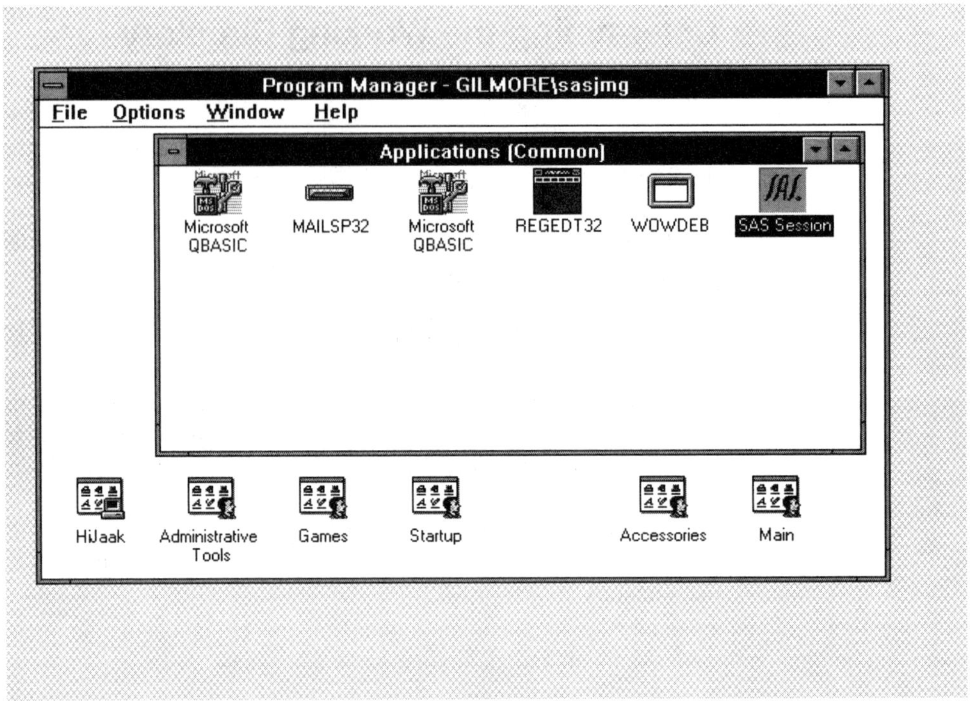

Figure 1.1 *Starting the SAS System from the Applications Group*

Figure 1.2 shows the PROGRAM EDITOR and LOG windows with a sample SAS program ready to be submitted. This program creates a SAS data set called ORANGES, which contains the results of a taste test on four varieties of oranges. Then the program sorts the data set by the total test score and prints the data set.

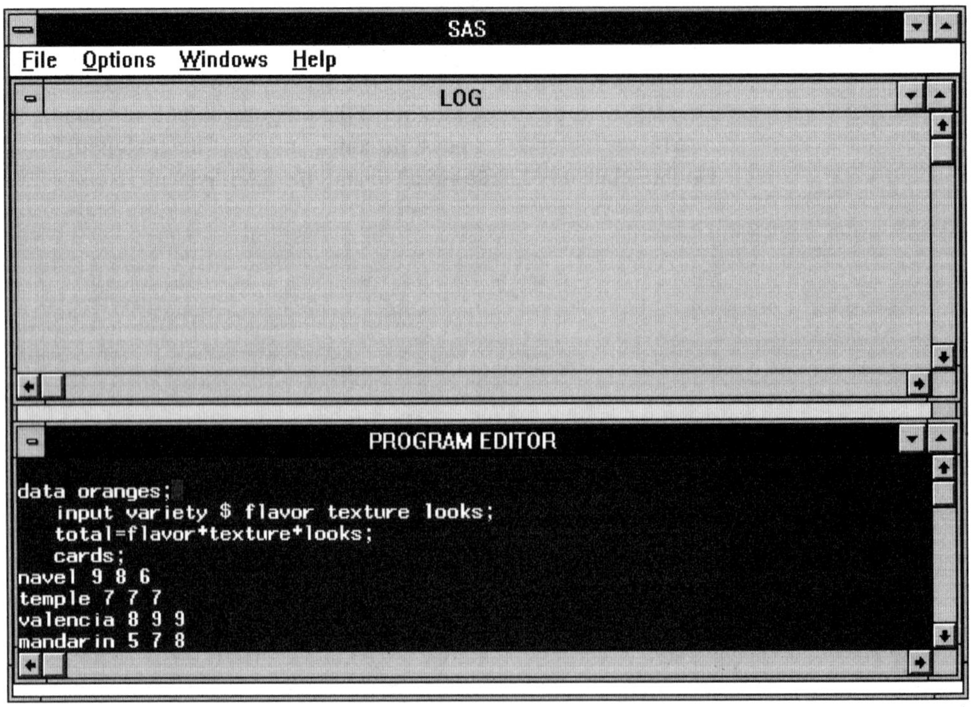

Figure 1.2 *Submitting the Sample SAS Program*

You can only see a portion of the SAS program in the PROGRAM EDITOR window. Here is the entire program:

```
data oranges;
   input variety $ flavor texture looks;
   total=flavor+texture+looks;
   cards;
navel 9 8 6
temple 7 7 7
valencia 8 9 9
mandarin 5 7 8
;

proc sort data=oranges;
   by descending total;
run;

proc print data=oranges;
   title 'Taste Test Results for Oranges';
run;
```

Once you submit the program, the output appears in the OUTPUT window, as shown in Figure 1.3.

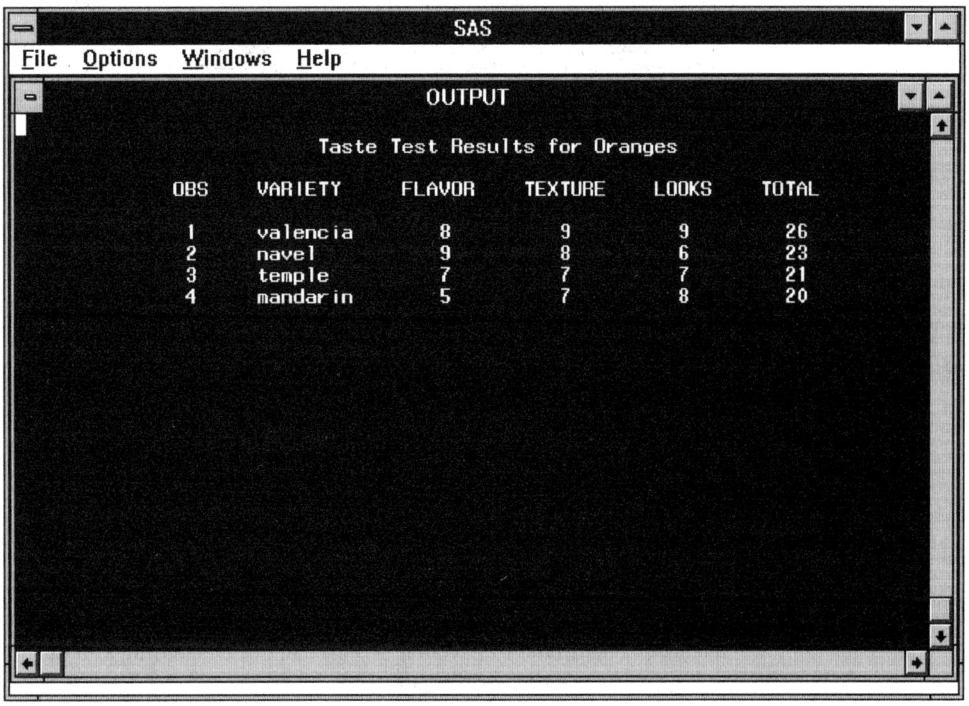

Figure 1.3
Looking at the Program Output

As mentioned previously, only the main SAS AWS menu bar at the top of the SAS window is visible by default. To see pop-up menus, click the right mouse button with the cursor in the window for which you want to see menus. Figure 1.4 shows a series of menus in the PROGRAM EDITOR window. This series was generated by first clicking the right mouse button with the cursor in the PROGRAM EDITOR window, then clicking on `File`, and then clicking on `Open`.

Figure 1.4
Pop-up Menus

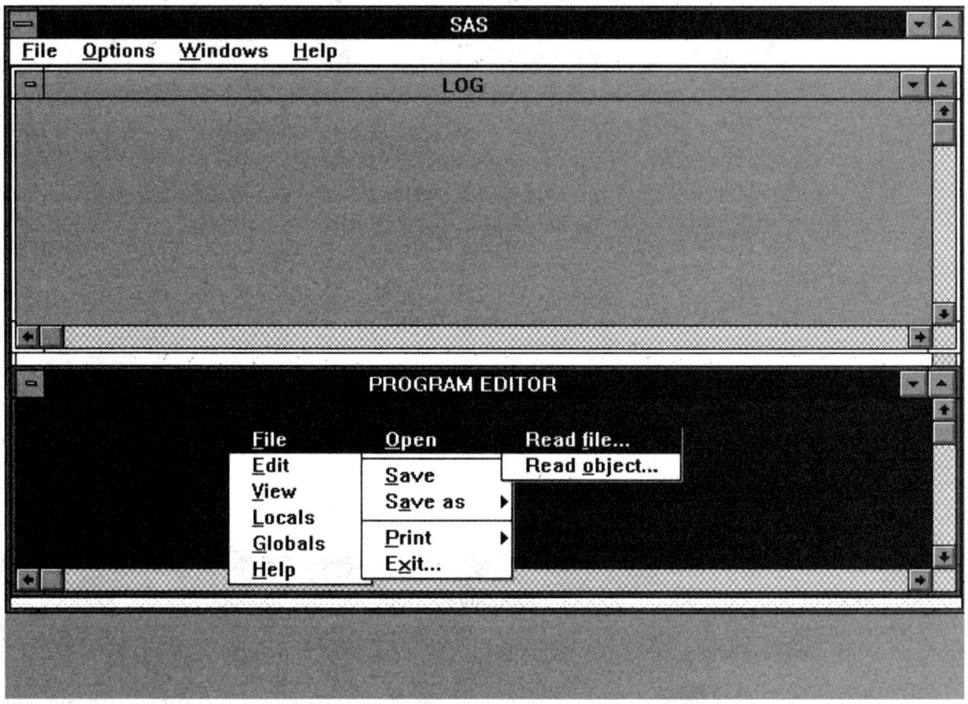

When you are ready to end your SAS session, double-click on the SAS AWS Control menu (the horizontal bar in the upper-left corner of the SAS AWS) and choose [OK] when the dialog box verifies your request. Choosing [OK] returns you to the program group window from which you started (in this example, the Main group).

Note: If you have disabled the **`Confirm Exit of SAS`** option in the Preferences dialog box, your SAS session ends without asking if you are sure you want to end the session. See "Preferences Item" on page 41 for more information on the Preferences dialog box.

Submitting SAS Code

You can submit SAS code from display manager or use the Windows NT File Manager to submit code. In the File Manager, you can either use drag and drop or double-click on a file with a file extension of .SS2 or .SAS. For drag-and-drop and double-clicking, you need the appropriate file association. This file association is created by the Install application when you install the SAS System.

Submitting Code in Display Manager

When you are using display manager to run the SAS System, you can choose to submit your code from the PROGRAM EDITOR window, or you can choose to submit code stored in the Clipboard.

The SUBMIT command, which is described in *SAS Language: Reference*, submits SAS code from the PROGRAM EDITOR window. To issue the SUBMIT command, select **`Locals`** from the pop-up menu in the PROGRAM EDITOR window and then select **`Submit`**. An alternate method of issuing the SUBMIT command is to press F3 or F8 from the PROGRAM EDITOR window.

To submit SAS code stored in the Clipboard (that is, the paste buffer), select **`Locals`** from the pop-up menu in the PROGRAM EDITOR window and then select **`Submit clipboard`**. The code is submitted from the Clipboard directly to the SAS System, and notes and results are sent to the SAS log and to the OUTPUT window, respectively. This feature enables you to copy or cut code from other applications, such as a text editor, and easily submit the code to the SAS System for execution.

You can also use the GSUBMIT command to submit SAS code that is stored in the Clipboard. See "Submitting SAS Code from the Clipboard" on page 54 for more information about the GSUBMIT command.

Submitting Code with the Drag-and-Drop Feature

Another method of submitting SAS programs is to use the drag-and-drop feature of the SAS System under Windows NT. You can submit a SAS program from the Windows NT File Manager by using the mouse to drag and drop the program's icon onto a SAS window or an iconed SAS session. If the SAS System is already running, the program is submitted in your display manager session. If the SAS System is not running, the program is submitted in batch mode.

For example, dragging and dropping the program icon for MYPROG.SAS onto any window of an open SAS session executes the following display manager command:

```
gsubmit "%include 'c:\myprog.sas'";
```

You can submit more than one program file at once by selecting a group of SAS program icons and dragging and dropping them on the open SAS session. The order in which the programs are run when they are submitted as a group is determined by the file manager application. Therefore, if order is important, you should drag and drop each program file separately.

Note: If the SAS System is busy when you drop a SAS program icon, the dropped file is ignored. The only indication that this has happened is a warning beep.

Submitting Code in .SS2 or .SAS Files

If you have SAS code stored in a file with a file extension of .SS2 or .SAS, you can run the code by double-clicking on the file's icon in the Windows NT File Manager (or a third-party File Manager replacement). A file association created by the Install application when you install the SAS System makes this feature possible.

When you double-click on a file, the SAS System is invoked in batch mode. If you already have a SAS session running, double-clicking on a file begins a second SAS session; it does not use the already-existing session.

Interrupting Your SAS Session

You can press the CTRL BREAK keys to interrupt processing in your SAS session. Depending on what tasks the SAS System is performing at the time of the interrupt, you can cancel submitted statements or cancel an upload or download request. Your various choices (such as to continue the interrupt or cancel it) are displayed in a dialog box.

Note: Depending upon what tasks are in progress when you issue an interrupt sequence, the SAS System may require several seconds to terminate processing.

The SAS System also supports the common Windows NT methods of issuing interrupts: you can click on the Control menu icon and choose to close the application, or you can choose `End Task` from the Task List. If you use either of these methods, a dialog box appears to verify your selection.

Exiting Your SAS Session Temporarily

You can submit the X statement to exit your SAS session temporarily and gain access to the Windows NT command processor specified by the Windows NT COMSPEC environment variable. The X statement takes the following form:

X <'*command*'>;

The optional *command* argument is used either to issue an operating system command or to invoke a Windows NT application such as Notepad. This discussion concentrates on using the X statement to issue operating system commands; however, you should be aware that the X statement can also be used to invoke Windows NT applications.

Note: The X statement is similar to the X command in display manager. The major difference between the two is that the X statement is submitted like any SAS statement; however, the X command is issued as a display manager command. This section uses the X statement in its examples, but the information applies to the X command as well.

If you want to execute only one operating system command, include the command as an argument to the X statement. When you submit the X statement, the command is executed, and you cannot issue any additional commands.

If you want to execute several operating system commands, submit the X statement without an argument. A command prompt appears where you can execute an unlimited number of operating system commands. Remember, however, that the commands you issue from the command prompt do not affect the SAS process. For example, if you change from the SAS working directory to MYDATA at the command prompt, the SAS System still uses the SAS directory as its working directory. Also, any environment variables you define are not available to the SAS System. If you submit an X statement or command without a *command* argument, type EXIT to return to your SAS session.

Other methods of exiting your SAS session temporarily include the following:

- Use the Command dialog box (discussed in Chapter 2) to issue the X command.
- Choose

  Globals ► Command ► Host command

  from the pop-up menu. From the Host command dialog box, issue the operating system command you want to execute.
- Choose the C:> tool from the default Toolbox or Toolbar.

Changing the SAS Working Directory

You can change the working drive and directory during your SAS session. To do this, you must include the change directory or change drive commands in the X statement. The SAS System intercepts the change directory (CD or CHDIR) and change drive commands.

Note: If you want to change both the working directory and the working drive, you must submit two separate X statements. You cannot change the working directory and working drive in the same X statement.

For example, if you submit the following statement, the working directory for your SAS session is changed to the MYDATA directory:

```
x 'cd \mydata';
```

In this example, you do not see a command prompt. Nor do you see a command prompt if you submit the following X statement; however, the working drive is changed to A:

```
x 'a:';
```

Note: The working directory is not changed if you specify the root directory of the A: drive (A:\).

Changing the working directory is useful if the external files you need are stored in a directory different than the one from which you invoke the SAS System. When you need to access these external files, you can either use a fully qualified pathname, or you can submit an X statement that changes the working directory to the directory where these external files reside.

If you have your DOS session configured so that when you change directories the subdirectories are shown in the command prompt, you can determine the current SAS System working directory by issuing an X statement or command without any arguments, as follows:

```
x;
```

The command prompt (such as C:\MYDATA>) indicates the current working directory. Type EXIT at the command prompt to return to your SAS session.

Executing Operating System Commands Conditionally

If you want to execute operating system commands conditionally, use the CALL SYSTEM routine, as in the following example:

```
options noxwait;

data _null_;
   input flag $ name $8.;
   if upcase(flag)='Y' then
      do;
         command='md c:\'||name;
         call system(command);
      end;
   cards;
Y mydir
Y junk2
N mydir2
Y xyz
;
```

This example uses the value of the variable FLAG to conditionally create directories. After the DATA step executes, three directories have been created: C:\MYDIR, C:\JUNK2, and C:\XYZ. The directory C:\MYDIR2 is not created because the value of FLAG for that observation is not `Y`.

The X command is a global SAS statement; therefore, it is important to realize that you cannot conditionally execute the X command. For example, if you submit the following code, the X statement is executed:

```
data _null_;
   answer='n';
   if upcase(answer)='y' then
      do;
         x 'md c:\extra';
      end;
run;
```

In this case, the directory C:\EXTRA is created regardless of whether the value of ANSWER is equal to `'n'` or `'y'`.

See "System-Dependent CALL Routines" on page 255 and Chapter 12, "SAS CALL Routines," in *SAS Language: Reference* for more information on the CALL SYSTEM routine.

XWAIT System Option

The XWAIT system option is used to control whether you have to type EXIT to return to your SAS session after an X statement or command has finished executing an operating system command. (The XWAIT system option is not used if an X statement is issued without a *command* argument or if the X statement invokes a Windows NT application such as Notepad.) This option and its negative form operate in the following ways:

XWAIT
: specifies that you must type EXIT to return to your SAS session. This is the default value.

NOXWAIT
: specifies that the command processor automatically returns to the SAS session after the specified command is executed; you do not have to type EXIT.

If you issue an X statement or command without a *command* argument, you must type EXIT to return to your SAS session, even if NOXWAIT is in effect.

When a window created by an X statement is active, reactivating the SAS System without exiting from the command processor causes the SAS System to issue a message box containing the following message:

```
The X command is active. Enter EXIT at the prompt in
the X command window to reactivate this SAS session.
```

If you receive this message box, press CTRL ESC to bring up the Task List. Choose **`C:\winnt\system32\cmd.exe`** and then choose [Switch To]. Enter the EXIT command from the prompt to close the window and return to your SAS session.

XSYNC System Option

The XSYNC option specifies whether the operating system command you submit executes synchronously or asynchronously with your SAS session. This option and its negative form operate in the following ways:

XSYNC
: causes the operating system command to execute synchronously with your SAS session. That is, control is not returned to the SAS System until the command has completed. You cannot return to your SAS session until the command prompt session spawned by the X command or statement is closed. This is the default value.

NOXSYNC
: indicates the operating system command should execute asynchronously with your SAS session. That is, control is returned immediately to the SAS System and the command continues executing without interfering with your SAS session. With NOXSYNC in effect, you can execute an X command or statement and return to your SAS session without closing the window spawned by the X command or statement.

Specifying NOXSYNC can be useful if you are starting applications such as Notepad or Excel from your SAS session. For example, suppose you submit the following X statement:

```
x notepad;
```

If XSYNC is in effect, you cannot return to your SAS session until you close the Notepad. But if NOXSYNC is in effect, you can switch back and forth between your SAS session and the Notepad. The NOXSYNC option breaks any ties between your SAS session and the other application. You can even end your SAS session; the other application stays open until you close it.

Comparison of the XWAIT and XSYNC Options

The XWAIT and XSYNC options have very different effects. An easy way to remember the difference is the following:

XWAIT
: means the command prompt session waits for you to type EXIT before you can go back to your SAS session.

XSYNC
: means the SAS System waits for you to finish with the other application before you can go back to your SAS session.

The various option combinations are summarized in Table 1.2.

Table 1.2 *Combining the XWAIT and XSYNC System Options*

Options in Effect	Result
XWAIT XSYNC	The command prompt window waits for you to type EXIT before closing, and the SAS System waits for the application to finish.
XWAIT NOXSYNC	The command prompt window waits for you to type EXIT before closing, and the SAS System does not wait for the application to finish.
NOXWAIT XSYNC	The command prompt window closes automatically when the application finishes, and the SAS System waits for the application to finish.
NOXWAIT NOXSYNC	The command prompt window closes automatically when the application finishes, and the SAS System does not wait for the application to finish.

Ending Your Display Manager Session

You can end your display manager session using several methods, including

- selecting `Close` from the SAS AWS Control menu
- double-clicking on the SAS AWS Control menu
- issuing the BYE or ENDSAS commands from a display manager command line
- submitting an ENDSAS statement
- closing the SAS session from the Task List by selecting the session process (the process name differs depending on how you started the SAS System) and selecting **`End Task`**

- selecting **`Exit SAS`** from the **`File`** menu in the SAS AWS menu bar.
- selecting **`Exit`** from the **`File`** pop-up menu
- pressing the ALT F4 accelerator-key combination defined by Windows NT.

Chapter Summary

This chapter provides important background information about how the SAS System and Windows NT complement each other. This chapter also describes some files the SAS System uses, including the SAS configuration and autoexec files, the user profile catalog, and the WORK data library. Finally, this chapter illustrates the fundamental tasks of starting the SAS System, issuing operating system commands from within your SAS session, and ending your SAS session. While this chapter discusses all of the methods of running the SAS System, including batch mode, Chapter 2 focuses on using the graphical interface features of the SAS System under Windows NT.

Chapter 2 Using Graphical Interface Features of the SAS® System under Windows NT

Introduction

The SAS System for the Microsoft Windows NT environment was developed in order to capitalize on the windowing features of the Windows NT graphical user interface. Like all applications developed under Windows NT, the SAS System provides a common graphical user interface. This makes it easier for you to learn new applications and to move between applications. This chapter focuses on running the SAS System using the SAS Display Manager System under Windows NT. It introduces you to the SAS Application Work Space (AWS), explains how you can use the SAS AWS menu bar to perform common tasks, and illustrates how to work within your SAS application, as well as how to customize it.

Note: When you see the `App4` icon, be sure to read the appropriate section in Appendix 4 as well as the information provided in this chapter. You can ignore the icon if you do not need to move files between Windows NT, OS/2, and DOS, or if your files do not contain national characters or graphics border characters.

Overview of the SAS System under Windows NT

The SAS application windowing environment consists of three types of windows:

- SAS Application Work Space (AWS)
- child windows
- dialog boxes.

The SAS *Application Work Space* (AWS) contains all SAS windows that are open, including those that have been minimized.

Child windows are the individual windows within the SAS AWS, such as the PROGRAM EDITOR, LOG, and OUTPUT windows. These windows behave like other windows in the Windows NT graphical interface in that you can maximize and minimize, scroll, and resize them. But because they are child windows of the SAS AWS, you cannot move them outside of the boundaries of the SAS AWS window.

Dialog boxes appear when the SAS System needs more information to complete a task. For example, when you exit your SAS session, a dialog box verifies your request. You may also see a dialog box if the SAS System cannot finish a task (for example, you may be out of disk space or a communications link may be down). In this case, a dialog box appears offering a list of choices such as **`Retry the operation`**, **`Abort`**, **`Ignore`**, and so forth. When a dialog box appears, you may have to respond to it before any further processing occurs, and you may be unable to switch windows within the SAS System until the dialog is completed.

Window Components

Each window within the SAS AWS contains a standard set of window components, including a Control menu icon, title bar and window title, minimize and maximize push buttons, vertical and horizontal scroll bars, and a sizing border, as shown in Figure 2.1:

Figure 2.1 *Major Window Components as Implemented within the SAS System*

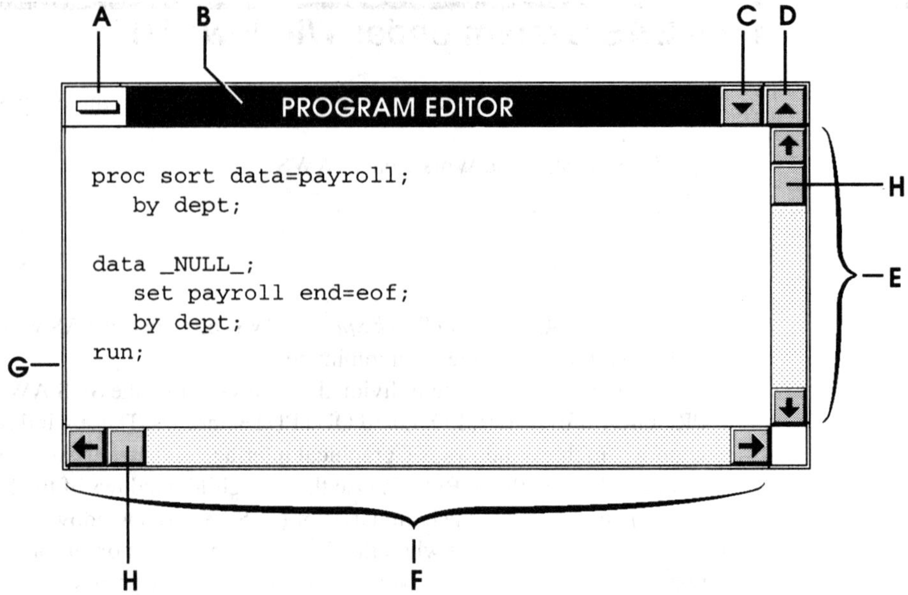

A	Control menu icon	**E**	Vertical scroll bar
B	Title bar and window title	**F**	Horizontal scroll bar
C	Minimize push button	**G**	Sizing border
D	Maximize push button	**H**	Scroll bar thumb

Using the SAS AWS Menu Bar

When you invoke the SAS System using display manager, the SAS System is contained in the SAS Application Work Space (AWS). Figure 2.2 shows the LOG and PROGRAM EDITOR windows as they first appear in the SAS AWS. Note the SAS AWS menu bar just above the LOG window.

Figure 2.2
The SAS Application Work Space (AWS)

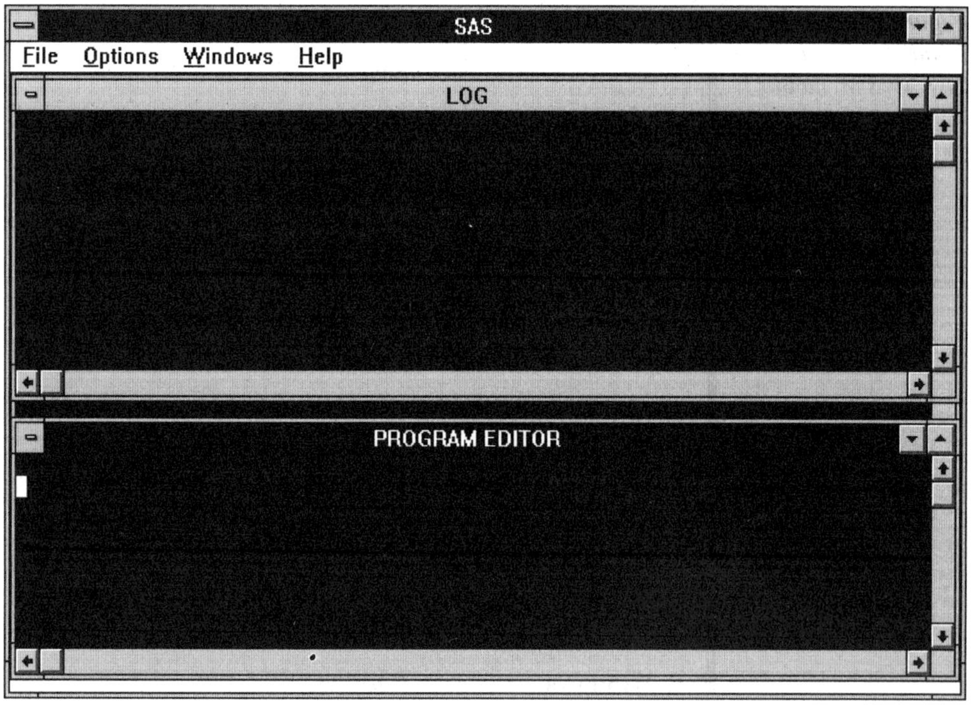

From the SAS AWS menu bar, you can access the `File`, `Options`, `Windows`, and `Help` menus of the SAS System. When you select one of these menus from the menu bar, you are in turn offered other options on a pull-down menu, as shown in the chart provided in Figure 2.3:

Figure 2.3
Road Map for the SAS AWS Menu Bar

- **File**
  - Open Into Pgm Editor...
  - Save As...
  - Print...
  - Release Print Requests
  - Printer Setup...
  - Run...
  - (*user-defined application list*)
  - Exit SAS...
- **Options**
  - Minimize All Windows
  - Fonts...
  - Preferences...
  - Edit Toolbox...
  - DDE Triplet...
- **Windows**
  - Cascade
  - Tile
  - Resize
  - (*window list*)
- **Help**
  - Extended Help
  - Keys
  - SAS System
  - Sample Programs
  - Installation Instructions
  - Install Application
  - Utility Application
  - About...

The following sections discuss each of the SAS AWS menu bar items. If an item in a pull-down menu is followed by an ellipsis (...), a dialog box requesting more information is opened whenever that item is selected.

If an item in a menu has an underlined letter, you can use that letter to perform that action. This letter is called an *accelerator key.* To use an accelerator key, press the ALT key to move your cursor to the first item of the SAS AWS menu bar, press the accelerator key for the menu you want to open (such as W for Windows). Now press the accelerator key to perform an action. For example, pressing ALT then typing `T` with the Windows menu open selects the `Tile` item. For more keyboard shortcuts, see “Keys Item” on page 46.

File Menu

The default `File` menu is shown in Figure 2.4:

Figure 2.4
SAS AWS File Menu

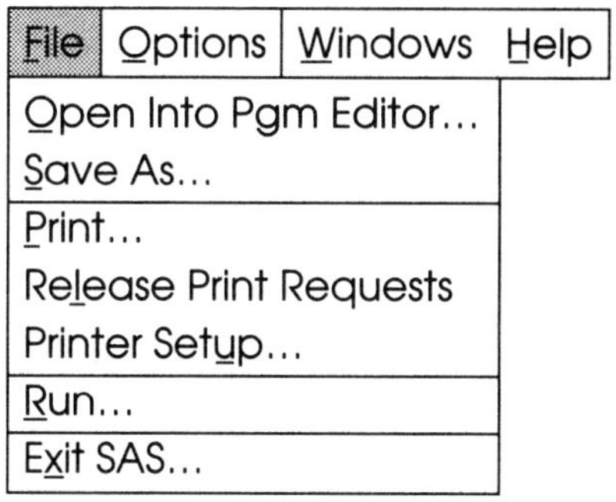

The `File` menu offers the following choices:

`Open Into Pgm Editor`
copies a program into the PROGRAM EDITOR window or immediately runs a program. This selection displays the Open dialog box.

`Save As`
saves the contents of a SAS window to a file. This selection displays the Save As dialog box.

`Print`
spools output to the Print Manager. This selection displays the Print dialog box.

`Release Print Requests`
releases print requests that have been held for later printing.

`Printer Setup`
enables you to choose and configure your default printer to be used with the SAS System. This selection displays the Printer Setup dialog box.

`Run`
asynchronously executes an operating system command or another application (similar to the **`File Run`** selection in the Windows NT Program Manager). This selection displays the Run dialog box.

user-defined application list
enables you to execute applications from this menu. If you have not defined any applications for this list, the list does not appear in the menu. (This is the case in Figure 2.4.) The REGISTER option, described on page 188 can be used to specify the applications that appear on this list.

`Exit SAS`
ends your SAS session. By default, a dialog box prompts you for verification of your action.

Each of these items is described in detail in the next several sections.

Note: Many child windows of the SAS AWS (such as the PROGRAM EDITOR and OUTPUT windows) also have a **File** menu that is similar to that of the SAS AWS **File** menu.

Open Into Pgm Editor Item

Open Into Pgm Editor helps you perform one of the most common tasks in the SAS System: copying external files into a SAS window, such as the PROGRAM EDITOR window. The Open dialog box is designed to perform this function. It is similar to using the INCLUDE display manager command.

Use the Open dialog box the same way you use the Open dialog box in other Windows NT applications to select the filename, drive, and directory of the file you want to copy into the PROGRAM EDITOR window. Choose [OK] to copy the program to the PROGRAM EDITOR window (the file is appended to the current contents of the window). Choose [Run] to run the file immediately.

Note: The PROGRAM EDITOR window can hold up to 256 characters on a single line. If you open a file with lines longer than 256 characters in the PROGRAM EDITOR window, the lines are truncated unless you use the INCLUDE command with an LRECL= value equal to the number of characters in the longest line, and you set either the AUTOWRAP or AUTOFLOW command to ON. If you want to use the Open dialog box to open a file with lines longer than 256 characters, use the FILENAME statement to set up a fileref with the appropriate options and use the fileref in the **File Name** field in the Open dialog box.

Save As Item

The Save As dialog box resembles the Open dialog box. However, rather than copying external files into the SAS System, the Save As dialog box writes text to disk. This dialog box enables you to select and save the text contents of a window. Using the Save As dialog box to save text is equivalent to using the FILE display manager command to save text.

Note: The Save As dialog box cannot be used to save graphics files. See "Producing Graphics" on page 123 for more information on using graphics in the SAS System under Windows NT.

Use the Save As dialog box the same way you use the Save As dialog box in other Windows NT applications. An added feature under the SAS System is the ability to specify which SAS window you want to save. Use the buttons in the **Window** area to specify the saved SAS window. For example, if you select **Log** before you choose [Save as], the contents of the LOG window are saved to the file you specify in the **File Name** field. The default is to save the contents of the active window. The active window is shown in the title bar of the dialog box.

Print Item

Print enables you to spool output to the Windows NT Print Manager. The Print dialog box is shown in Figure 2.5:

Figure 2.5
Print Dialog Box

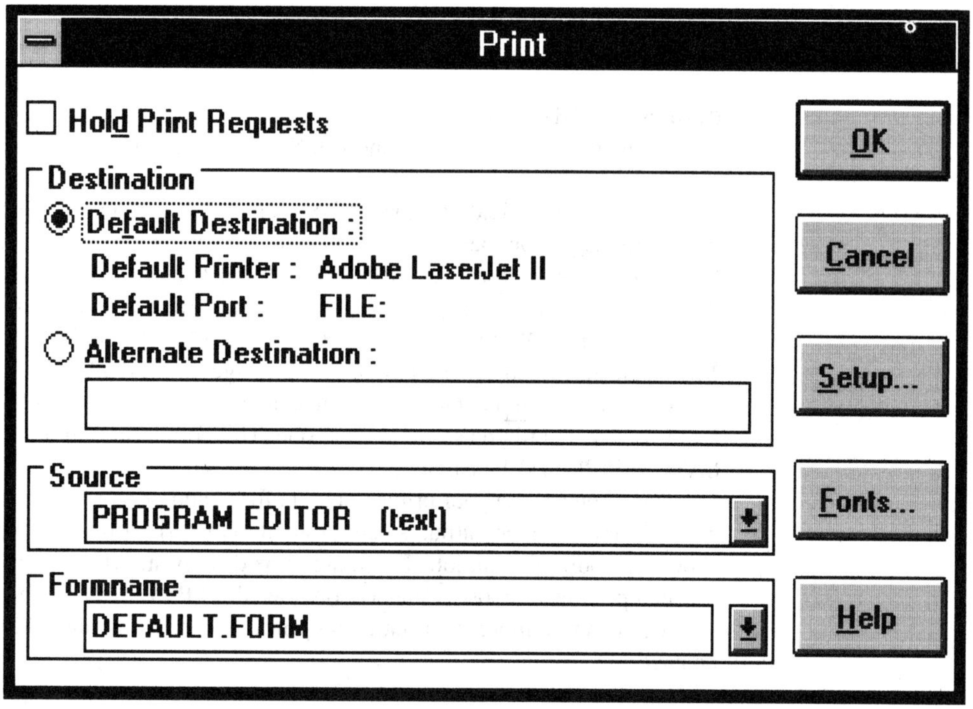

This dialog box shows the default printer and the default port the printer is attached to. You can change these defaults by choosing [Setup] to open the Printer Setup dialog box. (See "Printer Setup Item" on page 36 for instructions on changing the default printer information.)

The **`Hold Print Requests`** button is used to defer a print request for printing at a later time. When you choose **`Hold Print Requests`**, any print request you make is held until you choose **`Release Print Requests`** from the **`File`** menu of the SAS AWS menu bar. This feature enables you to queue up multiple print requests so that all print requests can be printed together, which eliminates unnecessary header pages.

You can override the default printer and port values by typing a filename in the **`Alternate Destination`** field. If you enter a filename in the **`Alternate Destination`** field, the output is routed to a file. The file contains all the printer control information that you specified in the Printer Setup dialog box, so you can print the file at a later time.

Use the **`Source`** field to choose what you want to print. The default value is the active window, but you can click on the arrow to the right of the field display the following values:

active window **`(text)`**
: prints the contents of the active SAS window.

active window **`(bitmap)`**
: prints a screen capture of the active SAS window.

`SAS AWS window (bitmap)`
: prints a screen capture of your SAS application work space. Your output does not include any images other than the SAS AWS.

`Entire screen (bitmap)`
: prints a screen capture of the entire display, including any non-SAS applications that are visible.

`Clipboard (text)`
prints the text stored on the Windows NT Clipboard.

`Clipboard (bitmap)`
prints the contents of the Windows NT Clipboard in bitmap format.

The `Formname` field lists the SAS System print form that is in effect. (Use the FSFORM display manager command to create print forms.) Clicking on the arrow displays all the SAS System print forms from the SASUSER.PROFILE and SASHELP.BASE catalogs. Choose the form you want to use by clicking on its name. For more information on printing with SAS forms under Windows NT, refer to "Using SAS System Print Forms" on page 120. You can also refer to "FORM Window" on page 287 and *SAS Language: Reference.*

Choosing [Font] enables you to select a printer font. The SAS System uses the printer font you select until you select another one. This font information is stored in your SASUSER.PROFILE2 catalog.

Once you choose your printer, source, form, and printer font, choose [OK]. A dialog box appears while the output is being routed to the Print Manager, which enables you to choose to abort the print job. This dialog box disappears when the routing is complete. To cancel a print job, choose [Cancel] from the Abort Printing dialog box.

You can find more information on printing from within the SAS System in "Printing" on page 116.

Release Print Requests Item

`Release Print Requests` enables you to release all print requests that were held when you chose `Hold Print Requests` from the Print dialog box. When you choose `Release Print Requests`, all deferred print requests are spooled to the Print Manager.

Printer Setup Item

`Printer Setup` enables you to define your default printer and specify printing attributes supported by the printer for text and graphics. An example of the Printer Setup dialog box is shown in Figure 2.6:

Figure 2.6
Printer Setup Dialog Box

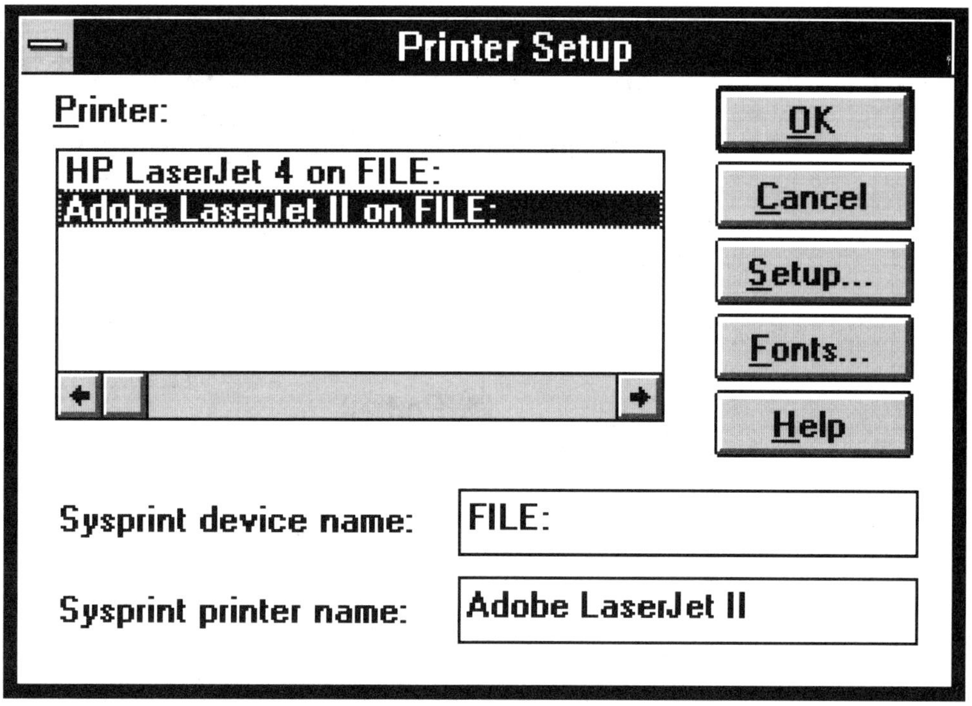

The printers listed in this dialog box are the printers installed at your site; therefore, the printers listed on your display probably differ from those shown in Figure 2.6. The dialog box shows the names of the printer device drivers you have installed and the ports (such as LPT1: and COM1:) on which they are installed. Also, the **`Sysprint Device Name`** and **`Sysprint printer name`** fields show the default port and printer. Note that the values displayed in these fields correspond to the value of the SYSPRINT system option. You can type a different value in one or both of the **`Sysprint device name`** and **`Sysprint printer name`** fields to create a special hybrid combination of printer devices and ports. For example, you can type a port like COM1: or a filename in the **`Sysprint device name`** field, or you can type a printer name such as HP Plotter in the **`Sysprint printer name`** field. See page 192 for a discussion of the SYSPRINT option.

When you choose Setup, a dialog box displays printer options supported by the selected printer. The contents of this dialog box depend on the printer device driver and are not controlled by the SAS System. An example of such a dialog box is shown in Figure 2.7:

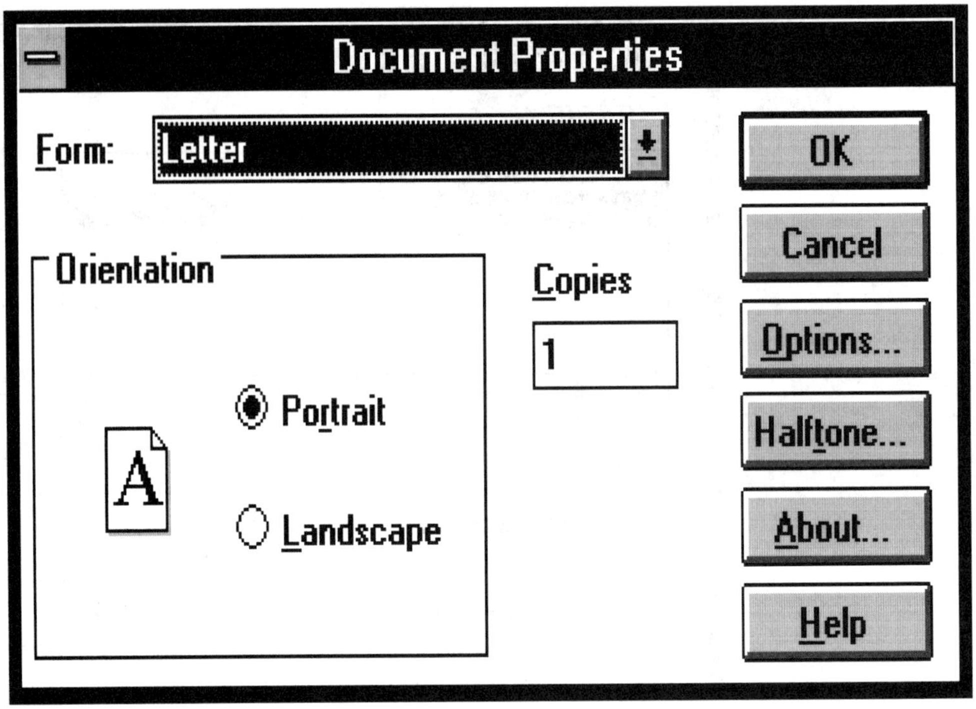

Figure 2.7
Sample Printer Options Dialog Box

Choosing Font enables you to select a printer font. The SAS System uses the printer font you select until you select another one. This font information is stored in your SASUSER.PROFILE2 catalog.

You can find more information on printing from within the SAS System in "Printing" on page 116.

Run Item

Run opens a dialog box that enables you to asynchronously execute an operating system command or a Windows NT application such as Excel. Type the command in the **Command Line** field and select OK. Figure 2.8 shows the Run dialog box:

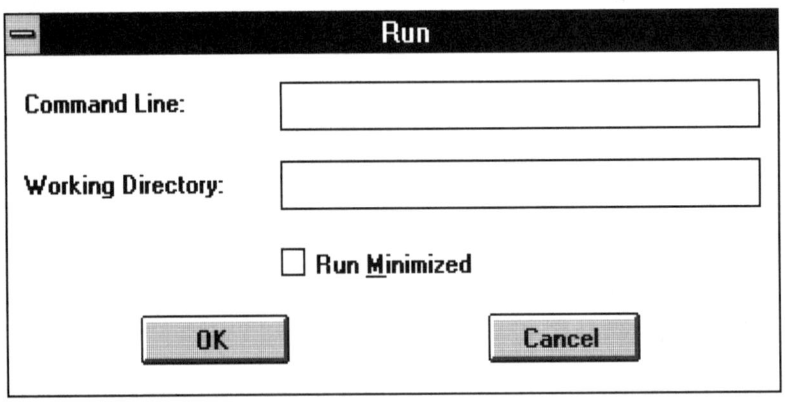

Figure 2.8
Run Dialog Box

Press the CTRL and ESC keys and then select **SAS** from the Task List window to return to your SAS session.

You are limited by Windows NT to a command of 256 characters or less. If the command that you enter is an executable Windows NT application, it runs as it would in the native Windows NT environment.

You can control whether a non-Windows NT application runs in a window or full screen with the PIF editor. Only DOS applications are affected by PIF files.

The working directory for commands executed from the Run dialog box is the SAS System working directory. This is the directory you specified in your SAS command unless you changed it with a CD or change drive command. If your application needs a different working directory, specify this directory in the `Working Directory` field. Not all applications require a special working directory; see your application's documentation for details.

If you select `Run Minimized`, the application or command you execute is invoked and becomes an icon.

Comparison between the Run dialog box and the X statement

There are some important differences between executing a command with the Run dialog box and executing the same command with the X command or statement. A command executed with the Run dialog box is an asynchronous execution. That is, the command is submitted to the operating system and control is immediately returned to the SAS System. In other words, launching an application with the Run dialog box is analogous to launching an application from the Program Manager. For example, if you use the Run dialog box to start Excel and then close your SAS session, the Excel session continues to execute. While you can get the same behavior from the X command or statement, it is not the default behavior. See "XWAIT System Option" on page 23 and "XSYNC System Option" on page 23 for more details.

User-Defined Application Items

You can customize the `File` menu to contain the names of up to eight applications, and you can launch one of these applications by clicking on its name. In this context, application means any file with a .EXE, .COM, or .BAT extension, or any operating system command; that is, an application is considered anything you can type at the operating system command prompt. Note that application here does not refer to applications that have been written with the SAS System.

To add applications to this list, use the REGISTER system option. "Adding Applications to the File Menu" on page 61 gives some examples of using this option.

As with applications or commands executed with the Run dialog box, any application you launch from the user-defined application list runs independently of the SAS System. Even if you close your SAS session, the launched application continues to exist.

Note: The SAS System does not check your REGISTER system option specifications. Therefore, if you make an error in a pathname or mistype a command, the error does not show up until you click on the application name to execute it.

Exit SAS Item

Choosing `Exit SAS` enables you to end your SAS session. When you choose `Exit SAS`, a dialog box verifies your request. If you do not want to be prompted for verification, disable `Confirm Exit of SAS` in the Preferences dialog box (see "Preferences Item" on page 41).

Options Menu

The `Options` menu is shown in Figure 2.9:

Figure 2.9
SAS AWS Options Menu

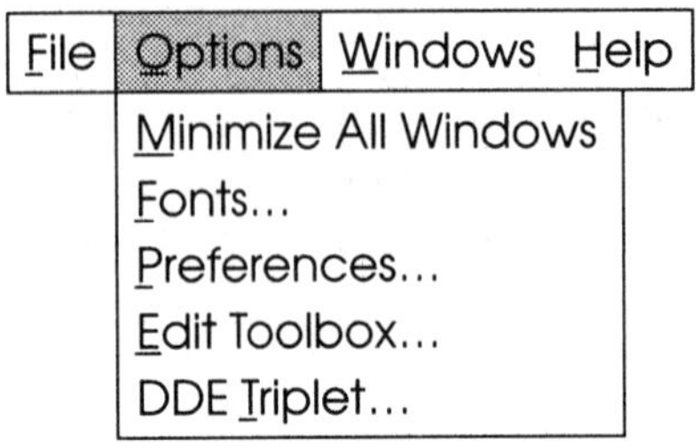

The `Options` menu offers the following choices:

`Minimize (Restore) All Windows`
minimizes all open SAS windows or restores minimized windows to full size.

`Fonts`
changes the text font and point size for text in SAS windows.

`Preferences`
enables you to choose and save your display configuration.

`Edit Toolbox`
edits existing toolboxes and defines new ones.

`DDE Triplet`
determines the DDE triplet for an application.

Each of these items is described in detail in the next four sections.

Minimize All Windows Item

Through the `Options` menu, you can minimize all open SAS windows except the SAS AWS. You may want to use this minimize feature to organize your display.

When you minimize all windows, the `Minimize All Windows` item in the `Options` menu changes to `Restore All Windows`. When you choose `Restore All Windows`, the SAS windows are restored to their previous size and position.

Choosing `Minimize All Windows` has no effect on the SAS AWS itself. For information on minimizing the SAS AWS, see "Customizing Your SAS Application" on page 58.

An alternate method of minimizing all open SAS windows is to use the ICON ALL command. This command can be issued as a display manager command or submitted as part of a SAS program, as in the following example:

```
dm 'icon all';
```

Fonts Item

To choose a different font or point size for text in SAS windows, select **`Fonts`** from the **`Options`** menu, which displays the Fonts Selection dialog box. The fonts available depend on what monospace fonts you have installed under Windows NT. For example, you might have the Courier font and System font available. When you select a font or point size, the **`Font Sample`** field displays a sample of the font you have selected. To save the selected font, choose [Save Workspace] in the Preferences dialog box.

If you purchase and install additional monospace fonts, these fonts are also displayed in the dialog box. You must install additional fonts in the Windows NT Control Panel for the SAS System to be able to find them.

You cannot use **`Fonts`** to select SAS/GRAPH fonts. For information about using hardware fonts under Windows NT, see "Using Hardware Fonts with SAS/GRAPH Software" on page 319.

Beware of changing certain display characteristics on low-resolution displays. If you select large font sizes on some monitors, you may not be able to see all the text in your SAS windows at one time. In some windows, such as the HELP and SAS/ASSIST windows where there are no scroll bars, large font sizes can cause some choices to be invisible. For these types of displays, large font sizes are not recommended. This same problem can occur if you use the Control Panel to change the window border thickness to a thick size. On low resolution displays, you should not use thick window borders. ■

Preferences Item

Choosing **`Preferences`** opens the Preferences dialog box, shown in Figure 2.10:

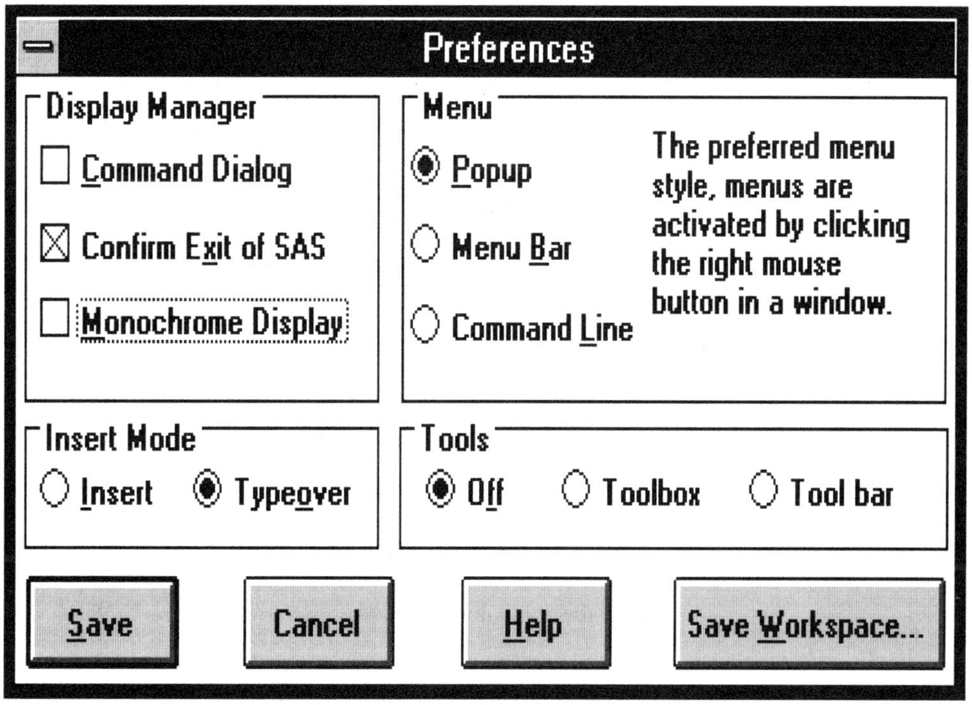

Figure 2.10 Preferences Dialog Box

This dialog box enables you to define interactive user preferences, as follows:

- choose `Command Dialog` to have the Command dialog box open. This enables you to have a command line always available, even when you are using pop-up menus or menu bars. For more information on this dialog box, see "Command Dialog Box" on page 57.
- in the `Tools` area, choose whether you want a Toolbox, Tool bar, or no tools. For more information, see "Using the Toolbox and Tool Bar" on page 62.
- choose `Confirm Exit of SAS` to have the SAS System prompt you for verification when you close your SAS session. Note that even if you have selected `Confirm Exit of SAS`, you can still bypass this verification process by using the BYE or ENDSAS command.
- choose `Monochrome Display` to select a monochrome display. If you do not select a monochrome display, a color display is used. To alter the color of graphics, such as those displayed by SAS/GRAPH software, use the application's color options instead of the Preferences dialog box.
- in the `Menu` area, choose the method of issuing display manager commands: `Popup`, `Menu Bar`, or `Command Line`. For more information, see "Issuing Display Manager Commands" on page 55.
- in the `Insert Mode` area, choose `Insert` or `Typeover` keyboard attributes for the default cursor mode. For more information, see "Using the Cursor" on page 49.
- choose [Save Workspace] to save your work space attributes, such as the size and position of the SAS AWS, WSAVE display manager command information for all displayed SAS windows, the current font and point size, and the current Toolbox and Command dialog box locations. When you choose [Save Workspace], an additional dialog box is opened, giving you the option to either save the work space or cancel.

Make your selections in the Preferences dialog box and choose [Save]. This saves your selections into your SASUSER profile and closes the dialog box. You can cancel your selections by choosing [Cancel] instead of [Save]. However, if you have saved the work space attributes by choosing [Save Workspace], choosing [Cancel] does not undo that save. If you need help on a Preferences dialog box item, choose [Help].

Edit Toolbox Item

`Edit Toolbox` enables you to define tools in the Toolbox and Tool bar. The Toolbox is a graphical key definition window. The Tool bar is similar, but is displayed in the menu bar of the SAS AWS. You can use an icon to represent any valid display manager command sequence. For more information on using and editing tool icons, see "Using the Toolbox and Tool Bar" on page 62.

DDE Triplet Item

`DDE Triplet` enables you to determine the DDE triplet for an application by way of the Clipboard. To use this item, follow these steps:

1. Invoke the application with which you want to use DDE.
2. Mark and copy an area from the application onto the Clipboard.
3. Choose `DDE Triplet`. An information window appears, showing the DDE triplet. You can mark and copy the DDE triplet by pressing CTRL V and then paste the triplet into a program.

Note: The application must be a DDE server. If it is not, the information window displays a message indicating the DDE triplet is not present. Also, not all applications support putting the DDE triplet on the Clipboard; check your application's documentation.

"Dynamic Data Exchange" on page 132 discusses using **`DDE Triplet`** in detail and also describes other features of DDE, such as a special fileref you can use in the FILENAME statement to represent the current DDE triplet stored on the Clipboard.

Windows Menu

The **`Windows`** menu is shown in Figure 2.11:

Figure 2.11
SAS AWS Windows Menu

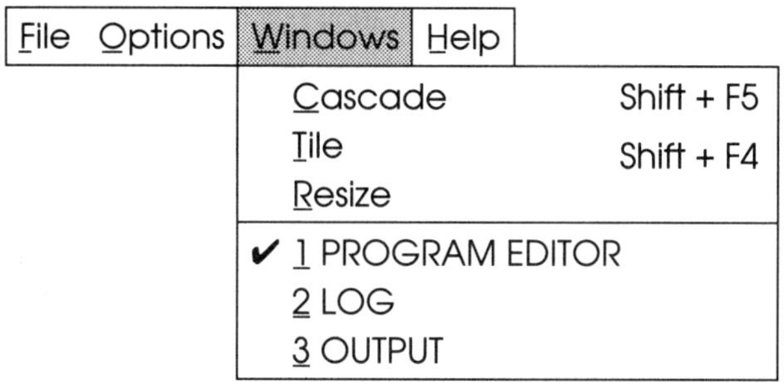

The **`Windows`** menu offers the following choices:

`Cascade`
: arranges the open SAS windows in layers.

`Tile`
: arranges the open SAS windows in a mosaic format.

`Resize`
: returns the display configuration to the last saved configuration, or to the default configuration if there is no saved configuration.

window list
: displays all the open SAS windows and indicates the active window with a check mark.

Each of these items is described in detail in the next four sections.

Cascade Item

`Cascade` layers the open SAS windows on top of one another. In some SAS applications, such as SAS/LAB software, only the application work space for that application is cascaded rather than the individual windows within the application.

Tile Item

`Tile` arranges the open SAS windows in a mosaic format. In some SAS applications, such as SAS/ASSIST software, only the application work space for that application is tiled rather than the individual windows within the application.

Resize Item

A default display configuration is provided at installation of the SAS System under Windows NT. If you change the display layout during a SAS session, you can restore the display to the SAS System default or last saved layout by selecting **`Resize`**. If you have saved your display layout using the WSAVE display manager command or [Save Workspace] in the Preferences dialog box, **`Resize`** restores the SAS System display configuration to the last display configuration saved, rather than the SAS System default display layout. If you want to delete the saved layout and restore your display layout to the SAS System default display configuration, use the CATALOG window to delete the WSAVE entries from your SASUSER.PROFILE catalog. To access the CATALOG window, select

[Globals] ▶ [Data management] ▶ [Catalog directory]

from the pop-up menu in any SAS window. The next time you invoke the SAS System, the SAS System default display layout is used.

Active Window Selection

Another feature of the **`Windows`** menu is a list of all open windows that indicates the active SAS window and enables you to change the active SAS window. The windows in the open window list are in order of the most recently opened window first. A check mark in front of a window name indicates the active window. For example, in Figure 2.12, the NOTEPAD window is the active window. To change the active window, click on the name of the window you want to activate.

Figure 2.12
SAS AWS Window List

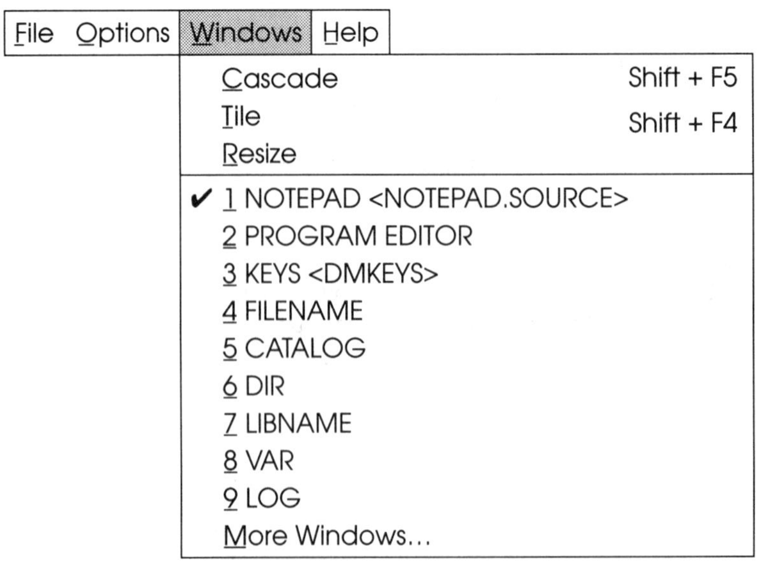

If more than nine windows are open concurrently within the SAS session, the last item on the `Windows` menu is `More Windows`. When you select `More Windows`, a dialog box displays all open SAS windows and prompts you to choose a new active window.

Help Menu

The SAS AWS menu bar contains a `Help` menu that includes several help categories, as shown in Figure 2.13.

The Help facility works like hypertext in that it enables you to select key words in the text about which you would like further information. Key words are highlighted in reverse video.

Note: Most child windows of the SAS AWS (such as the PROGRAM EDITOR and OUTPUT windows) also have a `Help` menu that is similar to the SAS AWS `Help` menu.

Figure 2.13
SAS AWS Help Menu

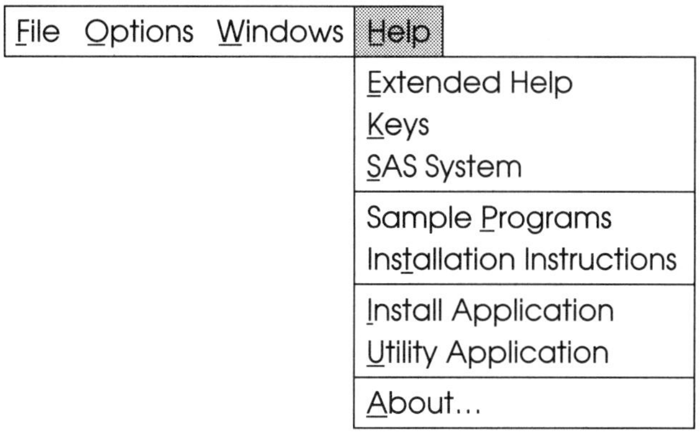

The `Help` menu offers the following choices:

`Extended Help`
displays help for the SAS AWS window.

`Keys`
enables you to display and change function display manager key definitions. The key definitions displayed by the `Keys` item are used in windows such as the PROGRAM EDITOR, LOG, and OUTPUT. To access key definitions for other SAS products such as SAS/FSP or SAS/INSIGHT software, select `Help` then `Keys` from the specific window, such as the FSEDIT window.

`SAS System`
provides general information about features of the SAS System.

`Sample Programs`
enables you to access many of the sample programs in the SAS Sample Library.

`Installation Instructions`
displays detailed help on how to install the SAS System under Windows NT.

`Install Application`
invokes the installation process.

`Utility Application`
: invokes various utility applications.

`About`
: includes information about the SAS System copyright, as well as details of your system configuration.

Each of these items is described in detail in the next six sections.

Extended Help Item

When you choose **`Extended Help`** from the SAS AWS **`Help`** menu, information about the SAS AWS window is displayed. Each time you click on a text string that is selectable, you branch off to additional help on that topic. To return to the previous frame, select [Goback] or close the window from the Control menu icon.

Note: When you select **`Extended Help`** from menus other than the SAS AWS **`Help`** menu, **`Extended Help`** displays the help frame that you get if you issue the HELP command from a SAS window command line. Usually, this is the information about that particular window; from the PROGRAM EDITOR, LOG, and OUTPUT windows, **`Extended Help`** displays the SAS System help window.

Keys Item

Choosing **`Keys`** displays the key definitions that are active for the SAS AWS, that is, the DMKEYS entry in your SASUSER.PROFILE catalog. These key definitions apply to the basic SAS windows, such as PROGRAM EDITOR, OUTPUT, and LOG windows. Other SAS products, such as SAS/FSP software, have their own key definitions. Use the pop-up menus in the specific product window, such as the FSEDIT window, to access key definitions for specific products.

Although the SAS System lets you define any key listed in the KEYS window, Windows NT reserves some keys for itself to maintain conformity among Windows NT applications. These reserved keys are not shown in the KEYS window.

To define or redefine a key within the SAS System, place the cursor in the **`Definition`** column across from the key or mouse button you want to define and type the display manager command or commands you want to associate with that key or button. The definition must be a valid SAS command or sequence of commands. For example, if you want to define the CTRL H key sequence to maximize a window and recall the last submitted program, specify the following commands in the **`Definitions`** column next to **`CTL H`**:

```
zoom; recall
```

The SAS System does not check the syntax of a command until it is used (that is, when the key is pressed). If you misspell a command or type an incorrect command, you do not discover your error until you use the key and receive an error message indicating that the command was unrecognized.

Your key definitions are stored in your SAS user profile catalog. As described in Chapter 1, a profile catalog is created each time you invoke the SAS System with a different value for the SASUSER option. Changes you make to one profile catalog are not reflected in any other. However, you can use the COPY command from the KEYS window or the CATALOG procedure to copy key definition members to other profile catalogs. See Chapter 8, "The CATALOG Procedure," in the *SAS Procedures Guide, Version 6, Third Edition* for more information about using the CATALOG procedure.

There are also some keys with special functions under Windows NT that the SAS System makes available for your use. These keys are especially important if you are not using a mouse.

ALT Spacebar
: opens the SAS AWS Control menu.

ALT
: toggles between the SAS AWS menu bar and the active window.

ALT –
: opens the Control menu of the active window.

CTRL ALT –
: opens the Control menu of a SAS application such as SAS/ASSIST software.

CTRL F6
: displays each open SAS window, one at a time, changing input focus to each window that is able to receive input.

ALT F6
: toggles between the active SAS windows and modeless dialog boxes such as the Command dialog box or the Toolbox. *Modeless* means that you do not have to close the dialog box before you can continue your SAS session. If you have two modeless dialog boxes open, ALT F6 toggles between the two open dialog boxes.

ESC
: returns one level from a menu.

For example, if you are using the keyboard rather than a mouse and you want to select **`Data management`** from the **`Globals`** pop-up menu in the PROGRAM EDITOR window, complete the following steps (assuming you are using pop-up menus, not menu bars):

1. Be sure your cursor is in the PROGRAM EDITOR window.
2. Press the ALT– keys to open the PROGRAM EDITOR's Control menu.
3. Press ENTER to access the window's menu (or press the U key, which is the accelerator key for **`Menu`**).
4. Use the down arrow key to move to **`Globals`**, and press ENTER (or press the G key, which is the accelerator key for **`Globals`**).
5. Use the down arrow key to move to **`Data management`** and press ENTER (or press the T key, which is the accelerator key for **`Data management`**). If at this point you decide you do not want to make a selection, press the ALT key to return to the work space area of the window or press the ESC key to return one level at a time from the menus to the active window.

SAS System Item

Choosing **SAS System** provides a help facility for the entire SAS System. The SAS System help facility is particularly useful when you need to review the syntax of SAS functions, procedures, or options. SAS System help is organized by topics, such as report writing and host information.

The **Host Information** help topic is of special interest to users of the SAS System under Windows NT because this is where you find all of the system-dependent details of the SAS System under Windows NT. These details include topics such as functions, SAS statements and statement options, and system options. Figure 2.14 shows the PC WORKSTATION HELP window:

Figure 2.14
PC WORKSTATION HELP Window

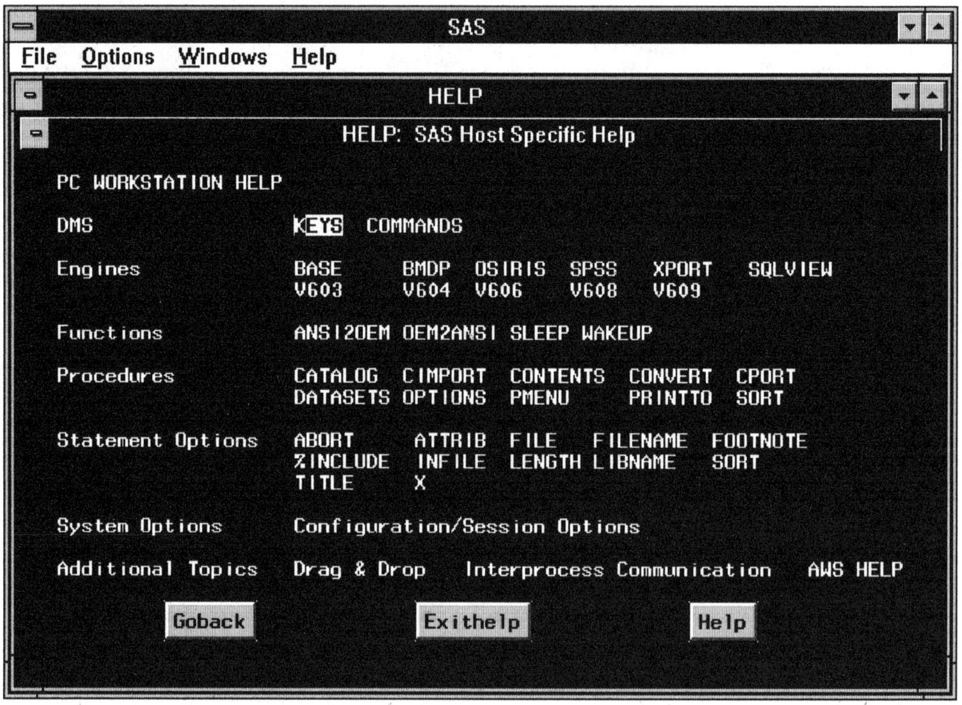

Sample Programs Item

Choosing **Sample Programs** displays (in native Windows NT help format) a list of SAS products, such as base SAS software, SAS/ACCESS software, and so on. Clicking on a product name displays an index of sample program titles. Click on a program title to see the program code. After the code appears, you can copy it to the Clipboard and submit it to the SAS System.

Installation Instructions Item

The **Installation Instructions** item provides (in the native Windows NT help format) detailed instructions on using the INSTALL application (discussed next). When you choose **Installation Instructions**, an index to installation topics is displayed. Click on a topic to display more details. The information displayed by choosing **Installation Instructions** corresponds to the information in *Installation Instructions for the SAS System, Release 6.09, under Microsoft Windows NT*.

Install Application Item

Choosing `Install Application` invokes the INSTALL application to assist you in installing or deleting products and components of SAS software. For more information on installing the SAS System, see your installation instructions.

Utility Application Item

Choosing `Utility Application` invokes utility applications that enable you to perform frequently used operations more easily. For example, if you have licensed SAS/GRAPH software, there is a utility that enables you to compress or decompress a map data set or add third party fonts for use with SAS/GRAPH software. See Appendix 6, "Utility Application" on page 343 for more information.

About Item

Choosing `About` provides you with details about your SAS environment, such as which versions of Windows NT and the SAS System you are running, whether you are using a math coprocessor, whether you are using the ANSI or OEM character set, and SAS System copyright information.

Working within Your SAS Session

This section provides information you need to use the SAS System efficiently under Windows NT. Topics include

- □ using the cursor for text entry
- □ using icons
- □ using the PROGRAM EDITOR
- □ using the Clipboard
- □ using ESC key and ALT key sequences
- □ issuing display manager commands.

Using the Cursor

Typeover mode is the default for SAS System text entry. In typeover mode, the cursor appears as a rectangular block, and characters are replaced as you type. When the cursor is in insert mode, it appears as a slender bar, called an *I-beam*. When you position the I-beam between two characters in insert mode, characters you type from the keyboard appear after the cursor.

You can toggle between insert and typeover mode by pressing the INSERT key. You can change the default cursor setting by opening the Preferences dialog box and choosing either `Insert` or `Typeover` in the `Insert Mode` area. Select [Save] and the cursor setting changes to the setting you choose.

Using Icons

Each SAS window (such as the PROGRAM EDITOR or OUTPUT window) has an icon associated with it. When a window is minimized, its icon appears at the bottom of the SAS AWS. These icons may be obscured by other open SAS windows, but you can activate them by using a window-call command (usually the name of the window). For example, if the PROGRAM EDITOR window is minimized, you can make the PROGRAM EDITOR window active by selecting the PROGRAM EDITOR window name in the SAS AWS `Windows` menu.

If you minimize the entire SAS AWS by selecting the minimize icon from the SAS AWS, the SAS icon appears at the bottom of the display. If the SAS System is currently processing any data, the SAS icon appears as an hourglass. (The hourglass is described in "Wait Cursor" on page 6.) Once processing is complete, the icon returns to its default appearance.

Individual windows inside a SAS application, such as SAS/ASSIST windows, may not have icons associated with them. In this case, only the application itself can be iconized.

Using the PROGRAM EDITOR Window

Under Windows NT, the SAS PROGRAM EDITOR window has been designed to work in a manner similar to other Windows NT editors such as Notepad. Thus you can edit your SAS code without learning how to use a new text editor. The following paragraphs explain some of the PROGRAM EDITOR window's features.

Line Numbers

If you are familiar with the SAS PROGRAM EDITOR window under other operating systems, such as MVS, notice that under Windows NT, line numbers are turned off by default. You can enter the NUMBERS ON command from the command line to display line numbers in the PROGRAM EDITOR window. You can also display line numbers by selecting `Edit` and then `Options` and `Numbers` from the PROGRAM EDITOR window pop-up menu.

To save your line number setting, choose

Options ▸ Preferences ▸ Save Workspace

from the AWS menu. An alternative method is to use the WSAVE command to save the settings for the PROGRAM EDITOR window only. One way to issue the WSAVE command is to choose `Save attributes` from the `View` menu in the PROGRAM EDITOR window.

Cursor Movement

The cursor movement keys (→, ←, ↑, ↓, PgUp, PgDn, and so on) function the same way in the PROGRAM EDITOR window as they do in other Windows NT applications.

Pressing the CTRL key with the ← (word left) or → (word right) causes the cursor to move one word at a time. When advancing through text, the word left and word right commands stop at the end of the text on a line and at the beginning of the first word on a new line. You can move to the top of a file by pressing CTRL PgUp or to the bottom of a file by pressing CTRL PgDn.

Pressing the HOME key causes the cursor to go to the beginning of the current line unless the command line is active. Pressing the HOME key when the command line is active causes the cursor to toggle between the current cursor position in the text and the command line.

Tab Key

Many text editors retain tab characters, while others expand tabs into space characters. The SAS PROGRAM EDITOR window expands tabs into space characters. Pressing the TAB key inserts spaces and moves any text to the right of the cursor.

By default, tabs are set on every 8th column. If you change the tab settings, the SAS System honors the new settings. If you remove all tab settings, the TAB key moves the cursor to the beginning of the next field and does not add any spaces to the text.

Line Breaks

Conceptually, line breaks are at the end of the line rather than at the beginning. Pressing the ENTER key creates a line break. To delete a line break, press the BACKSPACE key at the beginning of a line or press the DELETE key at the end of the line.

Marking Text

You can use the mouse or the SHIFT key in combination with the cursor movement keys to mark text. The marking of an area of text continues until you release the mouse button or press a key that is not a cursor movement key. Pressing an unshifted cursor movement key also ends the marked area.

If characters are marked and you start typing text, the marked area is replaced with the new text. This occurs even if you have moved the cursor away from the marked area. See "Using the Clipboard" on page 52 for information about marking and copying text with a mouse and in non-text windows.

Deleting Text

The DELETE key deletes a marked area of text if one exists; otherwise, the character to the right of the cursor is deleted. If the cursor is located past the last text character on the line, the next line is concatenated onto the end of the line containing the cursor.

Unique Features

The following features of the SAS PROGRAM EDITOR window are different from the standard features of other editors commonly used in the Windows NT environment:

- The SAS PROGRAM EDITOR window allows you to move the cursor past the last character entered on a line or past the last line of text entered.
- Extended marking is not supported. In some text editors, you can mark an area of text and then use the mouse to extend the mark.
- You can mark an area of text, move the cursor away from the marked area, and the marked text remains marked.
- You can use SHIFT TAB to delete blank space characters back to the last tab stop.

- Pasting from the Clipboard to a marked area is not supported. You must first cut, copy, delete, or unmark the area.
- Copying to the Clipboard removes text marking.

Using the Clipboard

The Windows NT Clipboard enables you to exchange text and graphics between applications. You can also submit SAS code stored on the Clipboard. The Clipboard uses operating system memory as an intermediate storage buffer for exchanging text and graphics. With the Clipboard, you can move text between

- windows within the SAS System
- the SAS System and other Windows NT applications
- two SAS sessions.

The SAS System under Windows NT can store information in seven formats:

the SAS text format
: preserves the text and color attributes between SAS sessions. This format is understood by the SAS System, but not necessarily by other Windows NT applications.

the Windows NT text format
: is understood by most Windows NT applications and is called the ANSI text format.

the OEM text format
: is used when running in OEM mode. The text format is based on the current codepage. See Appendix 4 for more information on using OEM fonts under Windows NT.

the Unicode text format
: is a universal text format that can represent all possible characters. The format is also referred to as a wide-character format. See your Windows NT documentation for more information on this text format.

the Windows NT bitmap format
: is for HELP windows, graphics, and windows in SAS/ASSIST software. This format is understood by most Windows NT applications and is called the BITMAP format.

the metafile format
: is used in many Windows NT applications that support the GSTORE command, such as the Graphics Editor in SAS/GRAPH software, SAS/QC software's ISHIKAWA procedure, and SAS/INSIGHT software. The metafile format provides more information about the image than the bitmap format, and is called the PICTURE format.

the DIB (Device Independent Bitmap) format
: is used with color bitmap files. When a bitmap is stored in the DIB format, colors map correctly from one device to another.

These formats enable you to copy SAS bitmapped information (for example, from a graphic) to another application.

Choosing [Font] enables you to select a printer font. The SAS System uses the printer font you select until you select another one. This font information is stored in your SASUSER.PROFILE2 catalog.

You can use the Clipboard only if both the source and destination applications provide support for the Clipboard facility and for the format you are using.

Marking and Copying Text

For windows that contain text, such as the PROGRAM EDITOR, LOG, OUTPUT, KEYS, and OPTIONS windows, you can hold down the left mouse button and drag the mouse to mark the area you want to cut or copy. The text area is immediately marked in reverse video while you are dragging the mouse. In text windows, you can scroll while you are dragging the mouse by moving the cursor beyond the border of the window in the direction you want to scroll. Release the mouse button when you have included all the text you want to copy.

To copy marked text to the Clipboard, select **`Copy to paste buffer`** from the **`Edit`** pop-up menu.

To paste text that is stored on the Clipboard, position the cursor in a text area in a window and select **`Paste text`** from the **`Edit`** pop-up menu. The text from the Clipboard is pasted to the area you indicate.

Marking and Copying in Non-Text Windows

For windows such as the HELP, GRAPH, and SAS/ASSIST windows, an area is marked by a box, not by reverse video. The box indicates that the area you are marking is in bitmap format. You cannot scroll in these windows while you are marking text. After you finish marking an area, you can copy it to the Clipboard. If the window you are working in has no **`Edit`** pop-up menu, you can use the following keys to perform the cut and paste functions (assuming you have not redefined them):

CTRL M	is the MARK command.
CTRL S	is the STORE (copy to paste buffer) command.
CTRL K	is the CUT command (only used with marked text, not graphics).
CTRL U	is the UNMARK command.
CTRL P	is the PASTE command.

Because the SAS System under Windows NT uses the Windows NT Clipboard, you do not have access to multiple paste buffers.

You can also use the PRT SCREEN and ALT-PRT SCREEN keys to copy information from you SAS session to the Clipboard. Pressing PRT SCREEN places the entire display in bitmap form on the Clipboard. Pressing ALT-PRT SCREEN places the active window (including any menus and scroll bars) on the Clipbard.

Using the GSTORE Command

SAS/QC software's ISHIKAWA procedure and the Graphics Editor support the storing of metafile graphics format as well as bitmap formats to the Clipboard. In the Graphics Editor, the area you mark is enclosed in a box, and you cannot scroll as you mark. The GSTORE command should be used to store the currently marked area (the entire screen when used with the ISHIKAWA procedure) to the Windows NT Clipboard in device-dependent bitmap

(BMP), device-independent bitmap (DIB), and metafile (PICTURE) graphical data formats. You can also choose **Copy to paste buffer** from the **Edit** menu to store the marked area to the Clipboard.

Pasting Bitmapped Information into Your SAS Session

Some windows, such as FRAME entries in SAS/AF software, enable you to paste into the window (unlike non-text windows, such as the HELP window).

Unless you license SAS/IMAGE software, you cannot paste bitmapped information from other applications into your SAS session.*

Submitting SAS Code from the Clipboard

The SAS System under Windows NT enables you to use the Windows NT Clipboard to submit SAS code. This feature can be used to copy or cut SAS code from another application, such as the Windows NT Notepad or another text editor, and submit it to the SAS System for execution.

To submit SAS code stored on the Clipboard, you can select

Locals ▶ Submit clipboard

from the pop-up menu in the PROGRAM EDITOR window. Alternatively, you can use the GSUBMIT command. The GSUBMIT command can be entered from the command line of any SAS display manager window, or it can be assigned to a function key. The following command submits SAS code stored on the Clipboard:

```
gsubmit buf=default
```

The GSUBMIT command can be used to submit SAS code stored on the Clipboard even if the PROGRAM EDITOR window is closed. If you use the GSUBMIT command often, you may want to define an icon for it in the Toolbox, or assign the GSUBMIT command to a function key. See "Adding a Bitmap to the Toolbox" on page 65 for more information about how to define Toolbox icons.

Using ESC and ALT Key Sequences

This section presents information on controlling text color in SAS applications with ESC key sequences and creating alternate ASCII characters with ALT key sequences.

---

* SAS/IMAGE software is a beta product in Release 6.09. For information about how to obtain SAS/IMAGE software, contact your SAS Site Representative.

Special Character Attributes

Extended color and highlight attribute keys are implemented for the NOTEPAD window and in SAS/AF and SAS/FSP applications. Press the ESC key and the indicated letter or number to turn a color or attribute on or off. With this feature, you can alter the color or attributes of entire lines or individual words or letters. Valid colors and attributes, as well as the keys you use to implement them, are listed in Table 2.1 and Table 2.2. You can type the letters for the colors in either uppercase or lowercase.

Table 2.1
Extended Color Key Sequences

Key	Color	Key	Color
ESC A	gray	ESC B	blue
ESC C	cyan	ESC G	green
ESC K	black	ESC M	magenta
ESC N	brown	ESC O	orange
ESC P	pink	ESC R	red
ESC W	white	ESC Y	yellow

Table 2.2
Extended Attribute Key Sequences

Key	Description
ESC 0	turns off all highlighting attributes.
ESC 2	turns on the underline attribute.
ESC 3	turns on the reverse-video attribute.

Alternate ASCII Characters

If you want to create alternate ASCII characters such as foreign language characters, you can use the ALT key in combination with the ASCII character code. Be sure to use the numeric keypad to enter the character code and have Num Lock on. See your Windows NT documentation for a list of ASCII character codes and instructions about how to use the ALT key sequences.

Issuing Display Manager Commands

You can choose among four methods of issuing commands to the SAS System:

- □ pop-up menus
- □ menu bars
- □ command line
- □ Command dialog box.

Choose `Preferences` in the SAS AWS `Options` menu to switch between and combine these methods of issuing commands. The next four sections give you some details on the differences between the methods. Which method you choose depends entirely on your personal preference and the needs of your application. A fifth method of issuing commands is called the Toolbox. This feature enables you to associate display manager commands with icons, and you click on the icons to execute the commands. See "Using the Toolbox and Tool Bar" on page 62 for more details. You can also use function keys to issue commands. See "Keys Item" on page 46 for more information.

Pop-Up Menus

Pop-up menus do not appear until you issue the WPOPUP command. By default, the WPOPUP command is assigned to the right mouse button. Pressing the right mouse button in a SAS window causes the menu to appear. After the menu appears, you can click on menu items to select them. You can assign the WPOPUP command to another mouse button or a function key if you want, using the KEYS window.

Selecting a pop-up menu item can lead you to a series of cascading menus. Appendix 5, "Pop-Up Menu and Menu Bar Map" on page 339 provides a road map of the pop-up menus of the primary display manager windows to assist you in finding the menu item you need.

Note: If you use the Preferences dialog box to choose pop-up menus, by default the PMENU display manager command toggles between the command line and pop-up menus. You can also enter the PMENU POPUP command from either the Command dialog box or the command line to select pop-up menus. See "System-Dependent Windowing Features" on page 280 for more information on the PMENU command under Windows NT.

Menu Bars

Menu bars use more system resources than pop-up menus; however, they have the advantage of always being displayed. To replace the pop-up menus with menu bars, select `Menu Bar` from the Preferences dialog box. See "Preferences Item" on page 41 for a discussion of the Preferences dialog box.

Selecting a menu bar item can lead you to a series of cascading menus. Appendix 5 provides a road map of the menus of the primary display manager windows to assist you in finding the menu item you need.

Note: If you use the Preferences dialog box to choose menu bars, by default the PMENU display manager command toggles between the command line and menu bars. You can also enter the PMENU MENUBAR command from either the Command dialog box or the command line to select menu bars. See "System-Dependent Windowing Features" on page 280 for more information on the PMENU command under Windows NT.

Command Line

If you want to use the command line to issue display manager commands, select `Command Line` from the Preferences dialog box. See "Preferences Item" on page 41 for a discussion of this dialog box. You can also use the PMENU OFF command to activate the command line. Issuing the PMENU ON command replaces the command line with pop-up menus or menu bars, depending on which was the last active method of issuing display manager commands. You can use the MENUBAR and POPUP options in the PMENU command to choose which type of menu you want to replace the command line with. See "System-Dependent Windowing Features" on page 280 for more information on the PMENU command under Windows NT.

Command Dialog Box

The Command dialog box enables you to have a command line for display manager commands at the same time you are using pop-up menus, menu bars, or command lines. Figure 2.15 shows the LOG and PROGRAM EDITOR windows along with the Command dialog box:

Figure 2.15
Command Dialog Box

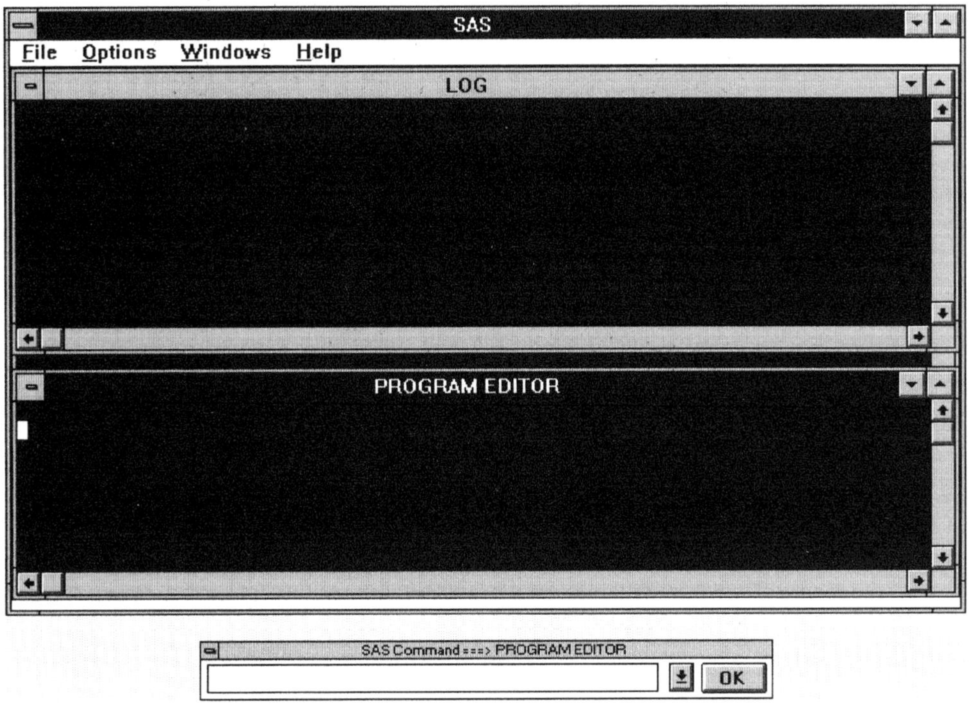

You open the Command dialog box in one of four ways:

- □ Choose **`Command Dialog`** in the Preferences dialog box.
- □ Select the following from any SAS window pop-up menu:

  Globals ▸ Command ▸ Command...

- □ Issue the following command:

  COMMAND WINDOW <'*title*'>

- □ press F11, which by default is defined as the COMMAND WINDOW command.

The *title* argument in the COMMAND WINDOW command is optional. If you do not specify a title, the default title is SAS Command ===> *active-window*. For example, if the PROGRAM EDITOR window is active, the title of the Command dialog box is SAS Command ===> PROGRAM EDITOR. Here is an example of issuing the COMMAND WINDOW command as part of a DM statement. Note the use of double quotes and single quotes because the title is more than one word.

```
dm "command window 'My SAS Command'";
```

If your title does not contain spaces, you can omit the quotes around the title, as in the following example:

```
dm 'command window CmdLine';
```

In this example, the title of the Command dialog box is CmdLine.

Note: If the Command dialog box is already open, the COMMAND WINDOW command causes the Command dialog box to be the active window. By default, F11 is defined as the COMMAND WINDOW command. The Command dialog box remains open until you close it. Issuing a command from the Command dialog box does not close it. The command you enter in the text field applies to the active window unless you specify the window as part of the command. For example, if you specify PRINT and the PROGRAM EDITOR window is active, the contents of the PROGRAM EDITOR window are printed. But if you specify OUTPUT; PRINT, the contents of the OUTPUT window are printed, because now the OUTPUT window is active. Use the ALT F6 key to toggle between the active window and the Command dialog box. For more information on the ALT F6 key, see "Keys Item" on page 46.

Clicking on the arrow in the Command dialog box displays the last ten commands you have entered. To reissue a command select the appropriate command in the list and choose [OK]. You can use F4 to toggle the list of commands on and off as long as the Command dialog box is active.

The END command ends the active window; it does not close the Command dialog box. To close the Command dialog box, use ALT F4. Be careful not to press ALT F4 twice—doing so will close your entire SAS session.

By default, the Command dialog box is not open when your SAS session begins. Use the Preferences dialog box to cause the Command dialog box to appear as the SAS System initializes. As an alternative to using the Preferences dialog box to ensure the Command dialog box opens when the SAS System initializes, you could use the INITSTMT system option in your CONFIG.SAS file to issue a DM statement with the COMMAND WINDOW command. Or put the DM statement in your AUTOEXEC.SAS file. You can also assign the COMMAND WINDOW command to a function key (by default, F11). When you press the key, the Command dialog box appears. Or if the Command dialog box is already open, the Command dialog box becomes the active window.

The default position of the Command dialog box is the bottom center of your display. You can move the Command dialog box anywhere you want, even outside of the SAS AWS, yet it is still tied to your SAS session. Therefore, if you iconize your SAS session, the Command dialog box disappears. Restoring the SAS icon restores the Command dialog box as well. You can save the Command dialog box position by choosing [Save Workspace] in the Preferences dialog box.

Note: You can use the COMDEF system option to set the position of the Command dialog box when the SAS System first initializes. The COMDEF option, which is described on page 181, does not cause the Command dialog box to open automatically.

Customizing Your SAS Application

The user interface for the SAS System under Windows NT is very flexible. You can customize the appearance and behavior of your SAS session by using display manager commands, system options, and commands to display and change the Toolbox (or Tool bar).

Customizing Your Windowing Environment

You can use several display manager commands to customize your SAS windowing environment. This section illustrates using some of these commands.

Using Display Manager Commands

In Chapter 1, Figure 1.2 shows the default display configuration of a display manager session: the LOG and PROGRAM EDITOR windows are the only two windows visible, and they are split evenly (the LOG window occupies the upper half of the display and the PROGRAM EDITOR window occupies the lower half). Although you can't see it in Figure 1.2, the OUTPUT window is also open and is positioned behind the LOG and PROGRAM EDITOR windows.

While the default display configuration is sufficient for efficient SAS System use, you may want to open a few more windows for easy access and rearrange the windows on your display. For example, you may want the FILENAME and LIBNAME windows open, but iconized, with the windows arranged in a mosaic pattern so you can see all of them at once. To accomplish this, submit the following statements:

```
dm 'filename; icon';
dm 'libname; icon';
dm 'tile';
```

These statements result in a display configuration similar to the one shown in Figure 2.16:

Figure 2.16
Customized Display Manager Session

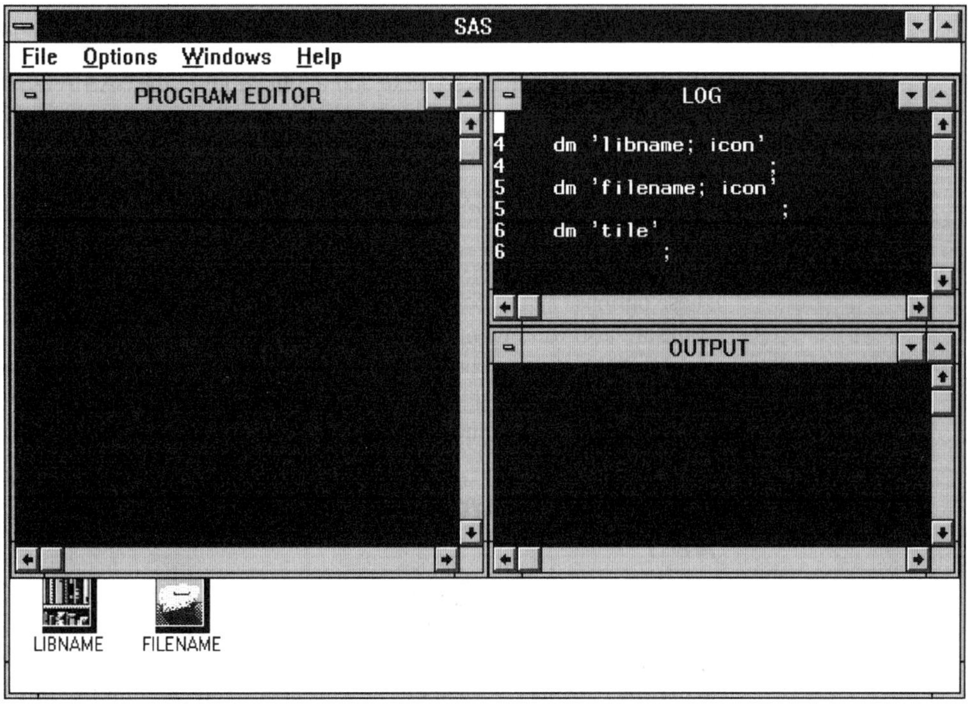

A complete list of display manager commands with system dependencies can be found in "System-Dependent Windowing Features" on page 280.

Changing the Window Colors

Changing the color of window components is a shared responsibility of Windows NT and the SAS System. You change the color of the following window parts by selecting `Color` from the Windows NT Control Panel:

application work space background	push buttons
menu text	title bar
scroll bars	menu bar
border	

Most other window component colors are controlled by the SAS System. To change a window component that is controlled by the SAS System, select `Colors` from the `View` menu. The specific window components available to you vary according to the window you are in. For more information on the color commands available, see Chapter 18, "SAS Display Manager Commands," in *SAS Language: Reference.*

Customizing Your SAS Session with System Options

Several SAS system options are available to enhance the windowing environment within the SAS System. The most commonly used options are the following:

AWSDEF
: specifies the location and dimensions of the SAS AWS when the SAS System initializes.

AWSTITLE
: specifies the text for the SAS AWS title bar.

ICON
: minimizes the SAS AWS when the SAS System initializes.

REGISTER
: enables you to add applications to the SAS AWS `File` menu so you can execute them by clicking on their names.

USERICON
: specifies user-defined icons to be incorporated into SAS/AF applications.

FONT
: specifies a font name and point size to use as the default display manager font.

These options can be specified in your SAS configuration file or in the SAS command. Some are also valid in an OPTIONS statement. For details on the syntax of these options and on where you can specify them, see Chapter 7. Other system options also affect your SAS display manager session, such as COMDEF, TOOLDEF, PFKEY, NUMMOUSEKEYS, and NUMKEYS. These options are also described in Chapter 7.

Changing the Size and Placement of the SAS AWS

The AWSDEF option enables you to control the placement and size of the SAS AWS when the SAS System initializes. By default, the SAS AWS takes up the entire display, except for space for icons at the bottom of the display. But suppose you want your SAS session always to occupy the upper-left quarter of your display. To accomplish this, specify the following AWSDEF option in your SAS configuration file:

```
-awsdef 0 0 50 50
```

For more information on the AWSDEF option, see page 179.

Changing the Title of Your SAS Session

By default, the SAS AWS title bar contains the text **SAS**. If you want a different title, you can use the AWSTITLE option. To set the title to **My SAS Session**, specify the following option in your SAS configuration file:

```
-awstitle "My SAS Session"
```

Minimizing Your SAS Session

The ICON system option causes the SAS System to be minimized at invocation. If you are running a batch job, you might want to use this option to save space on your display.

Adding Applications to the File Menu

The REGISTER system option enables you to add names of applications to the **File** menu of the SAS AWS. You can execute one of these applications by clicking on its name. The REGISTER option takes as arguments a menu name and an operating system command or a path specification for an executable file. You can also specify a working directory. Here is an example that adds a DIR command to the list. This command prints the contents of the SASUSER directory:

```
-register "Contents of SASUSER" "dir c:\sas\sasuser"
```

When you click on **Contents of SASUSER** from the **File** menu, the output of the DIR command is displayed in a command prompt window.

Here is an example of adding an .EXE file to the menu along with a specification of a working directory of C:\EXDATA:

```
-register "Excel" "excel.exe" "c:\exdata"
```

This adds **Excel** to the menu. When you click on **Excel**, the file EXCEL.EXE is invoked. Figure 2.17 shows the **File** menu with three application items added:

Figure 2.17
File Menu with Three User-Defined Application Items

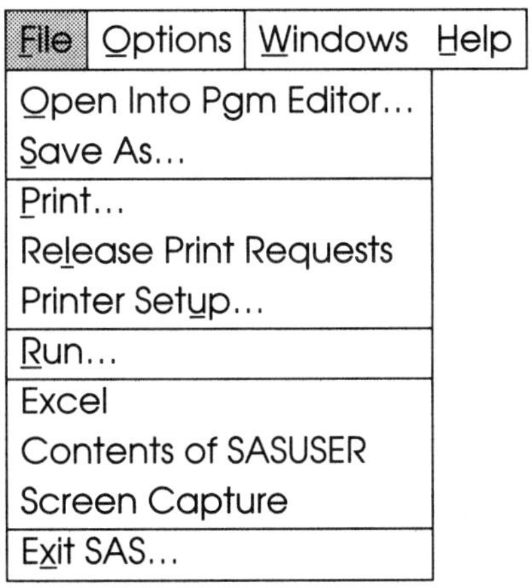

Note: The REGISTER system option is valid only in the CONFIG.SAS file and in the SAS command.

Adding User-Defined Icons to the SAS System

The USERICON option enables you to add your own icons to the SAS System. These icons can be used with SAS/AF and SAS/EIS applications. The syntax for the USERICON option is as follows:

-USERICON *icon-resource-file number-of-icons*

The *icon-resource-file* argument specifies the full path to a dynamic link library (DLL) file that contains the user icons. The *number-of-icons* argument specifies the number of icons found in the resource file. For example, the following option specifies that there are four icons located in an icon resource file named ICONS.DLL found in the C:\JUNK directory:

```
-usericon c:\junk\icons.dll 4
```

The DLL that is used as the icon resource file must be created using the Win32 Software Development Kit. Refer to the *Microsoft Win32 Software Development Kit* manual for more information on how to build a resource file.*

You can incorporate icons into your SAS/AF and SAS/EIS applications using a FRAME entry. Refer to *SAS/AF Software: FRAME Entry Usage and Reference, Version 6, First Edition* and *SAS/EIS Software: Reference, Version 6, First Edition* for more information.

Using the Toolbox and Tool Bar

The SAS System under Windows NT provides two methods of associating bitmaps with display manager commands: the Toolbox and the Tool bar. These two features are similar. The Toolbox is a window containing bitmaps. You can move the Toolbox around your display. The Tool bar is a sequence of bitmaps in the menu bar of the SAS AWS. You cannot move the Tool bar.

Note: Because the Toolbox and Tool bar are simply two visual representations of the same feature, the following text uses Toolbox for both, unless a difference between Toolbox and Tool bar behavior exists.

* Because Microsoft has changed the DLL format between Windows and Windows NT, you cannot use DLLs created under Windows in your Windows NT SAS session. You must rebuild your DLL files under Windows NT.

Understanding the Toolbox

The Toolbox is like a graphical KEYS window. Just as you can assign any valid sequence of SAS display manager commands to a mouse button or function key, you can also associate a bitmap with a display manager command or commands. Clicking on one or another of the tool bitmaps executes the command or commands associated with that bitmap. Figure 2.18 shows the Toolbox; the same bitmaps are available with the Tool bar.

Figure 2.18
Default Toolbox

By default, no tools are displayed when the SAS System initializes.

Choosing between the Toolbox and Tool Bar

Use the Preferences dialog box to specify whether you want the Toolbox or Tool bar active. If you prefer the Toolbox, choose `Toolbox` in the `Tools` area of the Preferences dialog box. When you choose [Save], the Toolbox opens. If you prefer the Tool bar, chose `Tool bar`. When you choose [Save], the tool bitmaps appear in the menu bar of the SAS AWS.

Defining the position of the Toolbox

You cannot change the position of the Tool bar; it is always in the menu bar of the SAS AWS. However, you can move the Toolbox wherever you want. The default position of the Toolbox is the top right corner of your display. You can move the Toolbox anywhere you want, even outside of the SAS AWS, yet it is still tied to your SAS session. Therefore, if you iconize your SAS session, the Toolbox disappears. Restoring the SAS icon restores the Toolbox as well. You can save the Toolbox position by choosing [Save Workspace] in the Preferences dialog box.

Note: You can also use the TOOLDEF system option to set the position of the Toolbox when the SAS System initializes. The TOOLDEF option, which is described on page 192, does not cause the Toolbox to open automatically.

Clearing Tool Bitmaps from Your Display

If you do not want any tools displayed, choose `Off` from the `Tools` area in the Preferences dialog box and choose [Save]. This causes the Toolbox or Tool bar to disappear from your display. Your SAS session configuration is also affected, in that the next time you open a SAS session, no toolbox is open.

If you want to clear tool bitmaps from your display for only this session, double-click on the Toolbox Control menu. If you are using the Tool bar, so that a Control menu is not available, issue the TOOLCLOSE display manager command. The TOOLCLOSE command does not affect your SAS session configuration.

Choosing a Set of Tool Bitmaps

When you invoke the SAS System, a default set of tool bitmaps is provided for your use. However, your SASUSER.PROFILE catalog does not contain any toolbox entries until you use the Toolbox Editor to edit a toolbox and save your changes. This behavior is similar to that of the KEYS window. By default, when you invoke the Toolbox Editor it loads the default Toolbox, which is named SASUSER.PROFILE.TOOLBOX.TOOLBOX. You can define additional toolboxes for other applications, such as SAS/AF applications, and store these in your SASUSER.PROFILE catalog (or another catalog) using another name.

You can make a specific toolbox from a catalog active by issuing the following display manager command:

TOOLLOAD <BOX|BAR> *libref.catalog.member*

Choose between BOX and BAR, depending on whether you want to load the bitmaps into a toolbox, or display them in the SAS AWS menu bar area.

Note: While you can issue the TOOLLOAD and TOOLCLOSE commands from the command line, they are most useful when you are developing SAS/AF applications. You can use the DM statement with these commands to enable your application to open and close the Toolbox and to give users of your applications access to several toolboxes during the course of their work.

Invoking the Toolbox Editor

If you want to change the default bitmaps available in the default Toolbox or define a new toolbox, use the Toolbox Editor. To bring up the Toolbox Editor, select `Edit Toolbox` from the SAS AWS `Options` menu. Alternatively, you can issue the TOOLEDIT display manager command.

Figure 2.19 shows the default appearance of the Toolbox Editor dialog box:

Figure 2.19 *Toolbox Editor Dialog Box*

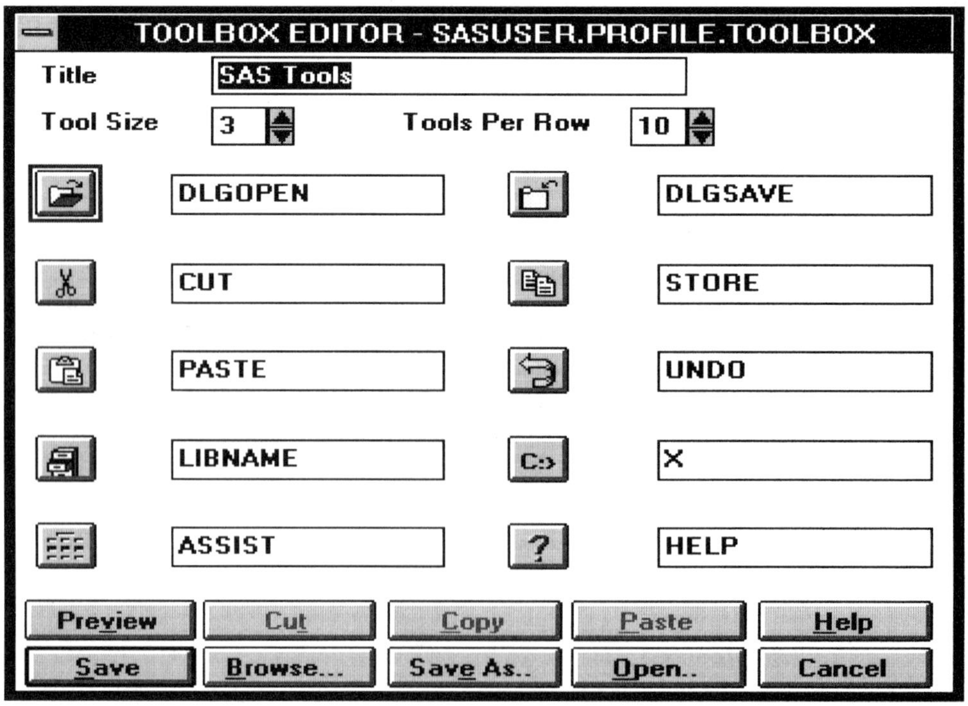

The default bitmaps have the following meanings:

DLGOPEN	opens the Open dialog box.
DLGSAVE	opens the Save As dialog box.
CUT	cuts marked text and graphics to the Clipboard.
STORE	copies marked text and graphics to the Clipboard.
PASTE	pastes the contents of the Clipboard into the active window at the cursor position.
UNDO	undoes the last line of text entry.
LIBNAME	opens the LIBNAME window.
X	opens a command prompt window where you can execute operating system commands.
ASSIST	invokes SAS/ASSIST software if you have SAS/ASSIST software installed.
HELP	invokes the SAS System help.

Here is a brief description of the various fields in the Toolbox Editor dialog box:

title bar
: displays the catalog entry you are editing.

`Title`
: specifies the title for the toolbox you are creating. The default Toolbox has a title of SAS Tools and is stored in your SASUSER directory. You can create a new toolbox by specifying a new name in this box and choosing [Save As]. You do not have to specify a name; you can leave this field blank.

`Tool Size`
: specifies the approximate size of the bitmaps in the toolbox. The size can range from 1 to 10 with 1 being a very small bitmap and 10 being a large bitmap. The default size is 3. The `Tool Size` field has no effect on the Tool bar; the menu bar height determines the Tool bar bitmap size.

`Tools Per Row`
: specifies how the bitmaps in the toolbox are arranged. For example, 10 tools per row creates a horizontal toolbox. This is the default. One tool per row creates a vertical toolbox. You can have up to 10 tools per row. The `Tools Per Row` field has no effect on the Tool bar; the Tool bar always displays a horizontal row of bitmaps.

Adding a Bitmap to the Toolbox

To add your own bitmap to the Toolbox, follow these steps:

1. Create a bitmap. For example, you could draw one with SAS/GRAPH software or any Windows NT graphics application that can paste bitmaps to the Clipboard.
   Note: If you plan to use the Tool bar, or a Toolbox with small bitmaps (for example, bitmaps with a size of 3), it is recommended that you design your bitmaps to be about 20 pixels wide and 16 pixels high. Also, a light grey background (RGB=192,192,192) is recommended.

2. Mark and copy your new bitmap to the Clipboard.
3. Open the Toolbox Editor and select the bitmap you want to replace by clicking on it.
4. Choose Paste to move your bitmap from the Clipboard into the Toolbox Editor.
5. Enter the text string or display manager command you want to associate with the bitmap. If you want to include more than one command, separate the commands with semicolons. You can use any display manager command available under Windows NT. For information on portable commands, see *SAS Language: Reference.* For information on commands specific to the Windows NT environment, see "System-Dependent Windowing Features" on page 280. For example, if you are developing a toolbox for a SAS/AF application, you could create a bitmap that opens the FORM window, allowing users to modify their SAS forms from within the SAS/AF application.

   Note: If you want a bitmap to place text at the cursor position instead of executing a display manager command, place a tilde (~) before the text. You can also use this technique with the KEYS window to define a key that places text at the cursor position. For example, defining a bitmap as `~SAS System` causes the text `SAS System` to be typed at the cursor position when you click on the bitmap.
6. Save your changes as described in "Saving Changes to the Toolbox" on page 67 and exit the Toolbox Editor.

Note: You can use the the PRT SCR key and the Paintbrush icon to capture icons from your display to paste into the Toolbox Editor.

Selecting a Tool from a Predefined Set

Use Browse to select a tool bitmap from a predefined set of bitmaps. A dialog box presents you with a set of bitmaps from which you can choose one for the currently selected tool in the Toolbox Editor. If there is already a bitmap for the selected too, it is replaced. Note that only the tool's picture is modified; the tool's text remains the same.

Creating a New Toolbox

To create an entirely new toolbox, choose Open. Then change the name in the `Title` field and add bitmaps as previously described. You can also use Open to open and edit an existing toolbox. Alternatively, you can use Save As to create a new toolbox then choose Save to close the Toolbox Editor.

Previewing Changes to the Toolbox

Clicking on Preview enables you to preview your changes to the Toolbox without saving them.

Close the the preview Toolbox before making more changes.
When you choose Preview, the Toolbox Editor remains open, but you cannot make any more changes until you close the Toolbox window that you are previewing. To close the preview, select the Control menu in the top left corner of the Toolbox and select `Close`. Control is then returned to the Toolbox Editor, and you can save your changes, make additional changes, or cancel your editing session. ■

Previewing always shows a Toolbox, regardless of whether you are currently using a Toolbox or Tool bar.

Saving Changes to the Toolbox

You can choose to make temporary changes to the active toolbox, save the changes to the default Toolbox (SASUSER.PROFILE.TOOLBOX), or create a new toolbox with a distinct name.

Permanent changes

[Save] saves the Toolbox information to the catalog entry shown in the title bar of the Toolbox Editor. Pressing ENTER is equivalent to choosing [Save]. When you choose [Save], the Toolbox Editor is closed.

Use [Save As] to save your changes to a catalog entry other than the currently open catalog entry. You can save your changes to another catalog entry in the same catalog or save the changes to another catalog entirely. For example, you may want to create a separate toolbox for a SAS/AF application and store the toolbox definition in the SAS/AF catalog. A dialog box prompts you for the catalog entry name. Be sure to specify a libref, catalog name, and entry name. The entry type is always TOOLBOX. When you choose [Save As], the Toolbox Editor remains open for further editing. The title bar changes to the name of the new entry.

Disabling a Tool

To define a tool as "do-nothing", enter a semicolon (;) as the command. The semicolon is necessary because if a bitmap has no command next to it, that tool is not displayed.

Removing a Bitmap from the Display

To prevent a bitmap from being shown in a toolbox, delete its command in the Toolbox Editor.

Chapter Summary

This chapter focuses on running the SAS System as a Windows NT application. First, it describes the SAS System Application Work Space (AWS) and the SAS AWS menu bar. Next, additional sections describe and illustrate how to perform common tasks in the SAS System such as entering text, cutting and pasting text and graphics, changing window colors, and using SAS system options to tailor your SAS session. Now that you understand how the SAS System operates under Windows NT, you are ready to learn the details of using SAS files under Windows NT. Chapter 3, "Using SAS Files" on page 69 provides this information.

Chapter 3 Using SAS® Files

Introduction

This chapter complements Chapter 6, "SAS Files," in *SAS Language: Reference, Version 6, First Edition* and Chapter 2, "SAS Files," in SAS Technical Report P-222, *Changes and Enhancements to Base SAS Software, Release 6.07*. This chapter briefly reviews SAS files, taking into account that your SAS files are stored in the Windows NT environment.

Note: When you see the `App4` icon, be sure to read the appropriate section in Appendix 4 as well as the information provided in this chapter. You can ignore the icon if you do not need to move files between Windows NT, OS/2, and DOS, or if your files do not contain national characters or graphics border characters.

What Is a SAS File?

The SAS System creates and uses a variety of specially structured files called *SAS files*. Although the operating system manages the file for the SAS System by storing it, the operating system cannot process it. For example, you can list SAS files with the DIR command, but you cannot use the Windows NT Notepad to edit SAS files. SAS files are different from external files. While external files can be processed by SAS statements and commands, they are not managed by the SAS System.

SAS files reside in SAS data libraries. Each SAS data library has an engine associated with it the first time a file in the library is accessed. The engine name specifies the access method that the SAS System uses to process the files in the data library. SAS data libraries are described in detail in "Using Data Libraries" on page 76.

Various engines enable the SAS System to access different formats or versions of SAS files and other vendors' files. For this reason, Release 6.09 of the SAS System is said to have Multiple Engine Architecture. Multiple Engine Architecture, combined with conversion utilities, provides access to Release 6.09, Release 6.08, Release 6.07, Release 6.06, Releases 6.03 and 6.04, and Version 5 SAS files, created under either Windows NT or other operating systems. Multiple Engine Architecture also provides access to files created by other vendors' products, including database files.

The following sections highlight information you need for creating and using SAS files with the various engines under Windows NT.

Types of SAS Files

SAS files are stored in SAS data libraries and are referred to as *members* of a library. Each member has a *member type*. The SAS System distinguishes between SAS files and external Windows NT files in a directory by using unique file extensions. The SAS System assigns certain Windows NT file extensions to a general set of SAS member types. Table 3.1 lists the Windows NT file extensions and their corresponding SAS member types for the V609 engine. For more information on engines, see "Multiple Engine Architecture" on page 74.

Table 3.1 *Windows NT File Extensions and Their Corresponding SAS Member Types*

Windows NT File Extension	SAS Member Type	Description
.SD2	DATA	specifies a SAS data file.
.SI2		specifies a data file index. Indexes are stored as separate files but are treated by the SAS System as integral parts of the SAS data file.
.SC2	CATALOG	specifies a SAS catalog.
.SS2	PROGRAM	specifies a stored program (DATA step).
.SV2	VIEW	specifies a SAS data view.
.SA2	ACCESS	specifies an access descriptor file.

Do not change the file extension of a SAS file; doing so can cause unpredictable results. The file extensions assigned by the SAS System to SAS files are an integral part of how the SAS System accesses these files. Also, you should not change the filename of a SAS file using operating system commands. If you want to change the name of a SAS file, use the DATASETS procedure. ■

Note: You may see files with other file extensions in your WORK and SASUSER data libraries. Most of these are temporary utility files, and you do not need to be concerned with them.

SAS Data Sets (Member Type DATA or VIEW)

SAS data set is an umbrella term for SAS data files and SAS data views. Both are discussed in this section. This section provides a brief overview of the concept of SAS data sets. See Chapter 6 of *SAS Language: Reference* for complete details.

Logically, a SAS data set consists of two types of information: descriptor information and data values. The descriptor information includes such things as data set name, data set type, data set label, and number of variables, as well as the names and labels of the variables in the data set, their types (character or numeric), their length, their position within an observation, and their formats. The data values contain values for the variables. A SAS data set can be visualized as a table consisting of rows of observations and columns of variable values. Figure 3.1 illustrates the SAS data set model:

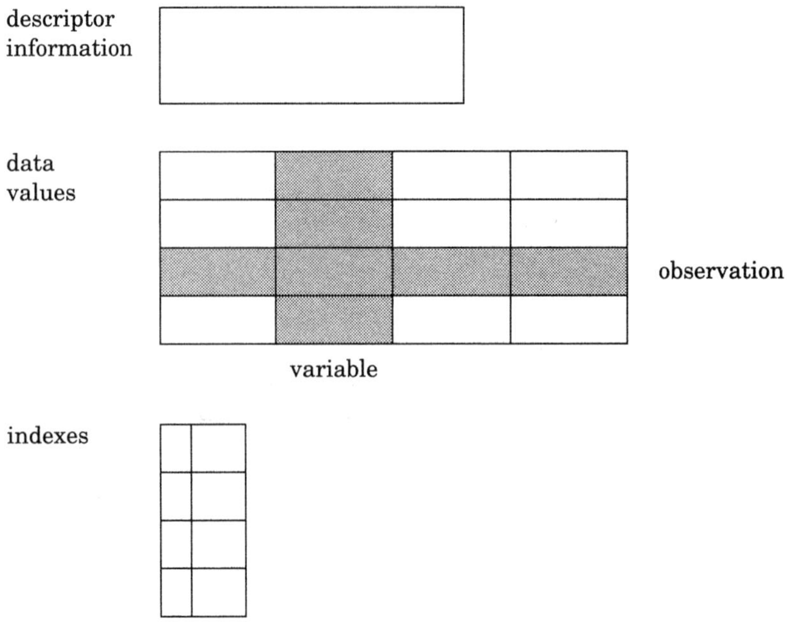

Figure 3.1
SAS Data Set Model

SAS data files (member type DATA)

The *SAS data file* is probably the most frequently used type of SAS file. SAS data files have a SAS member type of DATA and are created in the DATA step and by such SAS procedures as the FSEDIT procedure in SAS/FSP software and the RANK procedure in base SAS software.*

The SAS System defines two types of SAS data files, native and interface. Native data files store data values and descriptor information, as described earlier, in files formatted by the SAS System. These are the SAS data sets you may be familiar with from previous versions of the SAS System under other operating systems. In Release 6.09 of the SAS System, native SAS data files can be indexed. The *index* is an auxiliary file created in addition to the SAS data file. The index provides fast access to observations within a SAS data file through a variable or key. Under Windows NT, indexes are stored as separate files but are treated by the SAS System as integral parts of the SAS data file.

The maximum number of variables in a single SAS data set under Windows NT is 32,767. In addition, an observation under Windows NT cannot be longer than 1M. Therefore, if you want your data set to contain 32,767 character variables, the longest each variable can be is 32 bytes.

However, a DATA step can reference more than 32,767 variables, if you write only 32,767 or less variables to the data set. For example, you could drop some variables with a DROP= data set option. The maximum number of variables a DATA step can reference under Windows NT is 2,147,483,647.

---

* Both Release 6.04 and Release 6.09 SAS data files have a member type of DATA; however, the Windows NT file extension differs from the DOS file extension. Release 6.04 SAS data files have a file extension of .SSD, while Release 6.09 SAS data files have a file extension of .SD2. See "Using Release 6.04 SAS Files in Release 6.09" on page 89 for more information.

The second type of data file is the interface SAS data file. These files store data in a file formatted by other software. Examples of interface SAS data files are BMDP, OSIRIS, and SPSS files, which the SAS System can access as read-only files. See "Reading BMDP, OSIRIS, and SPSS Files" on page 91 for more information.

SAS data views (member type VIEW)

SAS data views have a member type of VIEW. They describe data values and tell the SAS System where to find the values, but they do not contain the actual data values themselves.

Views may be of two kinds, native or interface. A native SAS data view is created with the SQL procedure or with the DATA step and describes a subset or combination of the data in one or more SAS data files or SAS data views. For information on SQL views, see the *SAS Guide to the SQL Procedure: Usage and Reference, Version 6, First Edition* and Chapter 37, "The SQL Procedure" in SAS Technical Report P-222. For information on DATA step views, see Chapter 14, "Input DATA Step Views," in SAS Technical Report P-222.

Interface SAS data views contain descriptor information for data formatted by other software products, for example, a database management system. Such a view is created with the ACCESS procedure in SAS/ACCESS software. For more information, see *SAS/ACCESS Interface to PC File Formats: Usage and Reference, Version 6, First Edition* and other available SAS/ACCESS documentation.

SAS Catalogs (Member Type CATALOG)

A *SAS catalog* is a special type of SAS file that can contain multiple entries. Many different types of entries can be kept in the same SAS catalog. For example, catalogs can contain windowing applications, key definitions, toolbox definitions, SAS/GRAPH graphs, SAS/IML matrices, and so on.

You must convert SAS catalogs from earlier releases of the SAS System or from another operating system to Release 6.09 format before you can use them in a Release 6.09 SAS program. The only exception to this rule is catalogs created with Release 6.08 under OS/2. These catalogs can be read directly by your Windows NT SAS session.

See Appendix 1, "Transporting Files from the SAS System for Personal Computers to Release 6.06 of the SAS System," in SAS Technical Report P-195, *Transporting SAS Files between Host Systems*, for more information on how to convert SAS catalogs. You may also want to refer to "Converting Release 6.08 SAS Catalogs" on page 86, "Converting Release 6.06 SAS Catalogs" on page 88, "Converting Release 6.04 SAS Catalogs" on page 90, and "Using Version 5 and Other Remote Host SAS Files in Release 6.09" on page 90.

SAS Stored Program Files (Member Type PROGRAM)

A *stored program file* is a compiled DATA step generated by the Stored Program Facility. See Appendix 3, "Stored Program Facility," in *SAS Language: Reference*, as well as Chapter 13, "The Stored Program Facility," in SAS Technical Report P-222 for more information on this type of SAS file.

Access Descriptor Files (Member Type ACCESS)

Descriptor files created by the ACCESS procedure in SAS/ACCESS software have a SAS member type of ACCESS and are used when creating interface SAS data views. Descriptor files describe the data formatted by other software products supported by the SAS System under Windows NT. For more information, see *SAS/ACCESS Interface to PC File Formats* and other available SAS/ACCESS documentation.

Multiple Engine Architecture

All permanent and temporary SAS files are stored in SAS data libraries. To use a SAS data library in your SAS session, you must assign a *libref* (library reference) and an engine to the data library. The libref is the name you use to refer to the data library during a SAS session or job. It can be defined as an environment variable, or it can be assigned with the LIBNAME statement. (See Chapter 6 in *SAS Language: Reference* for a complete explanation of librefs.)

A *SAS data library* is a collection of SAS files within a Windows NT directory or a concatenation of directories. Although the directory can contain files that are not managed by the SAS System, only SAS files are considered part of the SAS data library. Any Windows NT directory can be treated as a SAS data library.

Access methods called engines provide access to many formats of data, giving the SAS System a *Multiple Engine Architecture.* Engines apply only to SAS data sets.

The engine identifies the set of routines that the SAS System uses to access the files in the data library. With this architecture, data can reside in different types of files, including SAS data files and data formatted by other software products, such as database management systems. By using the appropriate engine for the file type, the SAS System can write to or read from the file. For some types of files, you need to tell the SAS System what engine to use. For others, the appropriate engine is automatically chosen. More details on engines and Multiple Engine Architecture are found in Chapter 6 of *SAS Language: Reference.*

Engines are of two basic types, library and view. *Library engines* control access at the SAS data library level and can be specified in the LIBNAME statement. *View engines* enable the SAS System to read SAS data views described by the DATA step, SQL procedure, or SAS/ACCESS software. The use of SAS view engines is automatic because the name of the view engine is stored as part of the descriptor portion of the SAS data set. You cannot specify a view engine in the LIBNAME statement.

Library Engines

Library engines are of two types, native and interface. These engines support the SAS data library model. Library engines perform several important functions, including determining fundamental processing characteristics. For a more detailed description of library engines, see Chapter 6 in *SAS Language: Reference.*

Native Library Engines

Native library engines are those engines that access forms of a SAS file created and maintained by the SAS System. Native library engines include the default engine, the compatibility engine, and the transport engine. Table 3.2 lists the acceptable names (and nicknames) for these engines.

Table 3.2
Native Library Engines

Type	Name and Nickname	Description
default	V609 BASE V608	accesses Release 6.09 and 6.08 SAS data files
compatibility	V606	accesses Release 6.06 SAS data sets created under the OS/2 operating system
	V604 V603	accesses both Release 6.03 and 6.04 SAS data sets
transport	XPORT	accesses transport files

Because there is no difference between Release 6.04 and 6.03 SAS data sets and catalogs, the engine used to access them is the same: the V604 engine. When you see a reference to Release 6.04 SAS files in this book, it applies equally to Release 6.03 SAS files. Also, the V608 and V609 engines are identical. There is no difference between a SAS data set created under Release 6.08 and one created under Release 6.09 for the PC environments (OS/2, Microsoft Windows, and Microsoft Windows NT).

When using the default engine, choose which name, V609 or BASE, you use in your SAS jobs with an eye to the future. If your application is intended for Release 6.09 of the SAS System only, and you do not want to convert it to later releases, use the name V609. If, however, you plan to convert your application to new releases of the SAS System, use the name BASE because that refers to the latest default engine. Using the name BASE makes your programs easy to convert. The nickname BASE does not refer to base SAS software; rather, it refers to the base, or primary, engine. The BASE engine can be used with more than base SAS software.

Note: This book uses the term *default engine* to refer to the V609 engine. The V609 engine is the default engine for accessing SAS files under Release 6.09 of the SAS System unless the default engine is changed with the ENGINE system option. Use the OPTIONS procedure to see the value of the ENGINE system option.

Interface Library Engines

Interface library engines support access to other vendors' files. These engines allow read-only access to BMDP, OSIRIS, and SPSS files. You must specify the name of the interface library engine that you want to use as part of a LIBNAME statement. Table 3.3 lists the interface engine names:

Table 3.3
Interface Library Engines

Name	Description
BMDP	allows read-only access to BMDP files
OSIRIS	allows read-only access to OSIRIS files
SPSS	allows read-only access to SPSS files

See "Reading BMDP, OSIRIS, and SPSS Files" on page 91 for more information on these engines.

Rules for Determining the Engine

If you do not specify an engine name in a LIBNAME statement, the SAS System attempts to determine the engine (either the default or a compatibility engine) that should be assigned to the specified data library libref. Under Windows NT, the SAS System looks at the file extensions that exist in the given directory and uses the following rules to determine which engine the libref should be assigned to:

- If the directory contains SAS data sets from only one of the supported native library engines (not including XPORT), the libref is assigned to that engine.
- If there are no SAS data sets in the given directory, the libref is assigned to the default engine.
- If the directory contains SAS data sets from more than one engine, this is called a mixed mode library. The libref is then assigned to the default engine. A message is printed in the SAS log informing you the libref is assigned to a mixed mode library.

Note: It is always more efficient to specify the engine name than to have the SAS System determine the correct engine.

You can use the ENGINE system option to specify the default engine the SAS System uses when it detects a mixed mode library or a library with no SAS files. The valid values for the ENGINE option are V609, V608, V606, V604, V603, and BASE. By default, the ENGINE option is set to V609. See the description of the ENGINE option on page 182 for more information.

Using Data Libraries

Before you can use a SAS data library, you must assign a libref to it. The libref is a tag or label that is temporarily assigned to a directory so that the storage location (the full path, including drive and directory) is in a form that is recognized by the SAS System. A libref exists only during the session in which it is created. It is a logical concept describing a physical location, rather than something physically stored with the file. A libref follows the same rules of syntax as any SAS name. See Chapter 4, "Rules of the SAS Language," in *SAS Language: Reference* for more information on SAS naming conventions.

Assigning Librefs to SAS Data Libraries

There are two ways to specify a libref:

- □ Use the LIBNAME statement.
- □ Define an environment variable.

These two methods of assigning a libref to a SAS data library, as well as ways to list and clear the librefs you assign during a SAS session, are discussed in the next sections.

Using the LIBNAME Statement

You can use the LIBNAME statement to assign librefs and engines to one or more directories, including the working directory.

The LIBNAME statement has the following basic syntax:

LIBNAME *libref <engine-name> 'SAS-data-library'*;

A full explanation of all the arguments in this statement can be found on page 217.

There are other ways to use the LIBNAME statement; see *SAS Language: Reference* for complete documentation on the LIBNAME statement.

The words CON and NUL are reserved words under Windows NT.
Do not use CON or NUL as librefs. ■

Assigning a libref to a single directory

If you have Release 6.09 SAS data sets stored in the C:\MYSASDIR directory, you can submit the following LIBNAME statement to assign the libref TEST to that directory:

```
libname test V609 'c:\mysasdir';
```

This statement indicates that Release 6.09 SAS files stored in the directory C:\MYSASDIR are to be accessed using the libref TEST. Remember that the engine specification is optional.

Assigning a libref to the working directory

If you want to assign the libref MYCURR to your current SAS System working directory, use the following LIBNAME statement:

```
libname mycurr '.';
```

Assigning a libref to multiple directories

If you have SAS files located in multiple directories, you can treat these directories as a single SAS data library by specifying a single libref and concatenating the directory locations, as in the following example:

```
libname income ('c:\revenue','d:\costs');
```

This statement indicates that the two directories, C:\REVENUE and D:\COSTS, are to be treated as a single SAS data library. When you concatenate SAS data libraries, the SAS System uses a protocol for accessing the libraries, depending on whether you are accessing the libraries for read, write, or update. (A protocol is a set of rules.) See "Understanding How Concatenated SAS Data Libraries Are Accessed" on page 81 for more information.

Note: The concept of library concatenation also applies when specifying system options, such as the SASHELP and SASMSG options. See "System Option Syntax" on page 175 in Chapter 7, "SAS System Options" for information on how to specify multiple directories in options such as these.

Assigning engines

If you want to use another access method, or engine, instead of the V609 engine, you can specify another engine name in the LIBNAME statement. For example, if you want to access Release 6.04 SAS data sets from your Release 6.09 SAS session, you can specify the V604 engine in the LIBNAME statement, as in the following example:

```
libname oldlib V604 'c:\sas604';
```

As another example, if you plan to share SAS files between Release 6.09 under Windows NT and Release 6.06 under OS/2, you should use the V606 engine when assigning a libref to the SAS data library. In this manner, you can assure that any SAS data sets you create in this SAS data library are created in the Release 6.06 format, so Release 6.06 of the SAS System can read them. Here is an example of specifying the V606 engine in a LIBNAME statement:

```
libname lib606 V606 'c:\sas606';
```

The V606 engine is particularly useful if you are going to be accessing the same SAS files from your Release 6.09 SAS session and a Release 6.06 SAS session. Remember that while Release 6.09 can read Release 6.06 SAS data sets, Release 6.06 cannot read Release 6.09 SAS data sets.

For more information on using engine names in the LIBNAME statement, see "Using Release 6.04 SAS Files in Release 6.09" on page 89 and "Reading BMDP, OSIRIS, and SPSS Files" on page 91. You can also see Chapter 6 in *SAS Language: Reference.*

Using the LIBNAME statement in SAS autoexec files

If you prefer, you can store LIBNAME statements in your SAS autoexec file so that the librefs are available as soon as the SAS System initializes. For example, your SAS autoexec file may contain the following statements:

```
libname test 'c:\mysasdir';
libname mylib ('c:\mydata','d:\tempdata');
libname oldlib V604 'c:\sas604';
```

See "SAS Autoexec File" on page 8 for more information on how to create and use a SAS autoexec file.

Assigning multiple librefs and engines to a directory

If a directory contains SAS files created by several different engines, only those SAS files created with the engine assigned to the given libref can be accessed using that libref. You can assign multiple librefs with different engines to a directory. For example, the following statements are valid:

```
libname one V604 'c:\mydir';
libname two V609 'c:\mydir';
```

Data sets referenced by the libref ONE are created and accessed using the compatibility engine (V604), whereas data sets referenced by the libref TWO are created and accessed using the default engine (V609). You can also have multiple librefs (using the same engine) for the same SAS data library. For example, the following two LIBNAME statements assign the librefs MYLIB and INLIB (both using the V609 engine) to the same SAS data library:

```
libname mylib V609 'c:\mydir\datasets';
libname inlib V609 'c:\mydir\datasets';
```

Because the engine name and SAS data library specifications are the same, the librefs MYLIB and INLIB are identical and can be used interchangeably.

Using Environment Variables

You can also assign a libref to a SAS data library using environment variables instead of the LIBNAME statement. An *environment variable* equates one string to another within the Windows NT environment. The SAS System recognizes two kinds of environment variables, SAS environment variables and Windows NT environment variables. When you use a libref in a SAS statement, the SAS System first looks to see if that libref has been assigned to a SAS data library by a LIBNAME statement. If it has not, the SAS System searches first for any defined SAS environment variables and then for any Windows NT environment variables that match the specified libref. There are two ways of defining an environment variable to the SAS System:

- □ Use the SET system option. This defines a SAS (internal) environment variable.
- □ Issue a Windows NT SET command. This defines a Windows NT (external) environment variable. Alternatively, you can define Windows NT environment variables using the System dialog box, accessed from the Control Panel.

You cannot assign engines to environment variables.
If you use environment variables as librefs, you must accept the default engine. ■

The availability of environment variables makes it simple to assign resources to the SAS System prior to invocation.

SET system option

You can use the SET system option to define a SAS environment variable. For example, if you store your permanent SAS data sets in the C:\SAS\MYSASDATA directory, you can use the following SET option in the SAS command or in your SAS configuration file to assign the environment variable TEST to this SAS data library:

```
-set test c:\sas\mysasdata
```

When you assign an environment variable, the SAS System does not resolve the environment reference until the environment variable name is actually used. For example, if the TEST environment variable is defined in your SAS configuration file, the environment variable TEST is not resolved until it is referenced by the SAS System. Therefore, if you make a mistake in your SET option specification, such as mistyping a directory name, you do not receive an error message until you use the environment variable in a SAS statement.

You do not need quotation marks around the physical filename when specifying paths with the SET option when the option specification is in the SAS configuration file. If you use the SET option in an OPTIONS statement, use quotation marks around the filename. For complete syntax of the SET system option, see page 190.

Any environment variable name you use with a system option in your SAS configuration file must be defined as an environment variable before it is used. For example, the following SET option must appear before the SASUSER option that uses the environment variable TEST:

```
-set test d:\mysasdir
-sasuser !test
```

In the following example, environment variables are used with concatenated libraries:

```
-set dir1 c:\sas\base\sashelp
-set dir2 d:\sas\stat\sashelp
-sashelp (!dir1 !dir2)
```

Note that when you reference environment variables in your SAS configuration file or in a LIBNAME statement in your SAS programs, you must precede the environment variable name with an exclamation point (!).

It is recommended that you use the SET system option in your SAS configuration file if you invoke the SAS System through a program group window.

Windows NT SET command

You can execute a Windows NT SET command prior to invoking the SAS System to create a Windows NT environment variable. You must define the environment variable prior to invoking the SAS System; you cannot define environment variables for SAS System use from a command prompt window from within a SAS session.

The environment variables you define with the SET command can be used later within the SAS System as librefs. In the following example, the Windows NT SET command is used to define the environment variables PERM and BUDGET:

```
SET PERM=C:\MYSASDIR
SET BUDGET=D:\SAS\BUDGET\DATA
```

Note: When you reference an external environment variable (one assigned with the Windows NT SET command) in your SAS programs (such as in a DATA or MERGE statement), a note informing you the environment variable has been used is written to the SAS log.

Listing Libref Assignments

If you have assigned several librefs during a SAS session and need to refresh your memory as to which libref points where, you can use either the LIBNAME window or the LIBNAME statement to list all the assigned librefs.

If you are running the SAS System using the SAS Display Manager System, use the LIBNAME window to list the active librefs. There are two ways to open the LIBNAME window: issue the LIBNAME command or use the pop-up menus. Using pop-up menus, select

Globals ▶ Data management ▶ Libname list

The LIBNAME window lists all the librefs active for your current SAS session, along with the engine and the physical path for each libref. Any environment variables you have defined as librefs are listed, provided you have used them in your SAS session. If you have defined an environment variable as a libref but have not used it yet in a SAS program, the LIBNAME window does not list it.

If you are running the SAS System in batch mode, you can use the following LIBNAME statement to write the active librefs to the SAS log:

```
libname _all_ list;
```

Clearing Librefs

You can clear a libref by using the following form of the LIBNAME statement:

LIBNAME *libref* |_ALL_ CLEAR;

If you specify a libref, only that libref is cleared. If you specify the keyword _ALL_, all the librefs you have assigned during your current SAS session are cleared. (SASUSER, SASHELP, and WORK remain assigned.)

Note: When you clear a libref defined by an environment variable, the variable remains defined, but it is no longer considered a libref. (That is, it is no longer listed in the LIBNAME window). You can use the variable in a another LIBNAME statement to create a new libref.

The SAS System automatically clears the association between librefs and their respective data libraries at the end of your job or session. If you want to associate the libref with a different SAS data library during the current session, you do not have to end the session or clear the libref. The SAS System automatically reassigns the libref when you issue a LIBNAME statement for the new SAS data library.

Understanding How Concatenated SAS Data Libraries Are Accessed

When you use the concatenation feature to specify more than one physical directory for a libref, the SAS System uses the following protocol for determining which directory is accessed. (The protocol illustrated by these examples applies to all SAS statements and procedures that access SAS files, such as the DATA, UPDATE, and MODIFY statements in the DATA step and the SQL and APPEND procedures.)

Input and update

When a SAS file is accessed for input or update, the first SAS file found by that name is the one accessed. For example, if you submit the following statements and the file OLD.SPECIES exists in both directories, the one in the C:\MYSASDIR directory is printed:

```
libname old ('c:\mysasdir','d:\saslib');

proc print data=old.species;
run;
```

The same would be true if you opened OLD.SPECIES for update with the FSEDIT procedure.

Output

If the data set is accessed for output, it is always written to the first directory, provided that the directory exists. If the directory does not exist, an error message is displayed. For example, if you submit the following statements, the SAS System writes the OLD.SPECIES data set to the first directory (C:\MYSASDIR), replacing any existing data set with the same name:

```
libname old ('c:\mysasdir','d:\saslib');

data old.species;
   x=1;
   y=2;
run;
```

If a copy of the OLD.SPECIES data set exists in the second directory, it is not replaced.

Accessing data sets with the same name

One possibly confusing case involving the access protocols for SAS files occurs when you use the DATA and SET statements to access data sets with the same name. For example, suppose you submit the following statements and TEST.SPECIES originally exists only in the second directory, D:\MYSASDIR:

```
libname test ('c:\sas','d:\mysasdir');

data test.species;
   set test.species;
   if value1='y' then
      value2=3;
run;
```

In this case, the DATA statement opens TEST.SPECIES for output according to the output rules; that is, the SAS System opens a data set in the first of the concatenated libraries (C:\SAS). The SET statement opens the existing TEST.SPECIES data set in the second (D:\MYSASDIR) directory, according to the input rules. Therefore, the original TEST.SPECIES data set is not updated; rather, two TEST.SPECIES data sets exist, one in each directory.

Using the SASUSER Data Library

The SAS System automatically creates a data library with the libref SASUSER. This library contains, among other SAS files, your user profile catalog. By default under Windows NT, the SASUSER libref points to a directory called SASUSER, located under the working directory of your current SAS session. If a SASUSER directory does not exist, the SAS System creates one. You can use the SASUSER system option to make the SASUSER libref point to a different SAS data library. For more information on your profile catalog, see "Profile Catalog" on page 10. See page 190 for more information on the SASUSER system option. The SAS System stores other files besides the profile catalog in the SASUSER directory. For example, the sample data sets provided with SAS/ASSIST software are stored in this directory.

You cannot change the engine associated with the SASUSER data library.
The SASUSER data library is always associated with the V609 engine. If you try to assign another engine to this data library, you receive an error message. Therefore, even if you have set the ENGINE system option to V604, any SAS files created in the SASUSER data library are Release 6.09 SAS files. ■

Using the WORK Data Library

The WORK data library is the storage place for temporary SAS files. By default under Windows NT, the WORK data library is created as a subdirectory of the SASWORK directory. This subdirectory is named #TD*nnnnn*, as discussed in "WORK Data Library" on page 10. Temporary SAS files are available only for the duration of the SAS session in which they are created. At the end of that session, they are deleted automatically. By default, any file that is not assigned a two-level name is automatically considered to be a temporary file. A special libref of WORK is automatically assigned to any temporary SAS data sets created. For example, if you run the following SAS DATA step to create the data set SPORTS, a temporary data set named WORK.SPORTS is created:

```
data sports;
   input @1 sport $10. @12 event $20.;
   cards;
volleyball co-recreational
swimming   100-meter freestyle
soccer     team
;
```

If you display the LIBNAME window, you see a libref of WORK. You can display all the temporary data sets created during this session by typing an `s` in the field preceding the libref WORK and pressing the ENTER key, placing the cursor on the word WORK and pressing the ENTER key, or double-clicking on the word WORK.

You cannot change the engine associated with the WORK data library.
The WORK data library is always associated with the V609 engine. If you try to assign another engine to this data library, you receive an error message. Therefore, even if you have set the ENGINE system option to V604, any SAS files created in the WORK data library are Release 6.09 SAS files. ■

Using an Environment Variable

You can use an environment variable in your WORK data library specification, similar to what was illustrated earlier with the SASUSER system option. Use this technique when you do not want to use the default location for your WORK data library. You can put something similar to the following in your SAS configuration file to set up an environment variable to use for your WORK data library:

```
-set myvar c:\ tempdir
-work !myvar use
```

The SET option associates the MYVAR environment variable with the C:\TEMPDIR directory. Then the WORK option tells the SAS System to use that directory for the SAS WORK data library. The USE suboption in the WORK option tells the SAS System to store temporary SAS files in the directory specified by the WORK option. If you do not specify the USE suboption, by default the SAS System creates a subdirectory beneath the specified directory. This subdirectory is named #TD*nnnnn*, where *nnnnn* is a unique number associated with your SAS session.

Using the USER Libref

Although by default SAS files with one-level names are temporary and are deleted at the end of your SAS session, you can use the USER libref to cause SAS files with one-level names to be stored in a permanent SAS data library. For example, the following statement causes all SAS files with one-level names to be permanently stored in the C:\MYSASDIR directory:

```
libname user 'c:\mysasdir';
```

When you set the USER libref to a directory as in the previous example, if you want to create or access a temporary data set you must specify a two-level name for the data set with WORK as the libref. You can also assign the USER libref when you invoke the SAS System by using the USER system option. Refer to page 192 and Chapter 16, "SAS System Options," in *SAS Language: Reference* for more information on the USER system option.

Note: You can assign the V606 or V604 engines to the USER libref if you want data sets with one-level names saved in the Release 6.06 or Release 6.04 format.

Accessing SAS Files from Multiple SAS Sessions

If you are running multiple SAS sessions, whether on a single machine or across a network, you can have multiple access to the same SAS file only when you are reading from it. If one SAS session has write or update access to the file, no other session can access it. For example, you can have multiple users access the same SAS data set with an FSVIEW session in browse mode, but you cannot have more than one SAS session access the same data set if you invoke an FSVIEW session in edit mode.

The RSASUSER system option, described on page 189 allows you to share the SASUSER data library.

Using Release 6.09 SAS Files with Previous Releases of the SAS System for Windows and OS/2

It is possible to share and move SAS files between your Release 6.09 SAS session under Windows NT and Release 6.08 under both OS/2 and Microsoft Windows and Release 6.06 under OS/2.

Using Release 6.09 SAS Files in Release 6.08

There are different considerations for sharing SAS data sets and SAS catalogs, as described in the following sections.

SAS Data Sets

If your site has Release 6.08 of the SAS System installed under Windows or OS/2, you can transparently share SAS data sets between your Release 6.09 SAS session under Windows NT and Release 6.08 without using the CPORT and CIMPORT procedures.

SAS Catalogs

Because of the different internal structures of the operating systems, SAS catalogs cannot be shared between Windows NT and Windows or OS/2 without using PROC CPORT and PROC CIMPORT. Here are the basic steps to follow to convert your SAS catalogs from Release 6.09 to Release 6.08:

1. Using the CPORT procedure, create a transport file containing the SAS catalog from your Release 6.09 SAS session.
2. Transfer the file (perhaps on a network or diskette) to a place your Release 6.08 SAS session can read it.
3. Use the CIMPORT procedure from your Release 6.08 SAS session to read the transport file and create a converted SAS catalog.

Using Release 6.09 SAS Files in Release 6.06

If you want to use a Release 6.09 SAS file from Windows NT in a Release 6.06 application running under Release 6.06 of the SAS System under OS/2, you must first convert the file to Release 6.06 format. There are separate considerations for converting SAS data sets and SAS catalogs, as discussed in the following two sections.

SAS Data Sets

You can convert a SAS data set using the DATA step or COPY procedure and the V606 engine. Alternatively, you can use the CPORT and CIMPORT procedures. The conversion must be done from your Release 6.09 session because Release 6.06 of the SAS System cannot read Release 6.09 files. For example, you could submit the following code to convert the Release 6.09 SAS data set NTDATA.CUSTDATA to Release 6.06 format.

```
libname ntdata V609 'c:\customer';
libname data606 v606 'd:\os2cust';

proc copy in=ntdata out=data606 memtype=data;
   select custdata;
run;
```

After the conversion is complete, your Release 6.06 application can read the data set.

SAS Catalogs

Using Release 6.09 SAS catalogs in Release 6.06 applications generally is not recommended. Release 6.09 supports several catalog entry types that are not valid in Release 6.06. Also, many enhancements to various entry types make backward compatibility impossible or unpredictable. If you intend to use catalogs in existing Release 6.06 applications, you should create the catalogs under Release 6.06 and not try to use a Release 6.09 catalog in Release 6.06. For more information on using Release 6.09 catalogs under Release 6.06, see "SAS Catalogs" in Chapter 2 of SAS Technical Report P-222, *Changes and Enhancements to Base SAS Software, Release 6.07*.

Using Release 6.08 SAS Files in Release 6.09

App4

This section discusses accessing Release 6.08 SAS files from your Release 6.09 Windows NT SAS session. It also illustrates converting Release 6.08 SAS catalogs to Release 6.09 format.

Accessing Release 6.08 SAS Data Sets

You can transparently share SAS data sets between Release 6.08 and Release 6.09. The nicknames V608 and V609 refer to the same engine.

Converting Release 6.08 SAS Catalogs

Because of the internal architecture of Windows NT, SAS catalogs created by Release 6.08 under Microsoft Windows must be converted before the Release 6.09 of the SAS System can use them. You do not have to convert SAS catalogs created by Release 6.08 under OS/2; these catalogs can be read directly from your Windows NT SAS session.

Note: If you do not need to use the catalogs under both Release 6.08 and 6.09, it is recommended that you use PROC CPORT and PROC CIMPORT to convert Release 6.08 OS/2 catalogs, even though it is not generally required.

Here are the basic steps to follow to convert your SAS catalogs from Release 6.08 to Release 6.09:

1. Using the CPORT procedure, create a transport file containing the SAS catalog from your Release 6.08 SAS session.
2. Transfer the file (perhaps on a network or diskette) to a place your Release 6.09 SAS session can read it.
3. Use the CIMPORT procedure from your Release 6.09 SAS session to read the transport file and create a converted SAS catalog.

Using Release 6.06 SAS Files in Release 6.09

App4

This section discusses accessing Release 6.06 SAS files under OS/2 from your Release 6.09 Windows NT SAS session. It also illustrates converting Release 6.06 files to Release 6.09 format and creating Release 6.06 files from your Windows NT SAS session.

Accessing Release 6.06 Data Sets

You can access SAS data sets created with Release 6.06 of the SAS System under OS/2 from your Windows NT SAS session by using the V606 engine. For example, the following SAS statements (submitted from a Windows NT SAS session) print a Release 6.06 SAS data set named OS2DATA.SALEFIGS created under Version 1.2 of OS/2:

```
libname os2data v606 'c:\mydata';

proc print data=os2data.salefigs;
   title 'Sales Figures';
run;
```

Converting Release 6.06 Files to Release 6.09 Format

You may want to convert your Release 6.06 SAS files to Release 6.09 format. There are separate considerations for converting SAS data sets and SAS catalogs.

Converting Release 6.06 SAS Data Sets

While access to Release 6.06 SAS data sets is quite easy when you use the V606 engine, you may want to consider converting your SAS files to Release 6.09 format if you access them often and do not need to read the files from Release 6.06 any more. Release 6.09 of the SAS System offers a new data set format that is more efficient than the Release 6.06 format. For more information on the new format, refer to Chapter 2 in SAS Technical Report P-222.

The following SAS statements use the COPY procedure to convert all the Release 6.06 SAS data sets in the OS2DATA SAS data library to Release 6.09 and to format and store the new data sets in the NTDATA library:

```
libname os2data v606 'c:\mydata';
libname ntdata V609 'd:\newdata';

proc copy in=os2data out=ntdata memtype=data;
run;
```

Alternatively, you can use the DATA step to do the conversion, as in the following example. This technique works well if you want to convert only one or two data sets in a particular SAS data library.

```
libname os2data v606 'c:\mydata';
libname ntdata V609 'd:\newdata';

data ntdata.eggplant;
   set os2data.eggplant;
run;
```

You can also use the CPORT and CIMPORT procedures to perform the conversion. Remember that when you convert a data set to Release 6.09 format, you can no longer read that data set from Release 6.06. Do not convert your Release 6.06 files to Release 6.09 if you need to access the files from both releases.

Converting Release 6.06 SAS Catalogs

Because of the differences in the internal structures of the operating systems, you must use the CPORT and CIMPORT procedures to convert Release 6.06 SAS catalogs created under OS/2 to Release 6.09 format before you can use the catalogs in your Release 6.09 SAS session under Windows NT. Here are the basic steps to follow:

1. Using the CPORT procedure, create a transport file containing the SAS catalog from your Release 6.06 SAS session.
2. Transfer the file (perhaps on a network or diskette) to a place your Release 6.09 SAS session can read it.
3. Use the CIMPORT procedure from your Release 6.09 SAS session to read the transport file and create a converted SAS catalog.

Creating Release 6.06 Data Sets

You may need to create Release 6.06 SAS data sets from your Windows NT SAS session. This is similar to reading Release 6.06 data sets in that you use the V606 engine. For example, the following SAS statements use the V606 engine to create a SAS data set named QTR1. The raw data is read from the external file associated with the fileref MYFILE.

```
libname os2data v606 'c:\mydata';
filename myfile 'c:\qtr1data.dat';

data os2data.qtr1;
   infile myfile;
   input saledate amount;
run;
```

Using Release 6.04 SAS Files in Release 6.09

You can use your Release 6.04 SAS files (created under PC DOS) in Release 6.09 just as you can use Release 6.06 files in Release 6.09. This section discusses the considerations for using Release 6.04 SAS data sets and SAS catalogs. The information is also valid for Release 6.03 SAS files because there is no difference between Release 6.03 and Release 6.04 SAS files.

Accessing Release 6.04 Data Sets

The V604 engine enables you to read from and write to Release 6.03 and Release 6.04 SAS data sets directly from your Release 6.09 SAS session. (Remember that there are no differences between Release 6.04 and 6.03 SAS data sets.) This feature is useful when you have SAS data sets that you want to share between Release 6.04 for PCs and Release 6.09 under Windows NT. The V604 engine is supported only for SAS data sets (member type DATA). For example, if you have a Release 6.04 SAS data set named MYLIB.FRUIT that you want to print, you can submit the following statements from a Release 6.09 SAS session:

```
libname mylib V604 'c:\sas604';

proc print data=mylib.fruit;
run;
```

While it is useful to be able to access SAS data sets created in a previous release of the SAS System, you cannot take advantage of the full functionality of the Release 6.09 SAS System, which includes creating indexes and database views, unless you convert data sets created with earlier releases of the SAS System to Release 6.09 data sets.

Converting Release 6.04 SAS Files to Release 6.09

You may want to convert your Release 6.04 SAS files to Release 6.09 format. There are separate considerations for converting SAS data sets and SAS catalogs.

Converting Release 6.04 SAS Data Sets

If you want to convert Release 6.04 SAS data sets to Release 6.09 format, you can use the DATA step or the COPY procedure with the V604 engine specified in the LIBNAME statement. In the following example, the COPY procedure is used to convert several Release 6.04 SAS data sets to Release 6.09 format:

```
libname old V604 'c:\pcsas';
libname new V609 'd:\sas';

proc copy in=old out=new memtype=data;
   select revenue qtr1 qtr2 qtr3 qtr4 yearend;
run;
```

The COPY procedure is very efficient at converting either several data sets at a time or whole SAS data libraries. If you want to convert only one data set, you might use the DATA step instead, as in the following example:

```
libname old V604 'c:\pcsas';
libname new V609 'd:\sas';

data new.revenue;
   set old.revenue;
run;
```

Alternatively, you can use the CPORT and CIMPORT procedures to perform the conversion.

Converting Release 6.04 SAS Catalogs

If you want to convert Release 6.04 SAS catalogs to their Release 6.09 counterparts, see Appendix 1 of SAS Technical Report P-195, *Transporting SAS Files Between Host Systems.* While this appendix does not specifically discuss using the SAS System under Windows NT, you can nevertheless use the information to convert SAS catalogs.

Creating Release 6.04 Data Sets

You can also create Release 6.04 data sets from your Release 6.09 SAS session by specifying the V604 engine. These data sets can then be accessed directly by Release 6.04 of the SAS System. For example, if you want to create a Release 6.04 SAS data set named MYLIB.HIGHCOST, you can submit the following statements from your Release 6.09 SAS session:

```
libname mylib V604 'c:\sas604';

data mylib.highcost;
   input product $ cost;
   cards;
luggage 101.29
shoes 68.75
hats 38.97
;
```

Using Version 5 and Other Remote Host SAS Files in Release 6.09

You can directly access remote host SAS data sets, including Version 5, Release 6.07, and Release 6.08 SAS data sets created on a remote host. For example, you may have a Version 5 SAS data set on VSE, or a Release 6.07 data set on MVS. The following explanation uses Version 5, but also applies to these other releases.

To directly access a Version 5 SAS data set created on a remote host computer, use SAS/CONNECT software to establish a communication link between your local SAS session under Windows NT and a remote SAS session under the other host. Once you have established a link, you can remote submit SAS statements to process the Version 5 data on the remote host computer, or you can download the Version 5 data set to a Release 6.09 data set under Windows NT. SAS/CONNECT software provides a convenient one-step way to transport SAS files from system to system. For more information about downloading files, see *SAS/CONNECT Software: Usage and Reference, Version 6, First Edition*, SAS Technical Report P-224, *SAS/CONNECT Software: Changes and Enhancements for Release 6.08*, and SAS Technical Report P-255, *SAS/CONNECT Software: Changes and Enhancements, Release 6.09*.

As an alternative, you can create a transport data set from your Version 5 data set and transport your file from the host to Windows NT. Then you can use the XPORT engine to create a Release 6.09 file from this transport file. If you are accessing Version 6 remote SAS data sets, you can also use PROC CPORT to create the transport file.

The method for transporting data sets differs from the method for transporting SAS catalogs. For more information on transporting SAS files, see SAS Technical Report P-195.

Reading BMDP, OSIRIS, and SPSS Files

Release 6.09 of the SAS System provides three interface library engines that enable you to access external data files directly from a SAS program: the BMDP, OSIRIS, and SPSS engines. These engines are all read-only. Because they are sequential engines (that is, they do not support random access of data), these engines cannot be used with the POINT= option in the SET statement or with the FSBROWSE, FSEDIT, or FSVIEW procedures. You can use PROC COPY or a DATA step to copy the system file to a SAS data set and then perform these functions on the SAS data set. Also, because they are sequential engines, some procedures (such as the PRINT procedure) give a warning message that the engine is sequential. With these engines, the physical filename associated with a libref is an actual filename, not a directory. This is an exception to the rules concerning librefs.

You can also use the CONVERT procedure to convert BMDP, OSIRIS, and SPSS files to SAS data files; see page 227 for more information.

BMDP Engine

The BMDP interface library engine enables you to read BMDP DOS files from the BMDP statistical software package directly from a SAS program. The BMDP engine is a read-only engine. The following discussion assumes you are familiar with the BMDP save file terminology.*

To read a BMDP save file, you must issue a LIBNAME statement that explicitly specifies you want to use the BMDP engine. In this case, the LIBNAME statement takes the following form:

LIBNAME *libref* BMDP <'*filename*'>;

In this form of the LIBNAME statement, *libref* is a SAS libref and *filename* is the BMDP physical filename. If the libref appears previously as a fileref, you can omit *filename* because the physical filename associated with the fileref is used. This engine can only read BMDP save files created under DOS.

Because there can be multiple save files in a single physical file, you reference the CODE= value as the member name of the data set within the SAS language. For example, if the save file contains CODE=ABC and CODE=DEF and the libref is MYLIB, you reference

* See the documentation provided by BMDP Statistical Software Inc. for more information.

them as MYLIB.ABC and MYLIB.DEF. All CONTENT types are treated the same, so even if member DEF is CONTENT=CORR, it is treated as CONTENT=DATA.

If you know that you want to access the first save file in the physical file, or if there is only one save file, you can refer to the member name as _FIRST_. This is convenient if you don't know the CODE= value.

BMDP Engine Examples

In the following example, the physical file MYBMDP.DAT contains the save file ABC. This example associates the libref MYLIB with the BMDP physical file, then runs the CONTENTS and PRINT procedures on the save file:

```
libname mylib bmdp 'mybmdp.dat';

proc contents data=mylib.abc;
run;

proc print data=mylib.abc;
run;
```

The following example uses the LIBNAME statement to associate the libref MYLIB2 with the BMDP physical file. Then it prints the data for the first save file in the physical file:

```
libname mylib2 bmdp 'mybmdp.dat';

proc print data=mylib2._first_;
run;
```

OSIRIS Engine

Because the Inter-University Consortium on Policy and Social Research (ICPSR) uses the OSIRIS file format for distribution of its data files, the SAS System provides the OSIRIS interface library engine to support the many users of the data from ICPSR and to be compatible with PROC CONVERT, which is described in Chapter 9.

The read-only OSIRIS engine enables you to read OSIRIS data and dictionary files directly from a SAS program. These files must be stored in EBCDIC format. This means you must have downloaded the OSIRIS files from your host computer in binary format. The following discussion assumes you are familiar with the OSIRIS file terminology. * To read an OSIRIS file, you must issue a LIBNAME statement that explicitly specifies you want to use the OSIRIS engine. In this case, the LIBNAME statement takes the following form:

LIBNAME *libref* OSIRIS '*data-filename*' DICT='*dictionary-filename*';

In this form of the LIBNAME statement, *libref* is a SAS libref, *data-filename* is the physical filename of the OSIRIS data file, and *dictionary-filename* is the physical filename of the OSIRIS dictionary file. The *dictionary-filename* argument can also be an environment

* See documentation provided by the Institute for Social Research for more information.

variable name or a fileref. (Do not put it in quotes if it is an environment variable name or fileref.) The DICT= option must appear because the engine requires both files.

OSIRIS data files do not have member names. Therefore, you can use whatever member name you like. You can use the same OSIRIS dictionary file with different OSIRIS data files. Simply write a separate LIBNAME statement for each one.

The layout of an OSIRIS data dictionary is consistent across operating systems. This is because the OSIRIS software does not run outside of the MVS environment, but the engine is designed to accept an MVS data dictionary on any other operating system under which the SAS System runs. It is important that the OSIRIS dictionary and data files not be converted from EBCDIC to ASCII; the engine expects EBCDIC data. There is no specific file layout for the OSIRIS data file. The file layout is dictated by the contents of the OSIRIS dictionary file.

OSIRIS Engine Example

In the following example, the data file is MYOSIRIS.DAT, and the dictionary file is MYOSIRIS.DIC. The example associates the libref MYLIB with the OSIRIS files and then runs PROC CONTENTS and PROC PRINT on the data:

```
libname mylib osiris 'myosiris.dat' dict='myosiris.dic';

proc contents data=mylib._first_;
run;

proc print data=mylib._first_;
run;
```

SPSS Engine

The SPSS interface library engine enables you to read SPSS/PC files directly from a SAS program. This is a read-only engine. The following discussion assumes you are familiar with the SPSS save file terminology.[*]

To read an SPSS save file, you must issue a LIBNAME statement that explicitly specifies you want to use the SPSS engine. In this case, the LIBNAME statement takes the following form:

LIBNAME *libref* SPSS <'*filename*'>;

In this form of the LIBNAME statement, the *libref* argument is a SAS libref, and *filename* is the SPSS physical filename. If the libref appears also as a fileref, you can omit *filename* because the physical filename associated with the fileref is used. The SPSS/PC native file format, as well as the export file format, is supported. The engine determines which format is used and reads the save file accordingly. Native files must be created under PC DOS. Export files can originate from any operating system.

Because SPSS/PC files do not have internal names, you can refer to them by any member name you like, such as _FIRST_, if you want to be consistent with the BMDP engine.

* See documentation provided by SPSS Inc. for more information.

SPSS Engine Example

The following example associates the libref MYLIB with the physical file MYSPSS.DAT in order to run PROC CONTENTS and PROC PRINT on the save file:

```
libname mylib spss 'myspss.dat';

proc contents data=mylib._first_;
run;

proc print data=mylib._first_;
run;
```

Accessing Database Files with SAS/ACCESS Software

SAS/ACCESS software provides an interface between the SAS System and several database management systems (DBMS) that run under Windows NT. The interface consists of two procedures and an interface view engine, which can perform the following tasks:

ACCESS procedure
: creates SAS/ACCESS descriptor files that describe DBMS data to the SAS System. It also can create a SAS data file from DBMS data.

DBLOAD procedure
: loads SAS or other DBMS data into a DBMS file.

interface view engine
: enables you to use descriptor files in SAS programs to access DBMS data directly and enables you to specify descriptor files in SAS programs to update, insert, or delete DBMS data directly.

For more information on using SAS/ACCESS software under Windows NT, consult *SAS/ACCESS Interface to PC File Formats* and other available SAS/ACCESS documentation.

Chapter Summary

This chapter provides background information essential to using SAS files under Windows NT, including details on librefs and engines. It also illustrates accessing SAS files in various formats (such as Releases 6.09, 6.08, 6.06, and 6.04; Version 5; and transport files). SAS files are complemented by external files. Chapter 4, "Using External Files" on page 95 provides the specifics of using external files in your SAS programs under Windows NT.

Chapter 4 Using External Files

Introduction

External files are files that contain data or text, such as SAS programming statements, records of raw data, or procedure output. These files are not managed by the SAS System.

This chapter discusses how to access external files to read or write data lines and how to access external files containing SAS program statements that you want to read and execute in the Microsoft Windows NT environment.

The following SAS documentation contains basic, portable information on external files:

- *SAS Language: Reference, Version 6, First Edition*
- *SAS Language and Procedures: Usage, Version 6, First Edition*
- *SAS Language and Procedures: Usage 2, Version 6, First Edition.*

See SAS Technical Report P-195, *Transporting SAS Files between Host Systems*, for information on how to access external files containing transport data libraries.

Note: When you see the `App4` icon, be sure to read the appropriate section in Appendix 4 as well as the information provided in this chapter. You can ignore the icon if you do not need to move files between Windows NT, OS/2, and DOS, or if your files do not contain national characters or graphics border characters.

Referencing External Files

To access external files, you must tell the SAS System how to find the files. Use the following statements to access external files:

FILENAME
: associates a fileref with an external file that is used for input or output.

FILE
: opens an external file for writing data lines. Use the PUT statement to write lines.

INFILE
: opens an external file for reading data lines. Use the INPUT statement to read lines.

%INCLUDE
: opens an external file and reads SAS statements from that file. (No other statements are necessary.)

These statements are discussed later in this chapter; in Chapter 8, "SAS Statements" on page 201; and in Chapter 9, "SAS Language Statements," of *SAS Language: Reference.*

You can also specify external files in various SAS Display Manager System filename entry fields (for example, as a file destination in the OUTPUT MANAGER window) and in display manager commands, such as FILE and INCLUDE.

Depending on the context, any of the following point to an external file:

- a fileref assigned with the FILENAME statement.
- an environment variable defined with either the SET system option or the Windows NT SET command.
- a Windows NT filename enclosed in quotes.
- member name syntax. (This feature is also called aggregate syntax.)
- a single filename without quotes (a file in the working directory).

The following sections discuss these methods of specifying external files.

Because there are several ways to specify external files in the SAS System, the SAS System uses a set of rules to resolve an external file reference. The following list represents this order of precedence:

1. Check for a standard Windows NT file specification enclosed in quotes.
2. Check for a fileref defined by a FILENAME statement.
3. Check for an environment variable fileref.
4. Assume the file is in the working directory.

In other words, the SAS System assumes an external file reference is a standard Windows NT file specification. If it is not, the SAS System checks to see if the file reference is a fileref (defined by either a FILENAME statement or an environment variable). If the file reference is none of these, the SAS System assumes it is a filename in the working directory. If the external file reference is not valid for one of these choices, the SAS System issues an error message indicating that it cannot access the external file.

Using a Fileref

One way to reference external files is with a *fileref*. A fileref is a logical name associated with an external file. You can assign a fileref with the FILENAME statement, or you can use an environment variable to point to the file. This section discusses the different ways to assign filerefs and also shows you how to obtain a listing of the active filerefs and clear filerefs during your SAS session.

Using the FILENAME Statement

The FILENAME statement provides a means to associate a logical name with an external file, directory, or device. The simplest form of the FILENAME statement is as follows:

FILENAME *fileref 'external-file'*;

For example, if you want to read the file C:\MYDATA\SCORES.DAT, you can issue the following statement to associate the fileref MYDATA with the file C:\MYDATA\SCORES.DAT:

```
filename mydata 'c:\mydata\scores.dat';
```

Then you can use this fileref in your SAS programs. For example, the following statements create a SAS data set named TEST, using the data stored in the external file referenced by the fileref MYDATA:

```
data test;
   infile mydata;
   input name $ score;
run;
```

The words CON and NUL are reserved words under Windows NT.
Do not use CON or NUL as filerefs. ■

The FILENAME statement also enables you to concatenate directories of external files and to concatenate several individual external files into one logical external file. These topics are illustrated later in this chapter.

The FILENAME statement accepts various options that enable you to associate device names, such as printers, with external files and to control file characteristics, such as record format and length. Some of these options are illustrated in "Advanced External I/O Techniques" on page 110. For the complete syntax of the FILENAME statement, refer to page 206.

Using Environment Variables

Just as you can define an environment variable to serve as a logical name for a SAS data library (see "Using Environment Variables" on page 79), you can also use an environment variable to refer to an external file. You can choose either to define a SAS environment variable using the SET system option or to define a Windows NT environment variable using the Windows NT SET command. Alternatively, you can define Windows NT environment variables using the System dialog box, accessed from the Control Panel.

The words CON and NUL are reserved words under Windows NT.
Do not use CON or NUL as an environment variable. ■

The availability of environment variables makes it simple to assign resources to the SAS System prior to invocation. However, the environment variables you define for a particular SAS session are not available to other applications.

Using the SET system option

For example, to define a SAS environment variable that points to the external file C:\MYDATA\TEST.DAT, you can use the following SET option in your SAS configuration file:

```
-set myvar c:\mydata\test.dat
```

Then, in your SAS programs, you can use the environment variable MYVAR to refer to the external file:

```
data mytest;
   infile myvar;
   input name $ score;
run;
```

It is recommended that you use the SET system option in your SAS configuration file if you invoke the SAS System through a program group window.

Using the SET Command

An alternative to using the SET system option to define an environment variable is to use the Windows NT SET command. For example, the Windows NT SET command that equates to the previous example is

```
SET MYVAR=C:\MYDATA\TEST.BAT
```

(You can also select **System** in the Windows NT Control Panel to define your SET commands.)

You must issue all the SET commands that define your environment variables before you invoke the SAS System.

Note: When you reference an external environment variable (one assigned with the Windows NT SET command) in your SAS programs (such as in a FILE statement), a note informing you the environment variable has been used is written to the SAS log.

Assigning a Fileref to a Directory

The previous sections have illustrated assigning a fileref to a single external file. It is also possible to assign a fileref to a directory and then access individual files within that directory using member name syntax. (This feature is also called aggregate syntax.)

For example, if all your regional sales data for January are stored in the directory C:\SAS\MYDATA, you can issue the following FILENAME statement to assign the fileref JAN to this directory:

```
filename jan 'c:\sas\mydata';
```

Now you can use this fileref with a member name in your SAS programs. In the following example, you reference two files stored in the JAN directory:

```
data westsale;
   infile jan(west);
   input name $ 1-16 sales 18-25 comiss 27-34;
run;

data eastsale;
   infile jan(east);
   input name $ 1-16 sales 18-25 comiss 27-34;
run;
```

When you use member name syntax, you do not have to specify the file extension for the file you are referencing, as long as the file extension is the expected one. For instance, in the previous example, the INFILE statement expects a file extension of .DAT. Table 4.1 lists the expected file extensions for the various SAS statements and display manager commands:

Table 4.1 *Default File Extensions for Referencing External Files with Member Name Syntax*

Display Manager Command or SAS Statement	Display Manager Window	File Extension
FILE statement	PROGRAM EDITOR	.DAT
%INCLUDE statement	PROGRAM EDITOR	.SAS
INFILE statement	PROGRAM EDITOR	.DAT
FILE command	PROGRAM EDITOR	.SAS
FILE command	LOG	.LOG
FILE command	OUTPUT	.LST
FILE command	NOTEPAD	none
INCLUDE command	PROGRAM EDITOR	.SAS
INCLUDE command	NOTEPAD	none

For example, the following program submits the file C:\PROGRAMS\TESTPGM.SAS to the SAS System:

```
filename test 'c:\programs';
%include test(testpgm);
```

The SAS System searches for a file named TESTPGM.SAS in the directory C:\PROGRAMS.

If your file has a file extension different from the default file extension, you can use the file extension in the filename, as in the following example:

```
filename test 'c:\programs';
%include test(testpgm.xyz);
```

If your file has no file extension, you must enclose the filename in quotes, as in the following example:

```
filename test 'c:\programs';
%include test('testpgm');
```

To further illustrate the default file extensions the SAS System uses, here are some more examples using member name syntax. Assume the following FILENAME statement has been submitted:

```
filename test 'c:\mysasdir';
```

The following example opens the file C:\MYSASDIR\PGM1.DAT for output:

```
file test(pgm1);
```

The following example opens the file C:\MYSASDIR\PGM1.DAT for input:

```
infile test(pgm1);
```

The following example reads and submits the file C:\MYSASDIR\PGM1:

```
%include test('pgm1');
```

These examples use SAS statements. Display manager commands, such as the FILE and INCLUDE commands, also accept member name syntax and have the same default file extensions as shown in Table 4.1.

Another feature of member name syntax is that it enables you to reference a subdirectory in the working directory without using a fileref. As an example, suppose you have a subdirectory named PROGRAMS that is located beneath the working directory. You can use the subdirectory name PROGRAMS when referencing files within this directory. For example, the following statement submits the program stored in *working-directory*\PROGRAMS\PGM1.SAS:

```
%include programs(pgm1);
```

The next example uses the FILE display manager command to save the contents of the active window to *working-directory*\PROGRAMS\TESTPGM.DAT:

```
file programs(testpgm)
```

Note: If a directory name is the same as a previously defined fileref, the fileref takes precedence over the directory name.

Assigning a fileref to concatenated directories

Member name syntax is also handy when you use the FILENAME statement to concatenate directories of external files. For example, suppose you issue the following FILENAME statement:

```
filename progs ('c:\sas\programs','d:\myprogs');
```

This statement tells the SAS System that the fileref PROGS refers to all files stored in both the C:\SAS\PROGRAMS and the D:\MYPROGS directories. When you use the fileref PROGS in your SAS program, the SAS System looks in these directories for the member you specify. When you use this concatenation feature, you should be aware of the protocol the SAS System uses depending on whether you are accessing the files for read, write, or update. For more information, see "Understanding How Concatenated Directories Are Accessed" on page 102.

Summary of rules for resolving member name syntax

The SAS System resolves an external file reference that uses member name syntax by using a set of rules. For example, suppose your external file reference in a SAS statemetn or display manager command is the following:

```
progs(member1)
```

The SAS System uses the following set of rules to resolve this external file reference. This list represents the order of precedence:

1. Check for a fileref named PROGS defined by a FILENAME statement.
2. Check for a SAS or Windows NT environment variable named PROGS.
3. Check for a directory named PROGS beneath the working directory.

The member name must be a valid physical filename. If no extension is given (as in the previous example), the SAS System uses the appropriate default extension, as given in Table 4.1. If the extension is given or the member name is quoted, the SAS System does not assign an extension, and it looks for the filename exactly as it is given.

Assigning a Fileref to Concatenated Files

You can specify concatenations of files when reading external files from within the SAS System. Concatenated files consist of two or more file specifications, which may contain wildcard characters, separated by blanks or commas. Here are some examples of valid concatenation specifications:

- `filename allsas ('one.sas', 'two.sas', 'three.sas');`
- `filename alldata ('test1.dat' 'test2.dat' 'test3.dat');`
- `filename allinc 'test*.sas';`
- `%include allsas;`
- `infile alldata;`
- `include allinc`

When you use this concatenation feature, you should be aware of the protocol the SAS System uses depending on whether you are accessing the files for read, write, or update. For more information, see "Understanding How Concatenated Files Are Accessed" on page 103.

Note: Do not confuse concatenated file specifications with concatenated directory specifications, which are also valid and are illustrated in "Assigning a fileref to concatenated directories" on page 101.

Listing Fileref Assignments

If you have assigned several filerefs during a SAS session and need to refresh your memory as to which fileref points where, you can use either the FILENAME window or the FILENAME statement to list all the assigned filerefs.

If you are running display manager, use the FILENAME window to list the active filerefs. There are two ways to open the FILENAME window: either issue the FILENAME command or use the pop-up menus. To use pop-up menus, select

Globals ▶ Data management ▶ Filename list

The FILENAME window lists all the filerefs active for your current SAS session. Any environment variables you have defined as filerefs are listed, provided you have used them in your SAS session. If you have defined an environment variable as a fileref but have not used it yet in a SAS program, the fileref is not listed in the FILENAME window.

If you are running the SAS System in batch mode, you can use the following FILENAME statement to write the active filerefs to the SAS log:

```
filename _all_ list;
```

Clearing Filerefs

You can clear a fileref by using the following form of the FILENAME statement:

FILENAME *fileref* |_ALL_ CLEAR;

If you specify a fileref, only that fileref is cleared. If you specify the keyword _ALL_, all the filerefs you have assigned during your current SAS session are cleared.

Note: When you clear a fileref defined by an environment variable, the variable remains defined, but it is no longer considered a fileref. (That is, it is no longer listed in the FILENAME window). You can use the variable in a another FILENAME statement to create a new fileref.

The SAS System automatically clears the association between filerefs and their respective files at the end of your job or session. If you want to associate the fileref with a different file during the current session, you do not have to end the session or clear the fileref. The SAS System automatically reassigns the fileref when you issue a FILENAME statement for the new file.

Understanding How Concatenated Directories Are Accessed

When you associate a fileref with more than one physical directory, which file is accessed depends upon whether it is being accessed for input, output, or update.

Input and update

If the file is opened for input or update, the first file found that matches the member name is accessed. For example, if you submit the following statements, and the file PHONE.DAT exists in both the C:\SAMPLES and C:\TESTPGMS directories, the one in C:\SAMPLES is read:

```
filename test ('c:\samples','c:\testpgms');

data sampdat;
   infile test(phone.dat);
   input name $ phonenum $ city $ state $;
run;
```

Output

When you open a file for output, the SAS System writes to the file in the first directory listed in the FILENAME statement, even if a file by the same name exists in a later directory. For example, suppose you execute the following FILENAME statement:

```
filename test ('c:\sas','d:\mysasdir');
```

Then, if you issue the following FILE command, the file SOURCE.PGM is written to the C:\SAS directory, even if a file by the same name exists in the D:\MYSASDIR directory:

```
file test(source.pgm)
```

Understanding How Concatenated Files Are Accessed

When you associate a fileref with more than one physical file, the behavior of SAS statements and display manager commands depends on whether you are accessing the files for input, output, or update.

Note: You should not use concatenated files with some procedures, such as the FSLIST procedure in SAS/FSP software.

Input

If the file is opened for input, data from all files is input. For example, if you issue the following statements, the %INCLUDE statement submits 4 programs for execution:

```
filename mydata ('qtr1.sas','qtr2.sas','qtr3.sas','qtr4.sas');
%include mydata;
```

Output and update

If the file is opened for output or update, data is written to the first file in the concatenation. For example, if you issue the following statements, the PUT statement writes to MYDAT1.DAT:

```
filename indata 'dogdat.dat';
filename outdata ('mydat1.dat','mydat2.dat','mydat3.dat','mydat4.dat');

data _null_;
   infile dogdat.dat;
   input name breed color;
   file outdata;
```

```
   put name= breed= color=;
run;
```

Using a Quoted Windows NT Filename

Instead of using a fileref to refer to external files, you can use a quoted Windows NT filename. For example, if the file C:\MYDIR\ORANGES.SAS contains a SAS program you want to run, you can issue the following statement:

```
%include 'c:\mydir\oranges.sas';
```

When you use a quoted Windows NT filename in a SAS statement, you can omit the drive and directory specifications if the file you want to reference is located in the working directory. For instance, if in the previous example the working directory is C:\MYDIR, you can submit this statement:

```
%include 'oranges.sas';
```

Using Reserved Operating System Physical Names

You can use several reserved names as quoted physical filenames. Reserved operating system physical names enable you to do a variety of things, such as read data directly from the communications port (such as COM1) or write to a printer port (such as LPT1). *

Table 4.2 lists these physical names and their corresponding device-type keywords:

Table 4.2 *Reserved Windows NT Physical Names*

Physical Name	Device Type	Use
COM1–COM4	COMMPORT	Read/write from the communications port.
COM1–COM4	PLOTTER	Write data to the plotter or printer connected to the communications port.
LPT1–LPT3	PRINTER	Write data directly to the printer port.
NUL	DUMMY	Discard data. This name is useful in testing situations.

You can specify operating system physical names with or without a colon. For example, you can specify either COM1: or COM1. See your Windows NT manual for additional information.

The following example demonstrates how to use one of these physical names. The fileref PASSTEST points to the printer port, LPT1, and a null DATA step is used to read the SAS data set TEMPDATA and spool observations with passing scores to the Windows NT Print Manager:

* Note that you can attach printers to communications ports as well.

```
filename passtest printer 'lpt1';

data _null_;
   set tempdata;
   file passtest;
   where score ge 60;
   put _all_;
run;
```

Note the use of the device-type keyword PRINTER in the FILENAME statement in this example. Because the access protocols for devices are slightly different from the access protocols for files, you should always use the appropriate device-type keyword in combination with the reserved physical name in the FILENAME statement. If you do not use a device-type keyword, the SAS System defaults to using the access protocols for files, not for devices.

As an alternative to using a device-type keyword in the FILENAME statement, you can use the DEVICE= option in the FILE, INFILE, and %INCLUDE statements. Although this technique serves the same purpose as the device-type keyword, it is not as flexible an approach as using a device-type keyword in the FILENAME statement. For example, if you use a fileref in a PROC PRINTTO statement, no DEVICE= option is available.

For more information on available device-type keywords in the FILENAME statement and for valid values for the DEVICE= option in the FILE, INFILE, %INCLUDE statements, see the descriptions of these statements in Chapter 8.

"Data Acquisition" on page 167 discusses the access protocols for using a communications port device.

Using a File in Your Working Directory

If you store the external files you need to access in your working directory and they have the expected file extensions (see Table 4.1), you can simply refer to the filename, without quotes or file extensions, in a SAS statement. For example, if you have a file named ORANGES.SAS stored in your working directory and ORANGES is not defined as a fileref, you can submit the file with the following statement:

```
%include oranges;
```

Remember, though, that using this type of file reference requires that

- the file is stored in the working directory
- the file has the correct file extension
- the filename is not also defined as a fileref.

See "Determining the Working Directory for the SAS System" on page 15 and "Changing the SAS Working Directory" on page 21 for more information on how to determine and change the SAS System working directory.

Accessing External Files with SAS Statements

This section presents examples of using the FILE, INFILE, and %INCLUDE statements to access external files. These examples are simple; for more complex examples of using these statements under Windows NT, see "Advanced External I/O Techniques" on page 110. Also see Chapter 6.

Using the FILE Statement

The FILE statement enables you to direct lines written by a PUT statement to an external file.*

Here is a simple example using the FILE statement. This example reads the data in the SAS data set MYLIB.TEST and writes only those scores greater than 95 to the external file C:\MYDIR\TEST.DAT:

```
filename test 'c:\mydir\test.dat';
libname mylib 'c:\mydata';

data _null_;
   set mylib.test;
   file test;
   if score ge 95 then
      put score;
run;
```

The previous example illustrates writing the value of only one variable of each observation to an external file. The following example uses the _ALL_ option in the PUT statement to copy all variables in the current observation to the external file if the variable REGION contains the value `west`.

```
libname us 'c:\mydata';

data west;
   set us.pop;
   file 'c:\sas\pop.dat';
   where region='west';
   put _all_;
run;
```

This technique of writing out entire observations is particularly useful if you need to write variable values in a SAS data set to an external file so you can use your data with another application that cannot read data in SAS data set format.

Note: This example uses the _ALL_ keyword in the PUT statement. This code generates *named output*, which means that the variable name, an equals sign (=), and the variable value are all written to the file. Consider this when reading the data later. See the

* You can also use the FILE statement to direct PUT statement output to the SAS log or to the same destination as procedure output. See *SAS Language: Reference* for more information.

description of the PUT statement in Chapter 9 of *SAS Language: Reference* for more information on named output.

The FILE statement also accepts several options. These options enable you, among other things, to associate a device with the output file and to control the record format and length. Some of these options are illustrated in "Advanced External I/O Techniques" on page 110. See page 203 for the complete syntax of the FILE statement.

Note: The default record length used by the FILE statement is 132 characters. If the data you are saving have records longer than this, you must use the FILENAME statement to define a fileref and either use the LRECL= option in the FILENAME statement to specify the correct logical record length or specify the LRECL= option in the FILE statement. For details on the LRECL= option, see page 205.

Using the INFILE Statement

The INFILE statement is used to specify the source of data read by the INPUT statement in a SAS DATA step. The source can be either a text file or a device. The INFILE statement is always used in conjunction with an INPUT statement, which defines the location, order, and type of data being read.

Here is a simple example of the INFILE statement. This DATA step reads the specified data from the external file and creates a SAS data set named SURVEY:

```
filename mydata 'c:\mysasdir\survey.dat';

data survey;
   infile mydata;
   input fruit $ taste looks;
run;
```

Of course, you can use a quoted Windows NT filename instead of a fileref:

```
data survey;
   infile 'c:\mysasdir\survey.dat';
   input fruit $ taste looks;
run;
```

The INFILE statement also accepts other options. These options enable you, among other things, to associate a device with the input file and to control the record format and length. Some of these options are illustrated in "Advanced External I/O Techniques" on page 110. See page 213 for the complete syntax of the INFILE statement.

Note: The default record length used by the INFILE statement is 132 characters. If the data you are reading have records longer than this, you must use the FILENAME statement to define a fileref and either use the LRECL= option in the FILENAME statement to specify the correct logical record length or specify the LRECL= option in the INFILE statement. For details on the LRECL= option, see page 215.

Using the %INCLUDE Statement

When you submit a %INCLUDE statement, it reads an entire file into the current SAS program you are running and submits that file to the SAS System immediately. A single SAS program can have as many individual %INCLUDE statements as necessary, and you can nest up to ten levels of %INCLUDE statements. Using the %INCLUDE statement makes it easier for you to write modular SAS programs.

Here is an example that submits the statements stored in C:\SAS\MYJOBS\PROGRAM1.SAS using the %INCLUDE statement and member name syntax:

```
filename job 'c:\sas\myjobs';
%include job(program1);
```

The %INCLUDE statement also accepts several options. These options enable you, among other things, to associate a device with the input file and to control the record format and length. Some of these options are illustrated in "Advanced External I/O Techniques" on page 110. See page 211 for the complete syntax of the %INCLUDE statement.

Note: The default record length used by the %INCLUDE statement is 132 characters. If the program you are reading has records longer than this, you must use the FILENAME statement to define a fileref and either use the LRECL= option in the FILENAME statement to specify the correct logical record length or specify the LRECL= option in the %INCLUDE statement. For details on the LRECL= option, see page 212.

Accessing External Files with Display Manager Commands

This section illustrates how to use the FILE and INCLUDE display manager commands to access external files. Commands provide the same service as the Save As and Open dialog boxes discussed in "Open Into Pgm Editor Item" on page 34 and "Save As Item" on page 34. The method you use to access external files is a matter of personal preference.

Using the FILE Command

The FILE command has a different use than the FILE statement; the FILE command writes the current contents of a window to an external file rather than merely specifying a destination for PUT statement output in a DATA step.

For example, if you want to save the contents of the LOG window to an external file named C:\SASLOGS\TODAY.LOG, you can issue the following FILE command from the Command dialog box; however, the LOG window must be active:

```
file 'c:\saslogs\today.log'
```

If you have already defined the fileref LOGS to point to the SASLOGS directory, you can use the following FILE command:

```
file logs(today)
```

In this case, the file extension defaults to .LOG, as shown in Table 4.1.

If you use the FILE command to attempt to write to an already existing file, a dialog box gives you the option of replacing the existing file, appending the contents of the window to the existing file, or canceling your request.

If you issue the FILE command with no arguments, the contents of the window are written to the file referenced in the last FILE command. This is useful if you are editing a program and want to save it often. However, the dialog box that prompts you about overwriting or appending appears only the first time you issue the plain FILE command. Thereafter, unless you specify the filename in the FILE command, it uses the parameters you specified earlier (overwrite or append) without prompting you.

Choosing **Save As** from the SAS AWS **File** menu displays the Save As dialog box. This dialog box performs the same function as the FILE command, but it is more flexible in that it gives you more choices and is more interactive than the FILE command. For more information, see "Save As Item" on page 34.

The FILE command also accepts several options. These options enable you, among other things, to associate a device with the output file and to control the record format and length. Some of these options are illustrated in "Advanced External I/O Techniques" on page 110. See page 282 for the complete syntax of the FILE command.

Using the INCLUDE Command

The INCLUDE command, like the %INCLUDE statement, can be used to copy an entire external file into the PROGRAM EDITOR window, the NOTEPAD window, or whatever window is active. In the case of the INCLUDE command, however, the file is simply copied to the window and is not submitted.

For example, suppose you want to copy the file C:\SAS\PROG1.SAS into the PROGRAM EDITOR window. If you have defined a fileref SAMPLE to point to the correct directory, you can use the following INCLUDE command from the Command dialog box, assuming the PROGRAM EDITOR is the active window, to copy the member PROG1 into the PROGRAM EDITOR window:

```
include sample(prog1)
```

Another way to copy files into your display manager session is to use the Open dialog box. In addition to copying files, the Open dialog box gives you other options, such as running the program you are copying. The Open dialog box is the most flexible way for you to copy files into the PROGRAM EDITOR window. For more information, see "Open Into Pgm Editor Item" on page 34 for more information.

The INCLUDE command also accepts several options. These options enable you, among other things, to associate a device with the input file and to control the record format and length. Some of these options are illustrated in "Advanced External I/O Techniques" on page 110. See page 284 for the complete syntax of the INCLUDE command.

Issuing the INCLUDE command with no arguments includes the file referenced in the last INCLUDE command. If no previous INCLUDE command exists, you receive an error message.

Using the GSUBMIT Command

The GSUBMIT command can be used to submit SAS statements that are stored in the Windows NT Clipboard. To submit SAS statements from the Clipboard, use the following command:

```
gsubmit buffer=default
```

You can also use the GSUBMIT command to submit SAS statements specified as part of the command. See SAS Technical Report P-242, *SAS Software: Changes and Enhancements, Release 6.08* for more information on the GSUBMIT command.

Advanced External I/O Techniques

This section illustrates how to use the FILENAME, FILE, and INFILE statements to perform more advanced I/O tasks, such as altering the record format and length, appending data to a file, using the DRIVEMAP device-type keyword to determine which hard drives are available, and reading an external file created under the OS/2 operating system that contains national characters.

Altering the Record Format

Using the RECFM= option in the FILENAME, FILE, %INCLUDE, and INFILE statements enables you to specify the record format of your external files. The following example shows you how to use this option.

Usually, the SAS System reads a line of data until a carriage return and line feed combination ('0D0A'x) are encountered or until just a line feed ('0A'x) is encountered. However, sometimes data do not contain these carriage control characters but do have fixed-length records. In this case, you can specify RECFM=F to read your data.

To read such a file, you need to use the LRECL= option to specify the record length and the RECFM= option to tell the SAS System that the records have fixed-length record format. Here are the required statements:

```
data test;
   infile 'test.dat' lrecl=60 recfm=f;
   input x y z;
run;
```

In this example, the SAS System expects fixed-length records that are 60 bytes long, and it reads in the three numeric variables X, Y, and Z.

You can also specify RECFM=F when your data do contain carriage returns and line feeds, but you want to read these values as part of your data instead of treating them as carriage control characters. When you specify RECFM=F, the SAS System ignores any carriage controls and line feeds and simply reads the record length you specify.

Appending Data to an External File

Occasionally, you may not want to create a new output file, but rather append data to the end of an existing file. In this case, you can use the MOD option in the FILE statement as in the following example:

```
filename myfile 'c:\sas\data';

data _null_;
   infile myfile(newdata);
   input sales expenses;
```

```
   file myfile(jandata) mod;
   put sales expenses;
run;
```

This example reads the variables SALES and EXPENSES from the external data file C:\SAS\DATA\NEWDATA.DAT and appends records to the existing data file C:\SAS\DATA\JANDATA.DAT.

If you are going to append data to several files in a single directory, you can use the MOD option in the FILENAME statement instead of in the FILE statement. You can also use the PRINTTO procedure to append data to a file. See Chapter 28, "The PRINTTO Procedure" in the *SAS Procedures Guide, Version 6, Third Edition.*

Determining Your Hard Drive Mapping

You can use the DRIVEMAP device-type keyword in the FILENAME statement to determine which hard drives are available for use. Here is an example using this keyword:

```
filename myfile drivemap;

data mymap;
   infile myfile;
   input drive $;
   put drive;
run;
```

The information written to the SAS log looks similar to that shown in Output 4.1:

Output 4.1
Drive Mapping Information

```
filename myfile drivemap;

data mymap;
   infile myfile;
   input drive $;
   put drive;
run;
NOTE: The infile MYFILE is:
      FILENAME=DRIVEMAP,
      RECFM=V,LRECL=132

A:
C:
H:
J:
K:
L:
M:
N:
R:
S:
T:
U:
NOTE: 12 records were read from the infile MYFILE.
      The minimum record length was 2.
      The maximum record length was 2.
NOTE: The data set WORK.MYMAP has 12 observations and 1 variables.
NOTE: The DATA statement used 2.04 seconds.
```

You might use this technique in SAS/AF applications, where you could build selection lists to let a user choose a hard drive. You could also use the DRIVEMAP keyword to enable you to assign macro variables to the various available hard drives.

Using the DRIVEMAP device-type keyword in the FILENAME statement implies you are using the fileref for read-only purposes. If you try to use the fileref associated with the DRIVEMAP device-type keyword in a write or update situation, you receive an error message indicating you do not have sufficient authority to write to the file.

Reading External Files with National Characters

Characters such as the Â are considered national characters. Windows NT represents each character with a hexadecimal number. If your external file was created with a Windows NT editor (including applications such as WordPerfect) or in the SAS System under Windows NT, you do not need to do anything special. Simply read the file using the FILENAME or FILE statements, as you would normally do.

However, if the external file containing national characters (or graphics border characters) was created by a DOS or OS/2 editor, the binary values used to represent the characters are not interpreted correctly by Windows NT. (This is a Windows NT complication, not a restriction introduced by the SAS System.) Therefore, you must tell the SAS System to translate the file as it is being read.

Here is an example of a DATA step that reads a file created by a DOS editor. The OEM option in the INFILE statement alerts the SAS System to the fact that the file is in a different character set than what is expected by Windows NT. The OEM option (and its counterpart, the ANSI option) are briefly described in Chapter 8 in the descriptions of the FILE, FILENAME, %INCLUDE, and INFILE statements.

```
data readtest;
   infile 'd:\intldata\products.dat' oem;
   input country $20 topprod $20;
run;
```

This same example would work for reading a file created under OS/2.

If all the files in a directory are in the same format, specify the OEM option in the FILENAME statement and use member name syntax, as in the following example:

```
filename oemdata 'd:\intldata\' oem;

data readtest;
   infile oemdata(products);
   input country $20 topprod $20;
run;
```

You can modify your SAS environment under Windows NT so that the DOS and OS/2 character set is the default. This is done with the WINCHARSET system option, described briefly on page 193. Appendix 4, "Moving Files Containing ANSI or OEM Characters between Windows NT, OS/2, and DOS" on page 323 contains all the details on the character sets used by the various operating systems and how they affect users of the SAS System.

Chapter Summary

This chapter provides background information on using external files with the SAS System under Windows NT. You can learn what an external file is and how to refer to external files in SAS programs, and you can read through examples of using external files in SAS statements such as FILENAME, FILE, INFILE, and %INCLUDE, as well as display manager commands such as FILE and INCLUDE.

Once you have read Chapter 3, which discusses using SAS files, and this chapter, which discusses using external files, you can move on to Chapter 5, "Accomplishing Common Tasks with the SAS System under Windows NT" on page 115, which illustrates performing several common tasks with the SAS System (for example, printing, routing output to files, and producing graphics).

Chapter 5 Accomplishing Common Tasks with the SAS® System under Windows NT

Introduction

This chapter uses the information presented in the previous chapters to illustrate how to perform such tasks as printing output and creating graphics. These tasks involve using SAS files and external files and require an understanding of the different methods of running the SAS System. Therefore, be sure you have read Chapters 1 through 4 before proceeding with this chapter.

App4

Note: When you see the `App4` icon, be sure to read the appropriate section in Appendix 4 as well as the information provided in this chapter. You can ignore the icon if you do not need to move files between Microsoft Windows NT, OS/2, and DOS, or if your files do not contain national characters or graphics border characters.

Printing

The SAS System in the Microsoft Windows NT environment enables you to take advantage of the Windows NT Print Manager. This means you can spool printed output from your SAS session (such as the contents of the PROGRAM EDITOR and OUTPUT windows and results of procedures and the DATA step) to the Print Manager and manage this output in the same manner as you manage output from other Windows NT applications. You can also take advantage of fonts supported by your printers. For details on using the Print Manager, see your Windows NT documentation. "Producing Graphics" on page 123 discusses how to route graphics from your SAS session to printers.

Three items in the SAS AWS `File` menu facilitate printing: `Print`, `Release Print Requests`, and `Printer Setup`. These items and their associated dialog boxes are illustrated respectively in "Print Item" on page 34, "Release Print Requests Item" on page 36, and "Printer Setup Item" on page 36. This chapter provides more details than are provided in Chapter 2.

The first consideration in printing is identifying which printer drivers you have installed under Windows NT. This chapter does not teach you how to install printer drivers; see your printer and Windows NT documentation for that information. Once you have installed the printer drivers on the various available ports (such as LPT1-LPT3 and COM1-COM4), you are ready to print from your SAS session.

Choosing a Print Destination and Printer Attributes

Choose `Printer Setup` in the SAS AWS `File` menu and review the list of printer drivers and their port locations. The highlighted printer is your SAS System default printer. This is the printer that the SAS System spools your output to by default. You can use the `Sysprint device name` and `Sysprint printer name` fields to change the default printer. You can also change your default port and printer by using the SYSPRINT system option instead of the Printer Setup dialog box. See "Printing in Batch Mode" on page 120 and page 192 for a discussion of this option. Also refer to "Default Printer Details" on page 120.

Once you have chosen your default printer, choose [Setup] to display the printer attributes supported by that printer. The dialog box displayed is entirely dependent on the printer driver and is not created by the SAS System. However, the options you select in the dialog box (such as number of copies, page orientation, and so on) are saved from one SAS session to the next. Note that the options you select from your SAS session do not affect other applications outside the SAS System.

After you have completed adjusting the default printer and printer options, save your changes and close the Printer Setup dialog box by choosing [OK]. Next, choose `Print` from the SAS AWS `File` menu and either verify the default destination or supply an alternative destination, such as a filename. You can use the `Source` field to specify the source from which you want to print. When you choose [OK], the output is spooled to the Print Manager.

Once the output is in the Print Manager, you can manage it as you manage any other spooled output under Windows NT. You can delete queued jobs and monitor the queue's progress.

Deferring Print Requests

You can defer a print request by choosing **Hold Print Requests** from the Print dialog box. This causes all jobs to be held until you choose **Release Print Requests** from the SAS AWS **File** menu. Print requests are spooled to the Print Manager when you choose **Release Print Requests**. You can also use the HOLD option in the FILENAME or FILE statement to defer print requests. Consider the following example:

```
filename myfile printer 'lpt1:' hold;
filename printnow 'lpt1:';

data _null_;
   file myfile;
   put "Page 1";
run;

data _null_;
   file myfile;
   put "Page 2";
run;

data _null_;
   file printnow;
run;
```

It is not until the third DATA step executes that the output from all three DATA steps is sent to the printer.

You can use the pop-up menus in most SAS windows to submit a print job. Simply select **Print** from the **File** pop-up menu of that window. The Print dialog box appears.

Using SAS Display Manager System Commands

If you prefer using display manager commands to using pop-up menus or menu bars, you can use the PRINT display manager command to print the contents of the active window. For more information on these commands, refer to *SAS Language: Reference, Version 6, First Edition*. If you are using SAS/FSP software, you can use the SPRINT command. See *SAS/FSP Software: Usage and Reference, Verion 6, First Edition* for more information on the SPRINT command.

Sending DATA Step Output to a Printer

You may want to spool your DATA step output to a printer instead of to a file. Use the FILENAME statement and the PRINTER device-type keyword to accomplish this, as in the following example:

```
filename myfile printer 'lpt1:';

data _null_;
   set mydata;
```

```
      file myfile;
      where city='Cincinnati';
      put _all_;
   run;
```

In this example, the PRINTER device-type keyword is optional because the reserved printer port LPT1 is used. If you use a communications port instead, such as COM1, you must specify the PRINTER device-type keyword.

If you have specified the SYSPRINT system option (for example, in your SAS configuration file), thereby defining a default printing destination (such as LPT1 or COM2), you can leave off the quoted physical name in your FILENAME statement, as in the following example:

```
filename myfile printer;
```

In this case, the output is spooled to the default printer port as specified by the SYSPRINT system option.

Sending Printed Output to a File

You can send your printed output to a file by specifying a filename in the **Alternate Destination** field in the Print dialog box. This differs from simply specifying LPT1: or COM1: as the destination in the Save As dialog box because by using the Print dialog box, you ensure that the file contains all the printer control language necessary to support whatever options you have chosen with the Printer Setup dialog box, such as fonts and page orientation. Note that even when you specify a filename in the **Alternate Destination** field, the default printer driver is still used.

You can also route printed output to a file using the FILENAME statement, which is useful for routing DATA step output. Here is an example:

```
filename myfile printer 'c:\sas\results.dat';

data _null_;
   set qtr1data;
   file myfile;
   where sales ge 1000;
   put _all_;
run;
```

In this example, the output from the DATA step is routed to a file, yet still contains all the printer control information necessary for you to use your printer to produce formatted output.

Another method of sending printed output to a file is to use the Windows NT Control Panel and assign a specific filename or the device FILE: to a printer. If you assign the FILE: device to a printer, the SAS System prompts you for a filename each time you print. When you send output to a file, the contents of the file are overwritten if the file already exists.

Bypassing the Print Manager

To bypass the Print Manager, specify the SYSPRINT option with only the first argument, as in the following OPTIONS statement:

```
options sysprint='lpt1:';
```

Or specify a filename as the value, as in the following example:

```
options sysprint='myfile.dat';
```

If you do not specify the printer driver argument (the second argument) for the SYSPRINT option, the SAS System does not use the Print Manager.

You can also use the Printer Setup dialog box to bypass the Print Manager. Simply delete the value shown in the **Sysprint printer name** field and choose [OK]. This action is equivalent to specifying only the first parameter in the SYSPRINT option, and therefore the Print Manager is not used.

If during your session you want to alternately print with and without the Print Manager, you can issue OPTIONS statements to change the value of the SYSPRINT option or use the Printer Setup dialog box to go back to using the Print Manager. Note, however, that if you send output to a port different from the one you specify in the SYSPRINT option or in the Printer Setup dialog box, output is still routed to the Print Manager. For example, suppose you submit the following statements:

```
options sysprint='lpt1:';
filename myfile printer 'lpt1:';

data _null_;
   set tempdata;
   file myfile;
   put _all_;
run;
```

Because you are writing to the port referenced in the SYSPRINT option, and you specified only one parameter in the SYSPRINT value, the output from this DATA step is not routed through the Print Manager. However, if you submit a second FILENAME statement such as the following and then use this fileref in another FILE statement, the output is routed through the Print Manager because the FILENAME statement references a different port than was specified in the SYSPRINT option:

```
filename myfile printer 'lpt2:';

data _null_;
   set mydata;
   file myfile;
   put _all_;
run;
```

Printing in Batch Mode

When you run SAS jobs in batch mode, you do not have access to the Print and Printer Setup dialog boxes, but you can still take advantage of the Print Manager. Use the SYSPRINT system option to specify your default printer and port as described on page 192. For example, suppose your SAS configuration file contains the following option:

```
-sysprint lpt2 'HP LaserJet III'
```

Then, your SAS program might contain the following statements:

```
filename myfile printer;

data _null_;
   set schools;
   file myfile;
   where enrolled le 500;
   put _all_;
run;
```

When you submit your job, the SAS System uses the SYSPRINT specification to spool your output from the DATA step to the Print Manager, using the LPT2 port and the HP LaserJet III printer driver.

Default Printer Details

The SAS System looks for a default printer as follows (in order of precedence):

- the SYSPRINT system option value
- the SASUSER.PROFILE2 catalog information
- the system default printer (chosen from the Windows NT Control Panel).

The default printer is saved in the SASUSER.PROFILE2 catalog. The catalog is updated if during your SAS session you choose a different default printer (using the Printer Setup dialog box or the Windows NT Control Panel).

If no default printer exists, the SAS System uses the printer defined as the default printer in the Windows NT Control Panel. If no default Windows NT printer exists either, the default printer becomes LPT1:. If you want to override the default printer defined in your SASUSER.PROFILE2 catalog, use the SYSPRINT system option.

Using SAS System Print Forms

If you have defined SAS System print forms with the FSFORM display manager command, you can use these forms from the Print dialog box. Click on the arrow in the **Formname** field to display the print forms available in the SASUSER.PROFILE and SASHELP.BASE catalogs. Click on the form name you want to use.

Do not use a Sysprint printer name if you use a SAS form.
If you use a SAS System print form that controls printer characteristics such as fonts, numbers of copies, or page orientation, you must blank out the **`Sysprint printer name`** field in the Printer Setup dialog box before you print. ■

Controlling the Line and Page Size from Your SAS Form

When you print from display manager windows, your line size and page size are controlled by the active SAS form, through the **`Characters per line`**, **`Lines on first page`**, and **`Lines on following`** fields in the Text Body and Margin Information frame of the FORM window. If you set these fields to −99, the values of the LINESIZE and PAGESIZE system options are used to define the line size and page size of your output.

By default, under Windows NT the SASHELP.BASE.DEFAULT form uses −99 in these fields, so that the LINESIZE and PAGESIZE system option values are used to control the format of your output. (The other default forms, used by other products such as SAS/FSP software, do not use the special −99 value.) You can create your own SAS forms and set the line size and page size fields to −99 if you want. If you have a DEFAULT form in your SASUSER.PROFILE catalog and the line size and page size fields are set to −99, the LINESIZE and PAGESIZE system option values are used for all display manager output, including that from SAS/FSP applications, SAS/AF applications, and so on.

Routing Procedure Output and the SAS Log to a File

This section provides examples of routing SAS procedure output and the SAS log to a file. It does not attempt to illustrate every method of routing output; it illustrates the easiest or most common methods. Most of this task is the same across operating systems and is discussed fully in *SAS Language and Procedures: Usage, Version 6, First Edition.* However, the specification of external filenames and devices is system dependent. See "Referencing External Files" on page 96 for complete information on the various ways to reference external files.

You can route your SAS procedure output or the SAS log to a file in one of several ways. The method you choose depends on the method you use to run the SAS System, the moment at which you make your decision to route the output or SAS log, and your personal preference.

Some methods of sending SAS procedure output or the SAS log to a file include using

- □ the SAS AWS Save As dialog box
- □ the Save as dialog box from other pop-up menus
- □ the FILE command
- □ the PRINTTO procedure
- □ various system options.

The examples in this section illustrate only some of these printing methods. See Chapter 22, "Directing the SAS Log and Output" in *SAS Language and Procedures* for more information.

Using the Save As Dialog Box

Under display manager, selecting **Save As** from the SAS AWS **File** menu is the easiest way to send the contents of a window, including the OUTPUT and LOG windows, to a file. For more information on the Save As dialog box, see "Save As Item" on page 34.

Using the PRINTTO Procedure

In batch SAS sessions, the SAS procedure output and the SAS log are written by default to files named *filename*.LST and *filename*.LOG, respectively, where *filename* is the name of your SAS job. For example, if your SYSIN file is MYPROG.SAS, the procedure output file is named MYPROG.LST, and the log file is named MYPROG.LOG. However, you can override these default filenames and send your output and log to any file you choose. For example, suppose your job contains the following statements, which assign the fileref MYOUTPUT to the file C:\SAS\FIRST.TXT. Then the PROC PRINTTO statement tells the SAS System to send any upcoming SAS procedure output to the file associated with MYOUTPUT.

```
filename myoutput 'c:\sas\first.txt';

proc printto print=myoutput;
run;
```

Any PROC or DATA statements that follow these statements and that generate output send their output to the C:\SAS\FIRST.TXT file, not to the default procedure output file. If you want to change back to the default file, issue an empty PROC PRINTTO statement like the following example:

```
proc printto;
run;
```

Issuing these statements redirects the SAS procedure output to the default destination (*filename*.LST). In this way, you can send the output and log from different parts of the same SAS job to different files.

Note: If you route procedure output to a file and then look at it in the PROGRAM EDITOR window, it may contain carriage control characters. You can set the RECFM= option to P in the FILENAME statement to eliminate these characters from your file.

If you want to send the SAS log to a specific file, use the LOG= option in the PROC PRINTTO statement instead of the PRINT= option. For more information on the PRINTTO procedure, see Chapter 9, "SAS Procedures" on page 223 and Chapter 28 in the *SAS Procedures Guide, Version 6, Third Edition.*

Note: When you use the PRINTTO procedure to route SAS procedure output or the SAS log, the Status window does not reflect any rerouting of batch output but indicates it is routing the procedure output file and log to *filename*.LST and *filename*.LOG.

Using SAS System Options

You can use SAS system options to route your SAS output or SAS log to a file. For example, if you want to override the default behavior and send your procedure output from a batch SAS job to the file C:\SAS\PROG1.TXT, you can invoke the SAS System with the following command:

```
SAS -SYSIN C:\SAS\PROG1 -PRINT C:\SAS\PROG1.TXT
```

This SAS command executes the SAS program PROG1.SAS and sends the procedure output to the file C:\SAS\PROG1.TXT. You can treat the SAS log similarly by using the LOG system option instead of the PRINT system option. Two other related system options, the ALTPRINT and ALTLOG options, are explained on page 178.

Note: The Status window does reflect the PRINT and LOG system options values when recording where the procedure output and log are being sent.

Producing Graphics

This section describes basic steps for producing graphics with the SAS System under Windows NT. The following topics are covered:

- displaying graphics on your monitor
- sending graphs to a hardcopy device
- exporting graphics to other applications.

See *SAS/GRAPH Software: Reference, Version 6, First Edition, Volume 1* and *Volume 2* for full details on using SAS/GRAPH software. Also see Appendix 2, "Graphics Considerations" on page 319 for further details on using graphics and fonts with the SAS System under Windows NT.

Displaying Graphics on Your Monitor

In most cases, output is automatically displayed on your monitor when you run a SAS/GRAPH procedure; it is not necessary to specify a SAS/GRAPH device driver. Information about your graphics display is stored in a Windows NT information file and is automatically used by the SAS System if you are using display manager.

Here is a simple example of how to produce a graphic:

```
data hat;
   do x=-5 to 5 by .25;
      do y=-5 to 5 by .25;
         z=sin(sqrt(x*x+y*y));
         output;
      end;
   end;
```

```
proc g3d data=hat;
   plot y*x=z/ctop=red;
   title 'Cowboy Hat with G3D';
run;
quit;
```

Figure 5.1 shows the output for this program:

Figure 5.1
Cowboy Hat Program Output

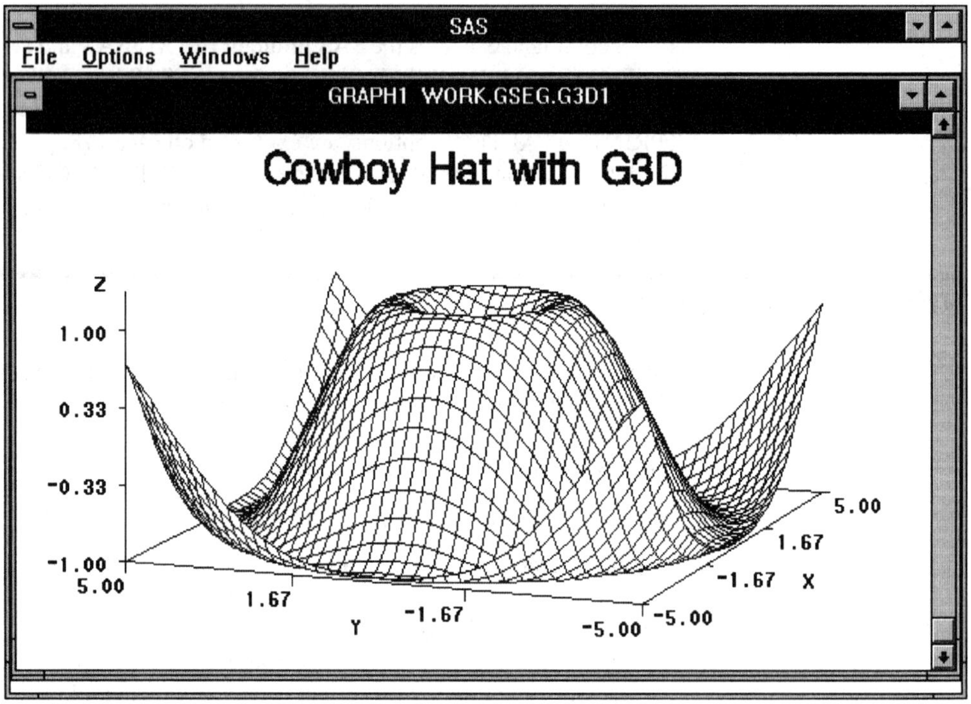

If you use the DEVICE= option in the GOPTIONS statement to route your graphics to a hardcopy device, and then you want to return to using your monitor to display graphics, you must specify a driver. Submit the following statement to display graphics output on your monitor:

```
goptions device=win;
```

The WIN device driver is also specified to display graphics on the monitor when you are running your SAS job in batch mode.

Directing Output to a Hardcopy Device

To send SAS/GRAPH output to a hardcopy device, you can use the PRINT command (or select **Print** from the **File** pop-up menu of the GRAPH window) to print a graph displayed on your monitor, or you can have the SAS/GRAPH procedure send the graph directly to your hardcopy device without first previewing the graph on your monitor.

Previewing and Printing from the GRAPH Window

When a graph is displayed in the GRAPH window, you can then send it to a hardcopy device using the PRINT command. To first preview the graph on your monitor as it would appear on the hardcopy device, specify the following:

GOPTIONS DEVICE=WIN TARGET=*hardcopy-driver*;

The *hardcopy-driver* specification is the SAS/GRAPH device driver for the hardcopy device. When the graph is displayed, issue the PRINT command to send the output to the device. If you have not specified the TARGET= option, you can still use the PRINT command to print the graph after it is displayed, but you are prompted to supply the name of a hardcopy driver.

See "Choosing a Hardcopy Driver" on page 125 for information on choosing specific hardcopy drivers and additional details on how output is sent to the device.

Sending the Graph Directly to the Device without Preview

If you do not want to preview your hardcopy output on your monitor, you can send the output from SAS/GRAPH procedures directly to your hardcopy device. This approach is useful in situations where you want to produce a large number of graphs without user intervention. To send output directly to the device, simply specify the name of the hardcopy driver (along with any other required options) in a GOPTIONS statement. For example, to send a SAS/GRAPH test pattern directly to a Hewlett Packard Laserjet III printer, specify the following:

```
goptions device=hpljs3;

proc gtestit;
run;
quit;
```

The next section provides information on choosing specific hardcopy drivers.

Choosing a Hardcopy Driver

SAS/GRAPH software provides two types of hardcopy device drivers: the WINPRT*x* series of drivers and SAS/GRAPH drivers. The WINPRT*x* series of drivers use the hardcopy drivers provided with Windows NT to generate the graphics data and send it to the device through the Windows NT Print Manager. SAS/GRAPH stand-alone drivers use internal SAS/GRAPH driver routines to generate the picture, and they can send the output either directly to a communications port or to the device through Windows NT Print Manager. The use of the WINPRT*x* series drivers is encouraged. The following sections describe the use of these drivers in more detail.

Using the WINPRT*x* series of drivers

The SAS/GRAPH WINPRT*x* series of hardcopy drivers use the Windows NT hardcopy driver for your printer
to generate hardcopy output. There are three WINPRT*x* drivers:

WINPRTC	is used for color printers.
WINPRTG	is used for gray-scale printers.
WINPRTM	is used for monochrome printers.

To use a WINPRT*x* driver with SAS/GRAPH software, first set your hardcopy device as the default system printer and destination by choosing **Printer Setup** from the SAS AWS **File** menu. To preview and then print your graph, specify DEVICE=WIN and specify the appropriate WINPRT*x* driver with the TARGETDEVICE= option in your SAS/GRAPH program and issue the PRINT command from the GRAPH window. Or you can select **Print** from the **File** pop-up menu when the graph is displayed. To send output directly to the device without preview, specify the appropriate WINPRT*x* driver with the DEVICE= option in your program.

Suppose you have a PostScript printer and you want to preview your graphics output, then send it to the printer using the WINPRTG driver. First, set up the PostScript printer as your default printer by choosing **Printer Setup** from the SAS AWS **File** menu and filling in the appropriate information. If the printer you are using is not listed, you can use the Windows NT Control Panel or the Print Manager to install the driver. For more information on installing printer drivers, refer to the *Microsoft Windows NT User's Guide*. Then, in your SAS/GRAPH program, specify the following:

```
goptions device=win target=winprtg;    /* gray-scale printer */

proc gplot;
   additional procedure statements
run;
quit;
```

The graph is displayed on your monitor as it will appear on the printer, using gray scales. To print the graph from the GRAPH window, issue the PRINT command or choose **Print** from the **File** pop-up menu in the GRAPH window. The output is then sent to the printer through the Windows NT Print Manager.

To send output directly to the printer without preview, specify DEVICE=WINPRTG instead of TARGET=WINPRTG in your GOPTIONS statement.

Note the following when using the WINPRT series of drivers:

- The ROTATE= option in your SAS/GRAPH program must be set to match the orientation of the printer in your Windows NT printer setup. The default orientation for WINPRT drivers is portrait. If you specify ROTATE=LANDSCAPE in a GOPTIONS statement in your SAS/GRAPH program, you should change the page orientation to landscape in your Windows NT printer setup to avoid unpredictable results.

- To use TrueType fonts with the WINPRT series of drivers, specify CHARTYPE=*x* in a GOPTIONS statement, where *x* is the number corresponding to the desired font listed in the following table:

Chartype	Font
1	Arial
2	Courier New
3	Times New Roman
4	Wingdings
5	Symbol

  To use multiple TrueType fonts in a single graph, specify FONT=HWDMX00*x* in the font specifications in your program, where *x* corresponds to the number of the specific font you want to use.

Using SAS/GRAPH stand-alone drivers

SAS/GRAPH stand-alone drivers use internal SAS/GRAPH driver routines instead of the Windows NT printer driver routines to generate hardcopy graphics output. Stand-alone drivers can route output to the device through the Windows NT Print Manager or can send output directly to the printer or serial port, bypassing the Print Manager. Note that TrueType fonts cannot be used with native drivers; to use TrueType fonts, you must use the WINPRT*x* series of drivers.

To use SAS/GRAPH stand-alone drivers, specify the appropriate driver name in the DEVICE= or TARGET= option in a GOPTIONS statement. Stand-alone drivers are available for a wide range of printers, plotters, and film recorders. For a current list of SAS/GRAPH stand-alone drivers, use the GDEVICE procedure. For information on the GDEVICE procedure, see Chapter 25, "The GDEVICE Procedure" in *SAS/GRAPH Software: Reference, Version 6, First Edition, Volume 2.*

If you use the SAS/GRAPH stand-alone device drivers to send graphics output to a hardcopy device through the Windows NT Print Manager (the default for most printer drivers), you must also install an associated Windows NT driver. This driver can be any Windows NT driver as long as the destination (such as LPT1: or COM1:) matches that of the output device.

For more information on installing Microsoft Windows NT printer drivers, refer to the *Microsoft Windows NT User's Guide.*

Use the Windows NT Print Manager to specify the port to which output is to be sent. In the Printer Properties dialog box, select a port.

Suppose you want to preview a graph on your display and then use a SAS/GRAPH native driver to print it on a Hewlett-Packard LaserJet Series III printer attached to LPT1. First, choose **`Printer Setup`** from the SAS AWS **`File`** menu and choose the associated printer driver as your printer selection. Then specify the following in your SAS/GRAPH program:

```
goptions device=win target=hpljs3;

proc gplot;
   additional procedure statements
run;
quit;
```

The graph is displayed on your monitor as it will appear on the printer. To print the graph from the GRAPH window, issue the PRINT command (or select **Print** from the **File** pop-up menu). The output is sent to the printer through the Windows NT Print Manager.

The destination of the output from SAS/GRAPH native drivers is determined by the DEVTYPE and GACCESS parameters in the device catalog entry for the driver. The DEVTYPE parameter dictates whether output is sent through the Windows NT Print Manager (DEVTYPE=PRINTER) or directly to the serial port (DEVTYPE=PLOTTER or DEVTYPE=DISK). The GACCESS parameter can be used with plotter drivers to dictate which port output is sent to. For most SAS/GRAPH printer drivers, the default value of DEVTYPE is PRINTER and the default GACCESS value is SASGASTD:, which causes output to be sent through the Print Manager to the port associated with the current Print Manager driver.

To send output from a SAS/GRAPH native printer driver directly to the printer port (bypassing the Windows NT Print Manager) select **Print Directly to Ports** in the Printer Details dialog box in the Windows NT Print Manager and specify GACCESS=SASGASTD>*port* in a GOPTIONS statement or in the SAS/GRAPH device driver entry.

Choosing between the SAS/GRAPH Stand-Alone and the WINPRT*x* Driver

When deciding whether to use SAS/GRAPH stand-alone drivers or the WINPRT*x* series of drivers, you need to consider such factors as the device you are using and the type of output you want to produce. Note the following specific considerations:

- If no Windows NT printer driver is available for your device, use a SAS/GRAPH stand-alone driver.
- If you have a device for which there is no SAS/GRAPH stand-alone driver, you should use the WINPRT*x* driver, provided there is a Windows NT printer driver available for the device. In cases where a new model of hardcopy device becomes available between releases of the SAS System and the hardware vendor provides a new Windows NT driver that uses new features of the device, you can use a WINPRT*x* driver to take advantage of those features.
- If you want to use options such as HSIZE=, VSIZE=, ROTATE= or COLORS= to customize the size, orientation, or colors used in your graph, using SAS/GRAPH stand-alone drivers usually produces more reliable results. If you do use these options with WINPRT*x* drivers, you should change the corresponding settings in your Windows NT Printer Setup to match (if they are available).
- To use TrueType fonts in your SAS/GRAPH output, use one of the WINPRT*x* drivers.

Exporting Graphics to Other Applications

To export SAS/GRAPH output to other graphics or word processing packages, you can use one of the following methods:

Sending Output to a Graphics Stream File (GSF)

SAS/GRAPH has a complete series of drivers that can produce files in many common formats such as CGM, TIFF, and HPGL. To create a file in one of these formats, specify the appropriate driver name with the TARGET= or DEVICE= option in a GOPTIONS statement. By default, these drivers write output to the file GRAPH.GSF in your current directory. You can redirect output to another file by changing the GACCESS value in the device catalog entry from SASGASTD>GRAPH.GSF to SASGASTD>*filename.ext*, where *filename.ext* is the file to receive output. You can also use a GOPTIONS statement to redirect output, as in the following example:

```
goptions device=hpgl gaccess='sasgastd>c:\mydir\hpgl.gsf';
```

Another way to create a graphics stream file is to use the **GSFNAME** field in the Host File Options window in a device catalog entry or the GSFNAME= option in a GOPTIONS statement. This causes output to be written to a specified fileref that you identify with a FILENAME statement. For example, to create the HPGL.GSF file as above, you can specify a value of **GRAFOUT** (this name is arbitrary) for the **GSFNAME** field in the device catalog entry. You then use a FILENAME statement for GRAFOUT to give the name of the file you want to create:

```
filename grafout 'c:\mydir\hpgl.gsf';
```

Alternatively, you can use a GOPTIONS statement:

```
filename grafout 'c:\mydir\hpgl.gsf';
goptions device=hpgl gsfname=grafout gsfmode=replace;
```

Saving Graphs to the Clipboard

From the GRAPH window, you can mark all or a portion of the graph to be copied to the Windows NT Clipboard by holding down the left mouse button and dragging the mouse to draw a rectangle around the part of the graph you want to copy. Once you have selected the part of the graph you want to save, select **Edit** and **Copy to Paste Buffer** from the GRAPH window pop-up menu. (This method currently is available only from the GRAPH window and the Graphics Editor; it may not work from other graphics windows in the SAS System.) From any SAS window, you can also press ALT-PRT SCREEN to place the entire window, including any menus and scroll bars, onto the Clipboard. Once you have copied the graph to the Windows NT Clipboard, you can save it as a bitmap image. You can then import the image into any other graphics package that can read a bitmap file.

Transferring SAS Files between Operating Systems

Because of the proprietary structure of SAS files, it is usually impossible to transfer SAS files between operating systems without first converting them to transport format (sequential) files or without using SAS/CONNECT software. If you attempt to use file transfer software (other than SAS/CONNECT software) to copy SAS files across operating systems without first converting them to sequential files by using the CPORT procedure, the files become corrupted and therefore, unreadable. See SAS Technical Report P-195, *Transporting SAS Files between Host Systems*, for more information on converting SAS files created with previous releases of the SAS System to Release 6.09 SAS files. You may also want to refer to Chapter 3, "Using SAS Files" on page 69.

Using SAS/CONNECT Software

SAS/CONNECT software is the cooperative processing facility of the SAS System. With SAS/CONNECT software, you can upload and download SAS files, graphics catalogs, and text and binary files between hosts, and you can submit programs from your PC to run on the remote host system, with your output and log messages returning to the SAS System on your PC.

You can use SAS/CONNECT software to transfer any version of SAS data sets from the remote host to your PC. For example, if your PC can communicate with a remote host running Version 5 or later of the SAS System, you can use SAS/CONNECT software to transfer SAS data sets from the remote host to your PC. If you are transferring Version 5 files to a Release 6.09 SAS session, they are automatically converted to their Release 6.09 counterparts.

You can also remotely submit SAS programs from the SAS System under Windows NT to the remote host for execution. For more information on using SAS/CONNECT software to transfer SAS files created with previous releases of the SAS System to Release 6.09 under Windows NT, see *SAS/CONNECT Software: Usage and Reference, Version 6, First Edition* and SAS Technical Report P-224, *SAS/CONNECT Software: Changes and Enhancements for Release 6.08.*

Note: The term *remote host* can refer to more than just a mainframe such as MVS. For example, the remote host could be the SAS System running under the OS/2 operating system on a 486-based machine.

Chapter Summary

This chapter discusses using the SAS System under Windows NT to accomplish common tasks such as printing, sending the SAS procedure output and SAS log to various destinations, and producing graphics. You are now ready to use the SAS System under Windows NT to meet all of your data access, management, analysis, and presentation needs. If you want to use the SAS System in a more advanced way (for example, performing interprocess communication), go on to Chapter 6, "Using Advanced Features of the SAS System under Windows NT" on page 131.

Chapter 6 Using Advanced Features of the SAS® System under Windows NT

Introduction

This chapter illustrates using some of the more advanced features of the SAS System in the Microsoft Windows NT environment, such as performing interprocess communication using Dynamic Data Exchange (DDE), unnamed and named pipes, and Object Linking and Embedding (OLE). It also illustrates using communications ports and DataMyte processing for data acquisition. These features allow you great flexibility in choosing where to get data and send data in your SAS programs. However, they also require a good understanding of the SAS System and the Windows NT operating system and the other applications you are using. Be sure you fully grasp the concepts covered in Chapters 1 through 5 before proceeding with this chapter. You also should have access to documentation for Windows NT and other application software.

Dynamic Data Exchange

Dynamic Data Exchange (DDE) is a method of dynamically exchanging information between Windows NT applications. DDE uses a client/server relationship to enable a client application to request information from a server application. In Release 6.09, the SAS System is always the client. In this role, the SAS System requests data from server applications, sends data to server applications, or sends commands to server applications.

You can use DDE with the DATA step, the SAS macro facility, SAS/AF applications, or any other portion of the SAS System that requests and generates data. DDE has many potential uses, one of which is to acquire data from a Windows NT spreadsheet or database application.

DDE Syntax

To use the DDE feature, issue a FILENAME statement of the following form:

FILENAME *fileref* DDE '*DDE-triplet*'|'CLIPBOARD' <*DDE-options*>;

You can use the following arguments with this form of the FILENAME statement:

fileref
: is a valid fileref as described in "Referencing External Files" on page 96.

DDE
: is the device-type keyword that tells the SAS System you want to use Dynamic Data Exchange.

'*DDE-triplet*'|'CLIPBOARD'
is the name of the DDE external file. If you know the DDE triplet for your application, you can specify it directly in the following form:

'*application-name*|*topic*!*item*'

Here is the explanation of these arguments:

application-name	is the name of the server application.
topic	is the topic of conversation.
item	is the range of conversation specified between the client and server applications.

The values for *application-name, topic*, and *item* are defined by the server application. A software package supporting DDE should list acceptable values for the triplet information in documentation supplied with the application. This argument is discussed in more detail in "Referencing the DDE External File" on page 133.

If you do not know the DDE triplet for your application, use CLIPBOARD as the filename. This is a reserved filename that tells the SAS System to determine the DDE triplet using the Windows NT Clipboard. More information on using the CLIPBOARD filename is presented in "Determining the DDE Triplet" on page 134.

DDE-options
can be any of the following:

HOTLINK	instructs the SAS System to use the DDE HOTLINK. For an example of using this option, see "Using the DDE HOTLINK" on page 137.
NOTAB	instructs the SAS System to ignore tab characters between variables. For an example of using this option, see "Using the NOTAB Option with DDE" on page 137.
COMMAND	allows remote commands to be issued to DDE server applications. For an example of using this option, see "Using DDE and the COMMAND Option to Execute Commands in an Application" on page 137.

Use caution when using DDE with data values that are blank or missing.
For sample code, see "Reading Missing Data" on page 139. ■

Referencing the DDE External File

When you define a fileref to use with DDE, the *DDE-triplet* argument refers to the DDE external file. In referencing the external file, *application-name* is the name of the Windows NT application managing the data (for example, Excel). The *topic* argument either can be the name of a spreadsheet or document, or it can be a special category called SYSTEM.

If you are using the Excel application and want to establish a DDE session with a specific spreadsheet, specify the name of the document as the topic name. You must then specify *item*, which is the range of information you want to include. For example, if you want to use DDE to link rows 1 through 3 and columns 1 through 5 in an Excel spreadsheet, specify the item name as R1C1:R3C5.

Alternatively, if you want to send commands to be executed by the server application, use the special topic name SYSTEM. When SYSTEM is specified, the item name is left blank. Commands to be executed are sent from the SAS session to the server application using the PUT statement. You can also use the SYSTEM topic name for input, using the INPUT statement.

For some server applications, such as Da Vinci eMail and the Windows NT Program Manager, you can use the COMMAND option in the FILENAME statement. When COMMAND is specified, the item name is left blank. Commands to be executed are sent from the SAS session to the server application using the PUT statement.

Determining the DDE Triplet

The DDE triplet is application-dependent; it is different for every application you run. You can look up the DDE triplet in your application's documentation or use the SAS System to determine the DDE triplet.

If you do not know the DDE triplet for the application you are communicating with, you can use the Windows NT Clipboard to get the name of the triplet. To do this, in the server application, mark the range of data you want to share with DDE and choose **Copy** from the server application's menu to store the information in the Windows NT Clipboard. Then select the **Options** menu in the SAS AWS menu bar and choose **DDE Triplet**. An information box appears showing you the DDE triplet for the application you copied to the Clipboard. Mark and copy the DDE triplet by pressing CTRL INS and paste the triplet into your FILENAME statement.

Alternatively, instead of using the SAS menus you can use the special filename CLIPBOARD along with a device type of DDE to reference the DDE triplet. The following example shows how to issue a generic FILENAME statement that enables you to read from several different applications:

```
filename mydata dde 'clipboard';

data test;
   infile mydata;
   input col1 $ col2 $ col3 $;
run;

proc print;
run;
```

Note: This method only works with applications that can function as DDE servers.

In the previous example, if you mark and copy three columns of a spreadsheet to the Clipboard and then submit this SAS code, the SAS System determines what the DDE triplet should be and reads the data. At this point, you could mark and copy three columns from another spreadsheet and submit the same SAS code to read in this second set of data.

DDE Examples

This section provides several examples of using the DDE feature of the SAS System under Windows NT. These examples use the Excel application as an illustration. Any application that supports DDE as a server can communicate with the SAS System. Before you run most of these examples, you must first invoke the server application and open the spreadsheet used in the example. The only exception to this requirement is found in the example shown in "Using DDE and the SYSTEM Topic to Execute Commands in an Application" on page 136. In this later example, you should not invoke Excel first because the example program invokes Excel for you.

If you did not start Excel before you began your SAS session, you can turn off the XWAIT and XSYNC options and use the X statement to start Excel, as in the following example:

```
options noxwait noxsync;
x excel;
```

Note: DDE examples are included in the sample library labeled DDE*n*.SAS, where *n* is the number of the example. Check with your SAS Software Representative for the location of the sample library.

Using DDE to Write Data

Suppose you want to send data from a SAS session to an Excel spreadsheet. You want to use rows 1 through 100 and columns 1 through 3. To do this, submit the following program:

```
   /* The DDE link is established using Microsoft Excel        */
   /* SHEET1, rows 1 through 100 and columns 1 through 3.       */
filename random dde 'excel|sheet1!r1c1:r100c3';

data random;
   file random;
   do i=1 to 100;
      x=ranuni(i);
      y=10+x;
      z=x-10;
      put x y z;
   end;
run;
```

Using DDE to Read Data

You can also use DDE to read data from an Excel application into the SAS System, as in the following example:

```
   /* The DDE link is established using Microsoft Excel        */
   /* SHEET1, rows 1 through 10 and columns 1 through 3.        */
filename monthly dde 'excel|sheet1!r1c1:r10c3';

data monthly;
   infile monthly;
   input var1 var2 var3;
```

```
run;

proc print;
run;
```

Using DDE and the SYSTEM Topic to Execute Commands in an Application

You can issue commands to Excel or other DDE-compatible programs directly from the SAS System using DDE. In the following example, the Excel application is invoked; a spreadsheet called SHEET1 is loaded; data are sent from the SAS System to Excel for row 1, column 1 to row 20, column 3; and the commands required to select a data range and sort the data are issued. The spreadsheet is then saved and the Excel application is terminated.

```
   /* This code assumes that Excel is installed on the current */
   /* drive in a directory called EXCEL.                       */
options noxwait noxsync;
x 'excel';

   /* Sleep for 60 seconds to give Excel time to come up.      */
data _null_;
   x=sleep(60);
run;

   /* The DDE link is established with Microsoft Excel SHEET1, */
   /* rows 1 through 20 and columns 1 through 3.               */
filename data dde 'excel|sheet1!r1c1:r20c3';

data one;
   file data;
   do i=1 to 20;
      x=ranuni(i);
      y=x+10;
      z=x/2;
      put x y z;
   end;
run;

   /* Microsoft defines the DDE topic SYSTEM to enable          */
   /* commands to be executed within Excel.                     */
filename cmds dde 'excel|system';

data _null_;
   file cmds;
   put '[SELECT("R1C1:R20C3")]';
   put '[SORT(1,"R1C1",1)]';
   put '[SAVE()]';
   put '[QUIT()]';
run;
```

Using DDE and the COMMAND Option to Execute Commands in an Application

For applications that do not use SYSTEM as a topic name, you can use the COMMAND option in the FILENAME statement to execute remote commands.

Using the NOTAB Option with DDE

The SAS System expects to see a TAB character placed between each variable that is communicated across the DDE link; similarly, the SAS System places a TAB character between variables when data are transmitted across the link. When the NOTAB option is placed in a FILENAME statement that uses the DDE device-type keyword, the SAS System accepts character delimiters other than tabs between variables.

The NOTAB option also can be used to store full character strings, including embedded blanks, in a single spreadsheet cell. For example, if a link is established between the SAS System and the Excel application, and a SAS variable contains a character string with embedded blanks, each word of the character string is normally stored in a single cell. To store the entire string including embedded blanks in a single cell, use the NOTAB option as in the following example:

```
   /* Without the NOTAB option, column1 contains 'test' and    */
   /* column2 contains 'one'.                                   */
filename test dde 'excel|sheet1!r1c1:r1c2';

data string;
   file test;
   a='test one';
   b='test two';
   put a $15. b $15.;
run;

   /* You can use the NOTAB option to store each variable       */
   /* in a separate cell. To do this, you must force a tab      */
   /* ('09'x) between each variable, as in the PUT statement.   */
   /* After this DATA step executes, column1 contains           */
   /* 'test one' and column2 contains 'test two'.               */
filename test dde 'excel|sheet1!r2c1:r2c2' notab;

data string;
   file test;
   a='test one';
   b='test two';
   put a $15. '09'x b $15.;
run;
```

Using the DDE HOTLINK

Unless the HOTLINK option is specified, DDE is performed as a single data transfer. That is, the values currently stored in the spreadsheet cells are those that are transferred. If the HOTLINK option is specified, the DDE link is activated every time the data in the specified spreadsheet range are updated. In addition, DDE enables you to poll the data when the HOTLINK option is specified to determine whether data within the range specified have been changed. If no data have changed, the HOTLINK option returns a record of 0 bytes. In the following example, row 1, column 1 of the spreadsheet SHEET1 contains the daily production total. Every time the value in this cell changes, the SAS System reads in the new value and outputs the observation to a data set. In this example, a second cell in row 5, column 1 is defined as a status field. Once the user completes data entry, typing any character in this field terminates the DDE link:

```
   /* Enter data into Excel SHEET1 in row 1 column 1. When you  */
   /* are through entering data, place any character in row 5   */
   /* column 1, and the DDE link is terminated.                 */
filename daily dde 'excel|sheet1!r1c1' hotlink;
filename status dde 'excel|sheet1!r5c1' hotlink;

data daily;
   infile status length=flag;
   input @;
   if flag ne 0 then stop;
   infile daily length=b;
   input @;

      /* If data have changed, then the incoming record length  */
      /* is not equal to 0.                                     */
   if b ne 0 then
      do;
         input total $;
         put total=;
         output;
      end;
run;
```

It is possible to establish multiple DDE sessions. The previous example uses two separate DDE links. When the HOTLINK option is used and there are multiple cells referenced in the *item* specification, if any one of the cells changes, then all cells are transmitted.

Using the !DDE_FLUSH String to Transfer Data Dynamically

DDE also enables you to program when the DDE buffer is dumped during a DDE link. Normally, the data in the DDE buffer are transmitted when the DDE link is closed at the end of the DATA step. However, the special string `'!DDE_FLUSH'` issued in a PUT statement instructs the SAS System to dump the contents of the DDE buffer. This function allows you considerable flexibility in the way DDE is used, including the capacity to transfer data dynamically through the DATA step, as in the following example:

```
   /* A DATA step window is displayed. Enter data as prompted. */
   /* When you are finished, enter STOP on the command line.   */

filename entry dde 'excel|sheet1!r1c1:r1c3';
dm 'pmenu off';

data entry;
   if _n_=1 then
      do;
```

```
         window ENTRY color=black
         #3 'This is data for Row 1 Column 1'
            c=cyan +2 var1 $10. c=orange
         #5 'This is data for Row 1 Column 2'
            c=cyan +2 var2 $10. c=orange
         #7 'This is data for Row 1 Column 3'
            c=cyan +2 var3 $10. c=orange;
      end;
   flsh='!DDE_FLUSH';
   file entry;

   do while (upcase(_cmd_) ne 'STOP');
      display entry;
      put var1 var2 var3 flsh;
      output;
      VAR1='';
      VAR2='';
      VAR3='';
   end;
   stop;
run;

dm 'pmenu on';
```

Reading Missing Data

This example illustrates reading missing data from an Excel spreadsheet called SHEET1. This example reads the data in columns 1 through 3 and rows 10 through 20. Some of the data cells may be blank. Here is an example of what some of the data look like:

```
.
.
.
10  John   Raleigh     Cardinals
11  Jose   North Bend  Orioles
12  Kurt   Yelm        Red Sox
13  Brent              Dodgers
.
.
.
```

Here's the code that can read these data correctly into a SAS data set:

```
filename mydata dde 'excel|sheet1!r10c1:r20c3';

data in;
   infile mydata dlm='09'x notab dsd missover;
   informat name $10. town $char20. team $char20.;
   input name town team;
run;

proc print data=in;
run;
```

In this example, the NOTAB option tells the SAS System not to convert tabs sent from the Excel application into blanks. Therefore, the tab character can be used as the delimiter between data values. The DLM= option specifies the delimiter character, and `'09'x` is the hexadecimal representation of the tab character. The DSD option specifies that two consecutive delimiters should represent a missing value. The default delimiter is a comma; for more information on the DSD option, see SAS Technical Report P-222, *Changes and Enhancements to Base SAS Software, Release 6.07*. The MISSOVER option prevents a SAS program from going to a new input line if it does not find values in the current line for all the INPUT statement variables. With the MISSOVER option, when an INPUT statement reaches the end of the current record, values that are expected but not found are set to missing.

The INFORMAT statement forces the DATA step to use modified list input, which is crucial to this example. If you do not use modified list input, you receive incorrect results. The necessity of using modified list input is not DDE specific; you would need it even if you were using CARDS data, whether your data were blank- or comma-delimited.

Using Unnamed Pipes

Unnamed pipes (also called anonymous pipes or simply pipes) enable you to run a program outside the SAS System and redirect the program's input, output, and error messages to the SAS System. This capability enables you to capture data from a program external to the SAS System without creating an intermediate data file.

For unnamed pipes to work with Windows NT applications external to the SAS System, the application program must read data from standard input (STDIN), write output to standard output (STDOUT), and write errors to standard error (STDERR). These files have numeric file handles associated with them, as follows:

File	File Handle
STDIN	0
STDOUT	1
STDERR	2

When the SAS System captures STDERR from another application, the error messages are routed by default to the SAS log. If you want to write to STDIN in another application, you can use a PUT statement in a SAS DATA step. Because the SAS System can write to STDIN and capture from STDOUT in the same application, unnamed pipes can be used to send data to an external program, as well as to capture the output and error messages of the same program. You can use redirection sequences to redirect STDIN, STDOUT, and STDERR. See "Using Redirection Sequences" on page 141 for more information. You can also refer to your Windows NT documentation.

Unnamed Pipe Syntax

To use an unnamed pipe, issue a FILENAME statement of the following form:

FILENAME *fileref* PIPE '*program-name*' *option-list*;

You can use the following arguments with this form of the FILENAME statement:

fileref
: is any valid fileref, as described in "Referencing External Files" on page 96.

PIPE
: is the device-type keyword that tells the SAS System you want to use an unnamed pipe.

program-name
: specifies the external Windows NT application program. This argument must fully specify the pathname to the program, or the path to the directory containing the program must be contained in the Windows NT PATH environment variable. This argument can also contain program options. For example, you can specify the following argument to indicate you want to run the STOCKMKT program on all stocks:

```
'stockmkt.exe -all'
```

option-list
: can be any of the options valid in the FILENAME statement, such as the LRECL= or RECFM= options. See page 206 for a complete list of options available for the FILENAME statement under Windows NT.

Using Redirection Sequences

Any Windows NT application that accommodates standard input, output, and error can use the unnamed pipe feature. Many Windows NT system commands work in this way, so these commands are available for your use. Unless you specify otherwise, an unnamed pipe directs STDOUT and STDERR to two different files. To combine the STDOUT and STDERR into the same file, use redirection sequences. Here is an example that redirects STDERR to STDOUT for the Windows NT DIR command:

```
filename listing pipe 'dir *.sas 2>&1';
```

In this example, if any errors occur in executing this command, STDERR (2) is redirected to the same file as STDOUT (1). This is an example of the SAS System's ability to capitalize on operating system capabilities; this feature of redirecting file handles is a function of the Windows NT operating system rather than the SAS System.

Unnamed Pipe Example

In the following example, you use the unnamed pipes feature of the SAS System under Windows NT to produce some financial reports. The example assumes you have a stand-alone C program that updates stock market information from a financial news bureau. You need the SAS System to run a stock market report with the most recently created data from the stock market program. Here is how you create and use the pipe within your SAS session:

```
filename stocks pipe 'stockmkt.exe -all';

data report;
   infile stocks;
   input stock $ open close change;
run;

proc print;
   var stock open close change;
   sum change;
   title 'Stock Market Report';
run;
```

In this example, the PIPE device-type keyword in the FILENAME statement indicates that the fileref STOCKS is an unnamed pipe. The STOCKMKT.EXE reference is the name of the stand-alone program that generates the stock market data. The INFILE statement causes the SAS System to execute the STOCKMKT.EXE program and read the data in the pipe from it. The STOCKMKT.EXE program is executed without your being aware that it is running. Because the fileref STOCKS has already been defined as an unnamed pipe, the standard output from STOCKMKT.EXE is redirected to the SAS System and captured through the INFILE statement. The SAS program reads in the variables and uses the PRINT procedure to generate a printed report. Any error messages generated by STOCKMKT.EXE appear in the SAS log.

Using Named Pipes

The *named pipes* capability is one of the most powerful tools available in the SAS System under Windows NT for communicating with other applications. The named pipes feature enables bidirectional data or message exchange between applications on the same machine or on separate machines across a network. Figure 6.1 illustrates these two basic methods of communication.

Figure 6.1 *Communication Using Named Pipes*

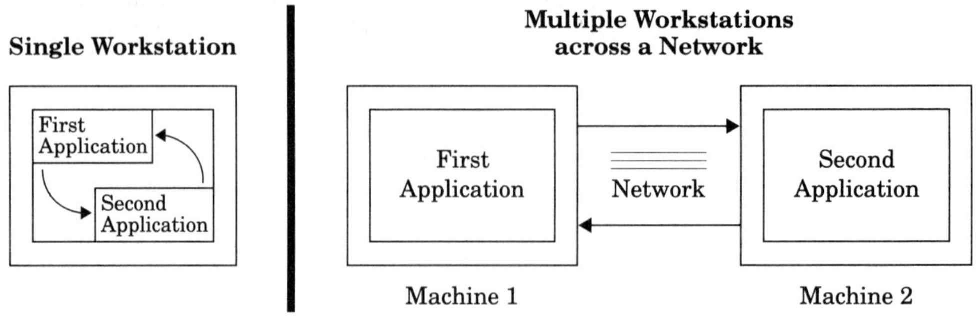

The applications can be SAS sessions or other Windows NT applications. For example, you can use the PRINTTO procedure to direct the results from SAS procedures to another Windows NT application, using a named pipe. Therefore, you have the choice of having multiple SAS sessions that communicate with each other or having one SAS session communicate with another Windows NT application.

Whether you are communicating between multiple SAS sessions or between a SAS session and another Windows NT application that supports named pipes, the pipes are defined in a client/server relationship. One process is defined as the *server*, while one or more other processes are defined as *clients*. In this configuration, you can have multiple clients send data to the server or the server send data to the various clients. Named pipes enable you to coordinate processing between the server and clients by using various options.

Named Pipe Syntax

You can use a named pipe anywhere you use a fileref in the SAS System. To use a named pipe, issue a FILENAME statement of the following form:

FILENAME *fileref* NAMEPIPE '*pipe-specification*' *<named-pipe-options>*;

You can use the following arguments with this form of the FILENAME statement:

fileref
: is any valid fileref as described in "Referencing External Files" on page 96.

NAMEPIPE
: is the device-type keyword that tells the SAS System you want to use a named pipe.

pipe-specification
: is the name of the pipe.

This argument has two mutually exclusive forms:

\\.\PIPE*pipe-name*
: indicates you are establishing a pipe on a single PC or defining a server pipe across a network. The *pipe-name* argument specifies the name of the pipe.

server-name\PIPE*pipe-name*
: indicates you are establishing a client pipe over a network named pipe server. Remember to include the double backslash (\\) in this situation. The *pipe-name* argument specifies the name of the client pipe. The *server-name* argument specifies the name of the named pipe server.

named-pipe-options
: can be any of the following. The default value is listed first:

SERVER|CLIENT
: indicates the mode of the pipe. SERVER is the default.

BLOCK|NOBLOCK
: indicates whether the client or server is to wait on reads if no data are currently available. BLOCK indicates to wait and is the default. NOBLOCK indicates not to wait; control is returned immediately to the program if no data are available in the pipe. Writing to the pipe always implies BLOCK.

(named-pipe-options continued)

BYTE|MESSAGE
: indicates the type of pipe. BYTE is the default. The difference between a BYTE pipe and a MESSAGE pipe is that a MESSAGE pipe includes an encoded record length, whereas a BYTE pipe does not.

RETRY=*seconds*
: indicates the amount of time the client or server should wait to establish the pipe. The minimum value for *seconds* is 10. This option allows time for synchronization of the client and server. The default waiting period is 10 seconds.

  There are two values for the *seconds* argument that indicate special cases:

  −2 indicates the client should wait the amount of time defined by the server's RETRY= option. If this option is used, the SERVER must always be active or the pipe connection fails.

  −1 indicates the client or server should wait indefinitely for the pipe connection.

EOFCONNECT
: is valid only when defining the server and indicates that if an end-of-file (EOF) is received from a client, the server should try to connect to the next client.

All of these options are consistent with terminology used in Windows NT programmers' reference guides such as the *Microsoft Win32 Preliminary SDK for Windows NT: Programmer's Reference: Overviews.*

Using the CALL RECONNECT Routine

There is a special SAS CALL routine that works with named pipes. The CALL RECONNECT routine enables the server to disconnect the current client and try to connect to the next available client. Normally, the pipe is terminated when the client side of the pipe sends an end-of-file to the server. To break the pipe connection at any time, the server SAS session can issue a CALL RECONNECT statement. "The CALL RECONNECT Routine" on page 150 illustrates using this routine. You can also refer to "System-Dependent CALL Routines" on page 255 for more information.

Named Pipe Examples

The best way to understand named pipes is to examine several different examples illustrating their use. In most of the examples in this section, the named pipe is established between two SAS sessions. However, named pipes work between the SAS System and other applications that support named pipes.

Simple Named Pipes: One Client Connected to One Server

The simplest named pipe configuration is one server connected to one client, as shown in Figure 6.2.

Figure 6.2
One Server Connected to One Client

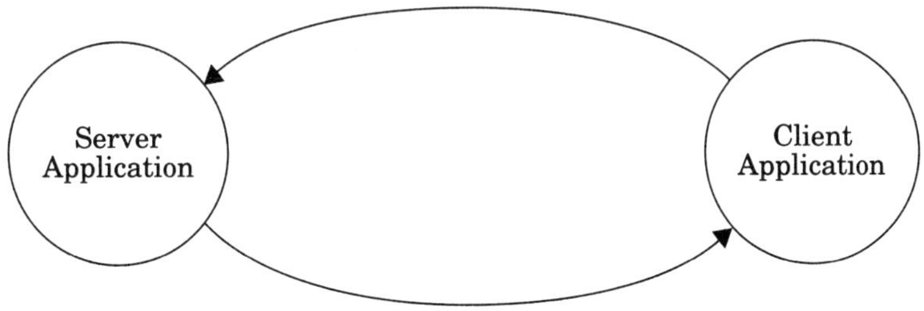

In the following example, a named pipe called WOMEN is established between two SAS sessions. The server SAS session selectively sends data to the client SAS session. You can start the server or the client first; one waits 30 seconds for the other to connect.

In the first SAS session, create a named pipe as a server:

```
   /* Creates a pipe called WOMEN, acting as a server. The server */
   /* waits 30 seconds for a client to connect.                  */
filename women namepipe '\\.\pipe\women' server retry=30;

   /* This code writes three records into the named pipe */
   /* called WOMEN.                                      */
data class;
   input name $ sex $ age;
   file women;
   if upcase(sex)='F' then
      put name age;
   cards;
MOORE M 15
JOHNSON F 16
DALY F 14
ROBERTS M 14
PARKER F 13
;
```

In the second SAS session, you can use SAS statements to exchange data between the two SAS sessions. For example, you can submit the following program from the client session:

```
   /* Creates a pipe called WOMEN, acting as a client.  The client */
   /* waits 30 seconds for a server to connect.                   */
filename in namepipe '\\.\pipe\women' client retry=30;

data female;
   infile in;
   input name $ age;
```

```
proc print;
run;
```

The following program is another example of a single client and server. This example illustrates using the PRINTTO procedure to direct results from the SUMMARY procedure to another Windows NT application, using a named pipe called RESULTS:

```
filename results namepipe '\\.\pipe\results' server retry=60;

proc printto print=results new;
run;

proc summary data=monthly;
run;
```

One Server Connected to Several Clients

You can choose to have one server connected to several clients. In this case, the named pipe configuration looks like that shown in Figure 6.3.

Figure 6.3
One Server Connected to Several Clients

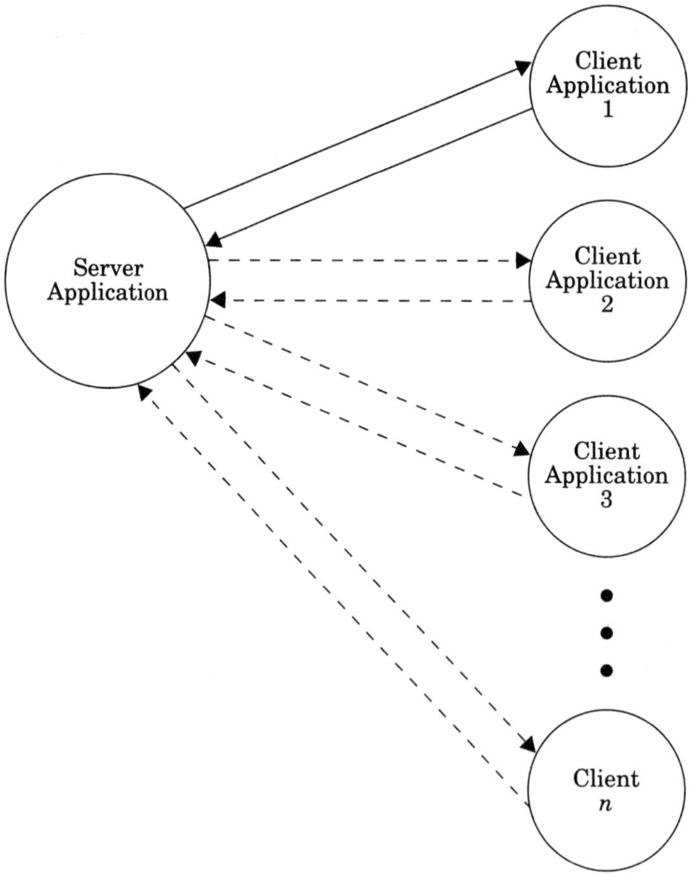

In this configuration, the data connection is initially between the server and the first client. When this connection is terminated, the server connects to the second client, and so on. The connection can return to the first client after the last client's connection is broken if your program is set up to do so.

You must use the EOFCONNECT option to cause the connection to move properly from one client to the next. Here is an example of using the EOFCONNECT option with one server SAS session and two clients. The clients can be on the same PC or on a PC connected across a network.

In the first SAS session, submit the following statements:

```
   /* Creates a pipe called SALES, acting as a server. The   */
   /* server waits 30 seconds for a client to connect.       */
   /* After the client has disconnected, this server SAS     */
   /* session tries to connect to the next available client. */
filename daily namepipe '\\.\pipe\sales' server eofconnect retry=30;

   /* This program reads in the daily sales figures sent from */
   /* each client.                                            */
data totsales;
   infile daily;
   input dept $ item $ total;
run;
```

In the second SAS session, submit the following statements:

```
   /* Creates a pipe called SALES, acting as a client.    */
   /* The client waits forever for a server to connect.   */
   /* After the first client has disconnected, the second */
   /* client connects with the server.                    */

   /* The first client is the TOYS department. */
filename dept1 namepipe '\\.\pipe\sales' client retry=-1;

data toys;
   input item $ total;
   dept='TOYS';
   file dept1;
   put dept item total;
   cards;
DOLLS 100
MARBLES 10
BLOCKS 50
GAMES 60
CARS 40
;

   /* The second client is the SPORTS department. These data */
   /* could come from a separate SAS session.                */
filename dept2 namepipe '\\.\pipe\sales' client retry=-1;

data sports;
   input item $ total;
   dept='SPORTS';
   file dept2;
   put dept item total;
```

```
   cards;
BALLS 30
BATS 65
GLOVES 15
RACKETS 75
FISHING 20
TENTS 115
HELMETS 45
;
```

The NOBLOCK Option

In the following example, the NOBLOCK option is used to specify that if no data are available when the pipe is read, then the program should continue to execute. If the default value of BLOCK had been used, then the pipe would wait indefinitely until data were found in the pipe. The EOFCONNECT option is also used to tell the server that when a client sends an end-of-file, the server should try connecting with a new client. The RETRY= option tells the server to look for any new clients for 20 seconds while the client waits indefinitely on a server. The clients can be on the same PC or on a PC connected across a network. A server connects to one client at a time, and the clients queue in a serial order waiting to connect to the server.

In the first SAS session, submit the following statements:

```
   /* Defines a named pipe called LINE. Use the NOBLOCK       */
   /* option to specify that if no data are available when    */
   /* the read is performed, then continue. Use the           */
   /* EOFCONNECT option to tell the server to try to connect  */
   /* with a new client if an end-of-file is encountered. Use */
   /* the RETRY= option to tell the server to look for any    */
   /* new clients for 20 seconds.                             */
filename data namepipe '\\.\pipe\line' server noblock eofconnect retry=20;

   /* This DATA step reads in all data from any clients */
   /* connected to the named pipe called LINE.          */
data all;
   infile data length=len;
   input @;

      /* If the length of the incoming record is 0, then no */
      /* data were found in the pipe; otherwise, read the   */
      /* incoming data.                                     */
   if len ne 0 then
      do;
         input machine $ width weight;
         output;
      end;
run;

proc print;
run;
```

Each of the following DATA steps below can be executed on several different PCs connected across a network:

```
   /* Defines a named pipe called LINE. The RETRY= option is   */
   /* set such that the clients wait forever until a server is */
   /* available (that is, RETRY=-1).                           */
filename data namepipe '\\.\pipe\line' client retry=-1;

   /* This is information from the first machine/client. */
data machine1;
   file data;
   input width weight;
   machine='LINE_1';
   put machine width weight;
   cards;
5.3 18.2
3.2 14.3
4.8 16.9
6.4 20.8
4.3 15.4
6.1 19.5
5.6 18.9
;

   /* This is information from the second machine/client. */
data machine2;
   file data;
   input width weight;
   machine='LINE_2';
   put machine width weight;
   cards;
4.3 17.2
5.2 18.4
6.8 19.9
3.4 14.5
5.3 18.6
4.1 17.1
6.6 19.5
;
```

Specifying the Named Pipe Using the FILEVAR= and DEVICE= Options in the FILE and INFILE Statements

In this example, the named pipe is established dynamically using the FILEVAR= option in the FILE and INFILE statements. The DEVICE= option enables you to define the named pipe from the FILE or INFILE statement. In this example, the server reads from a pipe called CONTROL to get the name of the client pipe (represented by the variable PIPENAME) that is transmitting data.

In the first SAS session, submit the following statements:

```
   /* The pipe named CONTROL indicates which client */
   /* is sending data.                              */                    */
filename control namepipe '\\.\pipe\control' server retry=-1;
```

```
data all;
   infile control;
   input pipename $25.;
   infile data filevar=pipename device=namepipe server
      retry=20 end=end;
   do until(end);
      input x;
      output;
      put pipename= x=;
   end;
run;
```

In the second SAS session, submit the following statements:

```
   /* The pipe named CONTROL indicates which client is sending */
   /* data.                                                    */
filename control namepipe '\\.\pipe\control' client retry=-1;

data line1;
   input fileout $25.;
   file control;
   put fileout $25.;
   file data filevar=fileout device=namepipe client retry=-1;
   if fileout='\\.\PIPE\LINE1' then
      do;
         do i=1 to 10;
            put i;
         end;
      end;
   else
      do;
         do i=11 to 20;
            put i;
         end;
      end;
   cards;
\\.\PIPE\LINE1
\\.\PIPE\LINE2
;
```

The CALL RECONNECT Routine

The following example demonstrates how to set up a named pipe server to establish a connection with two clients. (For this example, you need three active SAS sessions.) In this example, the CALL RECONNECT routine is used to reconnect to the next client on the named pipe if it has been at least 30 seconds since the previous client has sent any data. Each client is a data entry operator, sending data to the server SAS session.

In the server SAS session, submit the following statements:

```
filename data namepipe '\\.\pipe\orders' server noblock eofconnect retry=30;

data all;
   infile data length=len missover;
   input @;

      /* If the length of the incoming record is 0, then no */
      /* data were found in the pipe; otherwise, read the   */
      /* incoming data.                                     */
   if len ne 0 then
      do;
         input operator $ item $ quantity $;
         if item='' or quantity='' then
            delete;
         else
            output;
         put operator= item= quantity=;
      end;

      /* If no data are being transmitted, try reconnecting to */
      /* the next available client.                            */
   else
      do;

            /* Use the named pipe fileref as the argument of */
            /* CALL RECONNECT.                               */
         call reconnect('data');
      end;
   run;
```

In the second SAS session, which is the first data entry operator, submit the following statements:

```
filename data namepipe '\\.\pipe\orders' client retry=-1;

data entry1;
   if _n_=1 then
      do;
         window entry_1 #1 @2 'ENTER STOP WHEN YOU ARE FINISHED'
                        #3 @5 'ITEM NUMBER - ' item $3.
                        #5 @5 'QUANTITY - ' quantity $3.;
      end;

      do while (upcase(_cmd_) ne 'STOP');
         display entry_1;
         file data;
         put 'ENTRY_1' +1 item quantity;
         item='';
         quantity='';
      end;
   stop;
run;
```

In the third SAS session, which is the second data entry operator, submit the following statements:

```
filename data namepipe '\\.\pipe\orders' client retry=-1;

data entry2;
   if _n_=1 then
      do;
         window entry_2 #1 @2 'ENTER STOP WHEN YOU ARE FINISHED'
                        #3 @5 'ITEM NUMBER - ' item $3.
                        #5 @5 'QUANTITY - ' quantity $3.;
      end;
      do while (upcase(_cmd_) ne 'STOP');
         display entry_2;
         file data;
         put 'ENTRY_2' +1 item quantity;
         item='';
         quantity='';
     end;
   stop;
run;
```

Object Linking and Embedding

Object linking and embedding (OLE) is similar to Dynamic Data Exchange (DDE) in that it enables you to connect applications and share data between them. In other words, both OLE and DDE use a client/server model. However, OLE is much more powerful in that it allows the sharing of many types of data (objects), such as graphs, text, drawings, and charts. OLE treats as an object anything that can be transferred using the Clipboard. Also, OLE is more graphically oriented than DDE. With OLE, you accomplish the link between applications by using menu items and the mouse.

OLE is implemented in the SAS System through SAS/AF software, using the FRAME catalog entry type. You can also use OLE in your SAS/EIS applications. This section first describes the basic concepts of OLE. Then it presents an example of using an already-created SAS/AF application that contains OLE objects. Next it shows you how to add OLE objects to a SAS/AF application. The final discussion includes other considerations when using OLE with the SAS System, such as using SCL (Screen Control Language) methods with OLE objects and understanding OLE error messages.

Note: The SAS System implementation of OLE follows the industry standard for OLE as closely as possible. For example, the names of the OLE dialog boxes are standard, as is the information inside the dialog boxes. This similarity enables you to transfer your existing OLE knowledge to the SAS System with relative ease.

See your SAS/AF documentation for detailed information on using SAS/AF software in general. For information on using SAS/AF FRAME entries, see *SAS/AF Software: FRAME Entry Usage and Reference, Version 6, First Edition.* For application-specific information, such as information about Microsoft Windows NT Paintbrush, see your product documentation.

Note: The SAS System can act only as a client in OLE; it cannot be a server.

Object Linking versus Object Embedding

OLE consists of two distinct processes: object linking and object embedding. The type of connection between the client and server applications distinguishes a linked object from an embedded object.

Note: A third type of object, called a *static object*, also exists. A static object is neither linked nor embedded; it is simply a picture.

Object Linking

Object linking means that there exists a dynamic link between the server and client applications. The server information is stored in the linked object, but the data are not. Thus you are able to edit the data from either side of the link. For example, if you link a Microsoft Windows NT Paintbrush picture (the picture is the object in this case) to a SAS/AF application, you can either edit the picture from within the SAS/AF application (by double-clicking on the picture) or by invoking Paintbrush and opening the correct file. In either case, the changes you make are immediately reflected in the other side of the link by default.

Note: You can force the changes to be held until manually updated. See "Updating the Link Information" on page 166 for more information.

The link between the server and client applications exists only as long as the link's pathname is valid. If either the data file or the client application is moved, you must recreate the link. If you move the application to another machine, you must move the data file as well, making sure the pathname stays the same. If the data file is deleted, the link is lost. When you try to access a link that is no longer valid, the Links dialog box appears, which gives you the capability of re-establishing the link by specifying the new location of the file. "Updating the Link Information" on page 166 shows you how to use this dialog box.

Object Embedding

Object embedding differs from object linking in that changes can be made only from the client application. This restriction applies because in object embedding, both the server information and the data are stored in the embedded object. For example, if you embed a Paintbrush picture in a SAS/AF application, you can edit the picture only from within the SAS/AF application (by double-clicking on the picture). With embedded objects, the connection between the server and client applications does not depend on the original file. In fact, the original file can be deleted without harming the embedded object.

Choosing Which Approach to Use

As with choosing between OLE and DDE, choosing between object linking and object embedding depends on your preferences and application needs. If you need to be able to edit and manipulate objects both from the server application and from the SAS System, you should use object linking. If you do not need to edit the data outside of the SAS System, you can use object embedding. A third choice is using static objects, which are simply pictures that do not enable you to edit or manipulate the object at all.

Using a SAS/AF Application Containing OLE Objects

If someone has already created a SAS/AF application that uses OLE, you do not even need SAS/AF software installed on your machine. You can simply run the application.

The example in this section uses a SAS/AF application called MYAPP, stored in the SASUSER SAS data library. To invoke the application, issue the following SAS Display Manager System command:

```
af catalog=sasuser.myapp.main.menu
```

Alternatively, you can invoke the application using the pop-up menus, using the following path:

Globals
Invoke application
SAS/AF

Fill in the dialog box and choose [OK]. However you choose to invoke the MYAPP application, your display looks like the one in Figure 6.4.

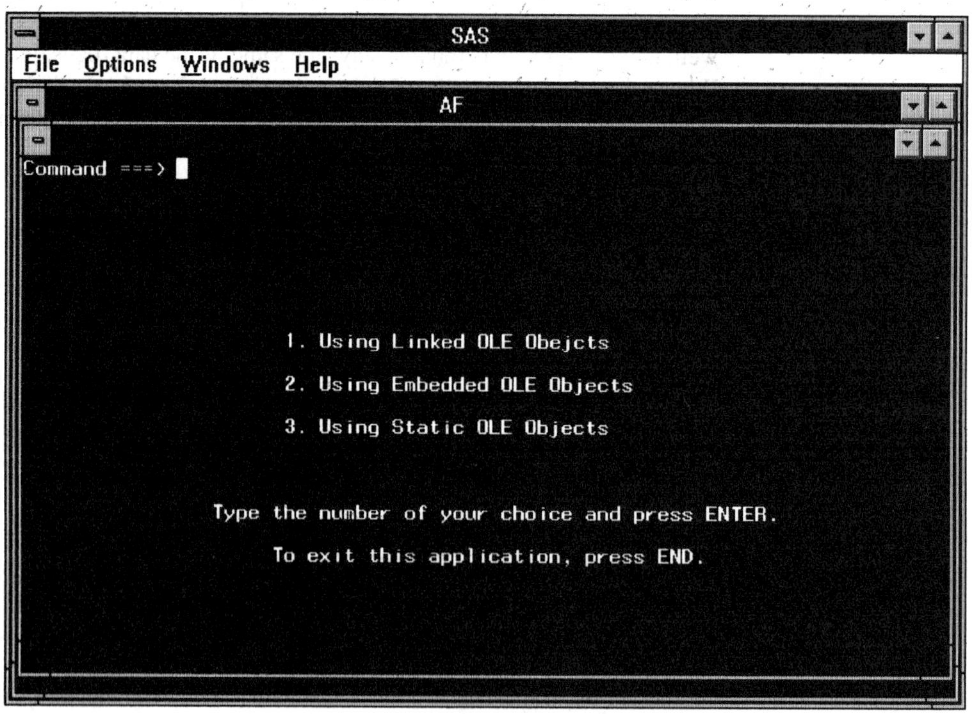

Figure 6.4
Sample SAS/AF Application Using OLE

The menu enables you to view linked, embedded, and static OLE objects. Each menu choice leads to a SAS/AF FRAME entry containing one or more OLE objects.

Using a Linked Object

Choosing **`Using Linked OLE Objects`** displays a SAS/AF FRAME entry that contains a Paintbrush picture, as shown in Figure 6.5.

Figure 6.5
SAS/AF FRAME Entry for Linked Objects

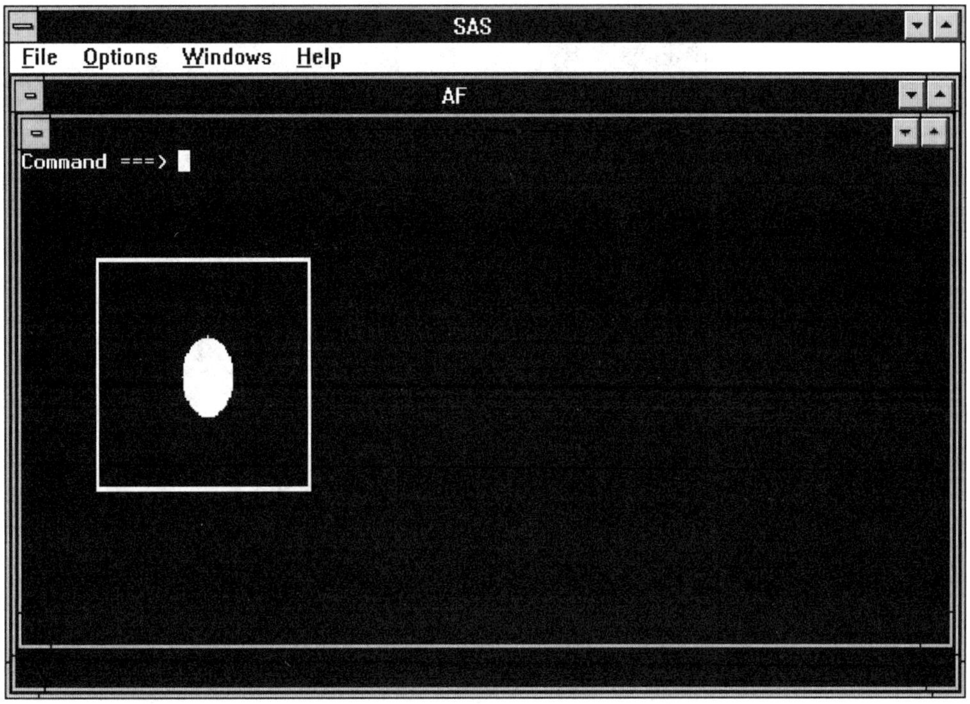

You can double-click on the linked Paintbrush object to invoke the Paintbrush program and display the picture for editing. Make some changes to the picture; by toggling between your AF window and the Paintbrush program, you can see the changes immediately displayed in the AF window. Note that the Paintbrush title bar displays the actual filename of the picture you are editing: **`Paintbrush - LINKED.BMP`**.

You could effect the same changes by invoking Paintbrush independently of the SAS System and editing the LINKED.BMP file. The next time you invoked the MYAPP application, the Paintbrush picture would reflect the changes you made. To try this, end your SAS session and invoke the Paintbrush application. Open the file named LINKED.BMP, and make any change you want. Close the file, and invoke the SAS System; then invoke the MYAPP application. Go to the **`Using Linked OLE Objects`** FRAME entry, and you will see the changes you made earlier.

Using an Embedded Object

Return to the main MYAPP application menu, and select **`Using Embedded OLE Objects`**. Your display should look like the one shown in Figure 6.6:

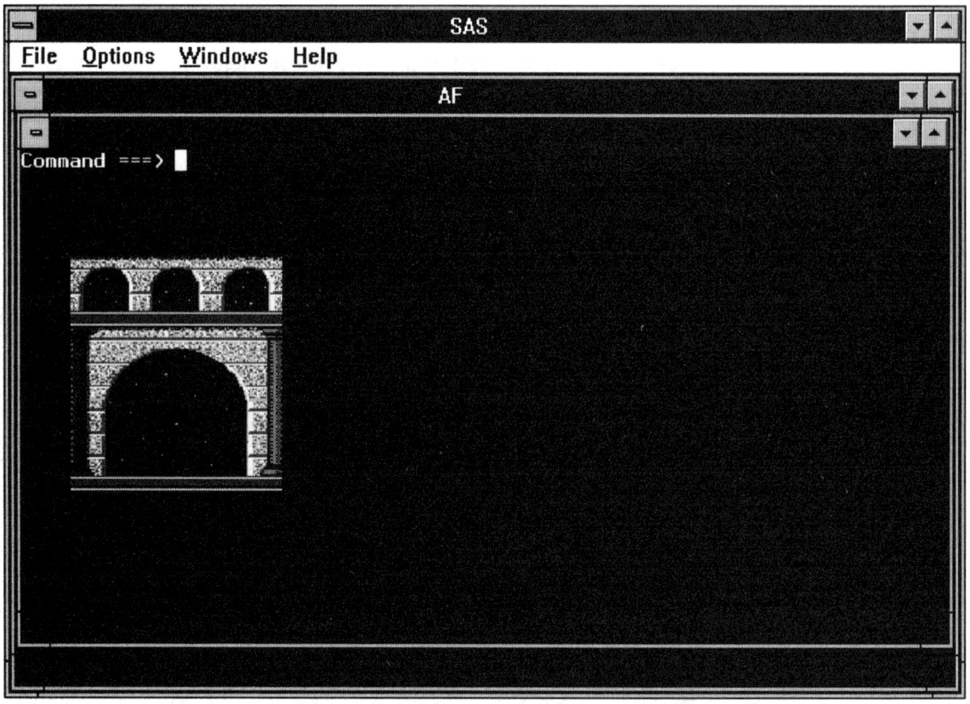

Figure 6.6
SAS/AF FRAME Entry for Embedded Objects

As discussed earlier, the difference between a linked object and an embedded object is where the data are stored. With an embedded object, the data are stored with the object. So when you double-click on the embedded Paintbrush picture, the Paintbrush program is invoked, but it is not the original file that is being edited. The Paintbrush title bar displays `Paintbrush - Paintbrush Picture in SAS Object`. Any changes you make to the picture displayed by Paintbrush are reflected in the SAS object. However, you cannot effect change in the SAS application by editing a file outside the SAS System, as you could with the linked Paintbrush picture.

Using a Static Object

Return to the main MYAPP application menu, and select `Using Static OLE Objects`. Your display should look like the one shown in Figure 6.7:

Figure 6.7
SAS/AF FRAME Entry for Static Objects

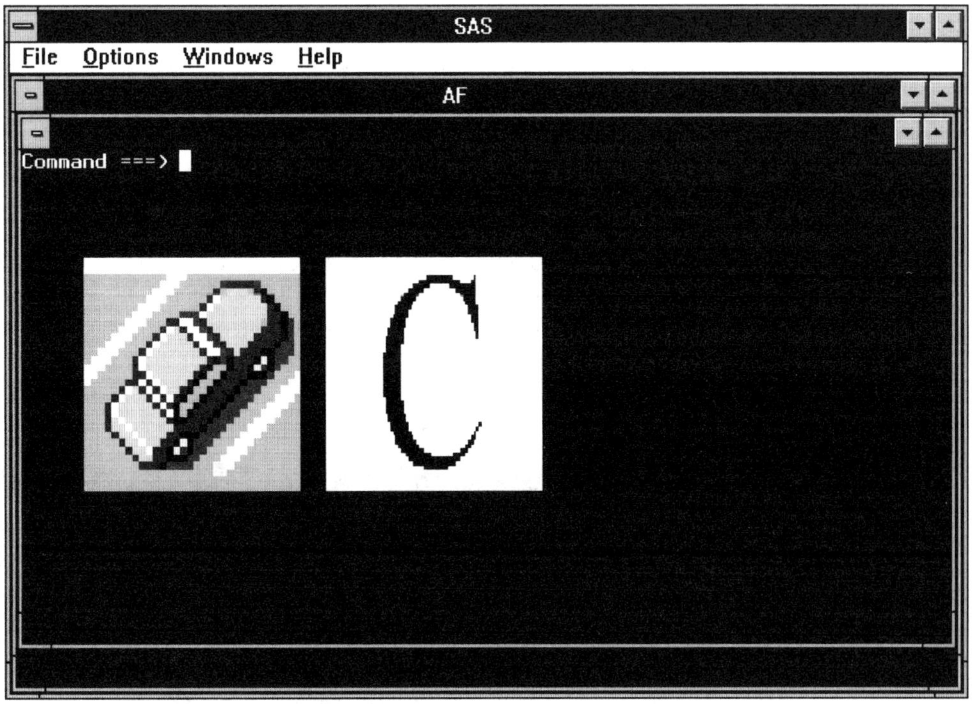

No actions are associated with a static object. For example, you cannot edit a static object. (Or, if the object is a sound file, you cannot play it.) It is just a picture. However, static objects can be used through SCL mechanisms, such as running labels. Static objects can be used for decorative or informational purposes. The only function of the objects in Figure 6.7 is informational, to show a piece of an online alphabet picture book (C for Car).

Adding an OLE Object to a SAS/AF Application

To add OLE objects to a SAS/AF or SAS/EIS application, you must have SAS/AF software licensed. There are three approaches to adding an OLE object to a FRAME entry: paste, insert, and read. The differences between these approaches are explained in the following list:

paste
: assumes you have something on the Clipboard. Using paste, you can create linked, embedded, or static objects.

insert
: lets you specify the type of server application you want to use to create an object (that is, you do not need to use the Clipboard). Using insert, you can create only embedded objects.

read
: indicates you want to add an existing object to a different FRAME entry; you do not need to use the Clipboard. A read object can be linked, embedded, or static, depending on the original object's type.

You must save your source file before copying it to the Clipboard.
If your source is temporary, you can create only embedded objects. ■

Pasting an Object

This section shows you how to add a linked sound object to the `Using Linked OLE Objects` FRAME entry, using the paste approach. Details on inserting and reading objects are presented later in this chapter.

First, put a sound object on the Clipboard by invoking the Sound Recorder that comes with Windows NT, opening a sound file, and copying it to the Clipboard. The sound recorder requires an installed sound driver such as a PC speaker driver.

Now invoke the SAS System, invoke the BUILD procedure on the MYAPP application, and choose to edit the LINKED.FRAME entry. Click your right mouse button (that is, issue the WPOPUP command) with your mouse cursor somewhere in the empty portion of the master region. Choose `Make` from the pop-up menu. Your display should look something like Figure 6.8:

Figure 6.8
Making a Region

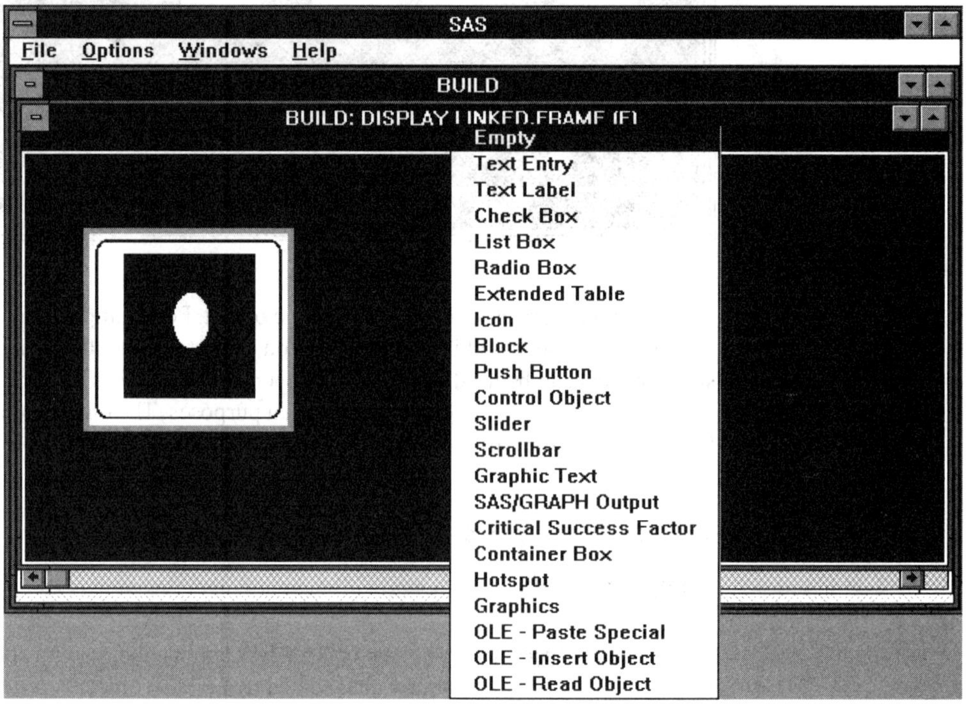

Note: Some OLE applications locate the paste and insert actions under the `Edit` item. In SAS/AF software, they are under the items `Fill` and `Make`.

Choose `OLE - Paste Special` and click the left mouse button to anchor the new object. The Paste Special dialog box opens, as shown in Figure 6.9:

Figure 6.9
Paste Special Dialog Box

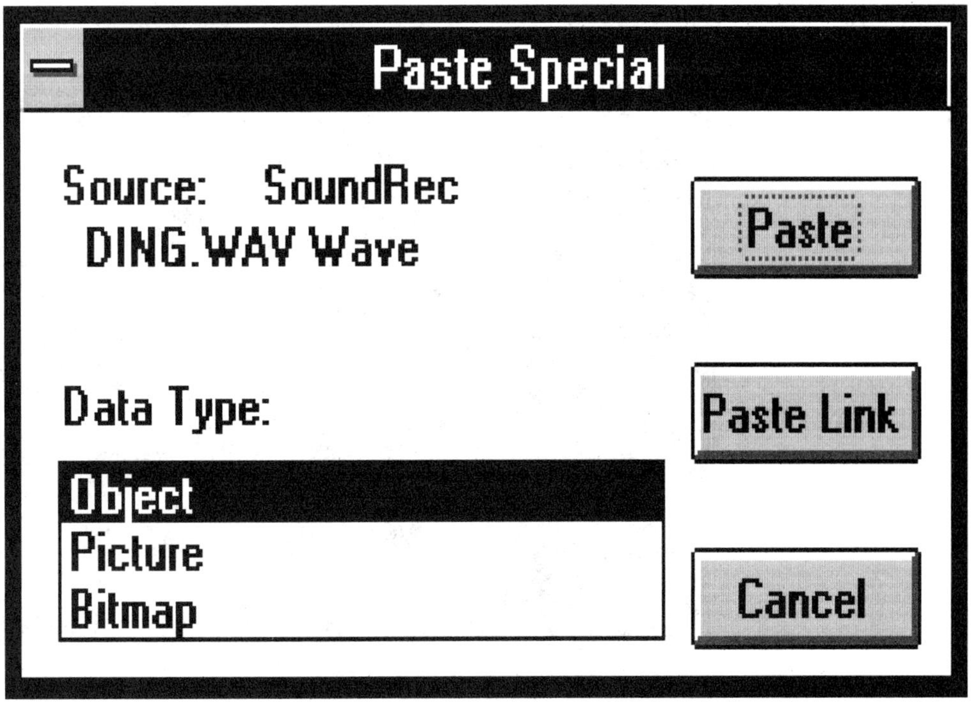

The `Source` field indicates the source of the pasted object (in this case, `SoundRec` for the Sound Recorder), as well as the filename (DING.WAV or another sound file). The `Data Type` listbox shows the available data types for the object you are pasting. To create a linked object, choose `Object` and then choose [Paste Link]. Table 6.1 shows the kind of object created by the various combinations of data type and [Paste] or [Paste Link].

Table 6.1
Data Types and Object Types

Data Type	Paste or Paste Link	Object Type
Object	Paste	Embedded
Object	Paste Link	Linked
Picture	Paste	Static
Picture	Paste Link	Linked
Bitmap	Paste	Static
Bitmap	Paste Link	Linked
DIB Bitmap	Paste	Static
DIB Bitmap	Paste Link	Linked

Once you choose [Paste Link], the OLE - Paste Special Attributes window appears as shown in Figure 6.10:

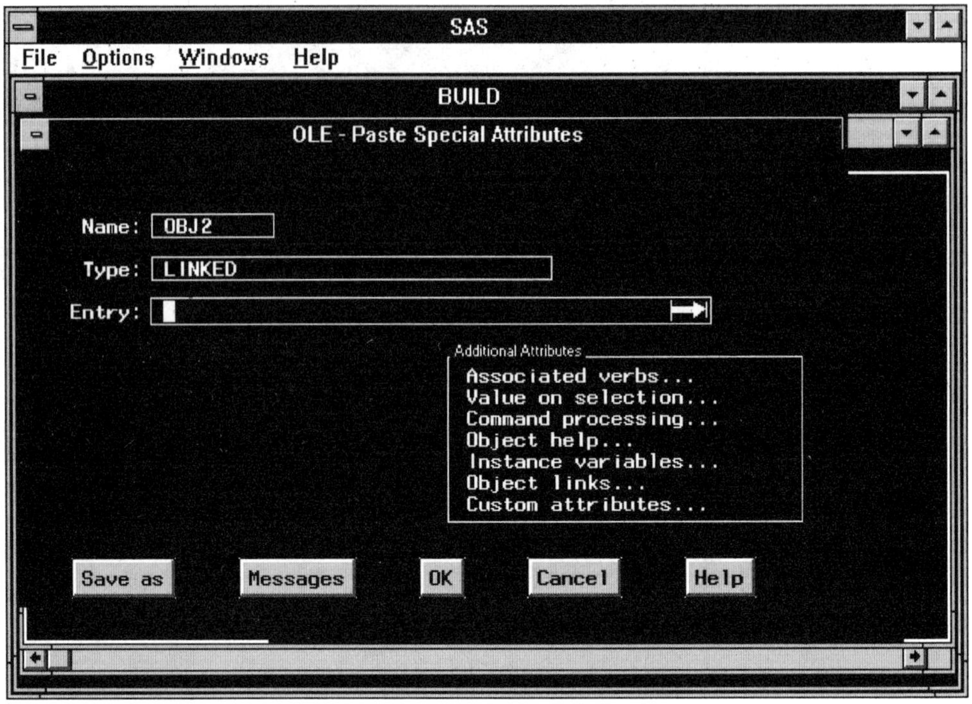

Figure 6.10 *Using the OLE - Paste Special Attributes Window*

Here is a description of the various fields in this window:

`Name` is the name of the object you are creating, in this case OBJ1. This is the name used in SCL code to manipulate the object.

If you do not assign a name, the default name is OBJ*n*, where *n* is the *n*th object (of any class) created in the FRAME entry. Each object, regardless of class, must have a unique name.

You can change the name of any OLE object by opening the Object Attributes window. Change the name and press ENTER. If an object by the same name exists, you receive a warning message to this effect on the message line.

`Type` is the type of object you are creating. In this case **`LINKED`** indicates the object is a linked object. If you had created an embedded object, the **`Type`** field would display **`EMBEDDED`**. For static objects, the **`Type`** field displays either **`PICTURE`** or **`BITMAP`**, depending on the data type you choose. You cannot edit this field.

`Entry` is the four-level name of the catalog entry that contains the OLE object. This is a required field, and you must specify the entry name level. However, the following default values are used if you do not specify the other three levels:

libref	defaults to the current catalog's libref (in this case, SASUSER).
catalog	defaults to the current catalog (in this case, MYAPP).
entry name	has no default value.
entry type	defaults to HSERVICE. You should not use any type except HSERVICE when saving OLE objects. The HSERVICE catalog entry type is not portable; you cannot use the CPORT or CIMPORT procedures with this entry type.

You can use the default values and simply type a one-level name in the **`Entry`** field. For example, if you specified a one-level name of MYOBJ, the following four-level name would be the default in this case:

```
sasuser.myapp.myobj.hservice
```

Click on the arrow to the right of the **`Entry`** field to display listboxes that enable you to choose available librefs, catalogs, and entry names.

If the SAS System detects another catalog entry by the same name that you specify, a dialog box appears, asking if you want to overwrite the object. If you want to overwrite the object, choose [OK]; otherwise, choose [Cancel].

Do not rename an OLE object in the catalog directory window.
Only use the OLE - Paste Special Attributes or OLE - Insert Object Attributes window to rename an object. If you use the catalog directory window, the next time you access the FRAME entry that uses the object, you receive an error message and the region will be empty. If you accidentally rename an object and then access the FRAME entry and receive an error message, you can cancel out of the FRAME entry and change the name back to the correct name. But if you END (which implies a SAVE) out of the FRAME entry, the object connection is lost and you must repaste or reinsert the object. ■

The information available from **`Additional Attributes`** is in general identical to the attribute information described in the documentation for the SAS/AF software's FRAME entry. The only additional attribute specific to OLE is the **`Associated verbs`** item. When you are creating an object, this item is inactive. If you open the Object Attributes window to see the object attributes of an existing object, the **`Associated verbs`** item is active. If you click on `Associated verbs`, it shows the OLE verbs you can use with the SCL _EXECUTE_ method to manipulate that object. The default verb is listed first. See "Using SCL Methods with OLE Objects" on page 165 for information on using SCL methods with OLE objects.

[Save as] enables you to save this object as a class. This action works as documented in *SAS/AF Software: FRAME Entry Usage and Reference.*

Once you have filled in the fields in the OLE - Paste Special Attributes window, choose [OK]. The object is created and fills the region you selected. Figure 6.11 shows the SAS/AF FRAME entry with the new object added:

Figure 6.11
New OLE Object

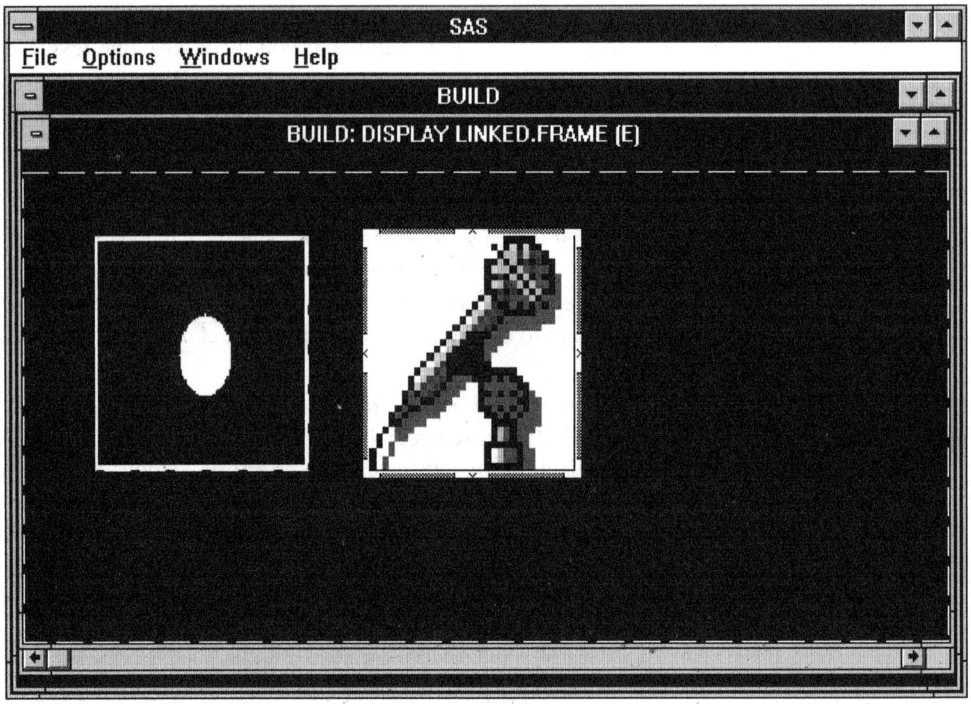

Be sure to use unique names in the Entry field of the various OLE attribute windows. If you are creating multiple FRAME entries and do not specify unique names explicitly, it is possible to overwrite existing object catalog entries. ■

Note: The HSERVICE entry associated with the region is written to your catalog whenever you save your action. A save is generated by several commands, including SAVE, END, and TESTAF, or when you change (edit) the object from the server application. If you create a new OLE object, the HSERVICE entry does not appear in the catalog listing unless you have saved your action.

Inserting an Object

The previous example illustrated pasting an OLE object into a SAS/AF FRAME entry. If you choose `OLE - Insert Object` from the `Make` menu, a different dialog box opens, called the Insert Object dialog box. This dialog box lists the OLE applications registered to Windows NT (an application is registered when you install it). Figure 6.12 shows an example of the Insert Object dialog box:

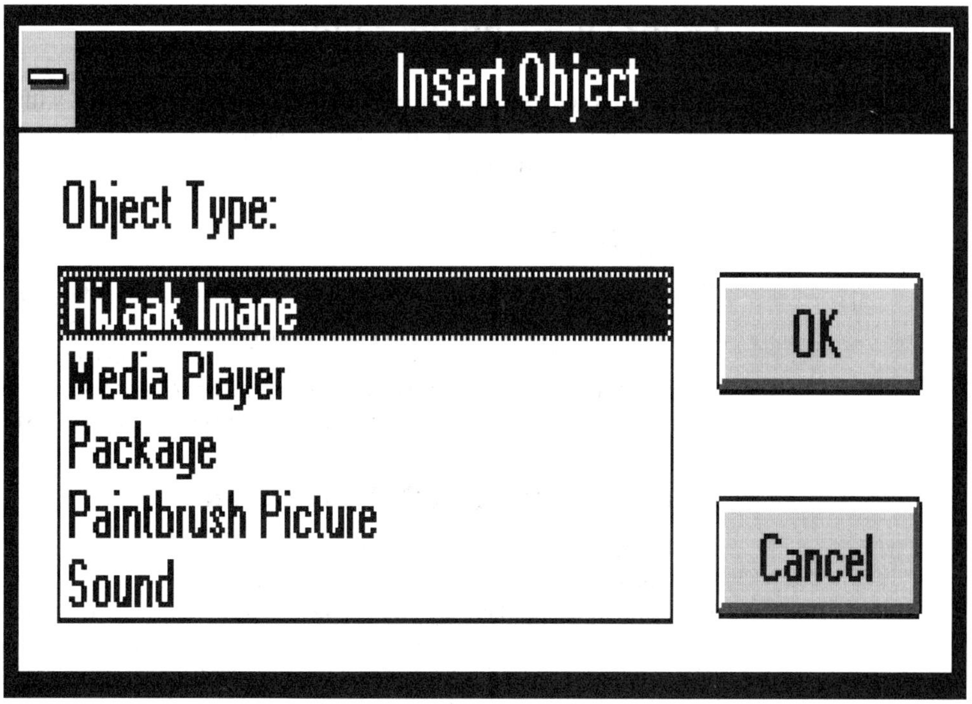

Figure 6.12
Insert Object Dialog Box

To insert the object, select the source application (such as `Paintbrush Picture`) and choose OK. This opens the OLE - Insert Object Attributes window, which works very similarly to the OLE - Paste Special Attributes window. Remember, however, that when inserting you can only create embedded objects. The **Type** field indicates **INSERT OBJECT** to remind you that this is not a pasted link. After you save the object, the **Type** field changes to **EMBEDDED**.

After you have filled in the fields in the OLE - Insert Object Attributes window, choose OK. The application you chose as the source is invoked. Each server application has different methods of inserting the object. For example, Paintbrush uses the `Update` item from the `File` menu. The Sound Recorder uses `Insert File`. Refer to your application's documentation on how to use its OLE features.

Reading an Object

If one of your SAS catalogs contains an HSERVICE entry that you want to use in another FRAME entry (either in that catalog or in another catalog), choose `OLE - Read Object` from the `Make` menu. This opens the OLE - Read Object Attributes window. (No intermediate dialog box is necessary.) This window is similar to the OLE - Paste Special Attributes window in that it enables you to specify the **Name** and **Entry** fields. These fields default in the same manner as in pasting. The **Name** field defaults to OBJ*n*, and you are required to enter at least the entry name of the object. The libref defaults to the libref of the current catalog, the catalog defaults to the current catalog, and the entry type defaults to HSERVICE. The **Type** field reflects the type (embedded, linked, picture, or bitmap) of the original object. When you have entered the information, choose OK. The object appears in your FRAME entry.

Note: When you choose OK, a dialog box informs you that the object already exists and will be overwritten. This box's purpose is to remind you that you now have two FRAME entries that use the same object, and changes in one FRAME entry affect the other. Simply choose OK to continue the read operation.

Other OLE Considerations

This section addresses advanced considerations for using OLE with the SAS System, such as using OLE verbs in SCL code and diagnosing OLE error messages you encounter as you create your SAS/AF applications.

Using TESTAF

If you issue the TESTAF command and make changes to an OLE object in the TESTAF window, the changes are not automatically reflected in the DISPLAY window. After you exit the TESTAF window, issue the UPDATE display manager command from the DISPLAY window, or choose **`Update`** from the **`Locals`** menu. These actions cause the changes you made in the TESTAF window to be copied to the DISPLAY window.

Using OLE Verbs in SCL Programs

One of the most powerful aspects of SAS/AF applications is the SCL code that runs behind your entries. You can write SCL code that manipulates OLE objects, just as you can write SCL code to manipulate any object (such as push buttons, extended tables, and so on).

An OLE verb is an action that you can perform on an object, using the _EXECUTE_ SCL method. The OLE verbs available with an OLE object vary, depending on the source of the object. For example, Paintbrush pictures have a single verb, Edit. Sound objects have two verbs, Play and Edit. Refer to your vendor documentation for the OLE verbs available with your particular application. Also, the verbs are listed in the Object Attributes window for an existing OLE object (choose the **`Associated verbs`** item in the **`Additional Attributes`** area).

To use an OLE verb in SCL code, use the CALL NOTIFY or CALL SEND routine. The syntax for these routines is as follows:

CALL NOTIFY('*object-name*','_EXECUTE_','*OLE-verb*');
CALL SEND(*object-ID*,'_EXECUTE_','*OLE-verb*');

For example, to play a sound object named OBJ1, use this code:

```
call notify('obj1','_execute_','play');
```

It is possible to pass more than one OLE verb at a time, as in the following example:

```
call notify('obj1','_execute_','play','edit','play');
```

You can use the DLGLINKS keyword in place of the *OLE-verb* to open the Links dialog box so that you can update the link information.

For more information on the CALL NOTIFY and CALL SEND routines, see *SAS/AF Software: FRAME Entry Usage and Reference, Version 6, First Edition.*

Using SCL Methods with OLE Objects

OLE objects inherit SCL methods from their parent class, SYSTEM, and from SYSTEM's parent class, WIDGET. For information on these classes, see *SAS/AF Software: FRAME Entry Usage and Reference, Version 6, First Edition.* In addition, the _GET_TYPE_, _EXECUTE_, and _UPDATE_ methods are available for OLE objects. "Using OLE Verbs in SCL Programs" on page 164 shows you how to use the _EXECUTE_ method. Information on the _GET_TYPE_ and _UPDATE_ methods follows.

_GET_TYPE_ method

The _GET_TYPE_ method returns a character string describing an object's type. In the case of OLE objects, _GET_TYPE_ returns one of the following, depending on the how the object was created:

"Embedded" "Bitmap"
"Linked" "Picture"

The syntax of the _GET_TYPE_ method is as follows:

CALL NOTIFY('*object-name*','_GET_TYPE_',*out-type*);
CALL SEND(*object-ID*,'_GET_TYPE_',*out-type*);

Here is an example using the _GET_TYPE_ method:

```
length type $30;
call notify('obj1','_GET_TYPE_',type);
_msg_="OBJ1 is a(n) "||type||" object.";
```

UPDATE method

When you manipulate OLE objects by using the _UPDATE_ method with the CALL NOTIFY and CALL SEND routines, you can use a third parameter. Here is the syntax of the _UPDATE_ method for use with OLE objects:

CALL NOTIFY('*object-name*','_UPDATE_'<,'*in-hservice*'>);
CALL SEND(*object-ID*,'_UPDATE_'<,'*in-hservice*'>);

The _UPDATE_ method recreates an object and updates its contents based on its current attributes. The *in-hservice* parameter is used only with OLE objects and is the name of an HSERVICE catalog entry. When you specify the *in-hservice* parameter, the object specified by *object-name* is changed to the object stored in the HSERVICE entry referenced by the *in-hservice* parameter.

Here is an example:

```
call notify('obj1','_update_','sasuser.examples.sound1.hservice');
```

When you execute this statement, the object stored in OBJ1 is replaced by the SASUSER.EXAMPLES.SOUND1.HSERVICE object.

Note: This version of the _UPDATE_ method overrides the _UPDATE_ method inherited by the WIDGET class.

Updating the Link Information

When you create a linked object, the only information stored with the object is the link information (that is, a pathname). The data are stored with the original file. If the original file is moved or renamed, you must tell the SAS System the new location of the file.

One way to do this is to double-click on the object. If the SAS System determines the link information is no longer valid, the Links dialog box appears. You can also open the Links dialog box by issuing the DLGLINKS display manager command. (A third method of opening the Links dialog box is to use SCL code. See "Other OLE Considerations" on page 164 for information on this.) An example of the Links dialog box is shown in Figure 6.13:

Figure 6.13
Links Dialog Box

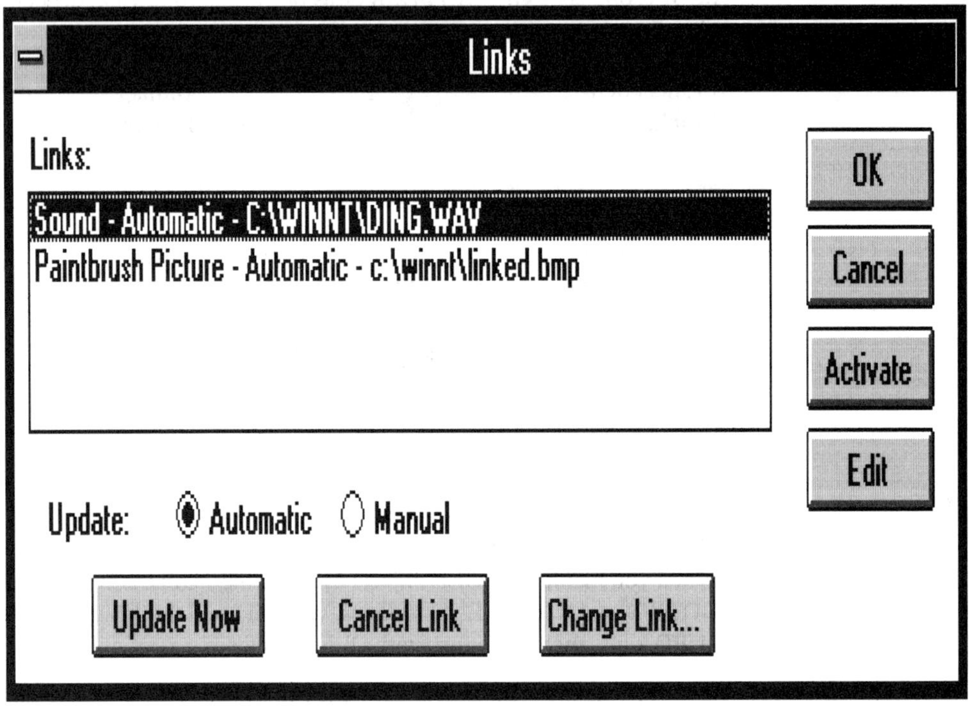

The `Links` listbox displays all the links for the current FRAME entry. Select the one you want to update and then choose Change Link to open the Change Link dialog box. Specify the correct filename and choose OK. Next, choose Update Now. The link is updated, but the Links dialog box does not close. If you want both to update the link and close the Links dialog box, choose OK from the Links dialog box. You can also use Update Now to refresh the object's data if you do not have the object set for automatic update.

You can perform the default method (or verb) on an object by choosing Activate in the Links dialog box. When you choose Activate, the Links dialog box closes and the default verb is invoked on that object. For example, the sound object plays; the Paintbrush picture opens for editing. Using Activate is a good way to test whether the link information is correct.

Choosing Edit enables you to edit the linked object. This is equivalent to double-clicking on a Paintbrush object. For other objects, such as sound objects, the default verb is Play. Using Edit from the Links dialog box is an easy way to edit objects whose default verb is not Edit.

Choosing [Cancel Link] deletes the link from the SAS System and transforms the linked object into a static object. Once you choose [Cancel Link] and then choose [OK], you cannot regain the link.

You can also use the Links dialog box to specify that changes not be reflected automatically through the link but be saved manually. If you want automatic updating (the default), select **Automatic**. If you want manual updating, choose **Manual**.

Choosing [Cancel] from the Links dialog box cancels any changes you have made and closes the dialog box.

Understanding OLE Error Messages

If the SAS System detects an error while opening an object, the Links dialog box is opened. No error message is given in this case.

At other times while you are using or creating a SAS application that uses OLE, you may see an occasional error message. "Using OLE" on page 306 lists the OLE error messages and describes the meaning of the messages.

Data Acquisition

This section illustrates data collection. The two methods discussed are using communications ports and using a DataMyte device.

Communications Ports

You can read data directly from the communications (serial) port on your machine. To set the serial communications parameters, use the Windows NT Control Panel to set up the communications port. The communications parameters you specify are specific to each data collection device.

To set up your communications port, you can choose between using the MODE command from the operating system prompt, or you can use the Control Panel. These techniques are equivalent, and which one you choose depends entirely on your preference. However, you must tell the SAS System which method you have chosen. Use the SETCOMM system option in your SAS configuration file to tell the SAS System how you are setting up your communications port. For example, to specify you are using the MODE command, include the following option in your SAS configuration file:

```
-setcomm mode
```

MODE is the default value for the SETCOMM option. To use the Control Panel, specify CONTROL as the value.

After you invoke the SAS System, submit a FILENAME statement to associate a fileref with the communications port, as in the following example:

```
filename test commport 'com1:';
```

This FILENAME statement defines the fileref TEST, uses the COMMPORT device-type keyword that specifies you are going to use a communications port, and specifies the COM1: reserved physical name.

Next, read the data from COM1: into a SAS data set using the TEST fileref. The following DATA step reads in the data, 1 byte at a time, until the SAS System encounters an end-of-file (the hex value of end-of-file is **'1a'x**):

```
data acquire;
   infile test lrecl=1 recfm=f unbuffered;
   input i $;
   if i='1a'x then stop;     /* Read until you find an end-of-file. */
run;
```

The communications port can be accessed multiple times. However, only one user at a time can write to the port, while multiple reads are allowed.

Two functions that are useful in data acquisition applications are SLEEP and WAKEUP. These functions enable you to control when your program begins to execute. For example, you can use the WAKEUP function to cause your program to begin executing at exactly 2:00 a.m. For more information on these two functions, see page 252 and page 253.

Communications Port Timeouts

By default, if you are reading from a communications port and a timeout occurs, an end-of-file (EOF) is returned to the program. You can specify how communications port timeouts are handled by using the COMTIMEOUT= option. The COMTIMEOUT= option is valid in the FILENAME and INFILE statements and must be used in conjunction with the COMMPORT device-type keyword in the FILENAME statement.

The COMTIMEOUT= option accepts the following values:

EOF
: returns an end-of-file when a timeout occurs. This is the default behavior. This causes the current DATA step to terminate.

WAIT
: instructs the communications port to wait forever for data. In other words, this value overrides the timeout. In this case, no record is returned to the DATA step until data are available. This can cause your program to go into an infinite loop, so use this value with caution.

ZERO
: returns a record length of 0 bytes when a timeout occurs. However, the DATA step does not terminate; it simply tries to read data again.

Here is an example of a FILENAME statement specifying that a record length of 0 bytes be returned to the program when a timeout occurs:

```
filename test commport 'com1:' comtimeout=zero;

data test;
   infile test length=linelen;
   input @;
   if linelen ne 0 then input value;
   else put 'Timeout reading from COM1:';
run;
```

DataMyte Processing

Release 6.09 of the SAS System under Windows NT supports DataMyte data collection devices through three SAS functions and one CALL routine. These functions are the DMYTECHC, DMYTECWD, and DMYTERVC functions. The CALL routine is DMYTECKS. These functions and CALL routines are described in Chapter 10 of this book.

A full discussion of DataMyte processing is beyond the scope of this book. However, the main points follow. A DataMyte is a data collection device you attach to your communications port. The DataMyte device is typically used to interface with precision instruments in industrial and factory applications.

You can send data to and request data from the DataMyte device. A chunk of data passed at one time is called a packet. Each packet can be up to 255 characters long and can consist of several components. Two of these components are used by the SAS functions that support DataMyte data collection:

- character count (CC), which is the number of characters in the packet excluding the start-of-text, the character count itself, and the checksum
- checksum (CS), which is the exclusive OR (XOR) of all the characters in the packet, excluding the checksum itself.

The following additional components are mentioned in the discussion of the SAS functions that support DataMyte data collection:

- start-of-text (STX) character, which is always CTRL-B (`'02'x`)
- end-of-transmission (EOT) character, which is always CTRL-D (`'04'x`).

For more information on DataMyte processing, see your DataMyte documentation.

Chapter Summary

This chapter shows you several different ways to share data between Windows NT applications using the SAS System and also illustrates two methods of data acquisition. These advanced features of the SAS System under Windows NT provide great flexibility in reading and writing data in SAS programs and are an important aspect of the SAS System under Windows NT.

Part 2

System-Dependent Features of the SAS® Language

Chapter 7 SAS® System Options

Introduction

SAS system options control many aspects of your SAS session, including output destinations, the efficiency of program execution, and the attributes of SAS files and data libraries. SAS system options can be specified in one or more ways: in the SAS command, in a SAS configuration file, in an OPTIONS statement (either in a SAS program or in a SAS autoexec file), or in the OPTIONS window. Table 7.1, at the end of this chapter, gives specific information on where each SAS system option can be specified.

Once a system option is set, it affects all subsequent DATA and PROC steps in a program or SAS session until it is respecified. For example, the CENTER option affects all subsequent output from a program, regardless of the number of steps in the program.

Some SAS system options have the same effect (and usually the same name) as other types of options. For example, the BUFSIZE system option is analogous to the BUFSIZE= data set option. In the case of overlapping options, the SAS System uses the following rules of precedence:

- □ The value specified in a statement option (for example, an external I/O statement option) takes precedence over the value specified in a system option.
- □ The value specified in a data set option takes precedence over the value specified in a statement option or a system option.

This chapter includes several sections. Of special importance are "Options for SAS Users under Windows NT" on page 177, which includes an alphabetic listing and discussion of all the SAS system options whose values are Microsoft Windows NT system-dependent, and "Summary of SAS System Options" on page 194, which includes a tabular listing of all SAS system options.

App4 **Note:** When you see the `App4` icon, be sure to read the appropriate section in Appendix 4 as well as the information provided in this chapter. You can ignore the icon if you do not need to move files between Windows NT, OS/2, and DOS, or if your files do not contain national characters or graphics border characters.

Displaying SAS System Option Settings

SAS system options are set to default values. To display the settings of the SAS system options in the SAS log, use the OPTIONS procedure. For example, the following statement produces a list of options, one option per line, with a brief explanation of what each option does:

```
proc options;
run;
```

Specifying the SHORT option in the PROC OPTIONS statement produces a list of options with no explanation. See Chapter 22, "The OPTIONS Procedure," in the *SAS Procedures Guide, Version 6, Third Edition* and Chapter 29, "The OPTIONS Procedure" in SAS Technical Report P-222, *Changes and Enhancements to Base SAS Software, Release 6.07* for more information on the OPTIONS procedure.

In the SAS Display Manager System, the OPTIONS window displays the settings of many SAS system options. However, the OPTIONS window does not list system options that are valid only at SAS invocation or system options that are not available on all operating systems.

Changing SAS System Option Settings

The default values for SAS system options are appropriate for many of your SAS programs. However, you can override a default setting in one (or more) of the following ways:

- You can specify SAS system options in the SAS command, as illustrated here:

  ```
  C:\SAS\SAS.EXE -NODATE -CONFIG MYCONFIG.SAS
  ```

  All SAS system options can be specified in the SAS command. See "Starting the SAS System" on page 12 for more information on issuing the SAS command.

- You can create a SAS configuration file (or edit the default CONFIG.SAS file) to specify values for SAS system options. The SAS configuration file must contain only option settings; it cannot contain SAS statements. For example, a configuration file named MYCONFIG.SAS may contain these option specifications (among others):

  ```
  -nocenter
  -noxwait
  -pagesize 60
  ```

  All SAS system options except the CONFIG option can appear in a SAS configuration file. For more information on SAS configuration files, see "SAS Configuration File" on page 6.

- You can specify many SAS system options in an OPTIONS statement at any point within a SAS session. For example, the following statement specifies that output is not to be labeled with a date and that the line size should be 132:

  ```
  options nodate linesize=132;
  ```

The options are set for the duration of the SAS session or until you change them with another OPTIONS statement. See Chapter 9, "SAS Language Statements," of *SAS Language: Reference, Version 6, First Edition* for more information on the OPTIONS statement.

Not all options can be specified in the OPTIONS statement. To find out whether an option can be specified in the OPTIONS statement, look up the option name in Table 7.1, at the end of this chapter, which summarizes all SAS system option information, including where you can specify the options.

- □ You can specify SAS options in a SAS autoexec file. A SAS autoexec file can contain any valid SAS statement or display manager command. Therefore, you can use an OPTIONS statement in your SAS autoexec file to set system options. For example, your SAS autoexec file can contain the following OPTIONS statement:

```
options xwait nodate pagesize=80;
```

  For more information on SAS autoexec files, see "SAS Autoexec File" on page 8.

- □ You can change some SAS system options in the OPTIONS window. To open the OPTIONS window select

  | Globals | ▸ | Global options | ▸ | SAS options |

  from the pop-up menu. Place the cursor on any option setting and either toggle the setting (by clicking on the box next to the option name to turn the option on or off) or type over the existing value. The value is saved for the duration of the SAS session only.

  Not all options appear in the OPTIONS window; therefore, some cannot be changed there. To find out whether an option can be altered in the OPTIONS window, bring up the OPTIONS window to see if the option is listed or look in Table 7.1, which summarizes all SAS system option information, including where you can specify each option.

System Option Syntax

It is important to remember the differences in syntax between specifying a system option in the SAS command or SAS configuration file and specifying it in the OPTIONS statement. The syntax for these situations is different, and if you use the wrong syntax, you receive an error message.

System Options in the SAS Command or SAS Configuration File

When you specify a system option in the SAS command, it must be preceded by a hyphen (-). For on/off options, just list the keyword corresponding to the appropriate setting. For example, the following SAS command invokes the SAS System and indicates output should not be centered:

```
C:\SAS\SAS.EXE -NOCENTER
```

For options that take a value, do not use an equals sign; follow the option name with a space and then the value. For example, the following SAS command invokes the SAS System with a line size of 132:

```
C:\SAS\SAS.EXE -LINESIZE 132
```

Physical names (that is, directory names or filenames) do not have to be enclosed in quotes when you use them in the SAS command or in the SAS configuration file. For example, the following SAS command invokes the SAS System and indicates that autocall macros are stored in the C:\SAS\CORE\SASMACRO directory:

```
C:\SAS\SAS.EXE -SASAUTOS C:\SAS\CORE\SASMACRO
```

To specify more than one option in the SAS command, simply separate each option with a space. For example, the following SAS command combines the three options shown previously in this section:

```
C:\SAS\SAS.EXE -LINESIZE 132 -NOCENTER -SASAUTOS C:\SAS\CORE\SASMACRO
```

Concatenating libraries

To provide more flexibility for storing SAS files across different drives, such as multiple logical drives on your hard disk or on a network, the SAS System lets you concatenate SAS libraries. The concept of concatenation within the SAS System means that you can specify multiple drives or directories when you specify options in the SAS configuration file or in the SAS command. To specify concatenated directories, specify the directory names inside parentheses, and separate the directory names with spaces.

One practical use of concatenation is the storage of SAS help catalogs. If you want to partition your SAS products among two or more directories, simply specify these multiple directories with the SASHELP option in the SAS configuration file, as in the following example:

```
-sashelp (c:\sas\core\sashelp d:\sas\stat\sashelp)
```

System Options in the OPTIONS Statement

When you specify a system option in the OPTIONS statement, do not precede the option name with a hyphen. Also, for options that take a value, use an equals sign, not a space. For example, the following OPTIONS statement indicates output should not be centered and the line size should be 132:

```
options nocenter linesize=132;
```

Physical names (that is, directory names or filenames) must be enclosed in quotes when used in the OPTIONS statement. For example, the following OPTIONS statement indicates that autocall macros are stored in the C:\SAS\CORE\SASMACRO directory:

```
options sasautos='c:\sas\core\sasmacro';
```

Any file specification not enclosed in quotes in the OPTIONS statement is assumed to be a logical name, that is, a fileref or an environment variable name. If no logical name is found, the SAS System issues an error message.

Processing Options Set in Several Places

When the same option is set in more than one place, the most recent specification is used. Therefore, the OPTIONS window or statement takes precedence over the SAS autoexec file; the SAS autoexec file takes precedence over the SAS command; and the SAS command takes precedence over the SAS configuration file.

Options for SAS Users under Windows NT

This section describes the system-dependent details of SAS system options.

Unapplicable Options in the Windows NT Environment

The following system options described in Chapter 16, "SAS System Options," in *SAS Language: Reference* are not applicable to the Windows NT environment:

- NODMS
- FSDEVICE
- OPLIST
- TAPECLOSE

Option List

The following is an alphabetic list of SAS system options that either apply only to the SAS System under Windows NT or have values that are specific to the Windows NT environment:

ALTLOG
ALTPRINT
AUTOEXEC
AWSDEF
AWSMENU
AWSTITLE
BUFNO
BUFSIZE
CATCACHE
CDE
CLEANUP
COMAMID
COMDEF
CONFIG
DBCSTYPE
DEVICE
ECHO
ENGINE
FONT
FULLSTIMER
ICON
LINESIZE
LOADLIST
LOG
LOGO
MAPS
MEMSIZE
MSGLEVEL
NEWS
NUMKEYS
NUMMOUSEKEYS
OBS
PAGESIZE
PATH
PATHDLL
PFKEY
PRINT
PROCLEAVE
REGISTER
REMOTE
RSASUSER
S
SASAUTOS
SASHELP
SASMSG
SASUSER
SET
SETCOMM
SITEINFO
SORTPGM
SORTSIZE
STIMER
SYSIN
SYSLEAVE

SYSPRINT	VERBOSE	XWAIT
TOOLDEF	WINCHARSET	
USER	WORK	
USERICON	XSYNC	

In the following list, syntax and a description are given for each option. The syntax both for specifying the option in the SAS command and SAS configuration file and for specifying the option in the OPTIONS statement is given where appropriate. (As explained earlier in this chapter, a hyphen before the option name and no equals sign following indicates the option is specified in the SAS configuration file or in the SAS command. No hyphen before the option name with an equals sign following indicates the option can be specified in the OPTIONS statement.) If the option cannot be specified in the OPTIONS statement, only the SAS command and configuration file syntax is given. All the default values given apply to the Windows NT environment. If no default value is given, there is no default value, or the value is set during the installation process and can vary from site to site.

If you need online help for a system option, select **SAS System** from the SAS AWS **Help** menu. Depending on whether the system option is portable or specific to the Windows NT environment, select **SAS Language** or **Host Information**, respectively. Table 7.1 on page 196 lists the default value for each system option, shows where each option can be specified (SAS command, SAS configuration file, OPTIONS window, and OPTIONS statement), and indicates where you can find more information on the option.

Here are the SAS system options that have operating system dependencies:

-ALTLOG *destination*|NOALTLOG
: specifies an alternate SAS log. By default, no copy of the SAS log is made.

ALTLOG *destination*
: specifies the destination for a copy of the SAS log. The *destination* argument can be a valid Windows NT pathname or filename (including device names) or an environment variable associated with a pathname. If you specify only a pathname, the copy is placed in a file in the specified directory, with a name of *filename*.LOG, where *filename* is the name of your SAS job. If you are using display manager and specify only a pathname, the filename is SAS.

NOALTLOG
: suppresses the creation of a copy of the SAS log.

-ALTPRINT *destination*|NOALTPRINT
: specifies an alternate SAS procedure output file. By default, no copy of the SAS procedure output file is made.

ALTPRINT *destination*
: specifies the destination for a copy of the SAS procedure output file. The *destination* argument can be a valid Windows NT pathname or filename (including device names) or an environment variable associated with a pathname. If you specify only a pathname, the copy is placed in a file in the specified directory, with a name of *filename*.LST, where *filename* is the name of your SAS job. If you are using display manager and specify only a pathname, the filename is SAS.

NOALTPRINT
: suppresses the creation of a copy of the procedure output file.

-AUTOEXEC *file-specification*|NOAUTOEXEC
specifies an alternate SAS autoexec file.

AUTOEXEC *file-specification*
specifies the SAS autoexec file to be used instead of the default AUTOEXEC.SAS file. The *file-specification* argument can be a valid Windows NT filename or an environment variable associated with a pathname. See "SAS Autoexec File" on page 8 for more information on the SAS autoexec file.

NOAUTOEXEC
indicates no SAS autoexec file is processed, even if one exists.

If no AUTOEXEC.SAS file is found, the default value for this option is NOAUTOEXEC. See "SAS Autoexec File" on page 8 for a discussion of the search rules for the SAS autoexec file.

-AWSDEF *row-percent column-percent height-percent width-percent*
AWSDEF=*row-percent column-percent height-percent width-percent*
specifies the location and dimensions of the SAS Application Workspace (AWS) window when the SAS System initializes.

The *row-percent* and *column-percent* arguments are screen percentages and control the position of the upper-left corner of the SAS AWS. For example, if you specify 50 for each of these, the upper-left corner of the SAS AWS is positioned in the middle of your display. The range for these parameters is 0 through 95. The *height-percent* and *width-percent* arguments are also screen percentages; these percentages control how big the SAS AWS is. For example, if you specify 100 for each of these, the SAS AWS is as large as your display. If you specify 50 for each, the SAS AWS is half as large as your display. The range for *height-percent* and *width-percent* is 10 through 100.

By default, the SAS AWS takes up most of the display, leaving room for icons at the bottom of the display.

An example of using this system option is given in "Customizing Your SAS Session with System Options" on page 60.

-AWSMENU|NOAWSMENU
controls whether the SAS Application Work Space (AWS) menu bar is displayed or not. This option is valid only at invocation and is usually used with a SAS/AF application to turn off the menu bar. The default value is AWSMENU.

-AWSTITLE "*title-text*"
specifies text string displayed in the SAS AWS title bar. If you do not specify the AWSTITLE option, the SAS AWS title is `SAS`. If your title contains no spaces or special characters, you can omit the quotes around the text string.

-BUFNO *number-of-buffers*
BUFNO=*number-of-buffers*
specifies the number of buffers to use for a SAS data set. Under Windows NT, there is no maximum number of buffers you can allocate, except for memory constraints. The default value is 1.

-BUFSIZE *n*|*n*K
BUFSIZE=*n*|*n*K
specifies the permanent buffer size for an output SAS data set. Under Windows NT, the value can range from 512 bytes through 1 megabyte. The value can be specified in bytes

(*n*) or kilobytes (*n*K). The default value is 0, which enables the engine to pick a value depending on the size of the observation.

You may want to vary the value of the BUFSIZE option if you are trying to maximize the number of observations per page. See "Calculating Data Set Size" on page 297 for more information.

-CATCACHE *n*
CATCACHE=*n*

specifies the number of SAS catalogs to keep open. The default value is 0. Non-zero values of CATCACHE can consume memory, causing adverse effects on the performance of the SAS System. See "Reducing the Number of Disk Accesses for SAS Files" on page 292 for more information about when you might want to use the CATCACHE option.

CDE =I<P>

displays SAS System image usage information in the SAS log. Specifying P (either by itself or in combination with I) purges from memory all images marked as deletable. If the P option is specified along with I, memory is purged before the information is printed. No space is allowed between the I and the P.

The CDE option can be specified in an OPTIONS statement, as a command entered on a display manager command line, or in a DM statement. The CDE option is ignored if it is specified in the SAS command or in a SAS configuration file. The CDE option is not displayed in the OPTIONS window or in the PROC OPTIONS output.

Here are some examples of specifying this option using the various methods of running the SAS System:

display manager

accepts the CDE option as a command:

`cde ip`	issued from the command line of any SAS window
`dm 'cde ip';`	submitted from the PROGRAM EDITOR window

batch mode

accepts the CDE option only in the OPTIONS statement:

```
options cde=i;
```

See "CDE System Option" on page 294 for further discussion of the CDE option.

-CLEANUP|NOCLEANUP
CLEANUP|NOCLEANUP

specifies how to handle out-of-resource conditions. The default value for this option is CLEANUP. When CLEANUP is on, you are not prompted for any out-of-resource condition except for out-of-disk-space conditions. If you do not want to be prompted for out-of-disk-space conditions, use the CLEANUP option in conjunction with the NOTERMINAL option.

If you specify NOCLEANUP, a dialog box prompts you for input when the SAS System runs out of a resource. On every menu except the out-of-disk-space menu, you can select **Continuous**. If you choose **Continuous**, the CLEANUP option is turned on, and you are not prompted again in out-of-resource conditions, unless the SAS System runs out of disk space.

-COMAMID *access-method-ID*
COMAMID=*access-method-ID*

specifies the communication access method to use for SAS distributed products, including SAS/CONNECT and SAS/SHARE software. See *SAS/CONNECT Software: Usage and Reference, Version 6, First Edition*, SAS Technical Report P-224, *SAS/CONNECT Software: Changes and Enhancements for Release 6.08* and SAS Technical Report P-255, *SAS/CONNECT Software: Changes and Enhancements, Release 6.09* for more information about this option under Windows NT.

-COMDEF TOP|CENTER|BOTTOM <LEFT|CENTER|RIGHT>

specifies the Command dialog box display location. The default position is BOTTOM CENTER. You must specify a vertical position first. You do not have to specify a horizontal position, but if you omit it, CENTER is used.

Note: The Command dialog box is positioned with respect to your entire display, not to the SAS AWS.

-CONFIG *file-specification*

specifies an alternative SAS configuration file (the default is CONFIG.SAS). The *file-specification* argument can be a valid Windows NT filename or an environment variable associated with a pathname. See "SAS Configuration File" on page 6 for more information on SAS configuration files.

-DBCSTYPE *encoding-method*

specifies a double-byte character set (DBCS) encoding method.

Under Windows NT, the valid values for *encoding-method* are as follows:

PCIBM specifies the IBM PC encoding method. This is the default value.

SJIS specifies the Shift-JIS encoding method. (Valid only if DBCSLANG=JAPANESE. See Chapter 16 in *SAS Language: Reference* for information on the DBCSLANG option.)

-DEVICE *device-driver*
DEVICE=*device-driver*

specifies an output device driver for SAS/GRAPH software. To see the list of available device drivers under Windows NT, you can use the GDEVICE procedure. If you want to use PROC GDEVICE interactively, submit the following code:

```
proc gdevice catalog=sashelp.devices;
run;
quit;
```

This displays a list you can scroll through.

If you want to write the device list to the SAS log, use the following code:

```
proc gdevice catalog=sashelp.devices nofs;
   list _all_;
run;
quit;
```

Your site may have defined additional device catalogs referenced by the GDEVICE0 libref; see your SAS Software Representative for more information.

If you do not specify the DEVICE option, the SAS System uses WIN as the generic output device.

-ECHO "*message*"|NOECHO

specifies a message to be echoed to the display while initializing the SAS System. For example, you can specify the following:

```
-echo "Release 6.09 of the SAS System under Windows NT is initializing."
```

The message appears in a dialog box before the SAS System initializes. You must choose OK before the SAS System can finish initializing. The default value for this option is NOECHO.

-ENGINE *engine-name*

specifies the default access method for SAS data libraries. Under Windows NT, the value for the *engine-name* argument can be one of the following:

V609 specifies the default SAS engine for Release 6.09. You can use the nicknames BASE and V608 for this engine.

V606 specifies the V606 engine. Note that this engine uses a different file format than the V609 engine. While the V609 engine can read V606 files, the V606 engine cannot read V609 files. Therefore, if you intend to share SAS files between Release 6.09 and Release 6.06, be sure to explicitly specify the V606 engine.

V604 specifies the Release 6.04 compatibility engine. You can use the nickname V603 for this engine.

The use of the SPSS, OSIRIS, BMDP, and XPORT engines with this option is not recommended.

-FONT '*font-name*' <*point-size*>
FONT='*font-name*' <*point-size*>

specifies a monospace font to use with the SAS System (the default font is Sasfont and the default point size is 8). If you specify a *point-size* that is not valid for a font, the *font-name* takes precedence.

The font name is case sensitive. Valid font names can be found in the Windows NT Control Panel. For example, the following option can be specified with the SAS command:

```
-font 'Sasfont' 12
```

The SAS System supports only monospace (fixed-pitch) fonts. If you use a proportional font with the SAS System, the text is displayed incorrectly.

If you are running in OEM mode and you specify an ANSI font, the FONT option overrides the OEM specification and the SAS System may display incorrect text.

-FORMCHAR *character-list*
FORMCHAR=*character-list*

is described in "FORMCHAR System Option" on page 329.

-FULLSTIMER|NOFULLSTIMER
FULLSTIMER|NOFULLSTIMER

generates memory usage and image usage statistics for each task the SAS System completes.

This option also gives you time-elapsed statistics, provided you have not turned off the STIMER option. If you do turn off the STIMER option, the FULLSTIMER option does not generate time statistics. The default value for this option is NOFULLSTIMER.

If you do not need statistics on such tasks as display manager (statistics for display manager are available only when the SAS System terminates), you should turn off the FULLSTIMER option before you end your SAS session. If you do not turn this option off, you see several dialog boxes displaying the statistics for SAS termination. If you have had a long or complex SAS session, there may be quite a few of these boxes.

Some statistics are not accurate unless the FULLSTIMER option is specified at startup time.

-ICON|NOICON
ICON|NOICON

minimizes the SAS System immediately after initialization if you put this option in the SAS command or the SAS configuration file. If you submit this option in an OPTIONS statement, the SAS System is immediately iconized; this is equivalent to clicking on the minimize button. The default value for this option is NOICON.

This option is especially useful for obtaining an iconized SAS session as soon as you boot your system. For example, the ICON option could be specified in the SAS command as follows:

```
c:\sas\sas.exe -icon
```

-LINESIZE *width*
LINESIZE=*width*

specifies the line size of SAS output under Windows NT. The default values are determined by the operating system based on the screen resolution, font, and point size. The values for this option can range from 64 through 256.

-LOADLIST|NOLOADLIST
LOADLIST|NOLOADLIST

enables you to see which SAS images you have loaded and purged during your SAS session. The information is written to the SAS log. The default value for this option is NOLOADLIST. For more information on this option, see Chapter "LOADLIST System Option" on page 294.

-LOG *destination*|NOLOG

controls the creation of the SAS log file for batch mode. By default, the log is sent to the LOG window in display manager; it is sent to a file named *filename*.LOG in batch mode, where *filename* is the name of your SAS job.

LOG *destination*

specifies the destination for the SAS log. The *destination* argument can be a valid Windows NT pathname or filename (including device names such as LPT1) or an environment variable associated with a pathname. If you specify only a pathname, the log file is created in the specified directory with the default name of *filename*.LOG, where *filename* is the name of your SAS job.

(-LOG continued)

NOLOG
: suppresses the creation of a SAS log. Do not use this value unless your SAS program is thoroughly debugged.

If you do not specify the LOG option, the log is routed by default to a file named *filename*.LOG in the SAS System working directory, where *filename* is the name of your SAS job.

This option is not valid under display manager.

-LOGO |NOLOGO
: controls whether a copyright window displays while the SAS System is initializing. The window closes as soon as the SAS AWS is created. LOGO is the default; if you do not want this window to display, specify NOLOGO.

-MAPS *library-specification*
MAPS=*library-specification*
: gives the name of the SAS library that holds the SAS/GRAPH map data sets. The *library-specification* argument can be a libref, a Windows NT pathname, or an environment variable associated with a pathname. Remember that a pathname is only to the directory or subdirectory level.

-MEMSIZE *n*|*n*K|*n*M
MEMSIZE=*n*|*n*K|*n*M
: specifies a limit on the total amount of memory the SAS System uses at any one time. The operating system may use additional amounts of memory. The default value is 0, allows the SAS System to use all available memory, up to the system limit.

The memory used by the SAS System includes virtual memory and is therefore not limited to RAM. It is not recommended that you use this option under Windows NT except in rare cases.

The MEMSIZE option accepts the following values:

n
: specifies a number in the range of 0 to 2,147,483,648. A value of 0 indicates that there is no limit, except the operating system limit.

*n*K
: specifies the number of kilobytes, from 0 to 2,097,152.

*n*M
: specifies the number of megabytes, from 0 to 2,048.

-MSGLEVEL *message-level*
MSGLEVEL=*message-level*
: controls the amount of information that the SAS System writes to the SAS log in certain situations. The *message-level* argument can be one of the following values:

N
: prints NOTE, WARNING, and ERROR messages. This is the default.

I
: prints INFORMATORY, NOTE, WARNING, and ERROR messages.

For example, if the SAS System uses an index to optimize a WHERE or BY statement, it normally does not generate a log message about the index. If MSGLEVEL=I, however, the system displays an informational message to the log whenever it uses an index to optimize a statement.

-NEWS *file-specification*|NONEWS

specifies a file that contains messages to be written to the SAS log after the SAS System initializes. The *file-specification* argument can be a valid Windows NT filename or an environment variable. By default, no news is printed.

-NUMKEYS *number-of-keys*

controls how many function keys are available to you. When the SAS System initializes, it queries your machine to find out how many function keys you have on your keyboard. You can override this setting by specifying a different value with the NUMKEYS option. For example, if you specify the following option, the SAS System displays 10 function keys in the KEYS window:

```
-numkeys 10
```

-NUMMOUSEKEYS *n*

specifies the number of mouse buttons you want the SAS System to use and display in the KEYS window. The value of *n* can range from 0 to 3. Specifying 0 or 1 as the value of this option is equivalent. If *n* is 0 or 1, the KEYS windows lists no mouse buttons (because the left, and in this case the only, mouse button is reserved by the SAS System). If *n* is 2, the KEYS window lists the right mouse button (RMB), as well as CTL RMB and SHF RMB. If *n* is 3, the KEYS window lists both the right mouse button and the middle mouse button (MMB).

Under Windows NT, the SAS System assumes you have three mouse buttons available, unless you specify the NUMMOUSEKEYS option. So, if you have a 1- or 2-button mouse and want the KEYS window to reflect this, put the NUMMOUSEKEYS option in your CONFIG.SAS file.

-OBS *n*|MAX
OBS=*n*|MAX

causes processing to end with the *n*th observation. The default value is MAX, which is 2,147,483,647.

-PAGESIZE *n*
PAGESIZE=*n*

specifies the page size of SAS output under Windows NT. The default values are determined by the operating system based on the screen resolution, font, and point size. The values for this option can range from 15 through 32,767.

-PATH *directory-specification*
PATH='*directory-specification*'

specifies one or more search paths for SAS executable files. You can specify multiple PATH options to define a search order. The *directory-specification* argument can be a valid Windows NT pathname or an environment variable associated with a pathname.

-PATHDLL *SAS-core-path*

specifies the location of the SAS System DLL files that interface with the operating system. This option takes only one path, not a string of paths.

The PATHDLL option is crucial to the boot process for the SAS System and is also searched at other key points in your SAS session. The set of images stored in the path specified by the PATHDLL option must be kept together. Typically, the INSTALL application takes care of setting the PATHDLL option, and you do not have to modify it.

Keep all !SASROOT\CORE\DLL files in the same directory.
If you move these DLL files, all the files must be moved at once, and you must change the value of the PATHDLL option accordingly. If the files are separated, the SAS System does not boot. The message you receive can vary. Some common messages in this situation are "Unable to load SASVWU" and "File not found: SASHOST.DLL". ■

-PFKEY *key-set*

enables you to map your function keys to the mainframe primary, alternate, or SAA keys. Use this option when you do not want the default SAS System key definitions under Windows NT, but rather want to use the mainframe key mappings (for example, the mappings used by the SAS System under MVS).

This option takes one of the following values:

PRIMARY

maps F1–F12 to the mainframe primary settings for PF1– PF12, and SHF F1–SHF F12 to PF13–PF24. The right mouse button (RMB) is mapped to MB2. If you have only 10 function keys, F11, F12, SHF F11, and SHF F12 are not available and are not shown in the KEYS window.

Here are the primary mainframe key definitions:

PC Key	Mainframe Definition	Key	Mainframe Definition
F1	mark	SHF F1	help
F2	smark	SHF F2	zoom
F3	unmark	SHF F3	zoom off; submit
F4	cut	SHF F4	pgm; recall
F5	paste	SHF F5	rfind
F6	store	SHF F6	rchange
F7	prevwind	SHF F7	backward
F8	next	SHF F8	forward
F9	pmenu	SHF F9	output
F10	command	SHF F10	left
F11	keys	SHF F11	right
F12	undo	SHF F12	home
RMB	zoom off; submit		

ALTERNATE

maps F1–F12 to the alternate mainframe key settings. That is, F1 – F12 map to PF13–PF24. The result is that F1–F12 are equivalent to SHF F1–SHF F12. The right mouse button (RMB) is mapped to MB2. If you have only 10 function keys, F11 and F12 are unavailable and are not shown in the KEYS window. F13–F24 are mapped to F1–F12 if your keyboard has only 12 function keys, not 24.

Here are the alternate mainframe key definitions:

PC Key	Mainframe Definition	Key	Mainframe Definition
F1	help	F2	zoom
F3	zoom off; submit	F4	pgm; recall
F5	rfind	F6	rchange
F7	backward	F8	forward
F9	output	F10	left
F11	right	F12	home
RMB	zoom off; submit		

SAA

maps F1–F12 to the mainframe SAA values for CUAPF1–CUAPF12, and SHF F1–SHF F12 to CUAPF13–CUAPF24. The right mouse button (RMB) is mapped to MB2. If you have only 10 function keys, F11, F12, SHF F11, and SHF F12 are unavailable and are not shown in the KEYS window.

Here are the SAA mainframe key definitions:

PC Key	Mainframe Definition	Key	Mainframe Definition
F1	help	SHF F1	cut
F2	keys	SHF F2	paste
F3	zoom off; submit	SHF F3	store
F4	home	SHF F4	mark
F5	pgm; recall	SHF F5	unmark
F6	zoom	SHF F6	smark
F7	backward	SHF F7	left
F8	forward	SHF F8	right
F9	prevcmd	SHF F9	rfind
F10	pmenu	SHF F10	rchange
F11	command	SHF F11	undo
F12	cancel	SHF F12	next
RMB	zoom off; submit		

WIN	specifies to use the default key definitions for the SAS System under Windows NT. This is the default value. For a list of key definitions, open the KEYS window.

Note that the function key values shown in the previous key map tables are for the display manager primary windows only. Other windowing SAS products, such as SAS/FSP, SAS/AF, and SAS/CALC software, have other key definitions.

If you do not specify the PFKEY option, or specify an invalid value, the SAS System loads the default Windows NT key definitions.

-PRINT *destination*|NOPRINT

controls the creation of the SAS procedure output file for batch mode. By default, the procedure output file is sent to the OUTPUT window in display manager; it is sent to a file named *filename*.LST in batch mode, where *filename* is the name of your SAS job.

PRINT *destination*

specifies the destination for the SAS procedure output file. The *destination* argument can be a valid Windows NT pathname or filename (including device names) or an environment variable associated with a pathname. If you specify only a pathname, the procedure output file is created in the specified directory, with the default name of *filename*.LST, where *filename* is the name of your SAS job.

NOPRINT

suppresses the creation of the SAS procedure output file.

If you do not specify the PRINT option, the procedure output is routed by default to a file named *filename*.LST in the SAS System working directory, where *filename* is the name of your SAS job.

This option is not valid in display manager.

-PROCLEAVE *n*K
PROCLEAVE=*n*K

specifies an amount of memory to reserve for normal SAS procedure termination. The value for the PROCLEAVE option is expressed in kilobytes. The default value is 30K; the range of values is from 30 through 64K.

-REGISTER '*menu-name*' '*command*' <'*working-directory*'>

adds an application to the SAS AWS `File` menu.

menu-name	specifies the name you want to appear in the menu.
command	specifies the command you want to execute. The *command* argument can either be a .EXE, .COM, or .BAT file, or can be an operating system command such as the DIR command.
working-directory	specifies the working directory to use for the application. This argument is optional. Read your application's documentation to see if the application requires a working directory specification.

You can add up to eight applications to the SAS AWS `File` menu. If your menu name or command does not include blanks or special characters, you can omit the quotes. For more information on adding applications to the run list, see "User-Defined Application Items" on page 39 and "Adding Applications to the File Menu" on page 61.

-REMOTE *session-ID*
REMOTE=*session-ID*

specifies the remote session ID used for SAS/CONNECT software. See *SAS/CONNECT Software: Usage and Reference* and SAS Technical Report P-224 for more information.

-RSASUSER |NORSASUSER

controls whether members of the SASUSER data library can be opened for update or for read-only access. The default is NORSASUSER.

RSASUSER

limits access to the SASUSER data library to read-only access. If you are running the SAS System under Windows NT on a network, it is common to have a SASUSER data library that is shared by a group of users. By default, if one user has a member of the SASUSER data library open for update, all other users are denied access to that SAS data library member. For example, if one user is writing to the SASUSER.PROFILE catalog, no other user can even read data from the PROFILE catalog.

Specifying RSASUSER enables a group of users to share SASUSER data library members by allowing all users read-only access to members. In the PROFILE catalog example, if RSASUSER is in effect, each user can open the PROFILE catalog for read-only access, allowing other users to concurrently read from the PROFILE catalog. However, no user can write information out to the PROFILE catalog; you receive an error message if you try to do so.

Specifying RSASUSER in a SAS session affects only that session's access to files. To enable a group of users to share members in the SASUSER data library, the system manager should set RSASUSER in the network version of the SAS configuration file, which is shared by all users who share the SASUSER data library.

If you specify RSASUSER but no PROFILE catalog exists in the SASUSER data library, the PROFILE catalog is created in the WORK data library.

NORSASUSER

prevents users from sharing members of the SASUSER data library, because it allows a user to open a file in the SASUSER library for update access. Update access requires exclusive rights to the data library member.

Note: The usefulness of the RSASUSER option depends on how the SAS System is being used. While the RSASUSER option is extremely useful when users must share information (such as the PROFILE catalog) stored in the SASUSER data library, it is not useful if these same users are using SAS/ASSIST software. SAS/ASSIST software requires update access to the SASUSER data library.

-S *n*|MAX
S=*n*|MAX

specifies the length of statements on each line of source statements and the length of data on the line following a CARDS statement. The value for this option can range from 0 through 2,147,483,647. The default value is 0, which enables the SAS System to read a file with any line length.

-SASAUTOS (*library-specification-1*<. . . *library-specification-n*)>
SASAUTOS=('*library-specification-1*'<. . . '*library-specification-n*')>

specifies the SAS autocall library or libraries. For more information on SAS autocall libraries and the SAS macro facility, see "SAS Macro Facility" on page 276.

The *library-specification* argument can be any valid Windows NT pathname or an environment variable associated with a pathname. Remember that a pathname is only to the directory or subdirectory level. Windows NT pathnames must be enclosed in quotes if you are using the OPTIONS statement. If you specify only one library specification, the parentheses are optional.

See *SAS Guide to Macro Processing, Version 6, Second Edition* for more information about the SAS macro facility.

-SASHELP (*library-specification-1* <. . . *library-specification-n*>)
: specifies the directory or directories to be searched for SAS help files, default forms, device lists, dictionaries, and other entries in the SASHELP catalog. Note that products and their corresponding files can be split across multiple drives and directories. The *library-specification* argument can be a Windows NT pathname or an environment variable associated with a pathname.

-SASMSG (*library-specification-1* <. . . *library-specification-n*>)
: specifies the directory or directories to be searched for SAS message files. Note that products and their corresponding message files can be split across multiple drives and directories. The *library-specification* argument can be a Windows NT pathname or an environment variable associated with a pathname.

-SASUSER (*library-specification-1* <. . . *library-specification-n*>)
: specifies the name of the SAS user profile library. The *library-specification* argument can be a Windows NT pathname or an environment variable associated with a pathname. If you list only one library specification, the parentheses are optional.

The default CONFIG.SAS file creates the SASUSER data library in the SASUSER directory under the working directory. If you do not use the SASUSER option when you invoke the SAS System, the SASUSER data library is set equal to the WORK data library, which is temporary. For more information on the SASUSER data library, see "Profile Catalog" on page 10 and "Using the SASUSER Data Library" on page 83.

-SET *SAS-variable path*|(*path-1* <. . . *path-n*>)
SET='*SAS-variable*' '*path*'|"('*path-1*' <. . . '*path-n*'>)"
: defines a SAS environment variable. This is analogous to defining a Windows NT environment variable with the Windows NT SET command. One way to use the SET option is to set up environment variables that represent commonly used external files. For example, the following code defines an environment variable for the sample source library:

```
-set sampsrc (!sasroot\base\sample
              !sasroot\stat\sample
              !sasroot\graph\sample)
```

Note: The words CON and NUL are reserved words under Windows NT. Do not use CON or NUL as environment variables.

For more information on using the SET option, see "Using Environment Variables" on page 79 and page 98.

-SETCOMM MODE|CONTROL
SETCOMM=MODE|CONTROL
: enables you to set your communications port.

MODE	indicates you want to set your communications port using the Windows NT MODE command, from the command prompt. This is the default value.
CONTROL	indicates you want to set your communications port using the Windows NT Control Panel.

-SITEINFO *file-specification*

specifies the file containing site information. The *file-specification* argument can be a valid Windows NT filename or an environment variable. The default SITEINFO file is !SASROOT\ CORE\SASINST\SITEINFO.TXT. For an example of the text stored in this file, see "The SITEINFO Window" on page 302.

-SORTPGM BEST|HOST|SAS
SORTPGM=BEST|HOST|SAS

specifies the name of the sort utility. Under Windows NT, all three values are accepted for the sake of compatibility, but the SAS sort utility is always used.

-SORTSIZE *n*|*n*K|*n*M
SORTSIZE=*n*|*n*K|*n*M

limits the amount of memory available to the SORT procedure. By default, this option is set to 1 megabyte. This option can reduce the amount of swapping the SAS System must do to sort the data set. If PROC SORT needs more memory than you specify, it creates a temporary utility file in your SASWORK directory in which to store the data. The SORT procedure's algorithm can swap unneeded data more efficiently than Windows NT can.

The value of the SORTSIZE option can be one of the following:

n	specifies the amount of memory in bytes.
*n*K	specifies the amount of memory in 1-kilobyte multiples.
*n*M	specifies the amount of memory in 1-megabyte multiples.

A value of 1M or 2M is optimal for a machine with 6 megabytes of physical memory. If your machine has more than 6 megabytes of physical memory, and you are sorting large data sets, setting the SORTSIZE option to a value greater than 2M may improve performance.

See "Improving Performance of the SORT Procedure" on page 295 for more details.

-STIMER|NOSTIMER
STIMER|NOSTIMER

specifies whether to display time elapsed statistics after each DATA step and procedure. The STIMER option prints the amount of time it took for the SAS System to complete a task. The default value for this option is STIMER.

-SYSIN *file-specification*|NOSYSIN

specifies a batch mode source file. The *file-specification* argument can be a valid Windows NT filename or an environment variable associated with a pathname.

You can test your SAS autoexec file by using the NOSYSIN value so that when the SAS System is invoked, the SAS autoexec file is processed, and then the SAS session is automatically terminated.

-SYSLEAVE *n*K
SYSLEAVE=*n*K

specifies an amount of memory to leave reserved for normal SAS System termination. The value for the SYSLEAVE option is expressed in kilobytes. The default value is 15K; the range of values is 15K through 64K.

-SYSPRINT *destination* <*driver*>
SYSPRINT='*destination*' <'*driver*'>

specifies a destination printer.

destination

is required and can be the name of a physical hardcopy device such as LPT2: or a file specification such as a fileref, an environment variable associated with a pathname or device, or a filename.

driver

is optional and is the name of a printer driver installed under Windows NT, such as ColorPro, or the name of a port such as LPT2:.

If you do not specify the *driver* argument, you are not able to take advantage of the Windows NT Print Manager. If you specify a port name instead of a printer name, the printer installed on that port is used.

If you enter a new value in the **`Sysprint device name`** field in the Printer Setup dialog box (discussed in Chapter 2), the value you enter is reflected in the SYSPRINT value (shown by PROC OPTIONS).

If you do not specify the SYSPRINT option, the *destination* and *driver* arguments use the default system printer values. If there is no default system printer, the value of both arguments is LPT1:.

For more information on printing, see Chapter 2 and "Printing" on page 116.

-TOOLDEF TOP|CENTER|BOTTOM <LEFT|CENTER|RIGHT>

specifies the Toolbox display location. The default position is TOP RIGHT. You must specify a vertical position first. You do not have to specify a horizontal position, but if you omit it, RIGHT is used.

Note: The Toolbox is positioned with respect to your entire display, not to the SAS AWS. This option has no effect if you are using the Tool bar instead of the Toolbox.

-USER *library-specification*
USER='*library-specification*'

specifies the name of the default permanent SAS data library. The *library-specification* argument can be a libref, an environment variable, or Windows NT pathname. Remember that a pathname is only to the directory or subdirectory level.

-USERICON *icon-resource-filename number-of-icons*

specifies the fully-qualified pathname of the resource file associated with your user-defined icons, as well as the maximum number of icons stored in this file. For example, the following option specifies 10 icons that are stored in C:\MYSTUFF\MYICONS.DLL:

```
-usericon c:\mystuff\myicons.dll 10
```

The icon resource file must be compiled using the Win32 Software Development Kit (SDK). Refer to SDK documentation for more information. User-defined icons can be incorporated into applications developed with SAS/AF or SAS/EIS software.

-VERBOSE|NOVERBOSE

specifies whether to write SAS configuration file system options to the display. This option is a good error diagnostic tool; if you receive an error message when invoking the SAS System, you can see if you have an error in your system option specifications. The default value for this option is NOVERBOSE.

-WINCHARSET ANSI|OEM

specifies the character set you want the SAS System to use for your display, as well as for reading and writing files. The default value is ANSI. If WINCHARSET is set to OEM, the SAS System obtains the current codepage number from the operating system. You can override the setting of this option by using the ANSI and OEM options in your I/O statements, such as FILE, FILENAME, %INCLUDE, and INFILE.

This system option is for advanced users only and requires you to know quite a bit about the internals of character sets under Windows NT, OS/2, and DOS. This option is of particular interest to SAS users in countries other than the United States.

-WORK (*library-specification-1* <. . . *library-specification-n*>) <USE>

specifies the pathname for the directory containing the WORK data library. The *library-specification* argument can be an environment variable or Windows NT pathname. Remember that a pathname is only to the directory or subdirectory level. If you list only one library, the parentheses are optional.

If you specify the USE suboption, the SAS System uses the directory you specify with the WORK option as the WORK data library. If you do not specify the USE suboption, the SAS System creates a subdirectory called #TD*nnnnn* under the directory you specify in the WORK option, where *nnnnn* is a unique number. The default behavior is to create a #TD*nnnnn* subdirectory.

If you have more than one library specification in the WORK option, the USE suboption is ignored, because for a concatenated WORK library, the SAS System does not create a subdirectory called #TD*nnnnn*. See "WORK Data Library" on page 10 for more information on the location of the WORK data library.

-XSYNC|NOXSYNC
XSYNC|NOXSYNC

controls whether an X command or statement executes synchronously or asynchronously.

XSYNC

is the default and causes the process you submit to execute synchronously. That is, control is not returned to the SAS System until the command has completed. You cannot return to your SAS session until the process spawned by the X command or statement is closed.

NOXSYNC

indicates the process should execute asynchronously. That is, control is returned immediately to the SAS System and the command continues executing without interfering with your SAS session. With NOXSYNC in effect, you can execute an X command or statement and return to your SAS session without closing the process spawned by the X command or statement.

The value of this option affects the execution of the following:

- X statement
- X command
- CALL SYSTEM routine
- %SYSEXEC statement.

For more information see "Exiting Your SAS Session Temporarily" on page 20.

-XWAIT|NOXWAIT
XWAIT|NOXWAIT
specifies whether you have to type EXIT at the DOS prompt before the DOS shell closes. This option does not affect Windows NT applications, such as Excel; it only applies to applications that execute in a DOS shell.

XWAIT
specifies that you have to type EXIT to return to your SAS session. This is the default value for this option.

NOXWAIT
specifies that the Windows NT shell goes away without your typing EXIT when the process is finished.

The XWAIT option affects the DOS shell started by any of the following:

- X statement
- X command
- CALL SYSTEM routine
- %SYSEXEC statement.

For more information see "Exiting Your SAS Session Temporarily" on page 20.

Summary of SAS System Options

Table 7.1 lists every system option available under Windows NT. Many of these options have no system-dependent behavior and are completely described in Chapter 16 of *SAS Language: Reference.* Other options have system dependencies and are described earlier in this chapter. Some options are described in both this book and in *SAS Language: Reference.* Use the following legend to determine where to find more information on an option:

COMP indicates the option is described completely earlier this chapter. (The only exception is the FORMCHAR option which is described in Appendix 4.) Some options are not applicable to the Windows NT environment; these options are listed in "Unapplicable Options in the Windows NT Environment" on page 177.

LR indicates the option is not described in this chapter but is described completely in *SAS Language: Reference.*

P-222	indicates the option is described in SAS Technical Report P-222, *Changes and Enhancements to Base SAS Software, Release 6.07*.
P-242	indicates the option is described in SAS Technical Report P-242, *SAS Software: Changes and Enhancements, Release 6.08*.
P-252	indicates the option is described in SAS Technical Report P-252, *SAS Software: Changes and Enhancements, Release 6.09*.

Table 7.1 *Summary of All SAS System Options*

Option Specification	Default	Specified in: SAS Command	CONFIG File	OPTIONS Window	OPTIONS Statement	See
ALTLOG *arg*	none	X	X			LR, COMP
ALTPRINT *arg*	none	X	X			LR, COMP
AUTOEXEC *arg*	AUTOEXEC.SAS if available	X	X			LR, COMP
AWSDEF *arg*	*	X	X		X	COMP
AWSMENU	AWSMENU	X	X			COMP
AWSTITLE *arg*	SAS	X	X			COMP
BATCH	NOBATCH (display manager); BATCH (batch)	X	X			LR, P-252
BUFNO *arg*	1	X	X	X	X	LR, COMP
BUFSIZE *arg*	0	X	X	X	X	LR, COMP
BYERR	BYERR	X	X	X	X	P-222
BYLINE	BYLINE	X	X	X	X	P-222
CAPS	NOCAPS	X	X	X	X	LR
CARDIMAGE	NOCARDIMAGE	X	X	X	X	LR
CATCACHE *arg*	0	X	X			LR, COMP
CDE *arg*	none				X**	COMP
CENTER	CENTER	X	X	X	X	LR
CHARCODE	NOCHARCODE	X	X	X	X	LR
CLEANUP	CLEANUP	X	X	X	X	LR, COMP
CMDMAC	NOCMDMAC	X	X		X	P-222
COMAMID *arg*	EHLLAPI	X	X		X	LR, COMP
COMDEF *arg*	BOTTOM CENTER	X	X			COMP
COMPRESS *arg*	NO	X	X	X	X	LR
CONFIG *arg*	CONFIG.SAS	X				LR, COMP
CPUID	CPUID	X	X			P-222
DATE	DATE	X	X	X	X	LR
DBCS	NODBCS	X	X		X	LR
DBCSLANG *arg*	none	X	X			LR

(continued)

* By default the SAS AWS takes up the entire display except for space for icons at the bottom of the display.
** This option can also be specified in a DM statement or on a window command line. It cannot be specified in the SAS command or in the SAS configuration file.

Table 7.1 (continued)

Option Specification	Default	Specified in: SAS Command	CONFIG File	OPTIONS Window	OPTIONS Statement	See
DBCSTYPE *arg*	PCIBM	X	X			LR, COMP
DETAILS	NODETAILS	X	X	X	X	P-222
DEVICE *arg*	none	X	X	X	X	LR, COMP
DKRICOND *arg*	ERROR	X	X	X	X	P-222
DKROCOND *arg*	WARN	X	X	X	X	P-222
DMR	NODMR	X	X			LR
DMSBATCH	NODMSBATCH	X	X			P-252
DSNFERR	DSNFERR	X	X	X	X	LR
ECHO *arg*	none	X	X			COMP
ECHOAUTO	NOECHOAUTO	X	X			LR
ENGINE *arg*	V609	X	X			LR, COMP
ERRORABEND	NOERRORABEND	X	X	X	X	LR
ERRORCHECK	NORMAL	X	X			P-242
ERRORS *arg*	20	X	X	X	X	LR
FIRSTOBS *arg*	1	X	X	X	X	LR
FMTERR	FMTERR	X	X	X	X	LR
FMTSEARCH *arg*	none	X	X	X	X	P-222
FONT *arg*	'Sasfont' 8	X	X		X	COMP
FORMCHAR *arg*	|----|+| ---+=|-/\<>*	X	X	X	X	LR, COMP
FORMDLIM *arg*	none	X	X	X	X	LR
FORMS *arg*	DEFAULT	X	X	X	X	LR
FULLSTIMER	NOFULLSTIMER	X	X		X	LR, COMP
GWINDOW	GWINDOW	X	X	X	X	LR
ICON	NOICON	X	X		X	COMP
IMPLMAC	NOIMPLMAC	X	X	X	X	LR
INITSTMT *arg*	none	X	X			LR
INVALIDDATA *arg*	•	X	X	X	X	LR
LABEL	LABEL	X	X	X	X	LR
LINESIZE *arg*	varies	X	X	X	X	LR, COMP

(continued)

Table 7.1 (continued)

Option Specification	Default	Specified in: SAS Command	CONFIG File	OPTIONS Window	OPTIONS Statement	See
LOADLIST	NOLOADLIST	X	X		X	COMP
LOCKWAIT *arg*	0	X	X	X	X	P-222
LOG *arg*	LOG window*	X	X			LR, COMP
LOGO	LOGO	X	X			COMP
LAST *arg*	_NULL_	X	X	X	X	LR
MACRO	MACRO	X	X			LR
MAPS *arg*	none	X	X		X	COMP
MAUTOSOURCE	MAUTOSOURCE	X	X	X	X	LR
MEMSIZE *arg*	0	X	X		X	COMP
MERROR	MERROR	X	X	X	X	LR
MISSING *arg*	•	X	X	X	X	LR
MLOGIC	NOMLOGIC	X	X	X	X	LR
MPRINT	NOMPRINT	X	X	X	X	LR
MRECALL	NOMRECALL	X	X	X	X	LR
MSGCASE	NOMSGCASE	X	X			P-222
MSGLEVEL *arg*	N	X	X	X	X	COMP, P-222
MSTORED	NOMSTORED	X	X	X	X	P-222
MSYMTABMAX *arg*	4,194,304	X	X	X	X	P-222
MVARSIZE *arg*	4,096	X	X	X	X	P-222
NEWS *arg*	none	X	X			LR, COMP
NOTES	NOTES	X	X	X	X	LR
NUMBER	NUMBER	X	X	X	X	LR
NUMKEYS *arg*	**	X	X			COMP
NUMMOUSEKEYS *arg*	3	X	X			COMP
OBS *arg*	MAX 2,147,483,647	X	X	X	X	LR, COMP
OVP	NOOVP	X	X	X	X	LR
PAGENO *arg*	1	X	X	X	X	LR

(continued)

* This default applies to display manager. The default value for batch mode is a disk file with a file extension of .LOG and the filename the same as the source filename. This file is stored in your working directory.

** The default value depends on your terminal.

Table 7.1 (continued)

Option Specification	Default	Specified in: SAS Command	CONFIG File	OPTIONS Window	OPTIONS Statement	See
PAGESIZE *arg*	varies	X	X	X	X	LR, COMP
PARM *arg*	none	X	X	X	X	LR
PARMCARDS *arg*	FT15F001	X	X	X	X	LR
PATH *arg*	none	X	X		X	COMP
PATHDLL *arg*	none	X	X			COMP
PFKEY *arg*	WIN	X	X			COMP
PRINT *arg*	OUTPUT window*	X	X			LR, COMP
PRINTINIT	NOPRINTINIT	X	X			P-252
PROBSIG *arg*	0	X	X	X	X	LR
PROC	PROC	X	X	X	X	P-222
PROCLEAVE *arg*	30K	X	X		X	LR, COMP
REGISTER *arg*	none	X	X			COMP
REMOTE *arg*	none	X	X	X	X	LR, COMP
REPLACE	REPLACE	X	X	X	X	LR
REUSE *arg*	NO	X	X	X	X	LR
RSASUSER	NORSASUSER	X	X			COMP, P-242
S *arg*	0	X	X	X	X	LR, COMP
S2 *arg*	0	X	X	X	X	LR
SASAUTOS *arg*	none	X	X	X	X	LR, COMP
SASFRSCR	none					P-222
SASHELP *arg*	none	X	X			LR, COMP
SASMSG *arg*	none	X	X			LR, COMP
SASMSTORE *arg*	none	X	X	X	X	P-222
SASSCRIPT *arg*	none	X	X	X	X	P-222
SASUSER *arg*	SASUSER subdirectory	X	X			LR, COMP
SEQ *arg*	8	X	X	X	X	LR
SERROR	SERROR	X	X	X	X	LR
SET *arg*	none	X	X		X	COMP
SETCOMM *arg*	MODE	X	X		X	COMP

(continued)

* This default applies to display manager. The default value for batch mode is a disk file with a file extension of .LST and the filename the same as the source filename. This file is stored in your working directory.

Table 7.1 (continued)

Option Specification	Default	Specified in: SAS Command	CONFIG File	OPTIONS Window	OPTIONS Statement	See
SETINIT	NOSETINIT	X	X			LR
SITEINFO *arg*	SITEINFO.TXT	X	X			LR, COMP
SKIP *arg*	0	X	X	X	X	P-222
SORTPGM *arg*	SAS	X	X		X	LR, COMP
SORTSEQ *arg*	none	X	X	X	X	P-222
SORTSIZE *arg*	1,048,576	X	X		X	COMP, P-222
SOURCE	SOURCE	X	X	X	X	LR
SOURCE2	NOSOURCE2	X	X	X	X	LR
SPOOL	SPOOL	X	X	X	X	LR
STIMER	STIMER	X	X		X	LR, COMP
SYMBOLGEN	NOSYMBOLGEN	X	X	X	X	LR
SYSIN *arg*	*	X	X			LR, P-252, COMP
SYSLEAVE *arg*	15K	X	X		X	LR, COMP
SYSPARM *arg*	none	X	X	X	X	LR
SYSPRINT *arg*	**	X	X		X	COMP
TERMINAL	TERMINAL	X	X			LR, P-252
TOOLDEF *arg*	TOP RIGHT	X	X			COMP
TRANTAB *arg*	***	X	X	X	X	P-222
USER *arg*	none	X	X	X	X	LR, COMP
USERICON *arg*	none	X	X			COMP
VERBOSE	NOVERBOSE	X	X			LR, COMP
VNFERR	VNFERR	X	X	X	X	LR
WINCHARSET *arg*	ANSI	X	X			COMP
WORK *arg*	SASWORK	X	X			LR, COMP
WORKINIT	WORKINIT	X	X			LR
WORKTERM	WORKTERM	X	X	X	X	LR
XSYNC	XSYNC	X	X		X	COMP
XWAIT	XWAIT	X	X		X	COMP
YEARCUTOFF *arg*	1900	X	X	X	X	LR

* The terminal is the default for display manager; *program-name*.SAS is the default value for batch mode.
** The default value for SYSPRINT is the default system printer. If no system default printer exists, the default is LPT1:.
*** The default value for TRANTAB is decided by internal default tables.

Chapter 8 SAS® Statements

Introduction

This chapter provides reference information on system-dependent features of SAS statements. The statements are listed alphabetically and include a description containing the following information:

- syntax
- Microsoft Windows NT specifics
- help
- other available information.

Note: When you see the `App4` icon, be sure to read the appropriate section in Appendix 4 as well as the information provided in this chapter. You can ignore the icon if you do not need to move files between Windows NT, OS/2, and DOS, or if your files do not contain national characters or graphics border characters.

System-Dependent Statements

If a statement is also described in Chapter 9, "SAS Language Statements," in *SAS Language: Reference, Version 6, First Edition*, that information is not repeated here. Instead, there is a "Windows NT Specifics" section that gives the details on how the statement behaves under Windows NT, and you are referred to *SAS Language: Reference.* Examples for most of these statements are provided in Part 1 earlier in this book. You may also want to refer to SAS Technical Report P-222, *Changes and Enhancements to Base SAS Software, Release 6.07* and SAS Technical Report P-242, *SAS Software: Changes and Enhancements, Release 6.08* for information on new and enhanced SAS statements.

ABORT

Stops executing the current DATA step, SAS job, or SAS session

Windows NT specifics: action of the ABEND and RETURN options; maximum value of *n*

HELP ABORT

Syntax

ABORT <ABEND|RETURN> <*n*>

Windows NT Specifics

Both the ABEND and RETURN options terminate the SAS job or session. The value of *n* (the condition code returned to the host system) can range from 0 to 65,535.

See Also

- Chapter 9, "SAS Language Statements," in *SAS Language: Reference, Version 6, First Edition*

ATTRIB

Associates a format, informat, label, and length with one or more variables

Windows NT specifics: length specification

HELP ATTRIB

Syntax

ATTRIB *variable-list-1 attribute-list-1* <. . . *variable-list-n attribute-list-n*>;

Windows NT Specifics

The length you can specify for a numeric variable under Windows NT ranges from 3 to 8 bytes.

See Also

- Chapter 9, "SAS Language Statements," in *SAS Language: Reference, Version 6, First Edition*

FILE

Specifies the current output file for PUT statements

Windows NT specifics: *file specification*; *host-option-list*

HELP FILE

Syntax

FILE *file-specification* <*option-list*> <*host-option-list*>;

Windows NT Specifics

The following arguments have system dependencies:

file-specification
can be any of the file specification forms discussed in "Referencing External Files" on page 96.

Note: The words CON and NUL are reserved words under Windows NT. Do not use CON or NUL as filerefs.

host-option-list
names external I/O statement options specific to Windows NT. They can be any of the following:

ANSI
indicates that the file should be written using the ANSI character set. OEM to ANSI translation is only valid for text format files (that is, either a variable-record or a print file). If the SAS System encounters a file during translation that has an invalid record format (for example, a fixed-record file or a binary file), you receive a warning message when the file is closed. This option is mutually exclusive of the OEM option. ANSI is the default character set.

BLKSIZE=*block-size*
BLK=*block-size*
is ignored, but is included for compatibility with previous versions of the SAS language.

BLOCK|NOBLOCK
is used only in the context of named pipes. This option indicates whether the client is to wait if no data are currently available. BLOCK is the default value.

BYTE|MESSAGE
is used only in the context of named pipes. This option indicates the type of pipe. BYTE is the default value.

COMMAND
is used only in the context of Dynamic Data Exchange (DDE). This option enables you to issue a remote command for applications that do not use the SYSTEM topic

FILE *continued*

(host-option-list continued)

name. Refer to "Referencing the DDE External File" on page 133 and "Using DDE and the COMMAND Option to Execute Commands in an Application" on page 137 for more information.

DEVICE=*device-name*
associates a device with the output file. The following are valid values:

COMMPORT	writes data to a communications port.
DDE	writes data to another application using Dynamic Data Exchange. See "Dynamic Data Exchange" on page 132 for more information.
DISK	writes data to a disk file. DISK is the default *device-name* under Windows NT.
DUMMY	throws data away to a null file.
PLOTTER	routes SAS/GRAPH output to a plotter. The Windows NT Print Manager is not used. The default device type for PLOTTER is COMMPORT.
NAMEPIPE	writes data to a named pipe. See "Using Named Pipes" on page 142 for more information.
PIPE	writes data to an unnamed pipe. See "Using Unnamed Pipes" on page 140 for more information.
PRINTER	writes data to the printer file or device. By default, the output is routed through the Windows NT Print Manager.

If you are using a device for output and do not use a device-type keyword in the FILENAME statement, you should use the DEVICE= option in the FILE statement so that the SAS System uses the correct access protocols for the device.

Note: The TAPE and TERMINAL device-type keywords (documented in *SAS Language: Reference*) are not applicable to the Windows NT environment. If you use one of these device-type keywords in your SAS program under Windows NT, you receive an error message. Also, while the DISK device-type keyword is accepted under Windows NT, it is ignored, because disk files are the default under Windows NT.

EOFCONNECT
is used only in the context of named pipes and is valid only when defining the server. This option indicates that if an end-of-file (EOF) is received from a client, the server should try to connect to the next client.

HOLD
specifies to defer print requests until you select `Release Print Requests` from the SAS AWS `File` menu. This option is useful if you want to hold printing from the DATA step or graphics output.

HOTLINK
is used only in the context of Dynamic Data Exchange (DDE). For a complete description and an example of using this option, see "Using the DDE HOTLINK" on page 137.

LRECL=*record-length*
specifies the record length (in bytes). Under Windows NT, the default is 132. The value of *record-length* can range from 1 to 1,048,576 (1 megabyte).

MOD
specifies that output should be appended to an existing file.

NOTAB
is used only in the context of Dynamic Data Exchange (DDE). This option enables you to use non-tab character delimiters between variables. For more information on this option, see "Using the NOTAB Option with DDE" on page 137.

OEM
indicates that the file should be written using the OEM character set. ANSI to OEM translation is only valid for text format files (that is, either a variable-record or a print file). If the SAS System encounters a file during translation that has an invalid record format (for example, a fixed-record file or a binary file), you receive a warning message when the file is closed. This option is mutually exclusive of the ANSI option. ANSI is the default character set.

RECFM=*record-format*
controls the record format. The following are valid values under Windows NT:

F — indicates fixed format.

N — indicates binary format and causes the file to be treated as a byte stream.

P — indicates print format.

S370V — indicates the variable S370 record format (V).

S370VB — indicates the variable block S370 record format (VB).

S370VBS — indicates the variable block with spanned records S370 record format (VBS).

V|D — indicates variable format. This is the default.

The S370 values are valid with MVS style files only. That is, files that are binary, have variable-length records, and are in EBCDIC format. If you want to use a fixed-format MVS file, first copy it to a variable-length, binary MVS file.

RETRY=*seconds*
is used only in the context of named pipes. This option specifies how long a named pipe client should wait for a busy pipe. The minimum (and default) value for *seconds* is 10.

SERVER|CLIENT
is used only in the context of named pipes. This option specifies the mode of a named pipe. The default value is SERVER.

FILE *continued*

See Chapter 6 and "Advanced External I/O Techniques" on page 110 for an example of using some of these options. See Chapter 9 in *SAS Language: Reference* for portable options available in the FILE statement.

See Also

- Chapter 4, "Using External Files" on page 95
- Chapter 6, "Using Advanced Features of the SAS System under Windows NT" on page 131
- Chapter 9, "SAS Language Statements," in *SAS Language: Reference, Version 6, First Edition*
- Chapter 20, "Working with External Files," in *SAS Language and Procedures: Usage 2, Version 6, First Edition*

FILENAME

Associates a SAS fileref with an external file

Windows NT specifics: *device-type*; *external-file*; *host-option-list*

HELP FILENAME

Syntax

FILENAME *fileref* <*device-type*> '*external-file*' <*host-option-list*>;
FILENAME *fileref device-type* <'*external-file*'> <*host-option-list*>;
FILENAME *fileref* <*device-type*> ('*directory-1*'<,. . .'*directory-n*'>)
<*host-option-list*>;

Note: This is a simplified version of the FILENAME statement syntax; see Chapter 9 in *SAS Language: Reference* for the complete syntax and its explanation.

Windows NT Specifics

You can use the following arguments with the FILENAME statement:

fileref
is any valid fileref, as discussed in Chapter 4. See "Assigning a Fileref to a Directory" on page 99 for examples of using filerefs in member name syntax (also called aggregate syntax). See "Understanding How Concatenated Directories Are Accessed" on page 102 for the rules the SAS System uses when accessing files through filerefs.

Note: The words CON and NUL are reserved words under Windows NT. Do not use CON or NUL as filerefs.

device-type
enables you to read and write data from devices rather than files. The following are valid values:

COMMPORT	reads data from and writes data to a communications port.
DDE	reads data from and writes data to another application using Dynamic Data Exchange. See "Dynamic Data Exchange" on page 132 for more information.
DISK	reads data from and writes data to a disk file. DISK is the default device type under Windows NT.
DRIVEMAP	enables you to determine which hard drives are available.
DUMMY	specifies a null output device. This value is especially useful in testing situations.
NAMEPIPE	writes data to a named pipe. See "Using Named Pipes" on page 142 for more information.
PIPE	writes data to an unnamed pipe. See "Using Unnamed Pipes" on page 140 for more information.
PLOTTER	indicates you are accessing a plotter. The Windows NT Print Manager is not used. This device-type keyword is used solely in conjunction with SAS/GRAPH software.
PRINTER	indicates you are accessing a printer file or device. By default, output is routed through the Windows NT Print Manager when you use this device-type keyword. See the discussion of the SYSPRINT system option on page 192 for more information on altering your default printer.

See Chapter 6 and "Advanced External I/O Techniques" on page 110 for an example of specifying a device type in the FILENAME statement.

Using a device-type keyword in the FILENAME statement is the recommended method of using devices for I/O processing. A device-type keyword ensures the SAS System uses the correct access protocols for the device you are using. You can specify a device with the DEVICE= option in the FILE, INFILE, and %INCLUDE statements. However, some device types are not valid in some statements. See the description of each statement for the valid device types for that statement.

Note: The TAPE and TERMINAL device-type keywords (documented in *SAS Language: Reference*) are not applicable to the Windows NT environment. If you use one of these device-type keywords in your SAS program under Windows NT, you receive an error message. Also, while the DISK device-type keyword is accepted under Windows NT, it is ignored, because disk files are the default under Windows NT.

external-file

can be any valid Windows NT file specification, enclosed in quotes. See "Using a Quoted Windows NT Filename" on page 104. Remember that you can use reserved operating system physical names such as LPT1 or COM2, as well as actual filenames.

The reserved filename, CLIPBOARD, is used with DDE. It tells the SAS System to use the Windows NT Clipboard to determine the DDE triplet.

host-option-list

names external I/O statement options specific to Windows NT. They can be any of the following:

FILENAME *continued*

ANSI
: indicates that the file should be written or read using the ANSI character set. OEM to ANSI translation is only valid for text format files (that is, either a variable-record or a print file). If the SAS System encounters a file during translation that has an invalid record format (for example, a fixed-record file or a binary file), you receive a warning message when the file is closed. This option is mutually exclusive of the OEM option. ANSI is the default character set.

BLKSIZE=*block-size*
BLK=*block-size*
: is ignored, but is included for compatibility with previous versions of the SAS language.

BLOCK|NOBLOCK
: is used only in the context of named pipes. This option indicates whether the client is to wait if no data are currently available. BLOCK is the default value.

BYTE|MESSAGE
: is used only in the context of named pipes. This option indicates the type of pipe. BYTE is the default value.

COMMAND
: is used only in the context of Dynamic Data Exchange (DDE). This option enables you to issue a remote command for applications that do not use the SYSTEM topic name. Refer to "Referencing the DDE External File" on page 133 and "Using DDE and the COMMAND Option to Execute Commands in an Application" on page 137 for more information.

COMTIMEOUT=*value*
: controls how a communications port timeout is handled. A timeout occurs when no data are available at the communications port for a period of time, usually 60 seconds. The COMTIMEOUT= option can have the following values:

EOF
: returns an end-of-file when a timeout occurs. This is the default behavior. This causes the current DATA step to terminate.

WAIT
: instructs the communications port to wait forever for data. In other words, this value overrides the timeout. In this case, no record is returned to the DATA step until data is available. This can cause your program to go into an infinite loop, so use this value with caution.

ZERO
: returns a record length of 0 bytes when a timeout occurs. However, the DATA step does not terminate; it simply tries to read data again.

The COMTIMEOUT= option is valid only if you also use the COMMPORT device-type keyword.

EOFCONNECT
: is used only in the context of named pipes and is valid only when defining the server. This option indicates that if an end-of-file (EOF) is received from a client, the server should try to connect to the next client.

HOLD
: specifies to defer print requests until you select `Release Print Requests` from the SAS AWS `File` menu. This option is useful if you want to hold printing from the DATA step or graphics output.

HOTLINK
: is used only in the context of Dynamic Data Exchange (DDE). For a complete description and an example of using this option, see "Using the DDE HOTLINK" on page 137.

LRECL=*record-length*
: specifies the record length (in bytes). Under Windows NT, the default is 132. The value of *record-length* can range from 1 to 1,048,576 (1 megabyte).

MOD
: specifies that output should be appended to an existing file.

NOTAB
: is used only in the context of Dynamic Data Exchange (DDE). This option enables you to use non-tab character delimiters between variables. For more information on this option, see "Using the NOTAB Option with DDE" on page 137.

OEM
: indicates that the file should be written or read using the OEM character set. ANSI to OEM translation is only valid for text format files (that is, either a variable-record or a print file). If the SAS System encounters a file during translation that has an invalid record format (for example, a fixed-record file or a binary file), you receive a warning message when the file is closed. This option is mutually exclusive of the ANSI option. ANSI is the default character set.

RECFM=*record-format*
: controls the record format. The following are valid values under Windows NT:

F	indicates fixed format.
N	indicates binary format and causes the file to be treated as a byte stream.
P	indicates print format.
S370V	indicates the variable S370 record format (V).
S370VB	indicates the variable block S370 record format (VB).
S370VBS	indicates the variable block with spanned records S370 record format (VBS).
V|D	indicates variable format. This is the default.

The S370 values are valid with MVS style files only. That is, files that are binary, have variable-length records, and are in EBCDIC format. If you want to use a fixed-format MVS file, first copy it to a variable-length, binary MVS file.

RETRY=*seconds*
: is used only in the context of named pipes. This option specifies how long a named pipe client should wait for a busy pipe. The minimum (and default) value for *seconds* is 10.

FILENAME *continued*

(host-option-list continued)

SERVER|CLIENT
: is used only in the context of named pipes. This option specifies the mode of a named pipe. The default value is SERVER.

See Chapter 6 and "Advanced External I/O Techniques" on page 110 for examples of using some of these options.

See Also

- Chapter 4, "Using External Files" on page 95
- Chapter 6, "Using Advanced Features of the SAS System under Windows NT" on page 131
- Chapter 9, "SAS Language Statements," in *SAS Language: Reference, Version 6, First Edition*
- Chapter 20, "Working with External Files," in *SAS Language and Procedures: Usage 2, Version 6, First Edition*

FOOTNOTE

Prints up to ten lines of text at the bottom of the procedure output

Windows NT specifics: maximum length of footnote

HELP FOOTNOTE

Syntax

FOOTNOTE<*n*> <'*text*'|"*text*">;

Windows NT Specifics

The maximum footnote length under Windows NT is 132 characters. If the specified footnote is greater than the LINESIZE system option, the footnote is truncated to the line size.

See Also

- Chapter 9, "SAS Language Statements," in *SAS Language: Reference, Version 6, First Edition*

%INCLUDE

Includes and executes SAS statements and data lines

Windows NT specifics: *source*, if a file-specification is used; *option-list*

HELP LANGUAGE

Syntax

%INCLUDE *source</option-list>*;

Note: This is a simplified version of the %INCLUDE statement syntax; see Chapter 9 in *SAS Language: Reference* for the complete syntax and its explanation.

Windows NT Specifics

You can use the following arguments with the %INCLUDE statement:

source
: describes the location of the information you want to access with the %INCLUDE statement. The two possible sources are a file specification or internal lines. Under Windows NT, you cannot use an asterisk (*) to specify keyboard entry. The file specification can be any of the file specification forms discussed in "Referencing External Files" on page 96.

option-list
: consists of statement options valid under Windows NT. Remember to precede the options list with a forward slash (/). Currently, the following options are available under Windows NT:

ANSI
: indicates that the file should be read using the ANSI character set. OEM to ANSI translation is only valid for text format files (that is, either a variable-record or a print file). If the SAS System encounters a file during translation that has an invalid record format (for example, a fixed-record file or a binary file), you receive a warning message when the file is closed. This option is mutually exclusive of the OEM option. ANSI is the default character set.

BLKSIZE=*block-size*
BLK=*block-size*
: is ignored, but is included for compatibility with previous versions of the SAS language.

DEVICE=*device-name*
: associates a device with the input file. The following are valid values:

DUMMY	causes an immediate end-of-file and may be useful in testing situations.

%INCLUDE *continued*

(option-list continued)

If you are using a device for input and do not use a device-type keyword in the FILENAME statement, you should use the DEVICE= option in the %INCLUDE statement so that the SAS System uses the correct access protocols for the device.

LRECL=*record-length*
: specifies the record length (in bytes). Under Windows NT, the default is 132. The value of *record-length* can range from 1 to 1,048,576 (1 megabyte).

App4

OEM
: indicates that the file should be read using the OEM character set. ANSI to OEM translation is only valid for text format files (that is, either a variable-record or a print file). If the SAS System encounters a file during translation that has an invalid record format (for example, a fixed-record file or a binary file), you receive a warning message when the file is closed. This option is mutually exclusive of the ANSI option. ANSI is the default character set.

RECFM=*record-format*
: controls the record format. The following are valid values under Windows NT:

F	indicates fixed format.
N	indicates binary format and causes the file to be treated as a byte stream.
P	indicates print format.
V|D	indicates variable format. This is the default.
S370V	indicates the variable S370 record format (V).
S370VB	indicates the variable block S370 record format (VB).
S370VBS	indicates the variable block with spanned records S370 record format (VBS).

The S370 values are valid with MVS style files only. That is, files that are binary, have variable-length records, and are in EBCDIC format. If you want to use a fixed-format MVS file, first copy it to a variable-length, binary MVS file.

See Also

□ Chapter 4, "Using External Files" on page 95

□ Chapter 9, "SAS Language Statements," in *SAS Language: Reference, Version 6, First Edition*

□ Chapter 20, "Working with External Files," in *SAS Language and Procedures: Usage 2, Version 6, First Edition*

INFILE

Specifies an external file to read with an INPUT statement

Windows NT specifics: *file-specification; host-option-list*

HELP INFILE

Syntax

INFILE *file-specification* <*option-list*> <*host-option-list*>;

Windows NT Specifics

The following arguments have system dependencies:

file-specification
identifies the source of input data records, usually an external file. The *file-specification* argument can be any of the file specification forms discussed in "Referencing External Files" on page 96. The reserved fileref CARDS enables the INFILE statement to reference in-stream data.

Note: The words CON and NUL are reserved words under Windows NT. Do not use CON or NUL as filerefs.

host-option-list
names external I/O statement options specific to Windows NT. They can be any of the following:

ANSI
indicates that the file should be read using the ANSI character set. OEM to ANSI translation is only valid for text format files (that is, either a variable-record or a print file). If the SAS System encounters a file during translation that has an invalid record format (for example, a fixed-record file or a binary file), you receive a warning message when the file is closed. This option is mutually exclusive of the OEM option. ANSI is the default character set.

BLKSIZE= *block-size*
BLK=*block-size*
is ignored, but is included for compatibility with previous versions of the SAS language.

BLOCK|NOBLOCK
is used only in the context of named pipes. This option indicates whether the client is to wait if no data are currently available. BLOCK is the default value.

BYTE|MESSAGE
is used only in the context of named pipes. This option indicates the type of pipe. BYTE is the default value.

COMTIMEOUT=*value*
controls how a communications port timeout is handled. This option can have the following values:

INFILE *continued*

(host-option-list continued)

EOF	returns an end-of-file when a timeout occurs. This is the default behavior.
WAIT	instructs the communications port to wait forever for data. In other words, this value overrides the timeout. In this case, no record is returned to the DATA step until data is available. This can cause your program to go into an infinite loop, so use this value with caution.
ZERO	returns a record length of 0 bytes when a timeout occurs.

The COMTIMEOUT= option is valid only if you also use the COMMPORT device-type keyword.

DEVICE=*device-name*
associates a device with the output file. The following are valid values:

COMMPORT	reads data from a communications port.
DDE	reads data from another application using Dynamic Data Exchange. See "Dynamic Data Exchange" on page 132 for more information.
DISK	reads data from a disk file. DISK is the default *device-name* under Windows NT.
DRIVEMAP	enables you to determine which hard drives are available.
DUMMY	causes an immediate end-of-file when used with the INPUT statement.
NAMEPIPE	writes data to a named pipe. See "Using Named Pipes" on page 142 for more information.
PIPE	writes data to an unnamed pipe. See "Using Unnamed Pipes" on page 140 for more information.

If you are using a device other than a disk file for input and do not use a device-type keyword in the FILENAME statement, you should use the DEVICE= option in the INFILE statement so that the SAS System uses the correct access protocols for the device.

Note: The TAPE and TERMINAL device-type keywords (documented in *SAS Language: Reference*) are not applicable to the Windows NT environment. If you use one of these device-type keywords in your SAS program under Windows NT, you receive an error message. Also, while the DISK device-type keyword is accepted under Windows NT, it is ignored, because disk files are the default under Windows NT.

EOFCONNECT
is used only in the context of named pipes and is valid only when defining the server. This option indicates that if an end-of-file (EOF) is received from a client, the server should try to connect to the next client.

HOTLINK
is used only in the context of Dynamic Data Exchange (DDE). For a complete description and an example of using this option, see "Using the DDE HOTLINK" on page 137.

LRECL=*record-length*
specifies the record length (in bytes). Under Windows NT, the default is 132. The value of *record-length* can range from 1 to 1,048,576 (1 megabyte).

NOTAB
is used only in the context of Dynamic Data Exchange (DDE). This option enables you to use non-tab character delimiters between variables. For more information on this option, see "Using the NOTAB Option with DDE" on page 137.

OEM
indicates that the file should be read using the OEM character set. ANSI to OEM translation is only valid for text format files (that is, either a variable-record or a print file). If the SAS System encounters a file during translation that has an invalid record format (for example, a fixed-record file or a binary file), you receive a warning message when the file is closed. This option is mutually exclusive of the ANSI option. ANSI is the default character set.

RECFM=*record-format*
controls the record format. The following are valid values under Windows NT:

F	indicates fixed format.
N	indicates binary format and causes the file to be treated as a byte stream.
P	indicates print format.
S370V	indicates the variable S370 record format (V).
S370VB	indicates the variable block S370 record format (VB).
S370VBS	indicates the variable block with spanned records S370 record format (VBS).
V|D	indicates variable format. This is the default.

The S370 values are valid with MVS style files only. That is, files that are binary, have variable-length records, and are in EBCDIC format. If you want to use a fixed-format MVS file, first copy it to a variable-length, binary MVS file.

RETRY=*seconds*
is used only in the context of named pipes. This option specifies how long a named pipe client should wait for a busy pipe. The minimum (and default) value for *seconds* is 10.

SERVER|CLIENT
is used only in the context of named pipes. This option specifies the mode of a named pipe. The default value is SERVER.

INFILE *continued*

See Chapter 6 and "Advanced External I/O Techniques" on page 110 for an example of using some of these options. See Chapter 9 in *SAS Language: Reference* for portable options available in the INFILE statement.

See Also

- Chapter 4, "Using External Files" on page 95
- Chapter 6, "Using Advanced Features of the SAS System under Windows NT" on page 131
- Chapter 9, "SAS Language Statements," in *SAS Language: Reference, Version 6, First Edition*
- Chapter 20, "Working with External Files," in *SAS Language and Procedures: Usage 2, Version 6, First Edition*
- Chapter 3, "SAS Language Statements," in SAS Technical Report P-222, *Changes and Enhancements to Base SAS Software, Release 6.07*

LENGTH

Specifies the number of bytes the SAS System uses to store a variable's values

Windows NT specifics: valid numeric variable lengths

HELP LENGTH

Syntax

LENGTH <*variable-1*> <*. . . variable-n*> <$> <*length*> <DEFAULT=*n*>;

Windows NT Specifics

You can use the following arguments with the LENGTH statement:

length
: can range from 3 to 8 bytes for numeric variables under Windows NT.

DEFAULT=*n*
: changes the default number of bytes used for storing the values of newly created numeric variables from 8 to the value of *n*. Under Windows NT, the value of *n* can range from 3 to 8 bytes.

See Also

- □ "Variable Precision and Storage Information" on page 275
- □ Chapter 9, "SAS Language Statements," in *SAS Language: Reference, Version 6, First Edition*

LIBNAME

Associates a libref with a SAS data library and lists file attributes for a SAS data library

Windows NT specifics: *engine-name*; *SAS-data-library*

HELP LIBNAME

Syntax

LIBNAME *libref <engine-name> 'SAS-data-library'*;
LIBNAME *libref <engine-name>* (*'SAS-data-library-1'*<,. . .*'SAS-data-library-n'*>);
LIBNAME *libref*|_ALL_ LIST;

Note: This is a simplified version of the LIBNAME statement syntax; see Chapter 9 in *SAS Language: Reference* for the complete syntax and its explanation.

The LIBNAME statement is also used to clear a libref. This use is completely documented in Chapter 9 of *SAS Language: Reference*, as well as in "Clearing Librefs" on page 81.

Windows NT Specifics

The LIBNAME statement associates a libref with a permanent SAS data library. It also can be used to list the file attributes of a SAS data library.

Note: The words CON and NUL are reserved words under Windows NT. Do not use CON or NUL as librefs.

Associating Librefs

Use this form of the LIBNAME statement to associate a libref or an engine with a SAS data library:

LIBNAME *libref <engine-name> 'SAS-data-library'*;
LIBNAME *libref <engine-name> 'SAS-data-library-1'*<,. . .*'SAS-data-library-n'*>);

You can use the following arguments with this form of the LIBNAME statement:

libref
is any valid libref, as documented in *SAS Language: Reference.*

engine-name
is one of the following library engines supported under Windows NT:

LIBNAME *continued*

V609	accesses Release 6.09 and Release 6.08 SAS data sets. You can use the nicknames BASE and V608 for this engine.
V606	accesses Release 6.06 SAS data sets.
V604	accesses Release 6.03 and Release 6.04 SAS data sets. You can use the nickname V603 for this engine.
XPORT	accesses transport format files.
BMDP	accesses BMDP system files.
OSIRIS	accesses OSIRIS data files.
SPSS	accesses SPSS system files.

See Chapter 3, “Using SAS Files” on page 69 and the discussion of engines in Chapter 9 of *SAS Language: Reference* for more information about these engines.

SAS-data-library
is the physical name of a SAS data library under Windows NT. It must be a valid Windows NT pathname. You can concatenate several Windows NT directories together to serve as a single SAS data library. See “Understanding How Concatenated SAS Data Libraries Are Accessed” on page 81 for more information on concatenated SAS data libraries.

Note: There are no engine/host options for the LIBNAME statement under Windows NT.

Listing Data Library Attributes

With the LIST option, you can use the LIBNAME statement to list attributes of SAS data libraries. Output 8.1 shows the results of the following LIBNAME statement:

```
libname sashelp list;
```

Output 8.1 *Data Library Attributes Listed by the LIBNAME Statement*

```
59   libname sashelp list;
NOTE: Libref=   SASHELP
      Engine=   V609
      Filefmt=  607
      Physical Name= c:\SAS\core\sashelp  c:\SAS\base\sashelp
      c:\SAS\access\sashelp  c:\SAS\af\sashelp
      c:\SAS\assist\sashelp  c:\SAS\calc\sashelp
      c:\SAS\connect\sashelp  c:\SAS\eis\sashelp
      c:\SAS\english\sashelp  c:\SAS\ets\sashelp
      c:\SAS\fsp\sashelp  c:\SAS\gis\sashelp
      c:\SAS\graph\sashelp  c:\SAS\image\sashelp
      c:\SAS\iml\sashelp  c:\SAS\insight\sashelp
      c:\SAS\lab\sashelp  c:\SAS\look\sashelp
      c:\SAS\maps\sashelp  c:\SAS\or\sashelp
      c:\SAS\phclin\sashelp  c:\SAS\qc\sashelp
      c:\SAS\share\sashelp  c:\SAS\stat\sashelp
      c:\SAS\toolkt\sashelp  c:\SAS\trader\sashelp
      c:\SAS\usage\sashelp  c:\SAS\test\sashelp
```

See Also

- □ Chapter 3, "Using SAS Files" on page 69
- □ Chapter 9, "SAS Language Statements," in *SAS Language: Reference, Version 6, First Edition*
- □ Chapter 3, "SAS Language Statements," in SAS Technical Report P-222, *Changes and Enhancements to Base SAS Software, Release 6.07*

TITLE

Specifies title lines for SAS output

Windows NT specifics: maximum length of title

HELP TITLE

Syntax

TITLE<*n*> <*'text'*|"*text*">;

Windows NT Specifics

The maximum title length under Windows NT is 132 characters. If the specified title is greater than the LINESIZE system option, the title is truncated to the line size.

See Also

- □ Chapter 9, "SAS Language Statements," in *SAS Language: Reference, Version 6, First Edition*
- □ Chapter 3, "SAS Language Statements," in SAS Technical Report P-222, *Changes and Enhancements to Base SAS Software, Release 6.07*

X

Issues an operating system command or specifies a Windows NT application from within a SAS session

Windows NT specifics: operating system command

HELP HOST

X *continued*

Syntax

X <'*command*'>;

Windows NT Specifics

The X statement issues a Windows NT command or specifies a Windows NT application (such as Notepad) from within a SAS session. The SAS System executes the X statement immediately. You can issue the X statement without the *command* argument.

no argument
: places you in a DOS session, with an operating system prompt. Here you can execute Windows NT commands in the context of the SAS System working directory. There are some things you cannot do from the DOS prompt in this situation, such as define environment variables for use by your SAS session. (Environment variables must be defined before you invoke the SAS System). Type EXIT at the DOS prompt and press ENTER to return to your SAS session.

command
: specifies a Windows NT command or a Windows NT application. This argument can be anything you can specify at a DOS prompt (including the SAS command). Therefore, you can use the X statement to execute Windows NT applications. The command can be enclosed in quotes, but this is not required.

  The command is passed to Windows NT and executed in the context of the working directory. If errors occur, the appropriate error messages are displayed. The command executes from the following command prompt:

```
[SAS][current-drive:\working-directory]
```

By default, you must type EXIT to return to your SAS session after the command has completed execution. Also by default, if you execute a Windows NT application such as Notepad, you must close the application before you can return to your SAS session. Specify NOXWAIT in an OPTIONS statement if you do not want to have to type EXIT. With NOXWAIT in effect, as soon as the command finishes execution, control is returned to your SAS session. Note, however, that if you execute a Windows NT application with the X statement, specifying NOXWAIT does not let you return to your SAS session until you close the application.

Another system option, XSYNC, controls whether you have to wait for the command to finish executing before you can return to your SAS session. If you specify NOXSYNC, you can start a Windows NT application with the X statement and return to your SAS session without closing the application. See "XWAIT System Option" on page 23 and "XSYNC System Option" on page 23 for more details on these two options.

Other methods of executing operating system commands exist under Windows NT besides the X statement (and X SAS Display Manager System command). See "Run Item" on page 38 and "Adding Applications to the File Menu" on page 61 for information on these additional methods. In addition, you can use the CALL SYSTEM routine and the %SYSEXEC statement. These are described in Chapter 10.

See Also

- □ "Exiting Your SAS Session Temporarily" on page 20
- □ XWAIT and XSYNC system options on page 194 and page 193, respectively
- □ Chapter 9, "SAS Language Statements," in *SAS Language: Reference, Version 6, First Edition*

Chapter 9 SAS® Procedures

Introduction

This chapter provides reference information on system-dependent features of base SAS procedures. The procedures are listed alphabetically and include a description containing the following information:

- Microsoft Windows NT specifics
- help
- other information available.

Note: When you see the App4 icon, be sure to read the appropriate section in Appendix 4 as well as the information provided in this chapter. You can ignore the icon if you do not need to move files between Windows NT, OS/2, and DOS, or if your files do not contain national characters or graphics border characters.

System-Dependent Procedures

If a procedure is also described in the *SAS Procedures Guide, Version 6, Third Edition*, that information is not repeated here. In particular, the syntax for the procedure is not repeated. Instead, there is a "Windows NT Specifics" section that gives the details on how the procedure behaves under Windows NT, and you are referred to the *SAS Procedures Guide*. The syntax and a full description are given for those procedures not described in the *SAS Procedures Guide*. Examples of most of these procedures are provided in *SAS Language and Procedures: Usage, Version 6, First Edition.*

CATALOG

Manages entries in SAS catalogs

Windows NT specifics: FILE= option in the CONTENTS statement

HELP CATALOG

Windows NT Specifics

The FILE= option in the CONTENTS statement of the CATALOG procedure accepts a file specification that is system-dependent. If an unquoted file specification is given in the FILE= option, but no FILENAME statement, SET system option, or Windows NT environment variable is used to define the file specification, the file is named *file-specification* .LST and is stored in the working directory. For example, if MYFILE is not a fileref defined by the FILENAME statement, the SET system option, or a Windows NT environment variable, and you submit the following statements, the file MYFILE.LST, containing the list of contents for SASUSER.PROFILE, is created in your working directory:

```
proc catalog catalog=sasuser.profile;
   contents file=myfile;
run;
```

See Also

- Chapter 8, "The CATALOG Procedure," in the *SAS Procedures Guide, Version 6, Third Edition*
- Chapter 17, "The CATALOG Procedure," in SAS Technical Report P-222, *Changes and Enhancements to Base SAS Software, Release 6.07*
- Chapter 2, "SAS Procedures," in SAS Technical Report P-242, *SAS Software: Changes and Enhancements, Release 6.08*

CIMPORT

Restores a transport file created by the CPORT procedure

Windows NT specifics: name and location of transport file

HELP CIMPORT

Windows NT Specifics

Coupled with the CPORT procedure, the CIMPORT procedure enables you to move catalogs and data sets from one operating system to another.

Note: PROC CIMPORT processes a file generated by PROC CPORT, not a transport file generated by the XPORT engine.

When you use the CIMPORT procedure under Windows NT, remember the following:

- The INFILE= option value can be a fileref defined in a FILENAME statement, a quoted Windows NT pathname, or an environment variable.
- If you omit the INFILE= option and have not defined the reserved fileref SASCAT, the SAS System tries to read from a file named SASCAT.DAT in your working directory. If no file by that name exists, the following error message is issued and the procedure terminates, assuming C:\SAS has been defined as the working directory:

```
ERROR: Physical file does not exist, C:\SAS\SASCAT.DAT.
```

- If you have not transferred the file created by PROC CPORT in binary format, PROC CIMPORT cannot read the file, and you receive the following message:

```
ERROR: Given transport file is bad.
```

See Also

- Chapter 10, "The CIMPORT Procedure," in the *SAS Procedures Guide, Version 6, Third Edition*
- SAS Technical Report P-195, *Transporting SAS Files between Host Systems*
- Chapter 19, "The CIMPORT Procedure," in SAS Technical Report P-222, *Changes and Enhancements to Base SAS Software, Release 6.07*
- SAS Technical Report P-252, *SAS Software: Changes and Enhancements, Release 6.09*

CONTENTS

Prints descriptions of the contents of one or more files from a SAS data library

Windows NT specifics: Engine/Host Dependent Information

HELP CONTENTS

Windows NT Specifics

While most of the printed output generated by the CONTENTS procedure is the same across all operating systems, the **`Engine/Host Dependent Information`** output depends on both the operating system and the engine. Output 9.1 shows an example of the **`Engine/Host Dependent Information`** generated for the V609 engine from the following statements:

```
proc contents data=oranges;
   title 'Contents for a Release 6.09 Data Set';
run;
```

CONTENTS *continued*

Output 9.1 *Engine/Host Dependent Information from PROC CONTENTS Using the V609 Engine*

```
                    Contents for a Release 6.09 Data Set                     1

                              CONTENTS PROCEDURE

Data Set Name: WORK.ORANGES                            Observations:         4
Member Type:   DATA                                    Variables:            5
Engine:        V609                                    Indexes:              0
Created:       14:29 Wednesday, March 17, 19xx         Observation Length:   40
Last Modified: 14:29 Wednesday, March 17, 19xx         Deleted Observations: 0
Protection:                                            Compressed:           NO
Data Set Type:                                         Sorted:               YES
Label:

                 -----Engine/Host Dependent Information-----

                      Data Set Page Size:       4096
                      Number of Data Set Pages: 1
                      File Format:              607
                      First Data Page:          1
                      Max Obs per Page:         101
                      Obs in First Data Page:   4

              -----Alphabetic List of Variables and Attributes-----

                      #    Variable    Type    Len    Pos
                      -----------------------------------
                      2    FLAVOR      Num       8      8
                      4    LOOKS       Num       8     24
                      3    TEXTURE     Num       8     16
                      5    TOTAL       Num       8     32
                      1    VARIETY     Char      8      0

                          -----Sort Information-----

                       Sortedby:      DESCENDING TOTAL
                       Validated:     YES
                       Character Set: ANSI
```

The engine name (V609) is listed in the header information. The **Engine/Host Dependent Information** describes attributes of the data set, such as the data set page size and the maximum number of observations per page. For more information on how to interpret the data set size information, see "Calculating Data Set Size" on page 297.

See Also

□ Chapter 4, "Starting with SAS Data Sets," in *SAS Language and Procedures: Usage, Version 6, First Edition*

□ Chapter 12, "The CONTENTS Procedure," in the *SAS Procedures Guide, Version 6, Third Edition*

□ Chapter 20, "The CONTENTS Procedure," in SAS Technical Report P-222, *Changes and Enhancements to Base SAS Software, Release 6.07*

□ Chapter 2, "SAS Procedures," in SAS Technical Report P-242, *SAS Software: Changes and Enhancements, Release 6.08*

CONVERT

Converts BMDP, OSIRIS, and SPSS/PC system files to SAS data sets

Windows NT specifics: all

HELP HOST

Syntax

PROC CONVERT *product-specification* <*option-list*>;

Description

The CONVERT procedure converts a data file from BMDP, OSIRIS, or SPSS/PC format into a SAS data set. PROC CONVERT produces one output data set, but no printed output. The new data set contains the same information as the input system file; exceptions are noted in "Output Data Sets" on page 228.

Because the BMDP, OSIRIS, and SPSS/PC products are maintained by other companies or organizations, changes may be made that make the system files incompatible with the current version of PROC CONVERT. SAS Institute only upgrades PROC CONVERT to support changes made to these products when a new version of the SAS System is available.

In the PROC CONVERT statement, the *product-specification* argument is required and can be one of the following:

BMDP=*fileref* <(CODE=*code* CONTENT=*content-type*)>

converts the first member of a BMDP save file created under DOS into a SAS data set. Here is an example:

```
filename save 'c:\mydir\bmdp.dat';

proc convert bmdp=save;
run;
```

If you have more than one save file in the BMDP file referenced by the *fileref* argument, you can use two options in parentheses after *fileref*. The CODE= option lets you specify the code of the save file you want, and the CONTENT= option lets you give the content of the save file. For example, if a file with CODE=JUDGES has a content of DATA, you can use the following statement:

```
filename save 'c:\mydir\bmdp1.dat';

proc convert bmdp=save(code=judges content=data);
run;
```

DICT=*fileref*

is valid only when used with the OSIRIS product specification. The DICT= option specifies the OSIRIS dictionary to use.

CONVERT *continued*

OSIRIS=*fileref*
: converts an OSIRIS file into a SAS data set. If you use this product specification, you must also use the DICT= option, which specifies the OSIRIS dictionary to use.

SPSS=*fileref*
: converts an SPSS/PC file into a SAS data set. The SPSS/PC file can be in the following formats:

- SPSS/PC format, created under DOS.
- SPSS Portable File Format (from any operating system). This format is also called export format.

In the syntax for PROC CONVERT, *option-list* can be one or more of the following and can be used with any *product-specification* argument:

FIRSTOBS=*n*
: gives the number of the observation where the conversion is to begin. This enables you to skip over observations at the beginning of the BMDP, OSIRIS, or SPSS/PC system file.

OBS=*n*
: specifies the number of the last observation to convert. This enables you to exclude observations at the end of the file.

OUT= *SAS-data-set*
: names the SAS data set created to hold the converted data. If the OUT= option is omitted, the SAS System still creates a data set and automatically names it DATA*n*, just as if you omitted a data set name in a DATA statement. If it is the first such data set in a job or session, the SAS System names it DATA1, the second is DATA2, and so on. If the OUT= option is omitted or if you do not specify a two-level name in the OUT= option, the data set converted to SAS format is stored in your WORK data library and by default is not permanent.

Missing Values

If a numeric variable in the input data set has no value or a system missing value, PROC CONVERT assigns it a missing value.

Output Data Sets

This section describes the attributes of the output SAS data set for each *product-specification* value.

Be sure that the translated names are unique.
As described below, variable names can sometimes be translated by the SAS System. To ensure the procedure works correctly, be sure your variables are named in such a way that translation results in unique names. ■

BMDP output Variable names from the BMDP save file are used in the SAS data set, but nontrailing blanks and all special characters are converted to underscores in the SAS variable names. The subscript in BMDP variable names, such as x(1), becomes part of the SAS variable name, with the parentheses omitted: X1. Alphabetic BMDP variables become SAS character variables of corresponding length. Category records from BMDP are not accepted.

OSIRIS output For single-response variables, the V1-V9999 name becomes the SAS variable name. For multiple-response variables, the suffix R*n* is added to the variable name, where *n* is the response. For example, V25R1 is the first response of the multiple-response variable V25. If the variable after V1000 has 100 or more responses, responses above 99 are eliminated. Numeric variables that OSIRIS stores in character, fixed-point binary, or floating-point binary mode become SAS numeric variables. Alphabetic variables become SAS character variables; any alphabetic variable of length greater than 200 is truncated to 200. The OSIRIS variable description becomes a SAS variable label, and OSIRIS print formats become SAS formats.

SPSS output SPSS variable names and variable labels become variable names and labels without change. SPSS alphabetic variables become SAS character variables. SPSS blank values are converted to SAS missing values. SPSS print formats become SAS formats, and the SPSS default precision of no decimal places becomes part of the variables' formats. SPSS value labels are not copied. DOCUMENT data are copied so that PROC CONTENTS can display them.

Comparison

The CONVERT procedure is closely related to the interface library engines BMDP, OSIRIS, and SPSS. (In fact, the CONVERT procedure uses these engines.) For example, the following two sections of code provide identical results:

```
filename myfile 'mybmdp.dat';

proc convert bmdp=myfile out=temp;
run;

libname myfile bmdp 'mybmdp.dat';
data temp;
   set myfile._first_;
run;
```

However, the BMDP, OSIRIS, and SPSS engines have more extensive capabilities than PROC CONVERT. For example, PROC CONVERT only converts the first BMDP member in a save file. The BMDP engine, in conjunction with the COPY procedure, copies all members.

CPORT

Writes SAS data sets and catalogs into a special format in a transport file

Windows NT specifics: name and location of transport file

HELP CPORT

Windows NT Specifics

The FILE= option value can be a fileref defined in a FILENAME statement, a quoted Windows NT pathname, or an environment variable.

If you do not use the FILE= option and have not defined the reserved fileref SASCAT, a file named SASCAT.DAT is created in your working directory.

See Also

- Chapter 16, "The CPORT Procedure," in the *SAS Procedures Guide, Version 6, Third Edition*
- SAS Technical Report P-195, *Transporting SAS Files between Host Systems*
- Chapter 22, "The CPORT Procedure," in SAS Technical Report P-222, *Changes and Enhancements to Base SAS Software, Release 6.07*
- Chapter 2, "SAS Procedures," in SAS Technical Report P-242, *SAS Software: Changes and Enhancements, Release 6.08*
- SAS Technical Report P-252, *SAS Software: Changes and Enhancements, Release 6.09*

DATASETS

Lists, copies, renames, and deletes SAS files and manages indexes for and appends SAS data sets in a SAS data library

Windows NT specifics: directory information; CONTENTS statement output

HELP DATASETS

Windows NT Specifics

The SAS data library information displayed in the SAS log by the DATASETS procedure depends on the operating system and the engine. Output 9.2 is an example SAS log showing the information (for the V609 engine) that the DATASETS procedure generates under Windows NT.

Output 9.2
SAS Data Library Information from PROC DATASETS

```
48    proc datasets library=work;
                                 -----Directory-----

                        Libref:         WORK
                        Engine:         V609
                        Physical Name: C:\SAS\SASWORK

                           #  Name      Memtype  Indexes
                           ----------------------------
                           1  HLPDS1    DATA
                           2  HLPDS2    DATA
                           3  ORANGES   DATA
                           4  RSW1      DATA
                           5  RSW2      DATA
                           6  TEST      DATA
49    run;
```

The output shows you the libref, engine, and physical name associated with the library, as well as the names of the SAS files contained in the library.

The CONTENTS statement of the DATASETS procedure generates the same `Engine/Host Dependent Information` as the CONTENTS procedure.

See Also

- □ Chapter 17, "The DATASETS Procedure," in the *SAS Procedures Guide, Version 6, Third Edition*
- □ Chapter 34, "Modifying Data Set Names and Attributes," in *SAS Language and Procedures: Usage, Version 6, First Edition*
- □ Chapter 23, "The DATASETS Procedure," in SAS Technical Report P-222, *Changes and Enhancements to Base SAS Software, Release 6.07*
- □ Chapter 2, "SAS Procedures," in SAS Technical Report P-242, *SAS Software: Changes and Enhancements, Release 6.08*

OPTIONS

Lists the current values of all SAS system options

Windows NT specifics: host options

HELP OPTIONS

Windows NT Specifics

The `PORTABLE` options displayed by the OPTIONS procedure are the same for every operating system (although the default values may differ slightly). However, the `HOST OPTIONS` displayed by this procedure are system-dependent. Output 9.3 shows the `HOST OPTIONS` displayed for the Windows NT environment.

OPTIONS *continued*

Output 9.3
Host Options Displayed by PROC OPTIONS

```
HOST OPTIONS:

 ALTLOG=            Specify an alternate log file in dms mode or batch mode.
 ALTPRINT=          Specify an alternate print file in dms mode or batch
                    mode.
 AUTOEXEC=          Specify a substitute AUTOEXEC file.
 AWSDEF=(  0    0  87 100)
                    Specify initial size and position of application work
                    space.
 AWSMENU            Specify to show the sas aws menu bar.
 AWSTITLE=          Specify the text string for SAS AWS title bar
 CODEGEN            Generate data step code instead of interpreting.
 COMAMID=EHLLAPI    Specify primary communication access method id.
 COMAUX1=           Specify auxiliary 1 communication access method id.
 COMAUX2=           Specify auxiliary 2 communication access method id.
 COMDEF=(BOTTOM CENTER)
                    Command dialog display location.
 CONFIG=C:\SAS\CONFIG.SAS
                    Specify a substitute CONFIG file.
 ECHO=              Echo a specific message to the terminal.
 NOEXITWINDOWS      Specify to close Windows 3.x session after sas
                    terminates.
 FONT=(Sasfont  8)  Specify facename and ptsize to use as the default dms
                    font.
 NOFULLSTIMER       Print timing information and system performance
                    statistics.
 NOICON             During startup, allows application work space to be
                    iconed.
 NOLOADLIST         Display full path of image names when loaded and purged.
 LOG=               Specify the LOG file for batch mode.
 NOLOGO             Specify to display SAS copyright message at startup
 NDP                Specify to force the use of numeric processor.
 NUMKEYS=12         Specify number of function keys.
 NUMMOUSEKEYS=3     Specify number of mouse keys.
 PATH=c:\SAS\core\sasexe
 PATH=c:\SAS\base\sasexe
 PATH=c:\SAS\access\sasexe
 PATH=c:\SAS\af\sasexe
 PATH=c:\SAS\assist\sasexe
 PATH=c:\SAS\calc\sasexe
 PATH=c:\SAS\connect\sasexe
 PATH=c:\SAS\eis\sasexe
 PATH=c:\SAS\english\sasexe
 PATH=c:\SAS\ets\sasexe
 PATH=c:\SAS\fsp\sasexe
 PATH=c:\SAS\gis\sasexe
 PATH=c:\SAS\graph\sasexe
 PATH=c:\SAS\image\sasexe
 PATH=c:\SAS\iml\sasexe
 PATH=c:\SAS\insight\sasexe
 PATH=c:\SAS\lab\sasexe
 PATH=c:\SAS\look\sasexe
 PATH=c:\SAS\maps\sasexe
 PATH=c:\SAS\or\sasexe
 PATH=c:\SAS\phclin\sasexe
 PATH=c:\SAS\qc\sasexe
 PATH=c:\SAS\share\sasexe
 PATH=c:\SAS\stat\sasexe
 PATH=c:\SAS\toolkt\sasexe
 PATH=c:\SAS\trader\sasexe
 PATH=c:\SAS\usage\sasexe
 PATH=c:\SAS\test\sasexe
 PATH=c:\SAS\internal\sasexe
                    Specify one of any number of search paths.
 PATHDLL=c:\SAS\core\sasdll
                    Specify the SAS System DLL search path.
 PFKEY=WIN          Key mappings.
 PRINT=             Specify the PRINT file for batch mode.
 PROCLEAVE=30K      Amount of memory to be reserved for procedures when an
                    out-of-memory condition has almost been reached.
 REGISTER=          Specify application (EXE, COM) to be launched from sas
                    AWS menu.
```

```
SET=(FT15F001 'FT15F001.DAT')
SET=(SASROOT c:\SAS)
SET=(SAMPSIO (                !sasroot\core\sample
                  !sasroot\base\sample
                  !sasroot\access\sample
                  !sasroot\af\sample
                  !sasroot\assist\sample
                  !sasroot\calc\sample
                  !sasroot\connect\sample
                  !sasroot\eis\sample
                  !sasroot\english\sample
                  !sasroot\ets\sample
                  !sasroot\fsp\sample
                  !sasroot\gis\sample
                  !sasroot\graph\sample
                  !sasroot\image\sample
                  !sasroot\iml\sample
                  !sasroot\insight\sample
                  !sasroot\lab\sample
                  !sasroot\look\sample
                  !sasroot\maps\sample
                  !sasroot\or\sample
                  !sasroot\phclin\sample
                  !sasroot\qc\sample
                  !sasroot\share\sample
                  !sasroot\stat\sample
                  !sasroot\toolkt\sample
                  !sasroot\trader\sample
                  !sasroot\usage\sample
                  !sasroot\test\sample        ))
SET=(SAMPSRC (                !sasroot\core\sample
                  !sasroot\base\sample
                  !sasroot\access\sample
                  !sasroot\af\sample
                  !sasroot\assist\sample
                  !sasroot\calc\sample
                  !sasroot\connect\sample
                  !sasroot\eis\sample
                  !sasroot\english\sample
                  !sasroot\ets\sample
                  !sasroot\fsp\sample
                  !sasroot\gis\sample
                  !sasroot\graph\sample
                  !sasroot\image\sample
                  !sasroot\iml\sample
                  !sasroot\insight\sample
                  !sasroot\lab\sample
                  !sasroot\look\sample
                  !sasroot\maps\sample
                  !sasroot\or\sample
                  !sasroot\phclin\sample
                  !sasroot\qc\sample
                  !sasroot\share\sample
                  !sasroot\stat\sample
                  !sasroot\toolkt\sample
                  !sasroot\trader\sample
                  !sasroot\usage\sample
                  !sasroot\test\sample        ))
SET=(INSTALL (                !sasroot\core\sastest
                  !sasroot\base\sastest
                  !sasroot\access\sastest
                  !sasroot\af\sastest
                  !sasroot\assist\sastest
                  !sasroot\calc\sastest
                  !sasroot\connect\sastest
                  !sasroot\eis\sastest
                  !sasroot\english\sastest
                  !sasroot\ets\sastest
                  !sasroot\fsp\sastest
                  !sasroot\gis\sastest
                  !sasroot\graph\sastest
                  !sasroot\image\sastest
                  !sasroot\iml\sastest
```

OPTIONS *continued*

```
                     !sasroot\insight\sastest
                     !sasroot\lab\sastest
                     !sasroot\look\sastest
                     !sasroot\maps\sastest
                     !sasroot\or\sastest
                     !sasroot\phclin\sastest
                     !sasroot\qc\sastest
                     !sasroot\share\sastest
                     !sasroot\stat\sastest
                     !sasroot\toolkt\sastest
                     !sasroot\trader\sastest
                     !sasroot\usage\sastest
                     !sasroot\test\sastest        ))
SET=(SASCBTA (                      !sasroot\sascbt
                     !sasroot\sascbt\cbt101
                     !sasroot\sascbt\cbt102
                     !sasroot\sascbt\cbt103
                     !sasroot\sascbt\cbt104
                     !sasroot\sascbt\cbt105
                     !sasroot\sascbt\cbt106       ))
                     Define the SAS system variable.
SETCOMM=             Source of comm port settings
SORTPGM=SAS          Name of sort program. (BEST, HOST or SAS)
STIMER               Print timing information after each step.
SYSIN=               Specify a batch mode SOURCE file.
SYSLEAVE=15K         Amount of memory to be reserved for system
                     out-of-memory condition.
SYSPRINT=(FILE: Adobe LaserJet II)
                     Specify file or device for printer.
TOOLDEF=(TOP RIGHT)
                     Toolbox display location.
USERICON=            Specify usericon resource file and maximum number of
                     usericons.
NOVERBOSE            Display the config options to the terminal.
WINCHARSET=ANSI      Specify the character set (OEM or ANSI) for Windows 3.x
                     to use.
XSYNC                Specify to run X command synchronously.
XWAIT                Specify that the X command is to wait.
$DEBUG XL_TRUNC
$STUBS

NOTE: The PROCEDURE OPTIONS used 6.82 seconds.
```

Note that the option values listed in Output 9.3 are examples only. The output of PROC OPTIONS depends on many things. Some option values depend on what method you use to run the SAS System. For example, the default line size under the SAS Display Manager System is 75 lines on a VGA display, while it is 132 lines in batch mode. Also, the way in which you have set up your process affects the default values of system options. For example, the default value of the SASAUTOS= option depends on where you store your autocall macros.

Using PROC OPTIONS, you can check the values of all system options. If you want more information on a particular Host option, use the HELP HOST command, or refer to Chapter 7, "SAS System Options" on page 173.

See Also

- Chapter 7, "SAS System Options" on page 173
- Chapter 22, "The OPTIONS Procedure," in the *SAS Procedures Guide, Version 6, Third Edition*
- Chapter 29, "The OPTIONS Procedure," in SAS Technical Report P-222, *Changes and Enhancements to Base SAS Software, Release 6.07*

PMENU

Defines PMENU facilities for windows created with SAS software

Windows NT specifics: ACCELERATE= option accepted for four key combinations

HELP PMENU

Windows NT Specifics

The PMENU procedure defines PMENU facilities for windows created by SAS applications. Under Windows NT, the ACCELERATE= option in the ITEM statement is accepted only for the following key combinations:

- Ctrl+C (COPY)
- Ctrl+V (PASTE)
- Ctrl+Z (UNDO)
- Ctrl+X (CUT).

You can use alternate key combinations if you want your program to be portable between Windows NT and OS/2. These alternate key combinations are the following:

- Ctrl+Insert
- Shift+Insert
- Alt+Backspace
- Shift+Delete.

If you use these alternate key combinations in your SAS program, the `Edit` menu shows the standard key combination; however, you can use either the standard or alternate key combination to activate the menu item.

See Also

- Chapter 26, "The PMENU Procedure," in the *SAS Procedures Guide, Version 6, Third Edition*
- Chapter 31, "The PMENU Procedure," in SAS Technical Report P-222, *Changes and Enhancements to Base SAS Software, Release 6.07*

PRINTTO

Defines destinations for SAS procedure output and the SAS log

Windows NT specifics: *destination*; UNIT= option

HELP PRINTTO

Windows NT Specifics

The specification of the output or log destination is system-dependent, as is the action of the UNIT= option.

destination
can be a fileref defined in a FILENAME statement, a quoted Windows NT pathname, or an environment variable. If the file specification you use is not a fileref defined by the FILENAME statement, the SET system option, or a Windows NT SET command, the destination is a file named *file-specification*.LST or *file-specification*.LOG stored in your working directory. To send your SAS output or log directly to the printer, use a FILENAME statement with the PRINTER device-type keyword. (See the first example in the next section.)

UNIT=*nn*
sends your SAS procedure output to the file FT*nn*F001.LST, where *nn* represents the UNIT= value, which can range from 1 to 99. The file is located in the SAS working directory.

Examples

The following statements redirect any SAS log entries generated after the RUN statement to an output file with a fileref of TEST, which is associated with the LPT1: device:

```
filename test printer 'lpt1:';

proc printto log=test;
run;
```

When these statements are issued, a dialog box is opened that informs you PROC PRINTTO is running. All SAS log entries are redirected to the TEST output file as specified; however, they are not printed on the LPT1: device until the output file is closed, either by redirecting the SAS log entries back to the default destination or to another file.

The following statements send any SAS log entries generated after the RUN statement to the external file associated with the fileref MYFILE:

```
filename myfile 'c:\mydir\mylog.log';

proc printto log=myfile;
run;
```

The following statements send any SAS procedure output to a file named MYPRINT.LST in your working directory (assuming MYPRINT is not a previously defined fileref or environment variable):

```
proc printto print=myprint;
run;
```

The following statements send any SAS procedure output to the printer port, which is usually defined by the system as LPT1:

```
proc printto print='lpt1:';
run;
```

The following statements (including a PROC PRINTTO statement with no options) redirect the SAS log and procedure output to the original default destinations:

```
proc printto;
run;
```

See Also

- □ Chapter 28, “The PRINTTO Procedure,” in the *SAS Procedures Guide, Version 6, Third Edition*
- □ Chapter 33, “The PRINTTO Procedure,” in SAS Technical Report P-222, *Changes and Enhancements to Base SAS Software, Release 6.07*

SORT

Sorts observations in a SAS data set by one or more variables, storing the resulting sorted observations in a new SAS data set or replacing the original data set

Windows NT specifics: sort utilities available; SORTSIZE= and TAGSORT statement options

HELP SORT

Windows NT Specifics

By default under Windows NT, the SORT procedure uses the ASCII collating sequence.

The SORT procedure uses the sort utility specified by the SORTPGM system option. Under Windows NT, although all three SORTPGM keywords (HOST, BEST, and SAS) are accepted for compatibility, the SAS sort is always used. You can use all the options available to the SAS sort utility, such as the SORTSEQ and NODUPKEY options. See the description of SORT procedure in Chapter 31, “The SORT Procedure,” of the *SAS Procedures Guide* for a complete list of all options available.

App4 For information on additional collating sequences supported under Windows NT, see “Sorting” on page 330.

SORT *continued*

SORTSIZE= Option

Under Windows NT, you can use the SORTSIZE= option in the PROC SORT statement to limit the amount of memory available to the SORT procedure. This option may reduce the amount of swapping the SAS System must do to sort the data set. If PROC SORT needs more memory than you specify, it creates a temporary utility file in your SASWORK directory to store the data in. The SORT procedure's algorithm can swap data more efficiently than Windows NT can.

The syntax of the SORTSIZE= option is as follows:

SORTSIZE=*n*|*n*K|*n*M

where

n specifies the amount of memory in bytes.

*n*K specifies the amount of memory in 1-kilobyte multiples.

*n*M specifies the amount of memory in 1-megabyte multiples.

By default, the CONFIG.SAS file sets this option to 1M using the SORTSIZE system option. A value of 1M or 2M is optimal for a machine with 6 megabytes of physical memory. If your machine has more than 6 megabytes of physical memory and you are sorting large data sets, setting the SORTSIZE= option to a value greater than 2M may improve performance.

You can override the default value of the SORTSIZE system option by specifying a different SORTSIZE= value in the PROC SORT statement, or by submitting an OPTIONS statement that sets the SORTSIZE system option to a new value.

The SORTSIZE= option is also discussed in "Improving Performance of the SORT Procedure" on page 295.

TAGSORT Option

The TAGSORT option in the PROC SORT statement is useful in situations where there may not be enough disk space to sort a large SAS data set. When you specify the TAGSORT option, only sort keys (that is, the variables specified in the BY statement) and the observation number for each observation are stored in the temporary files. The sort keys, together with the observation number, are referred to as tags. At the completion of the sorting process, the tags are used to retrieve the records from the input data set in sorted order. Thus, in cases where the total number of bytes of the sort keys is small compared with the length of the record, temporary disk use is reduced considerably. You should have enough disk space to hold another copy of the data (the output data set) or two copies of the tags, whichever is greater. Note that while using the TAGSORT option may reduce temporary disk use, the processing time may be much higher. However, on PCs with limited available disk space, the TAGSORT option may allow sorts to be performed in situations where they would otherwise not be possible.

Creating Your Own Collating Sequences

If you want to provide your own collating sequences or change a collating sequence that has been provided for you, use the TRANTAB procedure to create or modify translate tables. For complete details on the TRANTAB procedure, see SAS Technical Report P-197, *The TRANTAB Procedure, Release 6.06*, and Chapter 39, "The TRANTAB Procedure," in SAS Technical Report P-222, *Changes and Enhancements to Base SAS Software, Release 6.07*. When you create your own translate tables, they are stored in your PROFILE catalog and override any translate tables by the same name that are stored in the HOST catalog.

Note: System managers can modify the HOST catalog by copying newly created tables from the SASUSER.PROFILE catalog to the HOST catalog. Then all users can access the new or modified translate table.

If you want to see the names of the collating sequences stored in the HOST catalog and are using display manager, submit the following statement:

```
dm 'catalog sashelp.host' catalog;
```

SORT *continued*

Alternatively, you can select

Globals	▶	Data management}	▶	Catalog directory

from the pop-up menus. If you are not using display manager, you can use the following statements to generate a list of the contents of the HOST catalog:

```
proc catalog catalog=sashelp.host;
   contents;
run;
```

Entries of type TRANTAB are the collating sequences.

If you want to see the contents of a particular translate table, use the following statements:

```
proc trantab table=table-name;
   list;
run;
```

The contents of the collating sequence are displayed in the SAS log.

See Also

- □ SORTPGM system option on page 191
- □ "Improving Performance of the SORT Procedure" on page 295
- □ Appendix 4, "Moving Files Containing ANSI or OEM Characters between Windows NT, OS/2, and DOS" on page 323
- □ Chapter 10, "Working with Grouped or Sorted Observations," in *SAS Language and Procedures: Usage, Version 6, First Edition*
- □ Chapter 31, "The SORT Procedure," in the *SAS Procedures Guide, Version 6, Third Edition*
- □ SAS Technical Report P-197, *The TRANTAB Procedure, Release 6.07*
- □ Chapter 36, "The SORT Procedure," in SAS Technical Report P-222, *Changes and Enhancements to Base SAS Software, Release 6.07*

V5TOV6

Converts members of a SAS data library or a file of formats from Version 5 format to Version 6 format on the same operating system

Windows NT specifics: not supported

Windows NT Specifics

Operating systems that do not support Version 5 of the SAS System do not support this procedure. The V5TOV6 procedure is supported on the following operating systems: CMS, MVS, OpenVMS, and VSE.

See Also

- Chapter 43, "The V5TOV6 Procedure," in the *SAS Procedures Guide, Version 6, Third Edition*
- Chapter 40, "The V5TOV6 Procedure," in SAS Technical Report P-222, *Changes and Enhancements to Base SAS Software, Release 6.07*

Chapter 10 Other System-Dependent Features of the SAS® Language

Introduction

This chapter presents details on system-dependent features of the SAS language, such as functions, CALL routines, formats, and informats. It also discusses variable precision, the SAS macro facility, and system-dependent features of the SAS Display Manager System. Most of the information is in reference format, although some sections include examples.

Note: When you see the `App4` icon, be sure to read the appropriate section in Appendix 4 as well as the information provided in this chapter. You can ignore the icon if you do not need to move files between Microsoft Windows NT, OS/2, and DOS, or if your files do not contain national characters or graphics border characters.

System-Dependent Functions

This section describes functions available with the SAS System under Windows NT that are not described in Chapter 11, "SAS Functions," of *SAS Language: Reference, Version 6, First Edition*, as well as a few functions from *SAS Language Reference* that have system dependencies. The functions are listed alphabetically, and each includes a description that contains the following information:

- syntax
- help
- Windows NT specifics
- other information available.

If a function is also described in *SAS Language: Reference*, that information is not repeated here. Instead, there is a "Windows NT Specifics" section that gives the details on how the function behaves under Windows NT, and you are referred to Chapter 11 in *SAS Language: Reference.* You may also want to see Chapter 4, "SAS Functions," in SAS Technical Report P-222, *Changes and Enhancements to Base SAS Software, Release 6.07* and Chapter 1, "SAS Language," in SAS Technical Report P-242, *SAS Software: Changes and Enhancements, Release 6.08.*

BYTE

Returns one character in the ASCII collating sequence

HELP FUNCTIONS

Syntax

BYTE(*n*)

Windows NT Specifics

Because Windows NT is an ASCII system, the BYTE function returns the *n*th character in the ASCII collating sequence. The values of *n* can range from 0 to 255.

The character returned by the BYTE function depends on whether you are running the SAS System in OEM or ANSI mode. For more information on character sets under Windows NT, see the description of the WINCHARSET option on page 193 and Appendix 4.

Note: Any program using the BYTE function with characters above ASCII 127 (**'7F'x**) are not portable, because these are national characters and vary from country to country.

See Also

- Chapter 11, "SAS Functions," in *SAS Language: Reference, Version 6, First Edition*

COLLATE

Generates a collating sequence character string

HELP FUNCTIONS

Syntax

COLLATE(*start-pos*<,*end-pos*>)|(*start-pos*<,*length*>)

Windows NT Specifics

The COLLATE function returns a string of ASCII characters that range in value from 0 to 255. The string returned by the COLLATE function begins with the ASCII character specified by the *start-pos* argument. If the *end-pos* argument is specified, the string returned by the COLLATE function contains all the ASCII characters between the *start-pos* and *end-pos* arguments. If the *length* argument is specified instead of the *end-pos* argument, then the COLLATE function returns a string of length *length.* The returned string ends, or truncates, with the character having the value 255 if you request a string length that contains characters exceeding this value.

COLLATE *continued*

Unless you assign the return value of the COLLATE function to a variable with a length less than 200, the ASCII collating sequence string is padded with blanks to a length of 200. If you request more than 200 characters, the returned string is truncated to a length of 200.

The character string returned by the COLLATE function depends on whether you are running the SAS System in OEM or ANSI mode. For more information on character sets under Windows NT, see the descriptions of the WINCHARSET option on page 193 and in "Using the WINCHARSET System Option" on page 326.

App4 **Note:** Any program using the COLLATE function with characters above ASCII 127 (`'7F'x`) is not portable, because these are national characters and vary from country to country.

See Also

- □ Chapter 11, "SAS Functions," in *SAS Language: Reference, Version 6, First Edition*

DMYTECHC

Calculates the character count for a DataMyte packet

HELP HOST

Syntax

DMYTECHC('*string*')

Description

The DMYTECHC function accepts a text string as an argument and returns the character count for that string. This count represents the number of characters in the packet, excluding the STX (start-of-transmission) character, the character count itself, and the checksum. The return value is a 2-byte, hexadecimal number.

Example

Here is an example of using the DMYTECHC function. This example also uses the DMYTECKS CALL routine, which is described later in this chapter.

```
data dmyte1;
   length cs calccs $2;
   cs='00'x;
   stx='02'x;  /* This is the start-of-transmission character. */
   eot='04'x;  /* This is the end-of-transmission character. */
      /* The character count includes the text string and the EOT. */
   cmd='?SETUP'||eot;
   cc=dmytechc(cmd);
   put cc=;
   str=stx||cc||cmd;
```

```
      /* Call DMYTECKS to determine the checksum (CALCCS) */
      /* for the packet.                                  */
   call dmytecks(str,cs,calccs);
   put calccs=;
   dmytecmd=str||calccs;
run;
```

Next, you would send the value of the DMYTECMD variable to the DataMyte machine via the communications port.

See Also

- "DataMyte Processing" on page 168

DMYTECWD

Determines the total number of words in a DataMyte packet

HELP HOST

Syntax

DMYTECWD(*first-string,second-string*)

Description

The DMYTECWD function returns the number of tokens, or words, in a packet. Because data packets sent from DataMyte can be up to 256 characters long, but the SAS System can only process strings up to 200 characters long, you may have to break the packet up into two strings. *First-string* represents a less-than-200 character portion of the packet, while *second-string* represents the balance of the packet. Always break up the packet at a token delimiter, which is a semicolon (;). If the packet is 200 or less characters long, specify *second-string* as a null string (' ').

Both the *first-string* and *second-string* arguments can be a character variable, a character literal enclosed in quotes, or another character expression.

Example

Here is an example of using the DMYTECWD function. This program counts the words in the two character variables, FIRSTSTR and STR.

```
data dmyte2;
   length firststr str $ 200;
   firststr='07/16/83,14:00;M. Jones; Press 1;000;2.43;2.91;' ;
   str='2.83;2.80;';
   count=dmytecwd(firststr,str);
   put count=; /* This sample packet contains 18 words. */
run;
```

DMYTECWD *continued*

See Also

□ “DataMyte Processing” on page 168

DMYTERVC

Converts the DataMyte character count to an ASCII number

HELP HOST

Syntax

DMYTERVC(*hex-number*)

Description

The DMYTERVC function helps you convert a DataMyte character count, which is a 2-byte hexadecimal number, to an ASCII number. This number represents the number of characters the DataMyte is transmitting. This number does not include the STX (start-of-transmission) character, the 2-byte character count characters, or the 2-byte checksum.

Example

Here is an example of using the DMYTERVC function. The program uses the DMYTERVC function to calculate the character count. Once the character count is known, you can use it to process the incoming data, such as separate it into words and store those words in SAS variables.

```
data dmyte3;
   stx='02'x;  /* This is the start-of-transmission character. */
   infile 'com1:' lrecl=1 recfm=f;
   input x $char1.;
   if x eq stx then
      do;
         input cc $char2.;
         datacnt=dmytervc(cc);
      end;

      /* The character count tells us how many characters are in the   */
      /* packet being sent from the data collector (DATACNT is number   */
      /* of characters calculated by the DMYTERVC function.)            */
   do i = 1 to datacnt;
      index+1;
      input x $char1.;
      substr(str,index,1)=x;
```

```
      more data processing statements

   end;
run;
```

Some types of data you could expect in the packet include the date and time, identification information such as the name of the operator, and data values.

See Also

- "DataMyte Processing" on page 168

MCIPISLP

Causes the SAS System to wait for a piece of multimedia equipment to become active

HELP HOST

Syntax

MCIPISLP("*number-of-seconds*")

Description

The MCIPISLP function causes the SAS System to wait for a piece of multimedia equipment (such as a CD player or videodisc) to become active. This function is especially useful when you have used the MCIPISTR function to open a piece of equipment, but you know it is going to take a few seconds for the equipment to be ready.

The *number-of-seconds* argument must be an integer and represents how many seconds you want to wait.

The return value is the number of seconds slept.

The MCIPISLP function can be used in the DATA step and in SCL code.

Example

Here is an example that uses both the MCIPISTR and MCIPISLP functions to play a CD and a video. The PUT statements display the return values of these functions; this allows you to see in the SAS log whether there was a problem with any of your equipment.

```
data _null_;
      /* Open a CD player. */
   msg=mcipistr("open cdaudio alias mytunes");
   put msg=;

      /* Wait for the CD player to become active. */
   slept=mcipislp(1);

      /* Begin playing your favorite tunes from the beginning of the CD. */
   msg=mcipistr("play mytunes");
   put msg=;
```

MCIPISLP *continued*

```
      /* Now open a video file. */
   msg=mcipistr("open c:\movies\amovie.avs alias myshow");
   put msg=;

      /* Begin the show and wait for it to complete. */
   msg=mcipistr("play myshow wait");
   put msg=;

      /* When the show is complete, close the instance. */
   msg=mcipistr("close myshow");
   put msg=;

      /* Stop and close the instance of the CD player. */
   msg=mcipistr("stop mytunes");
   put msg=;

   msg=mcipistr("close mytunes");
   put msg=;
run;
```

MCIPISTR

Submits an MCI string command to a piece of multimedia equipment

HELP HOST

Syntax

MCIPISTR(*MCI-string-command*)

Description

The MCIPISTR function submits an MCI (Media Control Interface) string command. The *MCI-string-command* argument is any valid SAS string; that is, a character variable, a character literal enclosed in quotes, or another character expression.

You can use MCI to control many types of multimedia equipment, such as CD players, mixers, videodisc players, and so on. Windows NT provides MCI support; refer to your Win32 Software Development Kit documentation and your MCI-compliant device documentation for more information on valid MCI string commands.

The return value is a string that contains return information from the MCI string command. Examples of return information include "invalid instance" and "1".

The MCIPISTR function can be used in the DATA step and in SCL code.

Example

To use a CD player, you could submit the following statements in your DATA step:

```
msg=mcipistr("open cdaudio alias cd");
msg=mcipistr("play cd");
msg=mcipistr("stop cd");
msg=mcipistr("close cd");
```

See Also

□ MCIPISLP function

See Also

□ MCIPISTR function

RANK

Returns the position of a character in the ASCII collating sequence

HELP FUNCTIONS

Syntax

RANK(*x*)

Windows NT Specifics

Because Windows NT is an ASCII system, the RANK function returns an integer representing the position of a character in the ASCII collating sequence. The *x* argument must represent a character in the ASCII collating sequence. If the length of *x* is greater than 1, you receive the rank of the first character in the string.

The value returned by the RANK function depends on whether you are running the SAS System in OEM or ANSI mode. For more information on character sets under Windows NT, see the description of the WINCHARSET option on page 193 and Appendix 4.

Note: Any program using the RANK function with characters above ASCII 127 (**'7F'x**) are not portable, because these are national characters and vary from country to country.

See Also

□ Chapter 11, "SAS Functions," in *SAS Language: Reference, Version 6, First Edition*

SLEEP

Suspends execution of a SAS DATA step for a specified number of seconds

HELP HOST

Syntax

SLEEP(*x*)

Description

The SLEEP function suspends execution of a DATA step for a specified number of seconds. This function is useful for scheduling tasks, such as collecting data from the communications port.

The *x* argument is a numeric constant that must be greater than or equal to 0. Negative or missing values for *x* are invalid. The return value is the number of seconds slept. The maximum sleep period for the SLEEP function is approximately 46 days.

When you submit a program that calls the SLEEP function, a pop-up window appears telling you how long the SAS System is going to sleep. Your SAS session remains inactive until the sleep period is over. If you want to cancel the call to the SLEEP function, use the CTRL BREAK attention sequence.

You should use a null DATA step to call the SLEEP function; follow this DATA step with the rest of the SAS program. Using the SLEEP function in this manner enables you to use the CTRL BREAK attention sequence to interrupt the SLEEP function and continue with the execution of the rest of your SAS program.

Example

The SLEEP function is illustrated in the following example, which tells the SAS System to delay the execution of the program for 12 hours and 15 minutes:

```
data _null_;
   slept=sleep((60*60*12)+(60*15));
run;

data monthly;
   more SAS statements
run;
```

TRANSLATE

Replaces specific characters in a character expression

HELP FUNCTIONS

Syntax

TRANSLATE(*source,to-1,from-1*<, . . . *to-n,from-n*>)

Windows NT Specifics

Under Windows NT, you do not have to provide pairs of *to* and *from* arguments; however, if you do not use pairs, you must supply a comma as a place holder.

See Also

- Chapter 11, "SAS Functions," in *SAS Language: Reference, Version 6, First Edition*

WAKEUP

Specifies the time a SAS DATA step begins execution

HELP HOST

Syntax

WAKEUP(*x*)

Description

Use the WAKEUP function to specify the time a DATA step begins to execute. The return value is the number of seconds slept.

The *x* argument can be a SAS datetime value, a SAS time value, or a numeric constant, as explained in the following list:

- If *x* is a datetime value, the WAKEUP function sleeps until the specified date and time. If the specified date and time have already passed, the WAKEUP function does not sleep, and the return value is 0.
- If *x* is a time value, the WAKEUP function sleeps until the specified time. If the specified time has already passed in that 24-hour period, the WAKEUP function sleeps until the specified time occurs again.
- If *x* is a numeric constant, the WAKEUP function sleeps for that many seconds from the next occurring midnight. If the value of *x* is positive, the WAKEUP function sleeps for *x* seconds past midnight; if the value of *x* is negative, the WAKEUP function sleeps until *x* seconds before midnight.

Negative values for the *x* argument are allowed, but missing values are not. The maximum sleep period for the WAKEUP function is approximately 46 days.

When you submit a program that calls the WAKEUP function, a pop-up window appears telling you when the SAS System is going to wake up. Your SAS session remains inactive until the waiting period is over. If you want to cancel the call to the WAKEUP function, use the CTRL BREAK attention sequence.

You should use a null DATA step to call the WAKEUP function; follow this DATA step with the rest of the SAS program. Using the WAKEUP function in this manner enables

WAKEUP *continued*

you to use the CTRL BREAK attention sequence to interrupt the waiting period and continue with the execution of the rest of your SAS program.

Examples

The WAKEUP function is illustrated in the following example, which tells the SAS System to delay execution of the program until 1 p.m. on January 1, 1995:

```
data _null_;
   slept=wakeup('01JAN95:13:00:00'dt);
run;

data compare;
   more SAS statements
run;
```

The following example tells the SAS System to delay execution of the program until 10 p.m.:

```
data _null_;
   slept=wakeup("22:00:00"t);
run;

data compare;
   more SAS statements
run;
```

The following example tells the SAS System to delay execution of the program until 35 seconds after the next occurring midnight:

```
data _null_;
   slept=wakeup(35);
run;

data compare;
   more SAS statements
run;
```

The following example illustrates using a variable as the argument of the WAKEUP function:

```
data _null_;
   input x;
   slept=wakeup(x);
   cards;
1000
;
```

```
data compare;
   input article1 $ article2 $ rating;
   more SAS statements
run;
```

Because the instream data indicate that the value of X is 1000, the WAKEUP function sleeps for 1,000 seconds past midnight.

System-Dependent CALL Routines

This section describes the following CALL routines:

ANSI2OEM	OEM2ANSI	SYSTEM
DMYTECKS	SOUND	

The descriptions include the following information:

- syntax
- help
- Windows NT specifics
- other information available.

The CALL SYSTEM routine is also described in Chapter 12, "SAS CALL Routines," of *SAS Language: Reference*; this information is not repeated here. Instead, there is a "Windows NT Specifics" section that gives the details on how the routine behaves under Windows NT, and you are referred to Chapter 12 in *SAS Language: Reference.* You may also want to see Chapter 5, "SAS CALL Routines," in SAS Technical Report P-222.

ANSI2OEM

Translates a string of characters from the ANSI character set to the current OEM character set

HELP HOST

Syntax

ANSI2OEM(*string*,*dest*<,*length*>)

Description

The CALL ANSI2OEM routine translates a string of characters from the ANSI character set to the current OEM character set. The OEM character set is determined by the OEM codepage in effect. The following list explains the arguments to this CALL routine:

ANSI2OEM *continued*

string
is the character string to be translated. This argument can be a character variable, a character literal enclosed in quotes, or another character expression.

dest
is the variable that stores the translation result. Note that because this is a SAS character variable, any result longer than 200 characters is truncated.

If you do not specify the *length* argument, and the length of *string* is greater than the length of *dest*, you receive an error message and the translation does not complete.

length
is an optional argument that specifies the length of the string to be translated. If you do not specify *length*, all of the characters contained in the *string* argument are translated. If *length* is greater than the length of *string*, you receive an error message and the translation does not complete. Likewise, if you specify a length greater than the length of the *dest* variable, you receive an error message and the translation does not complete. The value of *length* must be positive.

The CALL ANSI2OEM routine is useful in cases where you are accessing data that are in ANSI format, and you are running the SAS System in OEM mode. For more information on ANSI versus OEM character sets, see Appendix 4, "Moving Files Containing ANSI or OEM Characters between Windows NT, OS/2, and DOS" on page 323.

Examples

The following example translates the three characters `abc` from the ANSI character set to the current OEM character set:

```
data _null_;
   length dest $3;
   call ansi2oem('abc',dest,3);
run;
```

The following example translates the single hexadecimal character `FF` from the ANSI character set to the current OEM character set:

```
data _null_;
   length dest $1;
   call ansi2oem('FF'x,dest,1);
run;
```

See Also

- Appendix 4, "Moving Files Containing ANSI or OEM Characters between Windows NT, OS/2, and DOS" on page 323

DMYTECKS

Calculates the checksum (exclusive OR) of all the characters in a DataMyte packet, excluding the checksum itself

HELP HOST

Syntax

DMYTECKS(*string,initial-cks,calculated-cks*)

Description

The CALL DMYTECKS routine calculates the checksum for a packet. The checksum is the exclusive OR (XOR) of all the characters in the packet (including the start-of-text character, the character count, and end-of-transmission character) excluding the checksum itself.

The CALL DMYTECKS routine takes three arguments:

string
: is the string for which the checksum is calculated. This argument can be a character variable, a character literal enclosed in quotes, or another character expression. A DataMyte can transmit a string consisting of up to 256 characters.

initial-cks
: is the initial checksum value. This value is **'00'x** if the string is under 200 characters.

Because the length of SAS character variables is limited to 200, if you want to calculate the checksum for a packet that is longer than 200 characters you have to call the CALL DYMTECKS routine twice. Call it once for the first 200 characters of the packet. Then pass the remaining characters to the CALL DYMTECKS routine and use the calculated checksum from the first call as the initial checksum value for the second call.

calculated-cks
: is the calculated checksum for *string*. This value is a 2-byte hexadecimal number.

For more information on DataMyte processing, see "DataMyte Processing" on page 168 and your DataMyte documentation.

Example

```
data _null_;
   length string1 string2 $200 checksm1 checksm2 calc_cs1 calc_cs2 $2;
      /* The string received from the DataMyte is longer than 200 */
      /* characters, so it is split into two strings, STRING1 and */
      /* STRING2. However, you must calculate the checksum for    */
      /* the entire string (STRING1||STRING2).                    */

      /* SAS statements reading in data from DataMyte until  */
      /* EOT is found.                                        */

   checksm1='00'x;   /* Initialize the first checksum.            */
```

DMYTECKS *continued*

```
      call dmytecks(string1,checksm1,calc_cs1);
      checksm2=calc_cs1;
      call dmytecks(string2,checksm2,calc_cs2);
   run;
```

The final checksum value is stored in CALC_CS2.

See Also

□ "DataMyte Processing" on page 168

OEM2ANSI

Translates a string of characters from the current OEM character set to the ANSI character set

HELP HOST

Syntax

OEM2ANSI(*string*,*dest*<,*length*>)

Description

The CALL OEM2ANSI routine translates a string of characters from the current OEM character set (determined from the OEM codepage in use) to the ANSI character set. The following list explains the arguments to this CALL routine:

string
: is the character string to be translated. This argument can be a character variable, a character literal enclosed in quotes, or another character expression.

dest
: is the variable that stores the translation result. Note that because this is a SAS character variable, any result longer than 200 characters is truncated.

  If you do not specify the *length* argument, and the length of *string* is greater than the length of *dest*, you receive an error message and the translation does not complete.

length
: is an optional argument that specifies the length of the string to be translated. If you do not specify *length*, all of the characters contained in the *string* argument are translated. If *length* is greater than the length of *string*, you receive an error message and the translation does not complete. Likewise, if you specify a length greater than the length of the *dest* variable, you receive an error message and the translation does not complete. The value of *length* must be positive.

The CALL OEM2ANSI routine is useful in cases where you are accessing data that are in OEM format, and you are running the SAS System in ANSI mode. For more information on ANSI versus OEM character sets, see Appendix 4.

Examples

The following example translates the three characters `abc` from the OEM character set to the ANSI character set:

```
data _null_;
   length dest $3;
   call oem2ansi('abc',dest,3);
run;
```

The following example translates the single hexadecimal character `FF` from the OEM character set to the ANSI character set:

```
data _null_;
   length dest $1;
   call oem2ansi('FF'x,dest,1);
run;
```

See Also

□ Appendix 4, "Moving Files Containing ANSI or OEM Characters between Windows NT, OS/2, and DOS" on page 323

SOUND

Generates a sound

HELP FUNCTIONS

Syntax

SOUND(*frequency,duration*)

Description

The CALL SOUND routine generates a sound of the desired frequency and duration. Frequency is specified in cycles per second by the *frequency* argument and duration is specified in 1/80ths of a second by the *duration* argument. The frequency must be within the range 20 ≤ *frequency* ≤ 20000.

SOUND *continued*

Example

The following statement produces a tone of frequency 523 cycles per second (middle C) lasting two seconds:

```
data _null_;
   call sound(523,160);
run;
```

SYSTEM

Issues operating system commands

HELP SYSTEM

Syntax

SYSTEM(*command*)

Windows NT Specifics

The CALL SYSTEM routine issues operating system commands. The *command* argument can be any of the following:

- an operating system command or the name of a Windows NT application enclosed in quotes
- an expression whose value is an operating system command or the name of a Windows NT application
- the name of a character variable whose value is an operating system command or the name of a Windows NT application.

In display manager, the command executes in a command prompt window. By default, you must type EXIT to return to your SAS session.

Comparison

The CALL SYSTEM routine is similar to the X command; however, the CALL SYSTEM routine is callable and can therefore be executed conditionally. An example of using the CALL SYSTEM routine is given in "Executing Operating System Commands Conditionally" on page 22.

The values of the XSYNC and XWAIT system options affect how the CALL SYSTEM routine works. For more information on these options see Chapter 1 and Chapter 7.

Example

Here is an example of using the CALL SYSTEM routine to obtain a directory listing:

```
data _null_;
   call system('dir /w');
run;
```

In this example, the /W option for the DIR command instructs Windows NT to print the directory in the wide format instead of a vertical list form.

See Also

- □ "Executing Operating System Commands Conditionally" on page 22
- □ XSYNC and XWAIT system options on page 23 and page 23, respectively
- □ Chapter 12, "SAS CALL Routines," in *SAS Language: Reference, Version 6, First Edition*

System-Dependent Informats and Formats

This section describes informats and formats that either are specific to Windows NT or have operating system dependencies. First, considerations for reading and writing binary data are given. Next, system-dependent informats and formats are described. This section closes with a discussion of storing user-written informats and formats under Windows NT.

For information on portable SAS informats and formats, see Chapter 13, "SAS Informats," and Chapter 14, "SAS Formats," in *SAS Language: Reference*; Chapters 6 and 7 in SAS Technical Report P-222; and Chapter 1, "SAS Language," in SAS Technical Report P-242.

Reading and Writing Binary Data

Different computers store numeric binary data in different forms. IBM 370, Hewlett-Packard 9000, Data General ECLIPSE, and Prime computers store bytes in one order. IBM-compatible microcomputers and some computers manufactured by Digital Equipment Corporation store bytes in a different order called byte-reversed. The SAS System provides a number of informats for reading binary data and corresponding formats for writing binary data. Some of these informats and formats read and write data in native mode, that is, using the byte-ordering system that is standard for the machine. Other informats and formats force the data to be read and written by the IBM 370 standard, regardless of the native mode of the machine. The informats and formats that read and write in native mode are IB*w.d*, PD*w.d*, PIB*w.d*, and RB*w.d*. The informats and formats that read and write in IBM 370 mode are S370FIB*w.d*, S370FPD*w. d*, S370FRB*w.d*, and S370FPIB*w.d*.

If a SAS program that reads and writes binary data runs on only one type of machine, you can use the native mode informats and formats. However, if you want to write SAS programs that can be run on multiple machines using different byte-storage systems, use the IBM 370 formats and informats. The purpose of the IBM 370 informats and formats is to enable you to write SAS programs that can be run in any SAS environment, no matter what the standard for storing numeric data.

For example, suppose you have a program that writes data with the PIB*w.d* format. You execute the program on a microcomputer so the data are stored in byte-reversed mode. Then you run another SAS program on the microcomputer that uses the PIB*w.d* informat to read the data. The data are read correctly because both the programs are run on the microcomputer, using byte-reversed mode. However, you cannot upload the data to a Hewlett-Packard 9000-series machine and read the data correctly because they are stored in a form native to the microcomputer, but foreign to the Hewlett-Packard 9000. To avoid this problem, use the S370FPIB*w.d* format to write the data; even on the microcomputer, this causes the data to be stored in IBM 370 mode. Then read the data using the S370FPIB*w.d* informat. Regardless of what type of machine you use when reading the data, they are read correctly.

Informats

The following informats have system dependencies:

HEX*w.*
$HEX*w.*
IB*w.d*
PD*w.d*
PIB*w.d*
RB*w.d*
ZD*w.d*

Each informat description includes the details for that informat in the Windows NT environment, as well as pointers to other sources of information.

HEX*w.*

Converts hexadecimal positive binary values to fixed-point or floating-point binary values

Numeric

Width range: 1–16

Default width: 8

HELP INFORMAT

Windows NT Specifics

The HEX*w.* informat converts the hexadecimal representation of positive binary values to floating-point binary values. The *w* value of the HEX*w.* informat determines whether the input represents an integer (fixed-point) or real (floating-point) binary number. When you specify a *w* value of 1 through 15, the input hexadecimal value represents an integer binary number. When you specify 16 for the *w* value, the input hexadecimal value represents a floating-point value.

The HEX*w.* informat expects input that is not byte-reversed, that is, not in Windows NT form. (The IB*w.*, PIB*w.*, and RB*w.* informats for binary numbers expect the bytes to be reversed.) This means you can use the HEX*w.* informat to read hex literals from SAS programs created in another environment.

See Also

□ Chapter 13, "SAS Informats," in *SAS Language: Reference, Version 6, First Edition*

$HEX*w.*

Converts hexadecimal data to character data

Character

Width range: 1–200

Default width: 2

HELP INFORMAT

Windows NT Specifics

The $HEX*w*. informat is like the HEX*w*. informat in that it reads values in which each hexadecimal digit occupies 1 byte. Use the $HEX*w*. informat to encode hexadecimal information into a character variable when your input data are limited to printable characters. The conversion is based on the ASCII character set.

See Also

□ Chapter 13, "SAS Informats," in *SAS Language: Reference, Version 6, First Edition*

IB*w.d*

Reads integer binary (fixed-point) data

Numeric

Width range: 1–8

Default width: 4

HELP INFORMAT

Windows NT Specifics

The IB*w.d* informat reads fixed-point binary values. For integer binary data, the high-order bit is the value's sign: 0 for positive values, 1 for negative. Negative values are represented in twos complement notation. If the informat includes a *d* value, the data value is divided by 10^d. The decimal range is 0 through 10.

Here is an example using the IB*w.d* informat. Suppose your data contain the following 6-byte (byte-swapped) value:

```
64 00 00 00 00 00
```

If you read this value using the IB6. informat, it is read as the fixed-point value 100.0. Suppose your data contain the following (byte-swapped) value:

IB*w.d* *continued*

```
01 80
```

Because the sign bit is set, the value is read as −32,767. Using this informat requires you to understand twos complements and byte-swapped data format. See "Reading and Writing Binary Data" on page 261 for more information on this informat. See Intel Corporation's *i486 Microprocessor Programmer's Reference Manual* for more information on microcomputer fixed-point values.

Comparison

The IB*w.d* informat and the PIB*w.d* informat give you different results, and you should differentiate carefully between these two informats. The IB*w.d* informat processes both positive and negative numbers and uses the high-order bit as the sign bit. In contrast, the PIB*w.d* informat is used only for positive numbers and does not look for a sign bit. As an example, suppose your data contain the following two-byte (byte-swapped) value:

```
01 80
```

When you read this value using the IB2. informat, the informat looks for the sign bit, sees that it is on, and reads the value as −32,767. However, if you read this value with the PIB2. informat, no sign bit is used, and the result is 32,769.

See Also

□ Chapter 13, "SAS Informats," in *SAS Language: Reference, Version 6, First Edition*

PD*w.d*

Reads packed decimal data

Numeric

Width range: 1–16

Default width: 1

HELP INFORMAT

Windows NT Specifics

The PD*w.d* informat reads packed decimal data. Each byte contains two digits in packed decimal data. The value's sign is in the first bit of the first byte (although the entire first byte is used for the sign). Although it is usually impossible to key in packed decimal data directly from a terminal, many programs write packed decimal data. The decimal range is 1 through 31.

Here is an example using the PD*w.d* informat. Suppose your data contain the following packed decimal number:

```
80 00 11 43
```

If you use the PD4. informat, this value is read as the double-precision value −1143.0. Similarly, the following value is read as 1500.0:

```
00 00 15 00
```

See Also

□ Chapter 13, "SAS Informats," in *SAS Language: Reference, Version 6, First Edition*

PIB*w.d*

Reads positive integer binary (fixed-point) data

Numeric

Width range: 1–8

Default width: 1

HELP INFORMAT

Windows NT Specifics

The PIB*w.d* informat reads integer binary (fixed-point) values. Positive integer binary values are the same as integer binary (see the IB*w.d* informat), except that all values are treated as positive. Thus, the high-order bit is part of the value rather than the value's sign. If the informat includes a *d* value, the data value is divided by 10^d. The decimal range is 0 through 10.

Here is an example using the PIB*w.d* informat. Suppose your data contain the following one-byte value:

```
FF
```

If you read this value using the PIB1. informat, it is read as the double-precision value 255.0. Using this informat requires you to understand twos complements and byte-swapped data format. See "Reading and Writing Binary Data" on page 261 for more information on this informat.

Comparison

The PIB*w.d* informat and the IB*w.d* informat give you different results, and you should differentiate carefully between these two informats. The IB*w.d* informat processes both positive and negative numbers and uses the high-order bit as the sign bit. In contrast, the PIB*w.d* informat is used only for positive numbers and does not look for a sign bit. As an example, suppose your data contain the following two-byte (byte-swapped) value:

```
01 80
```

When you read this value using the IB2. informat, the informat looks for the sign bit, sees that it is on, and reads the value as −32,767. However, if you read this value with the PIB2. informat, no sign bit is used, and the result is 32,769.

PIB*w.d* *continued*

See Also

- □ Chapter 13, "SAS Informats," in *SAS Language: Reference, Version 6, First Edition*

RB*w.d*

Reads real binary (floating-point) data

Numeric

Width range: 2–8

Default width: 4

HELP INFORMAT

Windows NT Specifics

The RB*w.d* informat reads numeric data that are stored in microcomputer real binary (floating-point) notation. Numeric data for scientific calculations are often stored in floating-point notation. (The SAS System stores all numeric values in floating-point notation.) A floating-point value consists of two parts, a mantissa giving the value and an exponent giving the value's magnitude. It is usually impossible to key in floating-point binary data directly from a terminal, but many programs write floating-point binary data. The decimal range for this informat is 0 through 10.

See "Reading and Writing Binary Data" on page 261 for more information on this informat.

See Also

- □ Chapter 13, "SAS Informats," in *SAS Language: Reference, Version 6, First Edition*

ZD*w.d*

Reads zoned decimal data

Numeric

Width range: 1–32

Default width: 1

HELP INFORMAT

Windows NT Specifics

The ZD*w.d* informat reads zoned decimal data. This is also known as an overprint trailing numeric format. Under Windows NT, the last byte of the field contains the sign information of the number. The conversion table for the last byte is as follows:

Digit	ASCII Character	Digit	ASCII Character
0	{	−0	}
1	A	−1	J
2	B	−2	K
3	C	−3	L
4	D	−4	M
5	E	−5	N
6	F	−6	O
7	G	−7	P
8	H	−8	Q
9	I	−9	R

See Also

□ Chapter 13, "SAS Informats," in *SAS Language: Reference, Version 6, First Edition*

Formats

The following formats have special considerations when used under Windows NT:

HEX*w.*
$HEX*w.*
IB*w.d*
PD*w.d*
PIB*w.d*
RB*w.d*
ZD*w.d*

Each format description includes the details for that format in the Windows NT environment, as well as pointers to other sources of information.

HEX*w.*

Converts real binary (floating-point) values to hexadecimal values

Numeric Width range: 1–16

Default width: 8

Alignment: left

HELP FORMAT

Windows NT Specifics

The HEX*w*. format converts a real binary (floating-point) number to its hexadecimal representation. When you specify a *w* value of 1 through 15, the real binary number is truncated to a fixed-point integer before being converted to hex notation. When you specify 16 for the *w* value, the floating-point value of the number is used; in other words, the number is not truncated.

See Also

□ Chapter 14, "SAS Formats," in *SAS Language: Reference, Version 6, First Edition*

$HEX*w.*

Converts character values to hexadecimal values

Character

Width range: 1–200

Default width: 4

Alignment: left

HELP FORMAT

Windows NT Specifics

The $HEX*w*. format is like the HEX*w*. format in that it converts a character value to hexadecimal notation, with each byte requiring two columns. Under Windows NT, the $HEX*w*. format produces hex representations of ASCII codes for characters.

See Also

□ Chapter 14, "SAS Formats," in *SAS Language: Reference, Version 6, First Edition.*

IB*w.d*

Writes integer binary (fixed-point) numbers

Numeric

Width range: 1–8

Default width: 4

Alignment: left

HELP FORMAT

Windows NT Specifics

The IB*w.d* format converts a double-precision number and writes it as an integer binary (fixed-point) value. Integers are stored in integer-binary, or fixed-point, form. If the format includes a *d* value, the data value is multiplied by 10^{d}. The decimal range is 0 through 10. See "Reading and Writing Binary Data" on page 261 for more information on this format. See Intel Corporation's *i486 Microprocessor Programmer's Reference Manual* for more information on microcomputer fixed-point values.

Here are two examples to help you understand how the IB*w.d* format works.

Processing a Positive Number

If you format 1.0 as the double-precision number, it is stored as an integer, like so:

```
01 00 00 00 00 00 00 00
```

(Remember, Windows NT stores binary data in byte-reversed order.) The value written depends on the *w* value you specify. Suppose you specify IB4. Then you receive the following value:

```
01 00 00 00
```

If you specify IB2., you receive

```
01 00
```

Processing a Negative Number

If you try to format −1 with the IB4., you see the following value:

```
FF FF FF FF
```

If you specify IB2., you receive

```
FF FF
```

IB*w.d* *continued*

See Also

□ Chapter 14, "SAS Formats," in *SAS Language: Reference, Version 6, First Edition*

PD*w.d*

Writes packed decimal data

Numeric

Width range: 1–16

Default width: 1

Alignment: left

HELP FORMAT

Windows NT Specifics

The PD*w.d* format writes double-precision numbers in packed decimal format. In packed decimal data, each byte contains two digits. The *w* value represents the number of bytes, not the number of digits. The value's sign is in the uppermost bit of the first byte (although the entire first byte is used for the sign). If the format includes a *d* value, the data value is multiplied by 10^d. See "Reading and Writing Binary Data" on page 261 for more information on this format. The decimal range is 1 through 31.

As an example, suppose you want to process the number 1143.0. If you specify PD2., you get the following value:

```
00 43
```

If you specify PD4., you get the following value:

```
00 00 11 43
```

As an example of a negative number, suppose you want to process −1143.0. If you specify PD2., you get

```
80 43
```

If you specify PD4., you get

```
80 00 11 43
```

See Also

□ Chapter 14, "SAS Formats," in *SAS Language: Reference, Version 6, First Edition*

PIB*w.d*

Writes positive integer binary data

Numeric

Width range: 1–8

Default width: 1

Alignment: left

HELP FORMAT

Windows NT Specifics

The PIB*w.d* format converts a fixed-point value to an integer binary value. If the fixed-point value is negative, the integer representation for −1 is written. If a *d* value is specified, the data value is multiplied by 10^d. See Intel Corporation's *i486 Microprocessor Programmer's Reference Manual* for more information on microcomputer fixed-point values. The decimal range is 0 through 10.

See Also

□ Chapter 14, "SAS Formats," in *SAS Language: Reference, Version 6, First Edition*

RB*w.d*

Writes real binary (floating-point) data

Numeric

Width range: 2–8

Default width: 4

Alignment: left

HELP FORMAT

Windows NT Specifics

The RB*w.d* format writes numeric data in real binary (floating-point) notation. Numeric data for scientific calculations are commonly represented in floating-point notation. (The SAS System stores all numeric values in floating-point notation.) A floating-point value consists of two parts, a mantissa giving the value and an exponent giving the value's magnitude. If the format includes a *d* value, the data value is multiplied by 10^d. The decimal range is 0 through 10.

RB*w.d* *continued*

Real binary is the most efficient format for representing numeric values because the SAS System already represents numbers this way and no conversion is needed. See "Reading and Writing Binary Data" on page 261 for more information on this format. See Intel Corporation's *i486 Microprocessor Programmer's Reference Manual* for more information on Windows NT floating-point notation.

See Also

□ Chapter 14, "SAS Formats," in *SAS Language: Reference, Version 6, First Edition*

ZD*w.d*

Writes zoned decimal data

Numeric

Width range: 1–32

Default width: 1

Alignment: left

HELP FORMAT

Windows NT Specifics

The ZD*w.d* format writes zoned decimal data. This is also known as an overprint trailing numeric format. In the Windows NT environment, the last byte of the field contains the sign information of the number. The conversion table for the last byte is as follows:

Digit	ASCII Character	Digit	ASCII Character
0	{	−0	}
1	A	−1	J
2	B	−2	K
3	C	−3	L
4	D	−4	M
5	E	−5	N
6	F	−6	O
7	G	−7	P
8	H	−8	Q
9	I	−9	R

See Also

- Chapter 14, "SAS Formats," in *SAS Language: Reference, Version 6, First Edition*

User-Written Informats and Formats

This section discusses creating Release 6.09 user-written informats and formats. It also describes what you must do to convert user-written informats and formats created in Release 6.04, Release 6.06, Release 6.08, and Version 5 to their Release 6.09 counterparts.

Creating Release 6.09 User-Written Informats and Formats

To create user-written informats and formats in Release 6.09, use the FORMAT procedure. The FORMAT procedure creates two kinds of formats:

- value formats that display output values in a different form (for example, displaying a numeric value as a character value). The VALUE statement generates value formats.

  For example, the following VALUE statement defines a format named TYPE. that displays numeric variable values as character values. Variable values written with the TYPE. format are stored as numbers (1 or 2) but displayed as character values (`DRAFT` or `PONY`):

  ```
  value type 1='DRAFT' 2='PONY';
  ```

- picture formats that specify templates for printing numbers, giving specifics such as leading zeros, decimal and comma punctuation, fill characters, prefixes, and negative number representation. Only numeric variables can have picture formats.

The FORMAT procedure also produces informats. Informats are especially useful when you want to transform the input data into more meaningful values. Value informats read variables and transform them into another value: character to numeric or character string to a different character string. The INVALUE statement generates value informats.

The INVALUE statement below defines an informat TYPE. that transforms a character variable's value to a numeric value. For instance, when the value of the variable read with the TYPE. informat is `DRAFT`, the variable's value is converted to 1:

```
invalue type 'DRAFT'=1 'PONY'=2;
```

The following INVALUE statement defines an informat that substitutes one character string for another. For instance, when the value of the variable read with the $FRENCH. informat is `OUI`, the variable's value is transformed to `YES`:

```
invalue $french 'OUI'='YES' 'NON'='NO';
```

User-written formats and informats are stored in a type of SAS file called a catalog. A catalog containing formats or informats has FORMATS as its second-level SAS name. You can have only one catalog named FORMATS in a SAS data library.

A catalog is composed of entries; an informat or format can be an entry. The names of informat or format entries in a catalog are identified by the informat name that is assigned with an INVALUE statement for informats and the format name that is assigned with either a PICTURE or VALUE statement for formats. The entry types of user-written informats are

INFMT (numeric) and INFMTC (character). The entry types of user-written formats are FORMAT (numeric) and FORMATC (character).

User-written informats and formats are either temporary or permanent, depending on whether they are stored in a temporary or permanent catalog. You can use temporary informats and formats only in the same SAS job or session in which they are created. Permanent informats and formats can be used in the job or session that creates them and in subsequent SAS jobs and sessions.

Formats and informats are temporary when you do not specify the LIBRARY= option in the PROC FORMAT statement because they are stored in your WORK data library in a temporary catalog, FORMATS.SC2. To retrieve a temporary format for writing a variable value, simply include the format's name in the appropriate SAS statement. The SAS System automatically looks for the format in the temporary catalog in the WORK data library.

For information on creating permanent informats and formats, see the description of the FORMAT procedure and the FMTSEARCH system option in SAS Technical Report P-222 and Chapter 18, "The FORMAT Procedure," in the *SAS Procedures Guide, Version 6, Third Edition.*

Converting User-Written Informats and Formats from Earlier Releases to Release 6.09

You must convert Release 6.04, Release 6.06, and Release 6.08 user-written informats and formats to their Release 6.09 counterparts before you can use them in a Release 6.09 SAS program. The only exception to this rule is user-written informats and formats created by Release 6.08 under OS/2; these informats and formats can be read directly from your Windows NT SAS session.*

Converting Version 6 user-written informats and formats

You can convert Release 6.04, 6.06, and 6.08 SAS catalogs containing user-written informats and formats using one of the following methods:

for converting Release 6.04 catalogs
: use the CNTLOUT= option in the PROC FORMAT statement in Release 6.04 to create an output data set and then use the CNTLIN= option in the PROC FORMAT statement in Release 6.09 to create the Release 6.09 informats or formats. You must use the V604 engine in your Release 6.09 SAS session to read the data set. This method also works for converting from Release Release 6.06 or Release 6.08.

for converting Release 6.06 or Release 6.08 catalogs
: use the CPORT and CIMPORT procedures to convert the informats and formats. For more information on these procedures, see Chapter 16, "The CPORT Procedure," and Chapter 10, "The CIMPORT Procedure," in the *SAS Procedures Guide*, as well as Chapters 19 and 22 in SAS Technical Report P-222. This method works for converting from Release 6.06 or Release 6.08 only; it does not work for converting from Release 6.04.

---

* However, it is recommended that you use PROC CPORT and CIMPORT to convert Release 6.08 OS/2 catalogs containing user-written informats and formats to Release 6.09 if you no longer need to use them in Release 6.08.

Converting Version 5 user-written informats and formats

You must also convert Version 5 user-written informats and formats to their Release 6.09 counterparts before you can use them in a Release 6.09 SAS program. (This implies that you are not only converting these files, but are also transferring them from a remote operating system to your PC). You can convert them using one of the following methods:

- □ Use the V5TOV6 procedure on the remote operating system to convert the informats and formats to Version 6 format. This implies that the remote operating system has access to Version 6 SAS software. Then, transport the converted informats and formats to your Windows NT machine and use the CIMPORT procedure to complete the conversion. For more information on the V5TOV6 procedure, refer to Chapter 43 in the *SAS Procedures Guide.*
- □ Use the SUGI supplemental procedure FMTLIB under Version 5 on the remote operating system to create an output data set, transport that data set to your PC, and then use the CNTLIN= option in the PROC FORMAT statement in Release 6.09 to create the Release 6.09 informats or formats.

Variable Precision and Storage Information

This section discusses variable precision under Windows NT and storage of numeric and character variable values. Note that the issue of numeric precision affects the return values of almost all SAS System math functions and many numeric values returned from SAS System procedures.

Note: The words CON and NUL are reserved words under Windows NT. Do not use CON or NUL as the name of a variable.

Numeric Variables

The default length of numeric variables in SAS data sets is 8 bytes. (You can control the length of SAS numeric variables with the LENGTH statement in the DATA step.) In the SAS System under Windows NT, the Windows NT data type of numeric values that have a length of 8 is LONG REAL. The precision of this type of floating-point values is 16 decimal digits. See Intel Corporation's *i486 Microprocessor Programmer's Reference Manual* for more information about the representation of the LONG REAL Windows NT data type.

Table 10.1 specifies the significant digits and largest integer that can be stored in SAS numeric variables.

Table 10.1 *Significant Digits and Largest Integer by Length for SAS Variables under Windows NT*

Length in Bytes	Largest Integer Represented Exactly	Exponential Notation
3	8,192	2^{13}
4	2,097,152	2^{21}
5	536,870,912	2^{29}
6	137,438,953,472	2^{37}
7	35,184,372,088,832	2^{45}
8	9,007,199,254,740,992	2^{53}

For example, if you know that a numeric variable always has values between 0 and 100, you can use a length of 3 to store the number and thus save space in your data set. Here is an example:

```
data mydata;
   length num 3;
   more SAS statements
run;
```

Note: *Dummy variables* (those whose only purpose is to hold 0 or 1) can be stored in a variable whose length is 3 bytes.

Use the 3-byte limit for only those variables whose values are small, preferably integers. If the value of a variable becomes large or has many significant digits, you may lose precision during arithmetic calculations if the length of a variable is less than 8 bytes. ■

The maximum number of variables in a single SAS data set under Windows NT is 32,767. In addition, an observation under Windows NT cannot be longer than 1M. Therefore, if you use the default length of 8 bytes for your numeric variables, you can have up to 4,095 variables.

However, a DATA step can reference more than 32,767 variables, if you write only 32,767 or less variables to the data set. For example, you could drop some variables with a DROP= data set option. The maximum number of variables a DATA step can reference under Windows NT is 2,147,483,647.

Character Variables

In the SAS System under Windows NT, character values are sorted using the ASCII collating sequence. As an alternative to the numeric dummy variables discussed previously, you can choose a character variable with a length of 1 byte to serve the same purpose.

The maximum number of variables in a single SAS data set under Windows NT is 32,767. In addition, an observation under Windows NT cannot be longer than 1M. Therefore, if you want your data set to contain 32,767 character variables, the longest each variable can be is 32 bytes.

However, a DATA step can reference more than 32,767 variables, if you write only 32,767 or less variables to the data set. For example, you could drop some variables with a DROP= data set option. The maximum number of variables a DATA step can reference under Windows NT is 2,147,483,647.

SAS Macro Facility

In general, the SAS macro language is portable and is documented in the *SAS Guide to Macro Processing, Version 6, Second Edition.* This section discusses those components of the macro facility that have system dependencies. You can get online help for the macro facility by selecting the SAS Language item from the SAS System HELP window and then selecting the SAS Macro Facility item. You may also want to refer to Chapter 41, "Macro Language Features" in SAS Technical Report P-222.

Note: The words CON and NUL are reserved words under Windows NT. Do not use CON or NUL as the name of a macro variable.

Automatic Macro Variables

The following automatic macro variables have system dependencies:

SYSDEVIC
: gives the name of the current graphics device. The current graphics device is determined by the DEVICE system option. Contact your system manager to determine which graphics devices are available at your site. (See page 181 and Chapter 16, "SAS System Options," in *SAS Language: Reference* for information about the DEVICE system option.)

SYSENV
: always contains the value `FORE` under Windows NT.

SYSJOBID
: returns a number that uniquely identifies the SAS task under Windows NT.

SYSRC
: holds the Windows NT status of Windows NT commands executed during your SAS session. The variable holds a character string that is the text form of the decimal value of the Windows NT command status. For example, consider the following statements:

```
options noxwait;

x 'dirf'; /* This is an invalid Windows NT command. */
%put This Windows NT status is &sysrc;

x 'dir'; /* This is a valid Windows NT command.  */
%put The corrected Windows NT status is &sysrc;
```

The following lines are written to the SAS log:

```
This Windows NT status is 1
The corrected Windows NT status is 0
```

The OPTIONS statement turns the XWAIT option off so that the Windows NT command prompt window disappears automatically without your having to type EXIT to return to your SAS session. If you run this example with the XWAIT option on, it does not work because you get a value of 0 in both cases; 0 is the return code for the EXIT command. If NOXSYNC is on, the value of SYSRC is automatically 0.

SYSSCP
: returns the operating system abbreviation WIN_NT.

Macro Statements

The following macro statements have system dependencies:

%KEYDEF

is analogous to the KEYDEF display manager command. It enables you to define function keys. The %KEYDEF statement takes the following form:

%KEYDEF *key-name*|'*key-name*' <'*definition*'>;

If the *definition* argument is omitted, a message is printed to the log showing the current definition of the key; otherwise, the key's definition is changed to whatever you specify.

Key names vary from terminal to terminal. You can define any key listed in the KEYS window, provided it is not reserved by Windows NT. You must enclose any key name that is hyphenated or contains a space, such as SHF F2 or CTRL Z, in quotes.

You can also use the %KEYDEF statement to define commands that are executed when the mouse buttons are pressed. The following key sequences are accepted as the *key-name* argument:

Key Name	Key Sequence
RMB	right mouse button
SHF RMB	shift key, right mouse button
CTL RMB	control key, right mouse button
MMB	middle mouse button
SHF MMB	shift key, middle mouse button
CTL RMB	control key, right mouse button

For example, to assign the ZOOM command to the CTL RMB key sequence, submit the following command:

```
%keydef 'ctl rmb' 'zoom';
```

%SYSEXEC

executes operating system commands immediately and places the return code in the SYSRC automatic macro variable. The %SYSEXEC statement is similar to the X statement described in Chapter 1. You can use the %SYSEXEC statement inside a macro or in open code. The %SYSEXEC statement takes the following form:

%SYSEXEC <*command*>;

The *command* argument can be any operating system command or any sequence of macro operations that generate an operating system command. You can also use the *command* argument to invoke a Windows NT application such as Notepad.

Omitting the *command* argument puts you into a Windows NT subprocess, which is interactive. To return to your SAS session, type EXIT at the DOS prompt and press ENTER. The SYSRC automatic variable is set to 0 if you omit the *command* argument in the %SYSEXEC statement.

Here is a simple example of %SYSEXEC:

```
%sysexec time;
```

This statement spawns a command prompt session that displays the following lines:

```
The current time is: 16:32:45.16
Enter new time:
```

Note: The %SYSEXEC statement uses the XSYNC and XWAIT system option values just like the X statement and X command do; for more information on these system options see Chapter 1 and Chapter 7.

Macro Functions

The following macro function has system dependencies:

%SYSGET
: returns the character string that is the value of the Windows NT environment variable passed as the argument. Both Windows NT and SAS environment variables can be translated using the %SYSGET function. A warning message is printed if the environment variable does not exist. The %SYSGET function takes the following form:

  %SYSGET(*environment-variable-name*);

  Here is an example of using the %SYSGET function:

```
%let var1=%sysget(comspec);
%put The COMSPEC environment variable is &var1;
```

  The following line is written to the SAS log:

```
The COMSPEC environment variable is C:\winnt\system\command.exe
```

Autocall Libraries

This section discusses the system dependencies of using autocall libraries. For general information, see the *SAS Guide to Macro Processing* and Chapter 41 in SAS Technical Report P-222.

An autocall library contains files that define SAS macros. SAS Institute supplies some autocall macros. To use the autocall facility, you must have the system option MAUTOSOURCE set. When the SAS System is installed, the SASAUTOS system option is used in the SAS configuration file to tell the SAS System where to find the default macros supplied by the Institute. You can also define your own autocall macros and store them in a Windows NT directory.

If you store autocall macros in a Windows NT directory, the file extension must be .SAS. Each macro file in the directory must contain a macro definition with a macro name the same as the filename. For example, a file named PRTDATA.SAS stored in a directory must define a macro named PRTDATA.

SASAUTOS System Option

To use your own autocall macros in your SAS programs, you must tell the SAS System where to find them using the SASAUTOS system option. The syntax of the SASAUTOS option is given in Chapter 7.

You can set the SASAUTOS system option when you start the SAS System, or you can use it in an OPTIONS statement during your SAS session. You should edit your SAS configuration file to add your autocall library to the library concatenation supplied by SAS Institute, as in the following example:

```
-sasautos (c:\mymacros
           !sasroot\core\sasmacro
           !sasroot\base\sasmacro
           !sasroot\stat\sasmacro
           more library specifications
           )
```

Autocall libraries are searched in the order you specify them. So if you use the above SASAUTOS option setting and call a macro named PRTDATA, the directory C:\MYMACROS is searched for the macro; then each of the !SASROOT libraries are searched.

System-Dependent Windowing Features

This section gives details on the system dependencies of the SAS windowing environment. These dependencies consist mainly of minor differences in the behavior of some windowing environment commands and in the information provided in the individual window frames of the FORM window.

Commands

The following windowing environment commands are not supported under Windows NT:

APPT
CALCULATOR (and DCALC)
PCLEAR
PLIST
SCROLLBAR
SMARK
WDRAG
WGROW
WMOVE
WSHRINK

These commands are not supported under Windows NT because it is more efficient to use the operating system's features. For example, the SCROLLBAR command and window sizing commands are superfluous in the Windows NT environment, where scrollbars and window sizing bars are an integral part of the graphical user interface.

The following commands are supported under Windows NT, but have system dependencies:.

AUTOSCROLL
: has system-dependent default values. The default value for the AUTOSCROLL command in the OUTPUT window under Windows NT is 0. In the LOG window, it is 1.

CAPS
: causes characters to be translated to uppercase when you move the cursor off the line or press the ENTER key.

COLOR
: controls the color of window components. Under Windows NT, you cannot use the COLOR command to change the colors of the following display components: border, menu bar, pop-up menu background, and title bar. Use the Windows NT Control Panel to change the colors of these display components.

  In addition, the HIGHLIGHT and BLINK attributes are not supported for any Windows NT window component.

COMMAND WINDOW <'*title* '>
: brings up the Command dialog box. This dialog box enables you to issue a display manager command. You can enter an optional title for the dialog box to display. If your title has no spaces in it you can omit the quotes.

  If you issue the COMMAND WINDOW command when the Command dialog box is already open, the Command dialog box becomes the active window. It may be convenient to assign this command to a function key, so switching to the Command dialog box is quick and efficient. By default, F11 is defined as the COMMAND WINDOW command. This command is not portable. See "Command Dialog Box" on page 57 for a discussion of how to use the Command dialog box.

CUT
: enables you to cut text from a window. The APPEND and BUFFER= options are not supported under Windows NT for the CUT command.

  Text cut with the CUT command is placed on the Windows NT Clipboard. See "Using the Clipboard" on page 52 for more information on the Windows NT Clipboard.

DLGABOUT
: opens the About dialog box. This command is not portable.

DLGFIND
: opens the Find dialog box. This command is not portable.

DLGFONT
: opens the Fonts Selection dialog box. This command is not portable.

DLGLINKS
: opens the Links dialog box. This command is not portable.

DLGOPEN
: opens the Open dialog box. This command is not portable.

DLGPREF
: opens the Preferences dialog box. This command is not portable.

DLGPRT
: opens the Print dialog box. This command is not portable.

DLGPRTSETUP
: opens the Printer Setup dialog box. This command is not portable.

DLGREPLACE
opens the Replace dialog box. This command is not portable.

DLGRUN
opens the Run dialog box. This command is not portable.

DLGSAVE
opens the Save As dialog box. This command is not portable.

FILE *file-specification* <*options*> <*host-options*>
saves the contents of a window to an external file. The *file-specification* argument can be an valid external file specification as documented in "Referencing External Files" on page 96. The portable *options* are documented in *SAS Language: Reference.* Under Windows NT, the FILE command also accepts the following *host-options* :

ANSI
indicates that the file should be written using the ANSI character set. OEM to ANSI translation is only valid for text format files (that is, either a variable-record or a print file). If the SAS System encounters a file during translation that has an invalid record format (for example, a fixed-record file or a binary file), you receive a warning message when the file is closed. This option is mutually exclusive of the OEM option.

BLKSIZE=*block-size*
BLK=*block-size*
is ignored, but is included for compatibility with previous versions of the SAS language.

DEVICE=*device-name*
associates a device with the output file. The following are valid values:

COMMPORT	writes data to a communications port.
DDE	writes data to another application using Dynamic Data Exchange. See "Dynamic Data Exchange" on page 132 for more information.
DISK	writes data to a disk device.
DUMMY	throws data away to the null file.
PLOTTER	routes SAS/GRAPH output to a plotter. The Windows NT Print Manager is not used.
PRINTER	writes data to the printer file or device. By default, the output is routed through the Windows NT Print Manager.

If you are using a device for input or output and do not use a device-type keyword in the FILENAME statement, you should use the DEVICE= option in the FILE command so that the SAS System uses the correct access protocols for the device.

HOTLINK
is used only in the context of Dynamic Data Exchange (DDE). For a complete description and an example of using this option, see "Using the DDE HOTLINK" on page 137.

LRECL=*record-length*
specifies the record length (in bytes). Under Windows NT, the default is 132. The value of *record-length* can range from 1 to 1,048,576 (1 megabyte).

NOTAB
is used only in the context of Dynamic Data Exchange (DDE). This option enables you to use non-tab character delimiters between variables. For more information on this option, see "Using the NOTAB Option with DDE" on page 137.

OEM
indicates that the file should be written using the OEM character set. ANSI to OEM translation is only valid for text format files (that is, either a variable-record or a print file). If the SAS System encounters a file during translation that has an invalid record format (for example, a fixed-record file or a binary file), you receive a warning message when the file is closed. This option is mutually exclusive of the ANSI option.

RECFM=*record-format*
controls the record format. The following are valid values under Windows NT:

F indicates fixed format.

N indicates binary format and causes the file to be treated as a byte stream.

P indicates print format.

V|D indicates variable format. This is the default.

See "Advanced External I/O Techniques" on page 110 for an example of using some of these options.

FILL
specifies the fill character. The default fill character under Windows NT is an underscore (_).

GSUBMIT BUF=*paste-buffer-name*|
"*SAS-statement-1; . . . SAS-statement-n;*" submits SAS code stored in the Windows NT Clipboard.

Under Windows NT, if the *paste-buffer-name* argument is specified it must be DEFAULT. The Windows NT Clipboard is the default paste buffer.

HOME
is equivalent to the HOME key on your keyboard, which toggles your cursor between the last cursor position and the home position in the window.

You can also define a function key to execute the CURSOR command, which positions the cursor at the home position in the window but has no toggle effect.

ICON <ALL>
iconizes the active display manager window. The appearance of window icons under Windows NT may be significantly different from the appearance of window icons under other operating systems. For example, the OUTPUT window icon is an image of a printer.

If the ALL option is specified, all SAS windows except the AWS are minimized to icons.

Do not confuse this command with the ICON system option, which iconizes the entire SAS AWS.

INCLUDE *file-specification* <*options*> <*host-options*>

copies lines from an external file into a window. The *file-specification* argument can be an valid external file specification as documented in “Referencing External Files” on page 96. The portable *options* are documented in *SAS Language: Reference.* Under Windows NT, the INCLUDE command also accepts the following *host-options*:

ANSI

indicates that the file should be read using the ANSI character set. OEM to ANSI translation is only valid for text format files (that is, either a variable-record or a print file). If the SAS System encounters a file during translation that has an invalid record format (for example, a fixed-record file or a binary file), you receive a warning message when the file is closed. This option is mutually exclusive of the OEM option.

BLKSIZE=*block-size*
BLK=*block-size*

is ignored, but is included for compatibility with previous versions of the SAS language.

DEVICE=*device-name*

associates a device with the input file. The following are valid values:

DDE	reads data from another application using Dynamic Data Exchange. See “Dynamic Data Exchange” on page 132 for more information.
DISK	reads data from a disk device.
DUMMY	causes an immediate end-of-file and may be useful in testing situations.

If you are using a device for input and do not use a device-type keyword in the FILENAME statement, you should use the DEVICE= option in the INCLUDE command so that the SAS System uses the correct access protocols for the device.

LRECL=*record-length*

specifies the record length (in bytes). Under Windows NT, the default is 132. The value of *record-length* can range from 1 to 1,048,576 (1 megabyte).

NOTAB

is used only in the context of Dynamic Data Exchange (DDE). This option enables you to use non-tab character delimiters between variables. For more information on this option, see “Using the NOTAB Option with DDE” on page 137.

OEM

indicates that the file should be read using the OEM character set. ANSI to OEM translation is only valid for text format files (that is, either a variable-record or a print file). If the SAS System encounters a file during translation that has an invalid record format (for example, a fixed-record file or a binary file), you receive a warning message when the file is closed. This option is mutually exclusive of the ANSI option.

RECFM=*record-format*
: controls the record format. The following are valid values under Windows NT:

F	indicates fixed format.
N	indicates binary format and causes the file to be treated as a byte stream.
P	indicates print format.
V|D	indicates variable format. This is the default.

MONOCHROME
: toggles the display between monochrome and color display. This command takes the following form:

MONOCHROME <ON|OFF>

This command is equivalent to choosing **Monochrome Display** in the Preferences dialog box. For more information on the Preferences dialog box, see "Preferences Item" on page 41. This command is not portable.

To alter the color of graphics, such as those displayed by SAS/GRAPH software, use the application's color options instead of the MONOCHROME command.

NEXTWIND
: steps forward through all open SAS windows.

PMENU <ON|OFF|POPUP|MENUBAR>
: controls the way you issue display manager commands, including pop-up menus, menu bars, and the command line.

no argument	toggles between the command line and either pop-up menus or menu bars, depending on which was last the active method of issuing display manager commands.
ON	replaces the command line with either pop-up menus or menu bars, depending on which was last the active method of issuing display manager commands.
OFF	turns pop-up menus or menu bars off and replaces them with a command line.
POPUP	replaces the command line with pop-up menus, regardless of what was the last active method of issuing display manager commands.
MENUBAR	replaces the command line with menu bars, regardless of what was the last active method of issuing display manager commands.

The PMENU command is also described in Chapter 18, "SAS Display Manager Commands," in *SAS Language: Reference.*

PREVWIND
: steps backward through all open SAS windows.

RESHOW
: redisplays the windows currently displayed. For example, if you receive a message from your network, the RESHOW command clears the message from the display but leaves the contents of the displayed windows unchanged.

STORE

enables you to copy text and graphics from one window to another. The APPEND and BUFFER= options are not supported under Windows NT for the STORE command. Text and graphics copied with the STORE command are placed in the Windows NT Clipboard. See "Using the Clipboard" on page 52 for more information on the Windows NT Clipboard.

TOOLCLOSE

closes the Toolbox or Tool bar. This command is not portable.

TOOLEDIT

brings up the Toolbox Editor. This command is not portable. For more information on using the Toolbox Editor, see "Using the Toolbox and Tool Bar" on page 62.

TOOLLOAD <BOX|BAR> *<libref.catalog.member>*

loads a specific toolbox. After this command completes, the specified toolbox is the active toolbox.

no arguments	loads SASUSER.PROFILE.TOOLBOX as a toolbox.
BOX|BAR	controls whether the icons are displayed as a toolbox or as a tool bar. The default is BOX.
libref.catalog.member	specifies the catalog entry to load. TOOLBOX is the default catalog entry type. If this argument is omitted, the SASUSER.PROFILE.TOOLBOX entry is loaded.

This command is not portable.

UNDO

undoes one line of text entry. If you have entered three lines of text, you must issue the UNDO command three times to undo all three lines. Lines removed using the CLEAR command cannot be replaced with the UNDO command if the lines have already been submitted. If you issue the CLEAR command before you submit statements, the UNDO command will replace the lines.

WPOPUP

causes the pop-up menus for a window to appear. By default under Windows NT, this command is associated with the right mouse button.

ZOOM

is implemented like the Maximize function in Windows NT. Under Windows NT, the ZOOM command zooms only the window from which you issue the command; it does not affect any other open SAS window.

Note: Several of these commands are illustrated in "Customizing Your Windowing Environment" on page 59.

FORM Window

The FSFORM command opens the FORM window, in which you can define print forms to use when you print SAS output. You can specify printer, page formats, margins, fonts, and printer control language in a FORM entry.

Do not use the Print Manager to print if you define a SAS form that contains printer control codes
If you use the Print Manager, the printer control codes are interpreted as text, not control codes. See "Using SAS System Print Forms" on page 120 for more information. ■

SAS print forms are especially useful when you use the PRINT command from display manager and when you print from SAS/AF, SAS/FSP, and SAS/CALC windows.

To invoke the FORM window, issue the following command:

FSFORM *<catalog-name.>form-name*

Refer to *SAS Language: Reference* for more information about the FSFORM command.

While the majority of the frames in the FORM window are the same across all operating systems, the first frame you see after issuing the FSFORM command, the Printer Selection frame, is system-dependent. This frame enables you to specify which printer you want to use. Figure 10.1 shows the default information for this frame under Windows NT. (To move from one FORM window frame to the next, use the NEXTSCR and PREVSCR commands. These commands are located under the `Locals` pop-up menu item.)

Figure 10.1
Printer Selection Frame

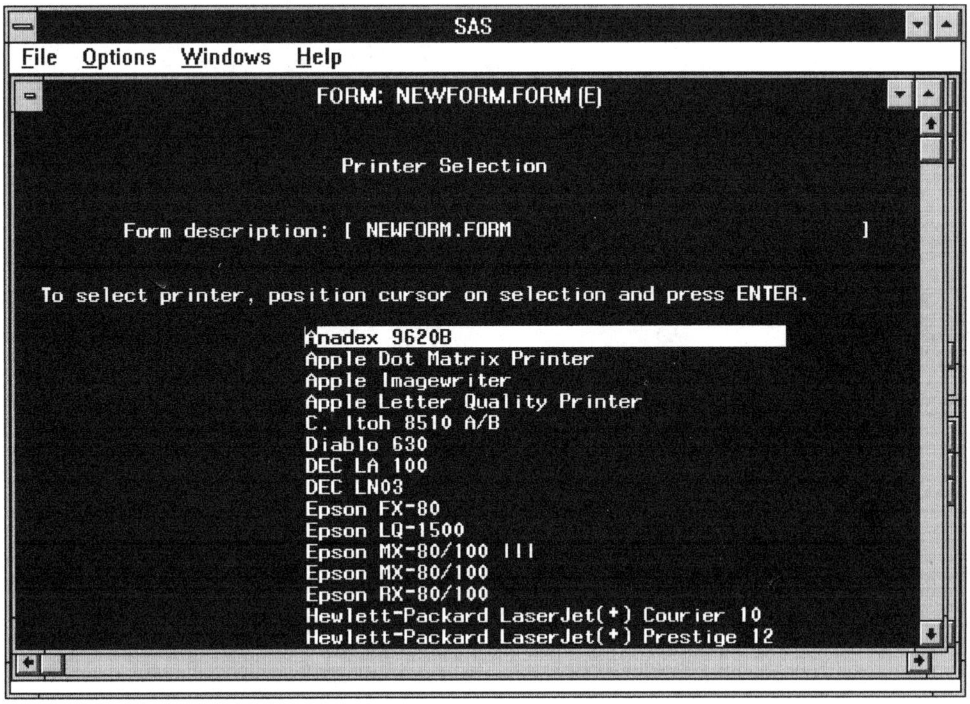

The information in the Printer Selection frame is also site-dependent, so the printer list at your site may be different from the one shown in Figure 10.1.

The Printer Selection frame appears only when you create a new print form. After you create a form, it is stored in your user profile catalog or whatever catalog was specified with the FSFORM command (entry type FORM). The next time you modify this form, the Printer Selection frame is skipped. You cannot return to the Printer Selection frame from the second FORM window frame.

Chapter 11 Performance Considerations

Introduction

This chapter discusses how to maximize the performance of the SAS System in the Microsoft Windows NT environment. Typically, you do not need to have customized PC configurations for increasing the SAS System performance; the SAS System is designed to be efficient and to take advantage of performance and hardware features where possible. But if you are running large, complicated applications or are running the SAS System on a network, you may want to read parts of this chapter.

Hardware Considerations

One obvious performance consideration is the type of processor your PC contains. The Windows NT environment is designed specifically for the Intel 80386 and 80486 architecture. The Windows NT operating system is powerful, but it requires a large amount of processing capability to support the graphical user interface. Upgrading to a more powerful 486-based PC can increase overall efficiency due to the decrease in execution time.

The SAS System takes full advantage of a math coprocessor. If a coprocessor is not installed, Windows NT emulation software emulates the floating-point instruction set. Math coprocessors increase performance of numerically-intensive applications such as those written with the DATA step or with SAS/ETS, SAS/IML, SAS/OR, SAS/QC, or SAS/STAT software.

Before installing a math coprocessor, make sure the coprocessor Mhz rating matches the clock cycle rating of the socket.
Operating the math coprocessor at speeds greater than that for which the chips are guaranteed can result in incorrect computations. ■

For more efficient I/O, you should have a fast hard disk available.

SAS System Features That Optimize Performance

I/O is one of the most important areas on which to concentrate when you are optimizing performance. The SAS System can be an I/O-intensive application. Most SAS jobs consist of repeated cycles through a particular set of data to perform a variety of data analysis and data manipulation techniques. The vast majority of I/O in a SAS job accesses a disk device. To improve the performance of a SAS job, you need to reduce the number of disk accesses.

You can do this in one of two ways: alter your SAS code to reduce the number of times you have to process the data, or reduce the number of data accesses by processing more data each time the disk is accessed. Sometimes you may be able to do both, making your SAS job even more efficient.

Note: For a comprehensive list of efficient programming tips, see *SAS Programming Tips: A Guide to Efficient SAS Processing.*

Reducing the Number of Times You Must Process the Data

There are several ways to reduce the number of times you have to process data, including using WHERE-clause processing, using indexes, accessing data through views, and using engines efficiently.

WHERE Clause

You can use the WHERE statement in a procedure to perform the same function as a DATA step with a subsetting IF statement. With the WHERE statement, you can eliminate extra data processing when performing certain analyses. For example, the following DATA step uses the SASUSER.MYDATA data set to create another data set, MIDLEVEL, that contains all observations with a value less than or equal to 50 in the SUMLEVEL variable and then prints the new data set.

```
data midlevel;
   set sasuser.mydata
   if sumlevel le 50;
run;

proc print;
run;
```

Output 11.1 shows the statistics generated for the creation of this data set, followed by the statistics generated by the PRINT procedure. (These numbers can vary from site to site.)

Output 11.1
Statistics When Using the Subsetting IF Statement in the DATA Step

```
NOTE: The DATA statement used 2 minutes 31.23 seconds.
      .
      .
      .
NOTE: The PROCEDURE PRINT used 13.85 seconds.
```

In contrast, you can get the same results from the PROC PRINT step without creating another data set if you use a WHERE statement in that step, as in the following example:

```
proc print data=sasuser.mydata;
   where sumlevel le 50;
run;
```

Output 11.2 shows the statistics generated by this program:

Output 11.2
Statistics When Using the WHERE Statement in the PRINT Procedure

```
NOTE: The PROCEDURE PRINT used 2 minutes 29.38 seconds.
```

As you can see, the WHERE clause saves resources by eliminating the number of times you process the data. In this example, you went from using about two minutes and 45 seconds to using about two minutes and 29 seconds. See Chapter 9, "SAS Language Statements," in *SAS Language: Reference, Version 6, First Edition* for more information on WHERE-clause processing.

Indexes

An index is an auxiliary data structure used in conjunction with WHERE-clause or BY-group processing to assist in the location and selection of observations specified by the value of the indexed variable. When an index is in place, the observation can be accessed by reading the desired observation directly. Without the index, the SAS System must start at the top of the data set, read each observation sequentially to the end of the data set, and apply the WHERE clause or BY statement to each value individually.

Indexing may or may not improve the performance of an application. If you are continuously rewriting a data set, the data set is not a good candidate for indexing because the index has to be recreated each time the data set is rewritten. See Chapter 6, "SAS Files," in *SAS Language: Reference* for more information about indexes.

Efficient Use of SAS Data Sets

If you find yourself processing the same raw data repeatedly, it is probably more efficient to convert the external file containing raw data into a SAS data set. The SAS System can process SAS data sets more efficiently than it can process external files.

Another efficiency consideration involves whether you are using Release 6.09 data sets or data sets created with a previous release of the SAS System. If you are processing a Release 6.04, Release 6.06, or Release 6.08 data set often, it is more efficient to convert that data set to its Release 6.09 counterpart. See Chapter 3, "Using SAS Files" on page 69 for more information on converting files to Release 6.09 format.

SQL Procedure

By setting up views of your data through the SQL procedure, you can use this procedure to do data subsetting and grouping. This eliminates extra passes through the data to preprocess or preformat the data. See the *SAS Guide to the SQL Procedure: Usage and Reference, Version 6, First Edition* and Chapter 37, "The SQL Procedure" in SAS Technical Report P-222, *Changes and Enhancements to Base SAS Software, Release 6.07* for more information on the SQL procedure.

Efficient Use of Engines

As mentioned before, one way to eliminate some of the data processing overhead is to store your data in a format that is directly accessible by an engine, that is, in a SAS data set. Storing your data in external files requires you to process the data before the SAS System can use it. By storing it in a directly accessible format, you reduce the number of steps and therefore, the resources required to perform the task.

If you do not specify an engine in the LIBNAME statement, extra processing is required for the SAS System to determine which engine to associate with the data library.
The SAS System must look at the extensions of all files in the directory until it has enough information to determine which engine to use. ■

For example, the following statement is more efficient because it explicitly tells the SAS System to use the V609 engine with the libref FRUITS:

```
libname fruits V609 'c:\sas\fruit';
```

When you submit this LIBNAME statement, the following note appears in the SAS log:

```
NOTE: Libref FRUITS was successfully assigned as follows:
        Engine:        V609
        Physical Name: C:\SAS\FRUIT
```

See Chapter 3 for more information on engines and the LIBNAME statement.

Reducing the Number of Disk Accesses for SAS Files

The following SAS system options can help you reduce the number of disk accesses needed for SAS files:

BUFNO
: adjusts the number of memory buffers you have open when processing a SAS data set. Increasing this option's value can improve your application's performance. The default value for this option is 1; experiment with other values to determine the optimal value for your needs. For more information on the BUFNO option, see Chapter 16, "SAS System Options," in *SAS Language: Reference.*

BUFSIZE

specifies the permanent buffer size for an output SAS data set. Adjusting this option's value can improve your application's performance. Under Windows NT, the value can range from 512 bytes to 1 megabyte. The default value is 0, which enables the engine to choose an optimal value, depending on the size of the observation. You may want to vary the value of the BUFSIZE option if you are trying to maximize the number of observations per page. For more information on the BUFSIZE option, see Chapter 16 in *SAS Language: Reference.*

CATCACHE

specifies the number of SAS catalogs to keep open at one time. That is, this option controls how many SAS catalogs are cached. The default value is 0, which means no catalogs are cached. Typically, you should leave this option set to 0. Increasing its value can use up memory, but it may be warranted if your application uses catalogs that are needed relatively soon by other applications (the catalogs closed by the first application are cached and can be accessed more efficiently by subsequent applications). If memory is a concern, leave the CATCACHE option set to 0.

Increasing the value for the CBUFNO option may result in fewer I/O operations when your application reads very large objects from catalogs. Increasing the value of the CBUFNO option can also improve your CPU time statistics.

Increasing the value of the CBUFNO option comes with the normal tradeoff between performance and memory usage. If memory is a serious constraint for you, you probably should not increase the value of the CBUFNO option. This is especially true if you have increased the value of the CATCACHE option.

COMPRESS

Storing your data sets in a compressed format can improve the performance of your application. Note, however, that using the COMPRESS option may require more CPU time to decompress the observations as they are made available to the SAS System. For more information on the COMPRESS option, including some of the processing limitations imposed by it, see Chapter 16 in *SAS Language: Reference.*

Another way to reduce the amount of data accessed and thus reduce the amount of I/O is to use the DROP, KEEP, and LENGTH statements to decrease the size of any given observation and to use the OBS= and FIRSTOBS= data set options to reduce the number of observations processed.

When you create and use temporary data sets, including only the required variables and observations uses fewer resources. By reducing the number and size of observations in temporary data sets, you can reduce the amount of I/O required to process the data. See Chapter 4, "Starting with SAS Data Sets," in *SAS Language and Procedures: Usage, Version 6, First Edition* for more information on the DROP, KEEP, and LENGTH statements, as well as the FIRSTOBS= and OBS= data set options.

Network Performance Considerations

Under Windows NT, loading application DLL (dynamic link library) files from a network drive can result in slower performance than loading the DLL files from a local drive.

To achieve optimum SAS System performance under Windows NT, run the SAS System from the local disk. Alternatively, you can put the most frequently used modules on the local disk. (See the discussion of the LOADLIST system option in "Obtaining Image Usage Information" on page 294 for a method of determining which modules are used most often.)

Advanced Topics

This section presents some advanced performance topics, such as monitoring the images the SAS System uses, improving the performance of the SORT procedure, and calculating data set size. This section assumes you are an experienced SAS user.

Obtaining Image Usage Information

The SAS System under Windows NT is designed to optimize memory management by minimizing image loading and purging. In general, you cannot observe this optimization. However, a few SAS system options that are intended for use by only experienced Windows NT and SAS users do display information about image loading. The LOADLIST and CDE options display information about which SAS modules are loaded to execute your SAS job.

LOADLIST System Option

The LOADLIST system option prints to the SAS log information about which SAS images are being loaded into memory. This information tells you which images are needed for your SAS jobs. Furthermore, if you are executing the SAS System from a network, you may want to copy the modules listed in the LOADLIST option output onto your local drive for faster access. Wherever you store these modules (on your hard disk, on a local network drive, or in another storage area), you must use the SAS system option, PATH, in your SAS configuration file to tell the SAS System where to find the modules. Be sure to add this option specification above the DO NOT EDIT BELOW THIS LINE mark in your SAS configuration file. For information on the PATH system option, see page 185. See "Specifying SAS System Options in the SAS Configuration File" on page 7 for more information on modifying the SAS configuration file.

In addition to the modules that have been loaded, the LOADLIST option also lists which modules have been purged from memory. The images listed as purged are the same images that were loaded during your SAS session and are no longer needed. These images are purged to make room for other images or data.

If you are executing the SAS System in batch mode, all image information generated during SAS System initialization and termination is directed to your display; information generated during the SAS job is written to the SAS log.

CDE System Option

The CDE system option produces information about the SAS images that have been loaded. If you specify CDE=I, information is printed about all of the images (DLLs) currently loaded into memory. For example, you can issue the following OPTIONS statement:

```
options cde=i;
```

From the information generated by this statement, you can determine whether a particular image is deletable.

If you specify CDE=P, then all images marked as deletable are purged from memory. It is important to note that the SAS System has been optimized in such a way that images are purged as needed. Inappropriate use of the CDE option can hamper performance and generate inefficient reloading of DLL images.

See page 180 for the complete CDE option syntax.

Improving Performance of the SORT Procedure

Two options for the PROC SORT statement are available under Windows NT, the SORTSIZE= and TAGSORT options. These two options control the amount of memory the SORT procedure uses during a sort and are discussed in the next two sections. Also included is a discussion of determining where the sorting process occurs for a given data set and determining how much disk space you need for the sort. For more information on the SORT procedure, see page 237.

SORTSIZE= Option

Under Windows NT, the PROC SORT statement supports the SORTSIZE= option. This option limits the amount of memory available for PROC SORT to use.

If you do not use the SORTSIZE= option in the PROC SORT statement, PROC SORT uses the value of the SORTSIZE= system option. If the system option is not set, PROC SORT uses all available memory and causes unnecessary amounts of swapping. If you use the SORTSIZE= option to limit the amount of available memory to about 1 or 2 megabytes, most of the SAS files and operating system files that are not needed are swapped out, and the 1 to 2 megabytes of sort buffers stay in memory for an optimum sort. If PROC SORT needs more memory than you specify, it creates a temporary utility file in your SASWORK directory to complete the sort.

The default value of this option is 1M (one megabyte). A value of 1M or 2M is optimal. If your machine has more than 12 megabytes of physical memory and you are sorting large data sets, setting this option to a value greater than 2M may improve performance.

Note: You can also use the SORTSIZE system option, which has the same effect as the SORTSIZE= option in the PROC SORT statement.

TAGSORT Option

The TAGSORT option is useful in situations where there may not be enough disk space to sort a large SAS data set. When you specify the TAGSORT option, only sort keys (that is, the variables specified in the BY statement) and the observation number for each observation are stored in the temporary files. The sort keys, together with the observation number, are referred to as tags. At the completion of the sorting process, the tags are used to retrieve the records from the input data set in sorted order. Thus, in cases where the total number of bytes of the sort keys is small compared with the length of the record, temporary disk use is reduced considerably. However, you should have enough disk space to hold another copy of the data (the output data set) or two copies of the tags, whichever is greater. Note that although using the TAGSORT option can reduce temporary disk use, the processing time may be much higher.

Determining Where the Sort Occurs

Where the physical sort occurs for a given data set depends on how you reference the data set name and whether you use the OUT= option in the PROC SORT statement. You may want to know where the sort occurs if you think there may not be enough disk space available for the sort. You always need free disk space that equals 3 times the SAS data set size. For example, if your SAS data set takes up 1M of disk space, you need 3M of disk space to complete the sort.

When you sort a SAS data set, a temporary utility file is opened in the WORK data library (that is, in a subdirectory of the SASWORK directory). This file has a .SU2 file extension. This file can be up to twice as big as your data set. Before you sort, be sure your WORK data library has room for this temporary utility file.

A second file with a .SO2 file extension is also created, which, if the sort completes successfully, is renamed to the data set name of the file being sorted (with a .SD2 file extension). The original data set is then deleted. This technique ensures data integrity. Be sure you have space for this .SO2 file. Use the following rules to determine where the .SO2 file and the resulting sorted data set is created:

- If you omit the OUT= option in the PROC SORT statement, the data set is sorted on the drive and in the directory or subdirectory where it is located. For example, if you submit the following statements (note the two-level data set name), the .SO2 file is created on the C: drive in the MYDATA subdirectory:

```
libname mylib 'c:\sas\mydata';

proc sort data=mylib.report;
   by name;
run;
```

  Similarly, if you specify a one-level data set name, the .SO2 file is created in your WORK data library.

- If you use the OUT= option in the PROC SORT statement, the .SO2 file is created in the directory associated with the libref used in the OUT= option. If you use a one-level name (that is, no libref), the .SO2 file is created in the WORK data library. For example, in the following SAS program, the first sort occurs in the SASWORK subdirectory, while the second occurs on the F: drive in the JANDATA directory:

```
proc sort data=report out=newrpt;
   by name;
run;

libname january 'f:\jandata';

proc sort data=report out=january.newrpt;
   by name;
run;
```

Calculating Data Set Size

You can create a dummy SAS data set containing one observation and the variables you need, and then you can determine the information needed to calculate the data set size by running the CONTENTS procedure.

For example, for a data set with two character variables, each 10 bytes long, and three numeric variables, each 8 bytes long, you would submit the following statements:

```
data test;
   length char1-char2 $ 10 num1-num3 8;
run;

proc contents;
   title 'Example for Calculating Data Set Size';
run;
```

These statements generate the output shown in Output 11.3.

Output 11.3 *Example for Calculating Data Set Size with PROC CONTENTS*

```
                    Example for Calculating Data Set Size                  1

                              CONTENTS PROCEDURE

Data Set Name: WORK.TEST                             Observations:         1
Member Type:   DATA                                  Variables:            5
Engine:        V609                                  Indexes:              0
Created:       14:27 Wednesday, March 17, 19xx       Observation Length:   44
Last Modified: 14:27 Wednesday, March 17, 19xx       Deleted Observations: 0
Protection:                                          Compressed:           NO
Data Set Type:                                       Sorted:               NO
Label:

                   -----Engine/Host Dependent Information-----

                       Data Set Page Size:      4096
                       Number of Data Set Pages: 1
                       File Format:             607
                       First Data Page:         1
                       Max Obs per Page:        92
                       Obs in First Data Page:  1

                -----Alphabetic List of Variables and Attributes-----

                      #    Variable    Type    Len    Pos
                      -----------------------------------
                      1    CHAR1       Char     10      0
                      2    CHAR2       Char     10     10
                      3    NUM1        Num       8     20
                      4    NUM2        Num       8     28
                      5    NUM3        Num       8     36
```

The size of the resulting data set depends on the data set page size and the number of observations. The following formula can be used to estimate the data set size:

number-of-data-pages = 1 + (floor(*number-of-obs* / `Max Obs per Page`))
size = 256 + (`Data Set Page Size` × *number-of-data-pages*)

Taking the information shown in Output 11.3, you can calculate the size of the example data set:

number-of-data-pages = 1 + (floor(1 / 92))
size = 256 + (4096 × 1) = 4352

Thus, the example data set uses 4,352 bytes of storage space.

Maximum Number of Variables

The maximum number of variables in a single SAS data set under Windows NT is 32,767. In addition, an observation under Windows NT cannot be longer than 1M. Therefore, if you want your data set to contain 32,767 character variables, the longest each variable can be is 32 bytes.

However, a DATA step can reference more than 32,767 variables, if you write only 32,767 or less variables to the data set. For example, you could drop some variables with a DROP= data set option. The maximum number of variables a DATA step can reference under Windows NT is 2,147,483,647.

Interactive Environment Considerations

If you are running a SAS job using the SAS Display Manager System and the job generates numerous log messages or extensive output, consider using the AUTOSCROLL command to suppress the scrolling of windows. This makes your job run faster because the SAS System does not have to use resources to scroll the LOG and OUTPUT windows during the job. For example, issuing AUTOSCROLL 0 in the LOG window causes the LOG window not to scroll until your job is finished. (For the OUTPUT window, AUTOSCROLL is set to 0 by default.)

Also, you can control the relative responsiveness of your SAS session by choosing `System` from the Windows NT Control Panel, then choosing [Tasking...]. Use these tasking options as follows:

- □ If you are running display manager and want your interactive session to have the best response time, choose `Best Foreground Application Response Time`.
- □ If you are running the SAS System in batch mode and you want your batch jobs to execute more quickly, choose `Foreground and Background Applications Equally Responsive`.

Optimizing Disk Access Using System Options

Three system options can help you optimize disk access during your SAS sessions. These options are PATHDLL, SASHELP, and SASMSG. Typically, you specify these options in your SAS configuration file.

PATHDLL Option

The PATHDLL system option tells the SAS System where to look for special DLL files that interface with the operating system. These files are stored in the !SASROOT\CORE\SASDLL subdirectory. These DLL files are used at boot time and at other key times during your SAS session.

Do not move your CORE\SASDLL DLL files or change your PATHDLL specification unless you are very sure of what you are doing.
These special DLL files must stay together. Moving one or two of the files, but not all of them, prevents the SAS System from booting. The location picked for these files during the INSTALL process is usually suitable. If you must move these files, be sure to move all of them and change your PATHDLL option value accordingly. ■

SASHELP Option

The SASHELP system option specifies a list of directories that contain SAS help files. Your default CONFIG.SAS file specifies a certain order for these directories. You can rearrange the directory specifications in the SASHELP option so that the most commonly accessed directories are listed first. For example, if you rarely access the SAS System help for base SAS software, but often invoke help for SAS/STAT and SAS/FSP software, place the SAS\STAT\SASHELP and SAS\FSP\SASHELP directories first in the SASHELP option value. Place the least commonly accessed directories last in the list of directories.

SASMSG Option

The SASMSG system option specifies a list of directories that contain SAS message files. Your default CONFIG.SAS file specifies a certain order for these directories. You can rearrange the directory specifications in the SASMSG option so that the most commonly accessed directories are listed first and the least commonly accessed directories are listed last in the list of directories.. For example, if you rarely access the SAS message system for SAS/GRAPH software, but use SAS/STAT and SAS/FSP software quite often (and therefore access the message files for these products), place the SAS\STAT\SASMSG and SAS\FSP\SASMSG directories first in the SASMSG option value and place the SAS\GRAPH\SASMSG directory last.

Chapter 12 Problem Determination and Resolution

Introduction

This chapter presents information to help you solve problems you encounter while running your SAS job. The SAS Technical Support Division is available to assist your SAS Software Representative and SAS Software Consultant with problems you encounter, and the first section of this chapter, "SAS Technical Support" on page 301 offers suggestions on what is needed to resolve problems. You can often solve your problem without Technical Support's assistance by looking at the SAS Notes, which are described in the second section. Finally, "Host System Subgroup Error Messages" on page 304 provide helpful details on diagnosing and fixing errors you encounter in your SAS jobs.

SAS Technical Support

Support for the SAS System is shared by SAS Institute and your SAS site representative. The Institute is responsible for maintaining the software, while the SAS Software Representative and SAS Software Consultant at your site are responsible for providing you with direct user support. If your representative cannot assist you, he or she can contact the Technical Support Division of SAS Institute. In order to provide the most efficient service possible, users are asked not to telephone Technical Support directly.

Technical Support can assist with suspected user errors in the SAS System; possible system incompatibilities; and questions about SAS statement syntax, general logic problems, and procedures and their output. However, Institute consultants cannot assist with special-interest applications, writing user programs, or teaching new users. They are also unable to provide support for general statistical methodology or design of experiments.

Information that Your SAS Software Representative Needs

When reporting problems to your SAS Software Representative, the following information assists him or her. The information is necessary if the Representative needs to contact Technical Support.

General Problems

When reporting any type of problem, have the following information available:

- the Microsoft Windows NT version and release numbers.
- the SAS software release number.
- the SAS statements for the PROC or DATA step causing the problem. Reducing the program to as little code as replicates the problem simplifies the task of locating the problem.
- the exact text of any error messages that appear in the SAS log or in a dialog box.
- a description of any changes made to SAS software on your system (if the same program ran successfully in the past).
- any recent upgrades or changes to the operating system or hardware.
- type of video monitor and adaptor you are using.

Windows NT Problems

When you have a problem you suspect relates to how the SAS System interacts with the operating system, report the following information:

- the version of Windows NT
- the difference in hardware or environment if the problem only happens for some users, but not for others. This information should include the processor type and speed, the presence or absence of a coprocessor, and the screen resolution and number of colors (that is, the video driver) that are selected.

The SITEINFO Window

Much of the information you need to provide to your SAS Software Representative may be contained in the SITEINFO window.* You call this window by issuing the SITEINFO command from any SAS window. Figure 12.1 shows an example of the SITEINFO window. Remember that this window is site-specific; therefore, the information displayed is different at every site.

* The information displayed in this window comes from a file specified with the SITEINFO system option. If your SITEINFO window is blank, contact your SAS Software Representative.

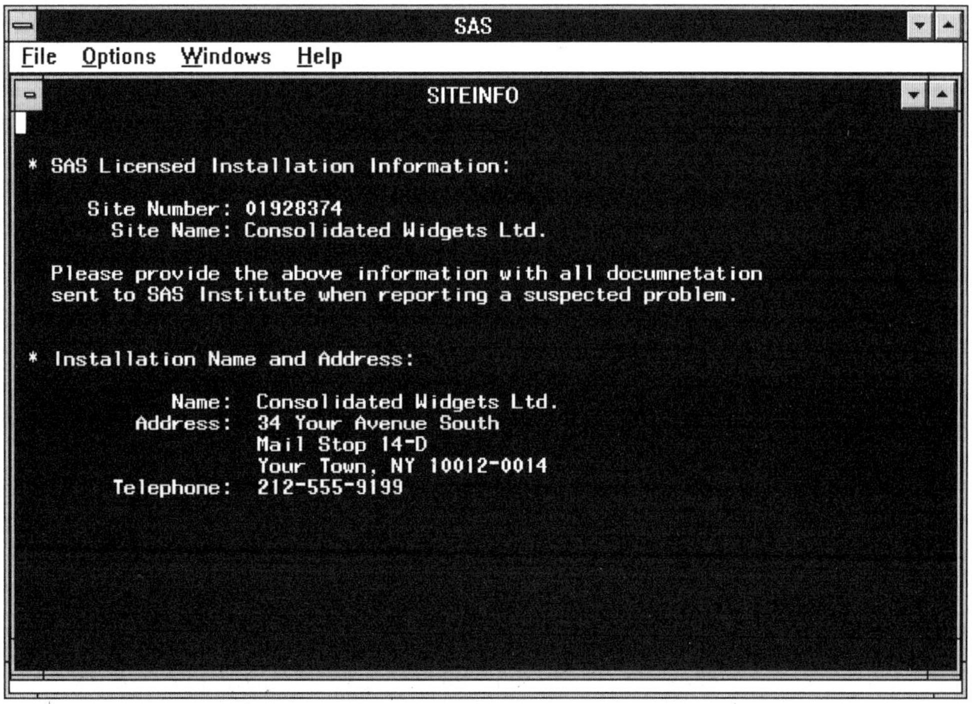

Figure 12.1
SITEINFO Window

Scroll forward in the SITEINFO window to see more information.

SAS Notes

The SAS Notes are part of the SAS System's Online Customer Support Facility.* The SAS Notes include the following information:

□ reports on known problems associated with SAS software

□ errors that users make frequently

□ fixes available for correcting errors.

Because the SAS Notes contain information about outstanding problems and common user errors, you should consult the SAS Notes whenever you encounter problems you cannot solve. Many problems result from not understanding how the SAS System works or from the use of incorrect syntax. Most of the time, you can probably locate the error quickly through the messages in the SAS log. If you cannot solve the problem, check the SAS Notes data set. If you still need assistance, your SAS Software Consultant should contact the Technical Support Division at SAS Institute.

Note: Because the SAS Notes are updated monthly, they are a good source for obtaining current information that has not yet been documented in manuals or technical reports.

* This facility is available only to customers in North America.

Obtaining the SAS Notes

The SAS Notes are distributed on separate diskettes by request. SAS Software Representatives can write SAS Institute's Distribution Center for a current copy of the notes. Copies are provided free of charge and should be requested three times a year. Requests for a current copy should be made by your SAS Software Representative. The Representative should send his or her request on company letterhead and include the site number, media requirements (such as disk density), and the name of the operating system.

For further information on the SAS Notes, see SAS Technical Report U-118, *A Guide to the SAS Notes, Sample Library, Support Application, and Application Services.*

Host System Subgroup Error Messages

The following is an alphabetic list of system-dependent messages that you may encounter during a SAS session. The error messages are divided into four groups: "Accessing Files" on page 304, "Using SAS System Features" on page 305, "Using OLE" on page 306, and "Using Networks" on page 307. The section "Resolving Internal Errors" on page 307 lists some special errors associated with the SAS System, as well as their causes. The final section, "Resolving Operating System and Windows NT Error Messages" on page 309 discusses what to do if you receive an unexpected Windows NT system error message in your SAS log.

In the following error message lists, the messages are in monospace. Words in italic in the messages represent items that are variable, such as a filename or number. Each description tells you where the message comes from and explains its meaning and what you can do to correct the possible problem, if anything.

Accessing Files

This section describes errors you may receive while trying to use the SAS System to access files (either external files or SAS files). Whenever you have trouble accessing files, always check the validity of your FILENAME and LIBNAME statements, to make sure they point to the right files. Also, be sure you are using the correct fileref or libref.

`Core catalog cannot be initialized. Please verify the system's date/time.`

The date or time stamp of the SAS System's CORE catalog is in the future. Make sure the date and time on your machine are set correctly. This message is issued in conjunction with internal error 602 (see "Resolving Internal Errors" on page 307).

`Error: Date/time is in the future.`

The date or time stamp of the file you are trying to access is in the future. Make sure the date and time on your machine are set correctly.

`Error: File is in use,` *`filename`*`.`

The file you are trying to access is in use by another Windows NT process, such as another Windows NT application.

`Error: File not found loading` *`filename-1`*`. File contributing to error:` *`filename-2`*`.`

A DLL-dependent file cannot be found when the requested file is loaded. For the SAS System, the !SASROOT\CORE\SASDLL file (usually specified with the PATHDLL system option in the SAS configuration file) may have become unavailable. This may be due to a network error or other drive failure. Ensure that PATHDLL specifies the location of !SASROOT\CORE\SASDLL.

`ERROR: Member or library` *`filename`* `unavailable for use.`

The file *filename* is being used by another Windows NT application.

`ERROR: Module` *`module-name`* `not found in search paths.`

This error is caused by one of the following reasons:

- incorrect PATH system option in the SAS configuration file
- the product you called is not installed
- a dependent image is not installed.

`ERROR: One or more members in library` *`library-name`* `are open.`

You are trying to reassign a libref while the library is in use.

`ERROR: Operating system error number` *`n`* `occurred while accessing` *`filename`*`.`

An unexpected return code has been received by the SAS System from the operating system. See "Resolving Operating System and Windows NT Error Messages" on page 309 for more information.

`ERROR: Physical file does not exist,` *`filename`*`.`

The file you are trying to access does not exist. Verify that you have specified the correct drive and directory. This error can also occur if you are trying to write to a write-protected diskette.

`ERROR: Write access to member` *`member-name`* `is denied.`

You are trying to update a file on a write-protected diskette or you are trying to update a file marked as read-only.

Using SAS System Features

This section describes errors you may receive while using features of the SAS language and procedures under Windows NT. Always check the syntax of the statement or procedure you are using. Also, if you do not get the results you expect, check the contents of any external files or SAS files to be sure they are correct.

`An interrupt has occurred.`

You have canceled a print job by choosing [Abort].

`ERROR: Out of disk space for spooling.`

Not enough disk space is currently available for spooling a print job. This message implies that no more disk space can be made available.

`ERROR: Not enough memory is available for spooling.`

Not enough memory is available for spooling. This message implies, however, that more space may become available at some point.

`ERROR: Option is valid only at invocation of the SAS System. Option is ignored.`

Several SAS system options can only be set in the SAS configuration file or in the SAS command. See Chapter 7, "SAS System Options" on page 173 for more information.

`ERROR: Unknown configuration option` *`option-name`*.

Check your SAS command and SAS configuration file for an invalid SAS system option. See Chapter 7 for more information on system options under Windows NT.

`ERROR: User terminated the job through the Print Manager.`

You terminated (that is, deleted) your print job by using the Print Manager.

`Invalid toolbox catalog:` *`catalog-name`*.

You have tried to load a nonexistent toolbox from a SAS catalog with the TOOLLOAD command. Check the spelling of the toolbox name and the catalog name in the command. You can use the DIR SAS Display Manager System command to see a listing of a SAS catalog.

`No tools defined.`

The toolbox you have attempted to load has no tools defined. You must have at least one tool defined in a toolbox.

`Sysprint device name is empty.`

The **`Sysprint device name`** field in the Printer Setup dialog box must have a value.

`Unable to access the specified printer driver.`

The SAS System cannot access the printer driver. Make sure the correct printer driver has been specified by either the SYSPRINT system option or with the Printer Setup dialog box.

`Unable to find the printer name.`

The SAS System cannot find the printer specified in the **`Sysprint device name`** field in the Printer Setup dialog box.

Using OLE

This section describes errors you may receive while using Window NT's object linking and embedding (OLE) capability in your SAS applications.

`An OLE error has occurred. OLE error:` *`nn`*

An OLE error not documented in this section has occurred. If you receive this error message, contact your SAS Software Representative, who can determine the cause of the error. The SAS Software Representative may have to call the SAS Institute Technical Support Division.

`OLE Links dialog already in use.`

You tried to open the Links dialog box when it is already open. Toggle through your windows to find the Links dialog box.

`Static Object - no OLE verbs associated with this object.`
: You have double-clicked on a static object. Static objects cannot perform any actions.

`Unable to execute OLE verb.`
: The OLE verb that was passed to the object was invalid or could not be sent. Check your SCL code for a misspelled verb.

`Unable to read/write the catalog entry.`
: The SAS System encountered an error reading or writing a catalog entry. If it is an error in reading a catalog, perhaps your catalog has been corrupted. Errors in writing could be caused by your accessing a catalog that is read-only.

`Unable to start OLE server.`
: The server application for the object could not be invoked. You may be missing some executables, or perhaps your network connection is down.

Using Networks

This section describes errors you may receive while using the SAS System on a network. For more information about using the SAS System on a network, see "Network Performance Considerations" on page 293 and Appendix 3, "Network Considerations" on page 321.

Any of the following errors can occur on a network if you do not have proper access rights:

```
ERROR: Deletion of old member filename failed.
ERROR: File deletion failed for filename.
ERROR: Rename of temporary member for filename failed.
ERROR: User does not have appropriate authorization level for file filename
```

Network software enables the network supervisor to control access to network files. Access rights can be set up so that you may be able to read a file, but are unable to update that file. The last message in this list can also appear if you try to access a directory as if it were a file.

Resolving Internal Errors

Internal errors are fatal errors that keep the SAS System from starting. While you should not usually see these error messages, you may be able to solve the problem that generated the message with a bit of investigation. The following list describes the most common of these messages:

`10 Host internal error: 10`
: CTRL BREAK was pressed during the initialization of the SAS System. Therefore, the SAS System terminated.

`11 Host internal error: 11`
: The SAS System needs more memory. To correct the problem, change swapping to a disk with more free space or delete enough files from the present swap disk to free up at least 20 megabytes of memory.

`12 Host internal error: 12`

The SAS System has determined that there is an error in the specified SAS System configuration. A descriptive message is displayed that indicates which system option is in error.

`13 Host internal error: 13`

Some part of the SAS System cannot be loaded. The part in question is indicated via a descriptive message. Restore the missing part to the appropriate directory.

`24 Host internal error: 24`

The SAS System was unable to initialize display manager. A descriptive message is displayed indicating the appropriate action.

`208 Unable to open profile catalog.`

The SAS System must have access to your SASUSER.PROFILE catalog or be able to create one if one does not exist. Check to be sure you have enough disk space, or if you are running the SAS System on a network, that you have access to the correct files. The SASUSER.PROFILE catalog is opened in the directory specified by the SASUSER system option, described on page 190. Also see "Profile Catalog" on page 10.

`301 WORK library is undefined.`
`SASUSER library is undefined.`
`SASHELP library is undefined.`

Check your SAS command or SAS configuration file to be sure that you have specified the directory path correctly for these libraries.

`302 SASMSG library is undefined.`

Check your SAS command or SAS configuration file to be sure that you have specified the directory path correctly for this library.

`305 Unable to initialize WORK library.`
`Unable to initialize SASUSER library.`

Check your SAS command or SAS configuration file to be sure that you have specified the correct directory for the WORK and SASUSER libraries. If you are running the SAS System on a network, be sure you have access to the necessary files.

`401 Unable to initialize the message subsystem.`

Check your SAS command or SAS configuration file to be sure that you have specified the directory path correctly for all SAS data libraries. Also check to see if your SAS configuration file is where it should be. If you are sure you have specified the directory paths correctly, contact your SAS Site Representative. It is possible that SAS message files have become corrupt, or have been inadvertently deleted.

`601 Invalid SETINIT information.`

Check your SETINIT information for errors. See Appendix 1, "Updating Your Licensing Information" on page 313 for more information.

`602 CORE catalog could not be accessed for options initialization.`

The CORE catalog cannot be accessed. This may be caused by having the date on your PC set incorrectly. Use the Windows NT DATE command to verify and set the date.

Resolving Operating System and Windows NT Error Messages

In situations where unexpected return codes are returned from Windows NT, the Windows NT error number is written to the SAS log. If you have access to Windows NT programming manuals or Windows NT user documentation, you can look up the error number to determine the cause of the error. Alternatively, you can report the error number to your SAS Software Representative.

Part 3
Appendices

Appendix 1 Updating Your Licensing Information

Introduction

In order to run each software product you license from SAS Institute, you must maintain current information about your licensing agreement with the Institute. This information is called *SETINIT information.* Your SAS software does not run without up-to-date SETINIT information. You must update your license information when you first license and install SAS software and whenever you renew your license or add new products.

The method you use for updating your licensing information depends on whether you are a new customer installing the SAS System for the first time, a customer adding SAS System products to your existing license, or a renewal customer. Both methods use the SETINIT.SAS file, which is a SAS program consisting of SETINIT procedure statements. The two methods for updating your licensing information are described in the next two sections.

New Customers

The installation process copies the SETINIT.SAS file into the !SASROOT\CORE\SASINST directory. (The SETINIT.SAS file can also be found on the install disk.) If the SETINIT.SAS file appears correct to the Install utility, the license update is executed automatically during the installation process. If the Install utility determines the SETINIT.SAS file is merely a template file, the utility stops and instructs you to edit the SETINIT.SAS file before continuing.* If you get such a message or a message indicating that your SAS System has expired, follow the editing procedure as outlined in "Renewal and Add-On Customers" on page 314.

* Such template files are often sent to non-U.S. customers to enable them to customize their SETINIT.SAS file with the correct information, such as European-format dates, and so on.

Renewal and Add-On Customers

When you renew your license or add SAS products to your license, you must update your licensing information contained in the SETINIT.SAS file. You receive a paper SETINIT when you receive your software package; your SETINIT.SAS file must reflect this information. To update the SETINIT.SAS file, follow these steps:

1. Locate the SETINIT.SAS file. Usually, this file is located in your !SASROOT\CORE\SASINST subdirectory. For example, if you installed SAS to C:\SAS, you would find SETINIT.SAS in the subdirectory C:\SAS\CORE\SASINST. If it is not there, you can copy the file from your installation diskette. It is recommended that you keep the SETINIT.SAS file in your !SASROOT\CORE\SASINST subdirectory.

2. The SETINIT.SAS file contains SETINIT procedure statements. Edit the statements so that they match the information contained in the paper SETINIT. You can use any ASCII editor (such as the Microsoft Windows NT Notepad or the SAS Text Editor) to make your changes. You need to modify the following information:

   - expiration date
   - password
   - product list.

   The syntax and meaning of each of the SETINIT procedure statements are explained in "SETINIT Procedure Syntax" on page 314.

3. Save your changes from step 2.

4. Enter the following command from your !SASROOT directory:

   ```
   SAS -SYSIN !SASROOT\CORE\SASINST\SETINIT.SAS -SETINIT
   ```

   This command submits a batch SAS program that updates your license information.
   Alternatively, you can issue the SAS command with the **Run** command in the Windows NT Program Manager or File Manager **File** menu.

To see if the update was successful, browse the file called SETINIT.LOG in your current directory and check for errors. If you find any error messages, verify the information in the SETINIT.SAS file and re-execute the batch SETINIT job as described previously.

SETINIT Procedure Syntax

The basic syntax of the SETINIT procedure under Windows NT is as follows:

PROC SETINIT RELEASE='*x.xx*';
SITEINFO NAME='*site-name*'
EXPIRE='*expiration-date*'D
PASSWORD=*password*
SITE=*site-number*
OSNAME='WIN_NT'
BIRTHDAY='*system-birth-date*'D
RECREATE;

CPU MODEL=' '
MODNUM=' '
SERIAL=' ';
EXPIRE '*prod-1*' . . . '*prod-n*' '*exp-date*'*D*;
SAVE;
<**SEC** NAME1='*text-string-1*'
NAME2='*text-string-2*'
INFO1='*text-string-3*'
INFO2='*text-string-4*'
INFO3='*text-string-5*'
PASSWORD=*password*;>
SAVE;

Each of these statements is described in the following sections:

PROC SETINIT Statement

The RELEASE= option specifies the current release of the SAS System. For Release 6.09, the option should read as follows:

release='6.09'

You should not have to change this line.

SITEINFO Statement

This statement identifies information about your site. You must edit the options that identify your the expiration date for your license and your primary password (the EXPIRE= and PASSWORD= options). The other options (NAME=, SITE=, OSNAME=, BIRTHDAY=, and RECREATE) are preset by SAS Institute, and you never need to edit them.

Here is an explanation of the four options you need to edit when updating your license information. Remember, the necessary information for these options is contained in your paper SETINIT.

EXPIRE='*expiration-date*'D
: specifies the expiration date for your license. The format of the date is '*ddMONyyyy*'D as in the following example:

```
expire='01may1993'd
```

PASSWORD=*password*
: specifies your primary password. This is a 9-digit number. Guard this information carefully.

Do not edit any options in the SITEINFO statement besides these two options.

CPU Statement

This statement is present for compatibility with other operating systems. Under Windows NT, all the options should have a quoted blank (' ') as the value. Do not edit this statement.

EXPIRE Statement

This statement specifies the expiration date for each SAS System product you are licensed to use. The basic format of the EXPIRE statement is a list of products followed by a date in the '*ddMONyyyy*'D format.

If you have multiple products due to expire on the same date, you can specify all of them in one EXPIRE statement, as in the following example:

```
expire 'base' 'stat' 'graph' 'ets' 'fsp' 'or' 'af' 'iml' 'qc'
       'calc' 'assist' 'connect' 'insight' 'eis'
       '01may1993'd;
```

Alternatively, if you have only a few SAS products licensed and they each have a different expiration date, you can have a separate EXPIRE statement for each product, as in the following example:

```
expire 'base'  '01may1993'd;
expire 'stat'  '01sep1993'd;
expire 'graph' '01dec1993'd;
```

The following example combines these methods by grouping products by expiration date:

```
   /* products licensed until December 1, 1993 */
expire 'base' 'stat' '01dec1993'd;
   /* products licensed on trial until June 1, 1993 */
expire 'graph' 'assist' '01jun1993'd;
```

Before saving your changes, reread your EXPIRE statements carefully, making sure you have not omitted any necessary quotes and all the dates are correct.

SAVE Statement

This statement tells the SAS System to verify the information specified in the other statements and save it. If the SAS System detects errors, they are recorded in the SAS log (SETINIT.LOG). If, after you run the SETINIT program, the SAS log file contains error messages, edit the SETINIT.SAS file again and verify all the information against your paper SETINIT. The second SAVE statement saves the SEC statement information.

SEC Statement

This statement is optional and enables you to customize the information that appears in the SAS log when the SAS System initializes. It also provides secondary SETINIT information that appears in the SETINIT SEC window. The SEC statement accepts six options: NAME1=, NAME2=, INFO1=, INFO2=, INFO3=, and PASSWORD=.

The NAME1= and NAME2= options specify information that appears in the SAS log. The INFO1=, INFO2=, and INFO3= options specify information that appears only in the SETINIT SEC window. The value for all these options is a text string up to 200 characters long.

The PASSWORD= option specifies your secondary SETINIT password and is a 9-digit number.

Note: The password specified with the PASSWORD= option in the SEC statement is completely separate from the primary password specified in the SITEINFO statement. A secondary password is not required to add new products or update your license.

Here is an example of using the SEC statement:

```
sec
   name1='Welcome to the SAS System at Consolidated Widgets, Ltd.'
   name2='If you need assistance, call ext. 9193.'

   info1='This copy is licensed for the Product Development Group.'
   info2='Only employees in that group should use this copy of'
   info3='the SAS System. Call x9090 for a list of employees.'
   password=000000000;
save;
```

The SAVE statement tells the SAS System to save the information you provide in the SEC statement. This statement is optional, as the RUN statement implies a save.

Appendix 2 Graphics Considerations

Introduction

This appendix discusses some special considerations you should remember when working with graphics in the SAS System under Microsoft Windows NT. The topics include using hardware fonts with the SAS Display Manager System and SAS/GRAPH software and using SAS/GRAPH map data sets. For a simple example of creating and displaying a graph and a discussion of routing graphics to hardcopy devices, see the section "Producing Graphics" on page 123.

Using Hardware Fonts with SAS/GRAPH Software

When you use display manager, in addition to the software fonts you receive with SAS/GRAPH software, you can take advantage of the hardware fonts provided with the Windows NT environment. Before you can use a hardware font (other than the default), you must identify its name. You do this by invoking the GDEVICE procedure. Refer to *SAS/GRAPH Software: Reference, Version 6, First Edition, Volume 2*, for more information about the GDEVICE procedure.

Once the GDEVICE window is displayed, type an `S` by the correct device name and press ENTER. This brings up the Detail window. From here select the Chartype window from the **`Locals`** pop-up menu. The Chartype window displays a list of all the available hardware fonts. Identify and remember both the chartype number of the font you want to use and whether it is scalable (if so, it has a `Y` in the **`Scalable`** column). Close the Chartype and GDEVICE windows.

To specify the font name you want to use in your SAS program, prefix the three-digit chartype number *nnn* with the string HW*xxx*, where *xxx* is the suffix of the **`Module`** value for the driver entry in the Detail window:

```
HWxxxnnn
```

If the chartype you identified in the Chartype window is not three digits, you must add leading zeros to it to form a three-digit number. For example, if you are using the WINPRTG driver (module SASGDDMX) and if the chartype is 15, add one leading zero to make the font name HWDMX015. You can use the font name in any valid SAS graphics statements that accept a font.

Note: TrueType fonts can be used only with the WIN and WINPRT*x* drivers.

In SAS/GRAPH programs, you can use the font name to specify a hardware font with the FONT= or F= option. For example, you can specify the following:

```
title2 font=hwdmx015 'This is hardware font 15';
```

See Chapter 6, "SAS/GRAPH Fonts," in *SAS/GRAPH Software: Reference, Version 6, First Edition, Volume 1,* for more information on the FONT= option, such as how to use alternate fonts with hardcopy devices and how to make an alternate font the default font.

Adding Fonts

Third party hardware fonts can be used with SAS/GRAPH software. To make a hardware font available to SAS/GRAPH procedures, use the SAS/GRAPH Font Management Utility.

To access this utility, select **Utility Application** from the SAS AWS **Help** menu. Then, select **SAS/GRAPH Font Management Utility** from the list of utilities and select [OK].

To display fonts on your monitor, in the Select a Device Type and Device Name dialog box choose **MONITOR** as the device type and enter **WIN** as the device name. Now select [OK]. If you want to print the fonts, choose **HARDCOPY** as the device type and enter the appropriate device driver name.

The default options in the subsequent dialog boxes should be sufficient for most situations. Simply select [OK] in each dialog box and follow the prompts.

Using SAS/GRAPH Map Data Sets

SAS/GRAPH map data sets are distributed in compressed format. You must decompress them by selecting **Utility Application** from the SAS AWS **Help** menu before you can use the map data sets in your SAS programs.

Often, these data sets are decompressed when the SAS System is installed. If you do not know whether your map data sets are decompressed, select **Help** from the SAS/GRAPH Map Data Sets Utility window. The number of bytes for each map are displayed for both compressed and decompressed modes. Check the file size of the specific map data set to determine if the map is decompressed. If you cannot invoke the SAS/GRAPH Map Data Sets Utility, contact your SAS Software Representative.

For more information on using SAS/GRAPH map data sets, see *SAS/GRAPH Software: Usage, Version 6, First Edition.*

Appendix 3 Network Considerations

Introduction

This appendix contains information for you to consider when using the SAS System under Microsoft Windows NT on a network. For network performance information, see "Network Performance Considerations" on page 293.

The implementation of the SAS System is independent of the network. If a network vendor properly supports Windows NT clients, the SAS System should work on that network.

Running the SAS System on a Network

The SAS System under Windows NT has no specific networking version. The SAS System for Windows NT performs all file I/O processing through the Windows NT kernel operating system calls and does not directly access any specific LAN I/O functions.

When you execute the SAS System on a network, you install a single copy of the software on a server. Individual users on the network can run directly from the network. Alternatively, users on the network can copy the most frequently used products to their local disk and execute less frequently used products from the network.

If several users are simultaneously running the SAS System from a common directory on the network, each user needs a unique SASWORK directory. To ensure this, check that the WORK option in the CONFIG.SAS file does not specify the USE suboption.

Installing the SAS System on a Network

Each individual network has a unique system configuration and particular hardware and software requirements. Each installation, therefore, must be customized to reflect these network attributes. In general, however, you install the SAS System on a LAN by performing the following steps:

1. Install the SAS System software on the server.
2. Set the file attributes on the server for all SAS executable files to read-only and shareable.
3. Establish a unique user directory (preferably on a local hard drive) for each LAN user. This ensures that each user has his or her own unique SASUSER and WORK data libraries. Alternatively, you can use the WORK or SASUSER system options.
4. Copy a CONFIG.SAS and AUTOEXEC.SAS file to each user's directory, so that users can tailor their SAS environment to their personal preferences.

If you are installing the SAS System for the first time, after you complete the previous steps your software should be ready to run. If you are reinstalling after adding a product or have let your license expire, you may need to update your SETINIT information. See Appendix 1, "Updating Your Licensing Information" on page 313 for more details on the SETINIT procedure.

Appendix 4 Moving Files Containing ANSI or OEM Characters between Windows NT, OS/2®, and DOS

Introduction

The information in this appendix supplements information found elsewhere in this book. The App4 icon, seen in previous chapters, indicates a section where you may need to read this appendix to have a full understanding of how the SAS System works in the Microsoft Windows NT environment.

Moving files (either SAS files or external files) between Windows NT, OS/2, and DOS is in general very easy. Typically, you can simply put a SAS file on a diskette, and, using the appropriate SAS engine, read the SAS file. The same is true of external files. You must be careful, however, when the files contain either national characters or graphics border-drawing characters (for box and line drawing), that is, characters with ASCII numbers greater than 127. Because Windows NT uses a different character set than either the OS/2 or DOS operating systems, these special characters do not translate well between the two systems.

In summary, you need to read this appendix only if you want to move files between Windows NT, OS/2, and DOS, and any of the following are true:

- you have SAS files that use the graphics border-drawing characters (such as SCL programs that draw boxes and borders)
- you have SAS output that contains border-drawing characters (such as REPORT and TABULATE procedure output)

- you have SAS programs that use national characters (such as in TITLE and FOOTNOTE statements)
- you have raw data files that contain national characters.

If you have any of these types of files, you need to read and understand the information contained in this appendix before you transfer and move files between SAS sessions running under Windows NT, OS/2, and DOS.

This appendix explains all the details and special considerations of moving files. First, the general difficulty is explained. Then, various solutions to the problem are explained, including a system option, I/O statement options, and SAS CALL routines. There are also some special considerations for configuration and autoexec file processing. The final section mentions some miscellaneous considerations, such as using SAS/CONNECT software in the context of moving files between Windows NT, OS/2, and DOS.

Note: For SAS files, you can always use the CPORT and CIMPORT procedures to transfer data sets and catalogs from one operating system to another. These procedures take care of translating one character set to the other. However, these procedures do not affect the transfer of external files.

Overview of Character Sets Used by Windows NT, OS/2, and DOS

Characters, such as the letters of the alphabet, numerals, punctuation, and even graphics characters, are represented internally by the operating system as hexadecimal numbers. Windows NT uses a different hexadecimal number than OS/2 and DOS to represent some characters.

Windows NT uses the ANSI (American National Standards Institute) character set. This set includes all the English alphabet and numerals, many graphics characters (such as smiley faces and arrows), and a fairly comprehensive set of national characters (such as Â or Æ). The ANSI character set does not, however, include graphics border-drawing characters (such as ┬ and ╟) and a few less common national characters.

OS/2 and DOS use a different character set called OEM (Original Equipment Manufacturer). In this scheme, several different character sets (called codepages) are available. Each character set is associated with a number. For example, the codepage that represents the standard US character set is 437. Other codepages include different sets of characters for use in other situations and countries. Some of the most common codepages are 437, 850, 860, 863, and 865.

When you compare the hex string representing a character in the ANSI character set to the hex string representing the same character in an OEM codepage, the differences become apparent. The letter A is represented in both schemes by the hex string '41'x. However, the hex string for Â in ANSI is 'C2'x, while in codepage 850 it is '86'x. This difference in hex representation is the source of difficulty when moving files containing special characters between Windows NT and OS/2, as well as between Windows NT and DOS. (For your convenience, the ANSI character set and the five supported OEM codepages are reproduced at the end of this appendix, in Figure A4.1 through Figure A4.6.)

The way to solve this difficulty varies depending on whether you want to move SAS files (such as data sets and catalogs) or external files (such as raw data or SAS programs) and whether such moving is an everyday occurrence or an occasional one.

Available Solutions

Release 6.09 of the SAS System under Windows NT provides four ways to handle the character set difficulty:

- the CPORT and CIMPORT procedures. These procedures create and read, respectively, a transport file. In the process of converting a SAS file to a transport file using the CPORT procedure and converting the transport file back to SAS format using the CIMPORT procedure, characters are translated. This is the most portable method of sharing SAS files between operating systems. However, you cannot use these procedures to transport external files.
- the WINCHARSET system option. This option sets the character set to either ANSI (the default) or OEM. Setting this option affects all input and output and enables you to move both SAS files and external files. This option affects how the SAS System interprets characters. It does not cause the SAS System to translate characters from one character set to the other.
  Select **`About`** from the SAS AWS **`Help`** menu to determine which mode your SAS session is using.
- the ANSI and OEM statement options, valid in the FILE, FILENAME, %INCLUDE, and INFILE statements and in the FILE and INCLUDE SAS Display Manager System commands. These options enable you to specify per file the character set for that file. The SAS System reads the file and translates it if necessary. These options are not applicable to SAS files.
- the ANSI2OEM and OEM2ANSI CALL routines. These CALL routines are used in the DATA step and in SCL programs. Using these CALL routines, you can translate a character string from one character set to the other.

More detailed analyses of these solutions are presented in the following four sections.

Using the CPORT and CIMPORT Procedures

The most portable method of moving SAS files from one operating system to another is to use the CPORT and CIMPORT procedures. These procedures enable you to move SAS files (but not external files) from one operating system to any other operating system. Therefore, they enable you to move SAS files between Release 6.09 of the SAS System under Windows NT and Release 6.06 or Release 6.08 of the SAS System under OS/2, or Release 6.04 of the SAS System under DOS (as well as between Windows NT and any other operating system, such as MVS or OpenVMS).*

The CPORT and CIMPORT procedures take care of character set translation as well as differences between releases of the SAS System. Therefore, they are the recommended method of moving SAS files between operating systems. These procedures are documented in the *SAS Procedures Guide, Version 6, Third Edition*, as well as in SAS Technical Report

* Remember that you should not attempt to move SAS catalogs to earlier releases of the SAS System. See Chapter 3 for more information on converting SAS catalogs.

P-222, *Changes and Enhancements to Base SAS Software, Release 6.07*. A few system dependencies of the CPORT and CIMPORT procedures are documented in Chapter 9 on page 230 and page 224, respectively.

The CPORT and CIMPORT procedures are not the only method of moving SAS files between Windows NT, OS/2, and DOS, however. Because all three of these environments are similar, and because it is common for users to expect to share files among these environments on a regular basis, the SAS System provides several other techniques that enable you to move files between these three systems. These techniques are discussed in the following sections.

Using the WINCHARSET System Option

This section explains the details of using the WINCHARSET system option to control which character set the SAS System uses. Setting this option to the correct value enables you to move both SAS files and external files between Windows NT, OS/2, and DOS.

Working in ANSI Mode

As explained earlier in this appendix, the default value for the WINCHARSET option is ANSI, which is the character set used by Windows NT. If you do nothing to your configuration file when you install the SAS System, you are working in ANSI mode. If you do not plan to transfer files (either SAS files or external files such as SAS programs or raw data files) between Windows NT and either OS/2 or DOS, you should not worry about the character set and the WINCHARSET option. Even if you do transfer files, if they do not contain any national characters or use graphics border-drawing characters, you can transfer the files without a problem.

If you plan to transfer data from your SAS session to other Windows NT applications, you should leave the WINCHARSET option set to ANSI because the ANSI character set is what most other Windows NT applications use.

ANSI fonts

If WINCHARSET=ANSI, the SAS System provides a default ANSI font named SASANSI.FON. This font is stored in the !SASROOT\CORE\SASDLL directory. You can use other ANSI monospace fonts supplied by the Microsoft Corporation or another vendor, such as the Fixedsys font or the Courier font.

When you invoke the SAS System, it tries to load the ANSI font for your display's resolution. If that font cannot be found, the SAS System tries to load the Windows NT System Monospace font. If that fails, a font is chosen arbitrarily.

Working in OEM Mode

Setting the WINCHARSET option to OEM enables you to move SAS files (including SAS data sets and SAS catalogs), SAS programs, and raw data files across DOS, OS/2, and Windows NT without worrying about whether the files contain national characters or graphics border-drawing characters.

When WINCHARSET is set to OEM, every keystroke is converted from ANSI to OEM format. This translation has no significant effect on the performance of the SAS System because the SAS System can translate faster than you can type. No translation is done on input and output. The SAS System assumes that all files read and written (both SAS files and external files) are in OEM format. Therefore, if you read an ANSI file while working in

OEM mode, it may be interpreted incorrectly unless you use the ANSI statement option (described in detail later in this appendix). There is no performance penalty for running in OEM mode.

If you have written SAS applications that use the border-drawing characters in the OEM character set, be sure to set WINCHARSET to OEM. Otherwise, the output of these applications will not be what you expect.

OEM fonts

The SAS System currently supports the following five OEM codepages:

437 (US)

850 (Multilingual)

860 (Portuguese)

863 (Canadian-French)

865 (Norwegian).

The SAS System queries the operating system to determine the current codepage. For each codepage, the following devices are supported:

EGA

VGA

XGA or 8514/A.

For each codepage, a SASFONT is available in at least three sizes. The font files are named according to the following convention, where *ccc* represents the codepage number:

SAS*ccc*.FON

All fonts are stored in the !SASROOT\CORE\SASDLL directory.

Using the ANSI and OEM I/O Statement Options

The ANSI and OEM statement options enable you to override on a per-file basis the character set used to read or write the file. The following SAS statements support the ANSI and OEM options:

FILE

FILENAME

%INCLUDE

INFILE

The FILE and INCLUDE display manager commands also support the ANSI and OEM options.

For example, suppose you have the WINCHARSET system option set to OEM but want to read a program that is stored in ANSI format. The following statements use the %INCLUDE statement and the ANSI option to accomplish this:

```
filename myfile 'c:\ansidata';

%include myfile(prog1)/ansi;
```

Alternatively, you can place the ANSI option in the FILENAME statement, in which case, all files in the C:\ANSIDATA directory are translated by the SAS System to ANSI format. The ANSI and OEM options apply to all external file input or output, so you can use them when reading data from serial ports as well.

Note: The SAS System does not translate files on input or output unnecessarily. If you are running in OEM mode and use the OEM option in a SAS statement, no translation is necessary and none is performed.

Using the ANSI2OEM and OEM2ANSI CALL Routines

While the ANSI and OEM statement options are used in external I/O statements, such as %INCLUDE and FILENAME, the ANSI2OEM and OEM2ANSI CALL routines are used in the SAS DATA step. The syntax of these CALL routines is described on page 255 and page 258. Basically, these two CALL routines enable you to translate a character string from the ANSI character set to the current OEM codepage, or from the current OEM codepage to the ANSI character set.

Use these CALL routines when you are running the SAS System in one mode but need to write data to an external file or SAS data set in the other mode.

SAS Configuration and Autoexec File Considerations

This section explains how the SAS System processes the SAS configuration and SAS autoexec files and how you should create these files.

The SAS System assumes that there are no national characters in the CONFIG.SAS file. National characters can be placed in the AUTOEXEC.SAS file.
If you are using the OEM character set, an OEM editor must be used to edit the SAS configuration or SAS autoexec files—that is, a DOS editor such as EDLIN or EDIT or an OS/2 editor, not a Windows NT editor. ■

For example, suppose your SAS configuration file specifies

```
-wincharset oem
```

This means you want to run the SAS System under Windows NT but use the OEM character set for input and output. In this case, the SAS System assumes that the SAS configuration file and the SAS autoexec file, if it exists, are in the OEM format. This implies that these files were created and edited using an OEM editor.

In the same way, if WINCHARSET is set to ANSI, the SAS System assumes the SAS configuration file and SAS autoexec file were created and edited using an ANSI editor (that is, a Windows NT editor, not a DOS or an OS/2 editor).

FORMCHAR System Option

Because the FORMCHAR system option specifies the graphics border-drawing characters, the specification of this option's value in the ANSI and OEM character set is different. The configuration file shipped with the SAS System contains two FORMCHAR specifications, with the OEM version commented out (because the default environment is ANSI). If you change your WINCHARSET option value to OEM, simply comment out the ANSI specification of FORMCHAR and remove the comments around the OEM version.

Do not type over the OEM values of the FORMCHAR option, either in your SAS configuration file or in the OPTIONS window.
If you do, you have to recreate the configuration file in an OEM environment. You cannot recreate the characters under Windows NT. Also, be careful not to edit the SAS configuration file with an inappropriate editor. If you do, the FORMCHAR values will be translated by the editor into incorrect characters. ■

Other Considerations

The previous sections in this appendix cover the main points of moving files containing special characters between Windows NT, OS/2, and DOS. This section covers minor details about the topic.

Using the Clipboard

No matter what mode (ANSI or OEM) your SAS session is using, when you copy things to the Clipboard, the copy in the Clipboard is in ANSI format.*

When you paste into your SAS session text stored in the Clipboard, the SAS session converts the Clipboard contents to the correct character set if necessary. For example, if you are running in OEM mode and paste into your SAS session data that did not originally come from the SAS System, translation is necessary because the data in the Clipboard are in the ANSI character set. However, if you are running in ANSI mode, no translation is necessary.

Printing

The Windows NT Print Manager only recognizes the ANSI character set. If the SAS System is running in OEM mode, text sent to the printer is translated to the ANSI character set automatically.

* Actually, two copies are made. One is in ANSI format, and another copy is kept in an internal SAS format. If you are running in OEM mode, the internal copy is kept in OEM format so that if you copy it back into your SAS session, no translation is necessary.

Sorting

Depending on what mode you are working in, ANSI or OEM, the national characters sort in a different order. If you are working in ANSI mode, the default sort order is ANSI. If you are working in OEM mode, you can specify a collating sequence that matches the codepage (language) you are using. For example, the collating sequence for the Portuguese language (codepage 860) differs from the collating sequence for the Norwegian language (codepage 865).

The SORT procedure accepts a SORTSEQ= option that enables you to specify a collating sequence for the SAS System to use. For example, the following statements tell the SAS System to use the OEM Swedish collating sequence when sorting the TOPPROD data set:

```
proc sort data=topprod sortseq=oemswed;
   by country;
run;
```

You do not have to use a specific collating sequence name if you do not want to. If you specify a generic collating sequence such as EBCDIC or SWEDISH, the SAS System automatically determines which collating sequence to use, OEM or ANSI, based on the mode in which you are running. If you are using an OEM codepage, the data set is sorted according to the OEM collating sequence. If you are running ANSI, a different collating sequence is used.

Table A4.1 summarizes the collating sequences supplied with the SAS System that relate to the ANSI and OEM character sets:

Table A4.1
ANSI and OEM Collating Sequences

Sequence Name	Meaning
ANSIDANI	ANSI to Danish
ANSISWED	ANSI to Swedish
ANSIEBCD	ANSI to EBCDIC
ANSIREVE	ANSI to reverse ANSI
ANSINATI	ANSI to national
OEMDANI	OEM to Danish
OEMSWED	OEM to Swedish
OEMEBCD	OEM to EBCDIC
OEMREVE	OEM to reverse OEM
OEMNATI	OEM to national

Note that the results returned by the BYTE, COLLATE, and RANK functions used in the DATA step depend on the collating sequence in use.

If a collating sequence that fits your needs is not supplied, you can define your own collating sequence using the TRANTAB procedure. You can also use the TRANTAB procedure to modify the collating sequence tables you were using with previous releases of the SAS System so they can be used with Release 6.09. This modification enables you to use existing SAS code without changing the name of the collating sequence specified by the

SORT procedure's SORTSEQ= option. When you used the TRANTAB procedure to modify an existing collating sequence, you should specify the old sequence name; you do not have to append ANSI or OEM to the name. See SAS Technical Report P-197, *The TRANTAB Procedure, Release 6.06* and Chapter 39, "The TRANTAB Procedure" in SAS Technical Report P-222, *Changes and Enhancements to Base SAS Software, Release 6.07* for more information. Also, in Release 6.09, the TRANTAB= system option is useful in this context. See SAS Technical Report P-222 for more information on this option.

Note: You should not mix character sets. For example, you should not run in ANSI mode but specify OEMSWED as a value for the SORTSEQ= option.

The SAS System does not unnecessarily re-sort data. For example, if you run in OEM mode under Windows NT and sort a data set, then transfer the data set to a SAS session under OS/2 and run PROC SORT on the data set, the SAS System determines that the data set is already sorted in OEM order and does not waste resources re-sorting the data. This same principle applies to other procedures, such as the IML and SQL procedures, that internally sort data. If the data are already in the correct sorted order, they are not re-sorted.

Entering Alternate ASCII Characters

You can enter characters from either the ANSI or OEM character set, as follows. Remember to use the numeric keypad, with Num Lock on, when entering ASCII character codes.

to enter an ANSI character
: hold down the ALT key and type a zero followed by the ASCII character code. For example, to enter a Ü, hold down the ALT key and type 0220.

to enter an OEM character
: hold down the ALT key and type the ASCII character code. For example, to enter a Ü, hold down the ALT key and type 154. Note that the OEM character is mapped to the appropriate ANSI character. Because of this, you can only enter OEM characters that have an exact match in the ANSI character set. (Some OEM characters do not have such a match.)

Using SAS/CONNECT Software

The problem of character translation is not unique to moving files between Windows NT and OS/2. Whenever you move a file from one operating system to another, character translation may be required. SAS/CONNECT software uses translation tables to perform character translation from one machine to another. If you feel it is necessary, you can use the TRANTAB system option to provide your own tables for SAS/CONNECT software to use.

Character Sets

Figure A4.1 through Figure A4.6 show the ANSI and OEM character sets that are supported by the SAS System in the Windows NT environment.

Figure A4.1
*ANSI Character Set**

	0	1	2	3	4	5	6	7	8	9	A	B	C	D	E	F
00:	█	█	█	█	█	█	█	█	█	█	█	█	█	█	█	█
10:	█	█	█	█	█	█	█	█	█	█	█	█	█	█	█	█
20:		!	"	#	$	%	&	'	(	)	*	+	,	-	.	/
30:	0	1	2	3	4	5	6	7	8	9	:	;	<	=	>	?
40:	@	A	B	C	D	E	F	G	H	I	J	K	L	M	N	O
50:	P	Q	R	S	T	U	V	W	X	Y	Z	[	\	]	^	_
60:	`	a	b	c	d	e	f	g	h	i	j	k	l	m	n	o
70:	p	q	r	s	t	u	v	w	x	y	z	{	|	}	~	█
80:	█	█	█	█	█	█	█	█	█	█	█	█	█	█	█	█
90:	█	‘	’	█	█	█	█	█	█	█	█	█	█	█	█	█
A0:		¡	¢	£	¤	¥	¦	§	¨	©	ª	«	¬	-	®	¯
B0:	°	±	²	³	´	µ	¶	·	¸	¹	º	»	¼	½	¾	¿
C0:	À	Á	Â	Ã	Ä	Å	Æ	Ç	È	É	Ê	Ë	Ì	Í	Î	Ï
D0:	Ð	Ñ	Ò	Ó	Ô	Õ	Ö	×	Ø	Ù	Ú	Û	Ü	Ý	Þ	ß
E0:	à	á	â	ã	ä	å	æ	ç	è	é	ê	ë	ì	í	î	ï
F0:	ð	ñ	ò	ó	ô	õ	ö	÷	ø	ù	ú	û	ü	ý	þ	ÿ

* Courtesy of Microsoft Press, a division of Microsoft Corporation.

Figure A4.2
*OEM Codepage 437 Character Set (United States)**

1 → 2 ↓	0-	1-	2-	3-	4-	5-	6-	7-	8-	9-	A-	B-	C-	D-	E-	F-
-0		►		0	@	P	`	p	Ç	É	á	░	└	╨	α	≡
-1	☺	◄	!	1	A	Q	a	q	ü	æ	í	▒	┴	╤	β	±
-2	☻	↕	"	2	B	R	b	r	é	Æ	ó	▓	┬	╥	Γ	≥
-3	♥	!!	#	3	C	S	c	s	â	ô	ú	│	├	╙	π	≤
-4	♦	¶	$	4	D	T	d	t	ä	ö	ñ	┤	─	╘	Σ	⌠
-5	♣	§	%	5	E	U	e	u	à	ò	Ñ	╡	┼	╒	σ	⌡
-6	♠	▬	&	6	F	V	f	v	å	û	ª	╢	╞	╓	µ	÷
-7	•	↨	'	7	G	W	g	w	ç	ù	º	╖	╟	╫	τ	≈
-8	◘	↑	(	8	H	X	h	x	ê	ÿ	¿	╕	╚	╪	Φ	°
-9	○	↓	)	9	I	Y	i	y	ë	Ö	⌐	╣	╔	┘	Θ	•
-A	◙	→	*	:	J	Z	j	z	è	Ü	¬	║	╩	┌	Ω	·
-B	♂	←	+	;	K	[	k	{	ï	¢	½	╗	╦	█	δ	√
-C	♀	∟	,	<	L	\	l	|	î	£	¼	╝	╠	▄	∞	ⁿ
-D	♪	↔	-	=	M	]	m	}	ì	¥	¡	╜	═	▌	ϕ	²
-E	♫	▲	.	>	N	^	n	~	Ä	Pt	«	╛	╬	▐	ε	■
-F	☼	▼	/	?	O	_	o	⌂	Å	ƒ	»	┐	╧	▀	∩	

* Courtesy of International Business Machines Corporation.

Figure A4.3
*OEM Codepage 850 Character Set (Multilingual)**

1 → 2 ↓	0-	1-	2-	3-	4-	5-	6-	7-		8-	9-	A-	B-	C-	D-	E-	F-
-0		►		0	@	P	`	p		Ç	É	á	░	└	ð	Ó	-
-1	☺	◄	!	1	A	Q	a	q		ü	æ	í	▒	┴	Đ	β	±
-2	☻	↕	"	2	B	R	b	r		é	Æ	ó	▓	┬	Ê	Ô	=
-3	♥	‼	#	3	C	S	c	s		â	ô	ú	│	├	Ë	Ò	¾
-4	♦	¶	$	4	D	T	d	t		ä	ö	ñ	┤	─	È	õ	¶
-5	♣	§	%	5	E	U	e	u		à	ò	Ñ	Á	┼	ı	Õ	§
-6	♠	▬	&	6	F	V	f	v		å	û	ª	Â	ã	Í	µ	÷
-7	•	↨	'	7	G	W	g	w		ç	ù	º	À	Ã	Î	þ	¸
-8	◘	↑	(	8	H	X	h	x		ê	ÿ	¿	©	╚	Ï	Þ	°
-9	○	↓	)	9	I	Y	i	y		ë	Ö	®	╣	╔	┘	Ú	¨
-A	◙	→	*	:	J	Z	j	z		è	Ü	¬	║	╩	┌	Û	·
-B	♂	←	+	;	K	[	k	{		ï	ø	½	╗	╦	█	Ù	¹
-C	♀	∟	,	<	L	\	l	|		î	£	¼	╝	╠	▄	ý	³
-D	♪	↔	-	=	M	]	m	}		ì	Ø	¡	¢	═	¦	Ý	²
-E	♫	▲	.	>	N	^	n	~		Ä	×	«	¥	╬	Ì	¯	■
-F	☼	▼	/	?	O	_	o	⌂		Å	ƒ	»	┐	¤	▀	´	

* Courtesy of International Business Machines Corporation.

Figure A4.4
OEM Codepage 860 Character Set (Portuguese) *

1 → 2 ↓	0-	1-	2-	3-	4-	5-	6-	7-	8-	9-	A-	B-	C-	D-	E-	F-
-0		►		0	@	P	`	p	Ç	É	á	░	└	╨	α	≡
-1	☺	◄	!	1	A	Q	a	q	ü	À	í	▒	┴	╤	β	±
-2	☻	↕	"	2	B	R	b	r	é	È	ó	▓	┬	╥	Γ	≥
-3	♥	‼	#	3	C	S	c	s	â	ô	ú	│	├	╙	π	≤
-4	♦	¶	$	4	D	T	d	t	ã	õ	ñ	┤	─	╘	Σ	⌠
-5	♣	§	%	5	E	U	e	u	à	ò	Ñ	╡	┼	╒	σ	⌡
-6	♠	▬	&	6	F	V	f	v	Á	Ú	ª	╢	╞	╓	µ	÷
-7	•	↨	'	7	G	W	g	w	ç	ù	º	╖	╟	╫	τ	≈
-8	◘	↑	(	8	H	X	h	x	ê	Ì	¿	╕	╚	╪	Φ	°
-9	○	↓	)	9	I	Y	i	y	Ê	Õ	Ò	╣	╔	┘	Θ	•
-A	◙	→	*	:	J	Z	j	z	è	Ü	¬	║	╩	┌	Ω	·
-B	♂	←	+	;	K	[	k	{	Ì	¢	½	╗	╦	█	δ	√
-C	♀	∟	,	<	L	\	l	¦	Ô	£	¼	╝	╠	▄	∞	ⁿ
-D	♪	↔	-	=	M	]	m	}	ì	Ù	¡	╜	═	▌	φ	²
-E	♫	▲	.	>	N	^	n	~	Ã	Pt	«	╛	╬	▐	ε	■
-F	☼	▼	/	?	O	_	o	⌂	Â	Ó	»	┐	╧	▀	∩	

* Courtesy of International Business Machines Corporation.

Figure A4.5
*OEM Codepage 863 Character Set (Canadian-French)**

1 → 2 ↓	0-	1-	2-	3-	4-	5-	6-	7-	8-	9-	A-	B-	C-	D-	E-	F-
-0		►		0	@	P	`	p	Ç	É	¦	░	└	╨	α	≡
-1	☺	◄	!	1	A	Q	a	q	ü	È	´	▒	┴	╤	β	±
-2	☻	↕	"	2	B	R	b	r	é	Ê	ó	▓	┬	╥	Γ	≥
-3	♥	‼	#	3	C	S	c	s	â	ô	ú	│	├	╙	π	≤
-4	♦	¶	$	4	D	T	d	t	Â	Ë	¨	┤	─	╘	Σ	⌠
-5	♣	§	%	5	E	U	e	u	à	Ï	¸	╡	┼	╒	σ	⌡
-6	♠	▬	&	6	F	V	f	v	¶	û	³	╢	╞	╓	μ	÷
-7	•	↨	'	7	G	W	g	w	ç	ù	¯	╖	╟	╫	τ	≈
-8	◘	↑	(	8	H	X	h	x	ê	¤	Î	╕	╚	╪	Φ	°
-9	○	↓	)	9	I	Y	i	y	ë	Ô	⌐	╣	╔	┘	Θ	•
-A	◙	→	*	:	J	Z	j	z	è	Ü	¬	║	╩	┌	Ω	·
-B	♂	←	+	;	K	[	k	{	ï	¢	½	╗	╦	█	δ	√
-C	♀	∟	,	<	L	\	l	|	î	£	¼	╝	╠	▄	∞	ⁿ
-D	♪	↔	-	=	M	]	m	}	‗	Ù	¾	╜	═	▌	φ	²
-E	♫	▲	.	>	N	^	n	~	À	Û	«	╛	╬	▐	ε	■
-F	☼	▼	/	?	O	_	o	⌂	§	ƒ	»	┐	╧	▀	∩	

* Courtesy of International Business Machines Corporation.

Figure A4.6
*OEM Codepage 865 Character Set (Norwegian)**

1 → 2 ↓	0-	1-	2-	3-	4-	5-	6-	7-	8-	9-	A-	B-	C-	D-	E-	F-
-0		►		0	@	P	`	p	Ç	É	á	░	└	╨	α	≡
-1	☺	◄	!	1	A	Q	a	q	ü	æ	í	▒	┴	╤	β	±
-2	☻	↕	"	2	B	R	b	r	é	Æ	ó	▓	┬	╥	Γ	≥
-3	♥	‼	#	3	C	S	c	s	â	ô	ú	│	├	╙	π	≤
-4	♦	¶	$	4	D	T	d	t	ä	ö	ñ	┤	─	╘	Σ	⌠
-5	♣	§	%	5	E	U	e	u	à	ò	Ñ	╡	┼	╒	σ	⌡
-6	♠	▬	&	6	F	V	f	v	å	û	ª	╢	╞	╓	µ	÷
-7	•	↨	'	7	G	W	g	w	ç	ù	º	╖	╟	╫	τ	≈
-8	◘	↑	(	8	H	X	h	x	ê	ÿ	¿	╕	╚	╪	Φ	°
-9	○	↓	)	9	I	Y	i	y	ë	Ö	⌐	╣	╔	┘	Θ	•
-A	◙	→	*	:	J	Z	j	z	è	Ü	¬	║	╩	┌	Ω	·
-B	♂	←	+	;	K	[	k	{	ï	ø	½	╗	╦	█	δ	√
-C	♀	∟	,	<	L	\	l	|	î	£	¼	╝	╠	▄	∞	ⁿ
-D	♪	↔	-	=	M	]	m	}	ì	Ø	¡	╜	═	▌	ϕ	²
-E	♫	▲	.	>	N	^	n	~	Ä	Pt	«	╛	╬	▐	ε	■
-F	☼	▼	/	?	O	_	o	⌂	Å	ƒ	¤	┐	╧	▀	∩	

* Courtesy of International Business Machines Corporation.

Appendix 5 Pop-Up Menu and Menu Bar Map

Introduction

This appendix provides a map of the pop-up menus for the PROGRAM EDITOR window. This map is also valid for the PROGRAM EDITOR menu bar, if you are using menu bars instead of pop-up menus. The menus for the other primary SAS Display Manager System windows are similar (LOG, OUTPUT, and OUTPUT MANAGER windows); the differences occur in the **`Edit`** and **`View`** menus because the editor options and the color items are window-specific. Also, not all primary windows have a **`Locals`** menu.

For a map of the SAS AWS menu bar, see Figure 2.3.

Map

Items followed by ellipses (. . .) indicate a dialog box appears when you choose this item. You fill in the dialog box with more information about what you want to do. Items without ellipses take immediate action.

Figure A5.1 *Pop-Up Menu Map*

- **File**
  - Open
    - Read file...
    - Read object...
  - Save
  - Save as
    - Write to file...
    - Write to object...
  - Print
    - Print file...
    - Open a form...
  - Exit...
- **Edit**
  - Undo
  - Unmark
  - Cut marked text
  - Copy to paste buffer
  - Paste text
  - Clear marked text
  - Clear text
  - Find...
  - Repeat find
  - Replace...
  - Check spelling
    - Spell all
    - Spell all suggest
    - Spell suggest
    - Spell remember...
    - Spell add...
    - Include dictionary...
    - Free dictionary...
    - Create dictionary...
  - Options
    - Numbers
    - Caps
    - Hor. scroll...
    - Ver. scroll...
    - Autoadd
    - Autoflow
    - Autosplit
    - Autowrap
    - Bounds...
    - Indent
    - Reset
- **View**
  - Colors
    - Background...
    - Banner...
    - Command...
    - Message...
    - Text...
    - Numbers...
  - Save attributes

Figure A5.2 *Figure A5.1 (continued)*

- ⋮
- **Locals**
  - Submit
  - Recall text
  - Submit top line...
  - Submit clipboard
  - Signon...
  - Remote submit
  - Signoff...
- **Globals**
  - SAS/ASSIST
  - SAS/EIS
  - Program Editor
  - Log
  - Output
  - Output Manager
  - Graph Manager
  - Access
  - Invoke application
    - SAS/AF...
    - Data analysis
      - Quality control
      - Experimental design
      - SAS/INSIGHT
      - SAS/LAB
      - SAS/GIS
    - Spreadsheet...
    - Project management
    - Forecasting
  - Data management
    - Directory
    - Libname list
    - SAS data libraries
    - Variable definition
    - Catalog directory
    - Edit
      - Table edit...
      - Record edit...
    - Browse
      - Table browse...
      - Record browse...
    - Filename list
    - External files
    - View file...
    - IMAGE window
  - Desktop
    - Notepad...
    - Personal letters...
    - Spreadsheet...
  - Command
    - Command...
    - Command line
    - Host command...
  - Global options
    - SAS options
    - Titles
    - Footnotes
    - Graphics axis
    - Graphics legend
    - Graphics symbol
    - Graphics pattern
- **Help**
  - Extended help
  - Keys
  - SAS System
  - SAS Window Index

Appendix 6 Utility Application

Introduction

The Utility Application provides a framework for invoking several utility features of the SAS System. The list of utility features is dynamic, and what you receive depends on the products and components of the SAS System that you license. When you install the CORE of the SAS System, the Utility Application is automatically installed for you.

Using the Utility Application

You can access the Utility Application through the SAS AWS **`Help`** menu. When you select **`Utility Application`**, the SAS System determines which utility features are installed, displays a list of them, and lets you make a selection. If no utility features are currently installed, a message to this effect is displayed in the UTILITY APPLICATION window.

An example of a utility feature of the SAS System is the ability to compress and decompress SAS/GRAPH map data sets. The map data sets must be decompressed before you can use them with SAS/GRAPH software.

Note: With Release 6.09 of the SAS System under Windows NT, if your distribution media is a CD-ROM, SAS/GRAPH map data sets are shipped decompressed and are ready to use as soon as you install the SAS System.

Click on **`SAS/GRAPH MAP Data Sets Utility`** to compress map data sets that you have previously decompressed but are not currently using. Compressing unused map data sets can save a great deal of disk space.

Figure A6.1 shows an example of the Utility Application window, listing two applications:

Figure A6.1
UTILITY APPLICATION Window

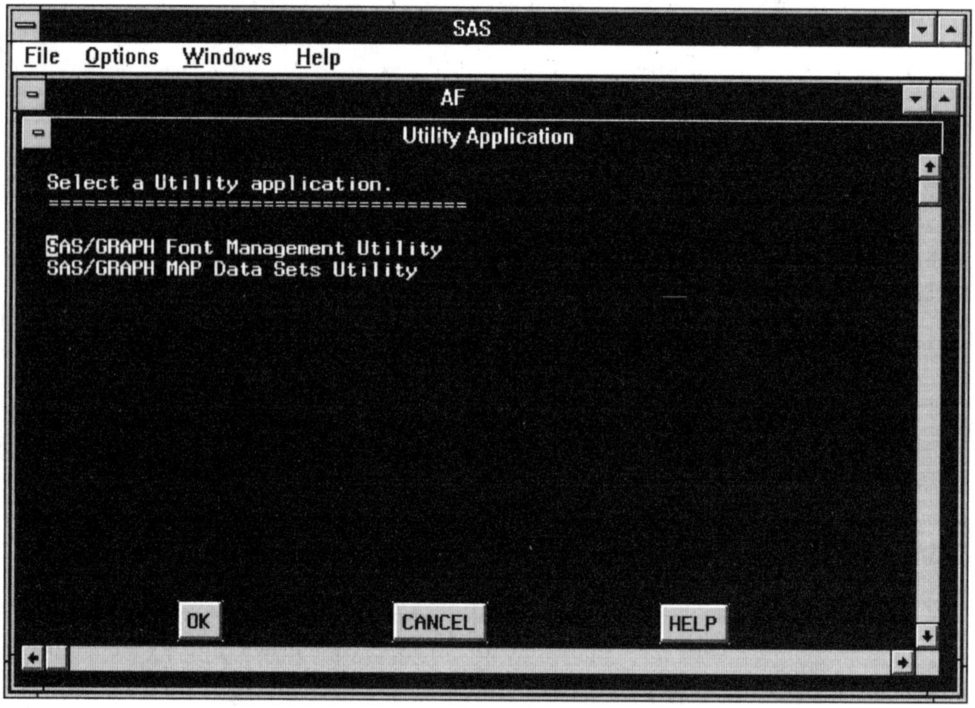

Glossary

This glossary provides definitions of SAS System and Windows NT terms used in this book. Note that only the most important terms are listed. If you need a definition for a SAS System term that is not included here, refer to *SAS Language: Reference, Version 6, First Edition.* For a definition of any Windows NT terms not included here, refer to the appropriate Windows NT documentation.

action bar
See menu bar.

active window
a window that is open, is displayed, and contains the cursor. Only one window can be active at a time.

application work space (AWS)
a graphics window that contains child windows. An example of an AWS in the SAS System is SAS/ASSIST software.

Under Windows NT, display manager SAS sessions are run in the SAS AWS, which provides all the regular features of any AWS under Windows NT. See also child window.

ASCII
an acronym for the American Standard Code for Information Interchange. ASCII is a 7-bit character coding scheme (8 bits when a parity check bit is included) including graphic (printable) and control (nonprintable) codes.

ASCII collating sequence
an ordering of characters that follows the order of the characters in the American Standard for Information Interchange (ASCII) character coding scheme. The SAS System uses the same collating sequence as its host operating system.

AUTOEXEC.SAS
a file containing SAS statements that are executed automatically when the SAS System is invoked. The autoexec file can be used to specify some SAS system options, as well as librefs and filerefs that are commonly used.

batch file
a file containing Windows NT commands organized for sequential processing. Batch files usually are identified with a .BAT extension.

batch mode
a method of executing SAS programs in which a file containing SAS statements and any necessary operating system commands is submitted for batch processing. While the program executes, control returns to the terminal or workstation environment where you can perform other tasks. Batch mode is sometimes referred to as running in the background. The job output can be written to files or printed on an output device.

Under Windows NT, a Status window associated with the SAS job reports what SAS job is running and where the log and procedure output files are written.

buffer
a memory area reserved for use in performing input/output (I/O) operations.

catalog
See SAS catalog.

catalog entry
See entry type.

child window
a window that is invoked from or contained in another window (the parent window). For example, each display manager window, such as the PROGRAM EDITOR and LOG window, is a child window of the SAS AWS. See also application work space (AWS).

client
(1) in a network, a workstation requesting services from the server. See also server.
(2) in pipes, unnamed pipes, DDE, and OLE, an application that sends data to or receives data from an application acting as a server. See also server.

Clipboard
a temporary storage place managed by Windows NT for data information that is being passed from one application to another. For example, you can use the Clipboard to pass information between Excel and your SAS session.

command prompt
the symbol after which you enter operating system commands. Under Windows NT, the default command prompt is C:\>.

CONFIG.SAS
under Windows NT, a file containing system options that are put into effect when the SAS System is invoked.

configuration file
in the SAS System, an external file containing SAS system options, often called CONFIG.SAS. The options in the file take effect when you invoke the SAS System. See also CONFIG.SAS.

Control menu
under Windows NT, the pull-down menu in the top left corner of most windows (including SAS display manager windows) that enables you to move and size windows. You can also use the Control menu to close a program and to select the Task List.

Control Panel
under Windows NT, an application that enables you to specify characteristics of your Windows NT session, such as mouse tracking speed and the color of the title bar. By default, the Control Panel is contained in the Main group.

converting SAS files
the process of changing the format of a SAS file from the format appropriate to one version of the SAS System to the format appropriate to another version running under the same operating system. The V5TOV6 procedure converts files from Version 5 to Version 6 format.

current directory
See working directory.

DDE
See Dynamic Data Exchange (DDE).

dialog box
a type of window that opens to prompt you for additional information, provide additional information, or ask you to confirm a request.

directory
(1) in the SAS System, either a list of the associated members and information in a SAS data set, or a list of entries and associated information in a SAS catalog.
(2) under Windows NT, a named subdivision on a disk or diskette used in organizing files. A directory also contains information about the file such as size and date of last change.

display manager
See SAS Display Manager System.

DLL
See dynamic link library (DLL).

download
to copy a file from the remote host to the local host.

drag
to press and hold a mouse button while moving the mouse.

dummy variable
(1) a variable used as a placeholder. Dummy variables usually do not have meaningful values.
(2) in some statistical applications, a numeric variable whose value is limited to 1 or 0.

Dynamic Data Exchange (DDE)
a standard mechanism in the PC environment for sharing data among Windows NT applications.

dynamic link library (DLL)
a collection of executable modules that are loaded at run time as needed.

engine
a part of the SAS System that reads from or writes to a file. Each engine allows the SAS System to access files with a particular format. There are several types of engines. See also interface engine, library engine, native engine, and view engine.

entry type
a characteristic of a SAS catalog entry that identifies its structure and attributes to the SAS System. When you create an entry, the SAS System automatically assigns the entry type as part of the name.

environment variable
under Windows NT, a variable that equates one string to another using the SET system option or the Windows NT SET command. The environment variables defined in one Windows NT application are not available to other Windows NT applications.

external file
a file created and maintained on the host operating system from which you can read data or stored SAS statements or in which you can store procedure output or output created by PUT statements in a DATA step. An external file is not a SAS data set.

file extension
under Windows NT, the classification of a file in a Windows NT directory that identifies what type of information is stored in the file. For example, .SC2 is the file extension for SAS catalogs. See also member type.

filename
under Windows NT, the identifier used for a file (including the file extension), such as PROFILE.SC2. See also fully qualified filename and pathname.

fileref
the name used to identify an external file to the SAS System.

Under Windows NT, you can assign a fileref with a FILENAME statement, the SET system option, or the Windows NT SET command.

font
a complete set of all the characters of the same design and style. The characters in a font can be figures or symbols as well as alphanumeric characters.

fully qualified filename
under Windows NT, a file specification that includes both the pathname and filename, such as C:\SAS\SASUSER\PROFILE.SC2. See also filename and pathname.

function key
a keyboard key that can be defined to have a specific action in a specific software environment.

group
in Program Manager, a collection of applications, such as Main or Accessories. You can run the SAS System by adding it to a group.

icon
in windowing environments, a pictorial representation of an object. An icon usually represents a window or an object associated with an action such as printing or filing.

Under Windows NT, double-click on the icon to expand the icon to the full form of the object or to choose the action.

index
in SAS software, a component of a SAS data set that enables the SAS System to access observations in the SAS data set quickly and efficiently. The purpose of SAS indexes is to optimize WHERE-clause processing and facilitate BY-group processing.

interface engine
a SAS System engine that reads and writes file formats supported by other vendors' software. See also engine and native engine.

library engine

an engine that accesses groups of files and puts them into the correct form for processing by SAS utility windows and procedures. A library engine also determines the fundamental processing characteristics of the library, presents lists of files for the library directory, and supports view engines. See also engine and view engine.

libref

the name temporarily associated with a SAS data library.

Under Windows NT, you can assign a libref with a LIBNAME statement, the SET system option, or the Windows NT SET command.

local SAS session

a SAS session running on the local host. The local session accepts SAS statements and passes those that are remote-submitted to the remote host for processing. The local session manages the output and messages from both the local session and the remote session.

maximize

to display a window at its largest size.

Media Control Interface (MCI)

an applications programming interface (API) developed by Microsoft and IBM that allows programs to access multimedia devices such as CD players, mixers, VCRs, video record/playback hardware, and so on.

Under Windows NT, host-specific SAS functions enable you to access this API.

member

a SAS file in a SAS data library.

member name

a name given to a SAS file in a SAS data library. A member name can reference a SAS data set, catalog, access descriptor, or stored program.

Under Windows NT, member name is equivalent to filename for files stored in a SAS data library.

member type

a name assigned by the SAS System that identifies the type of information stored in a SAS file. Member types include ACCESS, DATA, CATALOG, PROGRAM, and VIEW.

menu bar

the primary list of items in a window that represents the actions or classes of actions that can be executed. Selecting an item executes an action, opens a pull-down menu, or opens a dialog box requesting additional information. See also pop-up menu and pull-down menu.

methods of running the SAS System

standard methods of operation used to run SAS System programs. These methods are SAS/ASSIST software, display manager, interactive line mode, noninteractive mode, and batch mode.

Under Windows NT, only SAS/ASSIST software, display manager, and batch mode are supported.

minimize

to shrink a window to an icon.

Media Control Interface (MCI)
an applications programming interface (API) developed by Microsoft and IBM that allows programs to access multimedia devices such as CD players, mixers, VCRs, video record/playback hardware, and so on.

Under Windows NT, host-specific SAS functions enable you to access this API.

Multiple Engine Architecture (MEA)
a feature of the SAS System that enables it to access a variety of file formats through sets of instructions called engines. See also engine.

multitasking
the ability to execute more than one task running inside a single CPU.

named pipe
a named object that provides client-to-server, server-to-client, or duplex communication between unrelated processes. You can use named pipes to establish communication between Windows NT applications, including multiple SAS sessions. See also pipe.

native engine
an engine that accesses forms of SAS files created and processed only by the SAS System. See also engine.

network
an interconnected group of computers.

Object Linking and Embedding (OLE)
a method of interprocess communication supported by Windows NT that involves a client/server architecture. OLE enables an object created by one application to be embedded in or linked to another application.

OLE
See Object Linking and Embedding (OLE).

pathname
under Windows NT, a specification of a drive, directories, and subdirectories, such as C:\SAS\SASUSER.

permanent SAS data library
a library that is not deleted when the SAS session terminates; it is available for subsequent SAS sessions. Unless the USER libref is defined, you use a two-level name to access a file in a permanent library. The first-level name is the libref, and the second-level name is the member name. See also USER data library.

physical filename
the name the operating system uses to identify a file. See also file extension, filename, and pathname.

pipe
an object that provides direct access to STDIN, STDOUT, and STDERR between Windows NT processes. Pipe is synonymous with unnamed pipe. See also named pipe.

pop-up menu
a menu that appears when requested. Pop-up menus are context-specific, depending on which window is active and on the cursor location.

Under Windows NT, use the WPOPUP command to request a pop-up menu. The SAS System assigns the WPOPUP command to the right mouse button by default. See also menu bar and pull-down menu.

primary windows
in the SAS Display Manager System, the PROGRAM EDITOR, LOG, OUTPUT (LISTING), and OUTPUT MANAGER windows.

procedure output file
an external file that contains the result of the analysis or the report produced. Most procedures write output to the procedure output file by default. Reports that DATA steps produce using PUT statements and a FILE statement with the PRINT destination also go to this file.

PROFILE catalog
a SAS catalog in a special SAS data library that contains information used by the SAS System to control various aspects of your display manager session. See also SASUSER library.

Program Manager
a graphical user interface to applications and files under Windows NT.

program title
under Windows NT, the name of an application contained in a group window.

pull-down menu
the list of choices that appears when you choose an item from a menu bar or from another menu. See also menu bar and pop-up menu.

return code
a code passed to the operating system that reports the results of executing a command or job step.

SAS AWS
See application work space (AWS).

SAS catalog
a SAS file that stores many different kinds of information in smaller units called entries. A single SAS catalog can contain several different types of catalog entries.

Some catalog entries contain system information such as key definitions. Other catalog entries contain application information such as window definitions, help windows, formats, informats, macros, or graphics output.

SAS command
a command that invokes the SAS System. This command may vary depending on the operating system and site.

SAS data file
a SAS data set that contains both data values and the descriptor information.

SAS data library
in the SAS data model, a collection of SAS files accessed by the same library engine and recognized as a logical unit by the SAS System.

SAS data set
descriptor information and its related data values organized as a table of observations and variables that can be processed by the SAS System. A SAS data set can be either a SAS data file or a SAS data view.

SAS data view
a SAS data set in which the descriptor information and the observations are obtained from other files. SAS data views store only the information required to retrieve data values or descriptor information.

SAS Display Manager System
an interactive, windowing interface to SAS System software. Display manager commands can be issued by typing them on the command line, pressing function keys, or selecting items from menus or menu bars. Within one session, many different tasks can be accomplished, including preparing and submitting programs, viewing and printing results, and debugging and resubmitting programs.

SAS file
a specially structured file that is created, organized, and, optionally, maintained by the SAS System. A SAS file can be a SAS data set, a catalog, a stored program, or an access descriptor.

SAS log
a file that contains the SAS statements you enter and messages about the execution of your program.

SAS system option
an option that affects processing the entire SAS program or interactive SAS session from the time the option is specified until it is changed. Examples of items controlled by SAS system options include appearance of SAS output, handling of some files used by the SAS System, use of system variables, processing observations in SAS data sets, features of SAS System initialization, and the SAS System's interface with your computer hardware and with the operating system.

SASUSER library
a default permanent SAS data library that is created at the beginning of your first SAS session. It contains a PROFILE catalog that stores the tailoring features you specify for the SAS System. You can also store other SAS files in this library. See also PROFILE catalog and SAS data library.

scroll bar
an element of the windowing environment that enables you to scroll the contents of the window.

server
(1) in a network, a special workstation, machine, or computer reserved for servicing other computers in the network. Servers can provide file services, communication services, and so on. Servers enable users to access common resources such as disks, data, and modems. See also client.

(2) in pipes, unnamed pipes, DDE, and OLE, an application that sends or receives data from an application acting as a client. See also client.

swapping
the action of moving segments from memory to disk and vice versa.

system option
See SAS system option.

Task List
under Windows NT, the list of active tasks. You can access the list by using the CTRL ESC key sequence. You can use this list to switch from one task to another, stop a task, and so on.

temporary SAS data library
a library that exists only for the current SAS session or job. The most common temporary library is the WORK library. See also WORK data library.

title bar
under Windows NT, an element of a window that displays the title of the window. The title bar is at the top of the window and is highlighted if the window is active.

toggle
an option, parameter, or other mechanism that enables you to turn on or turn off a processing feature.

toolbar
under Windows NT, a feature of the SAS System that enables you to associate an icon with any SAS System command or macro. Selecting the icon executes its associated command or string of commands. The toolbar is located in the menu bar area of the SAS AWS. See also Toolbox.

Toolbox
under Windows NT, a feature of the SAS System that enables you to associate an icon with any SAS System command or macro. Selecting the icon executes its associated command or string of commands. The Toolbox is a dialog box and can be moved. See also toolbar.

unnamed pipe
See pipe.

Unrecoverable Application Error (UAE)
the Windows NT error message that appears when an application violates system integrity. The error can be caused by any application that is running or by the operating system.

upload
to copy a file from the local host to the remote host.

USER data library
a SAS data library defined with the libref USER. When the libref USER is defined, the SAS System uses it as the default libref for one-level names.

view engine
an engine that enables the SAS System to process SAS data views. A view engine performs in a transparent manner. See also SAS data view.

WORK data library
the SAS data library automatically defined by the SAS System at the beginning of each SAS session or job. It contains SAS files that are temporary by default. When the libref USER is

not defined, the SAS System uses WORK as the default library for SAS files created with one-level names.

working directory

the directory to which commands and actions apply when you are executing an application.

Under Windows NT, the working directory is the directory from which you invoked the SAS System.

Index

B

C

E

F

K

L

M

N

O

S

V

W

X

Z

Special Characters